So Far, So Good...
So Megadeth!

Martin Popoff

So Far, So Good... So Megadeth!

Martin Popoff

WYMER PUBLISHING
Bedford, England

First published in Canada in 2014.
This edition published in 2017 by Wymer Publishing
Bedford, England
www.wymerpublishing.co.uk
Tel: 01234 326691
Wymer Publishing is a trading name of Wymer (UK) Ltd

Copyright © 2017 Martin Popoff / Wymer Publishing.

ISBN 978-1-908724-61-8

The Author hereby asserts his rights to be identified
as the author of this work in accordance with sections
77 to 78 of the Copyright, Designs & Patents Act 1988.

All rights reserved. No part of this publication may be
reproduced or transmitted in any form or by any means,
electronic or mechanical, including photocopying, or any
information storage and retrieval system, without written
permission from the publisher.

This publication is sold subject to the condition that it shall not,
by way of trade or otherwise, be lent, re-sold, hired out or
otherwise circulated without the publishers prior consent in any
form of binding or cover other than that in which it is published
and without a similar condition including this condition
being imposed on the subsequent purchaser.

Front cover image © Chris Casella.
Back cover image © Kevin Estrada.

Printed and bound by
CMP Ltd, Poole, Dorset, England

A catalogue record for this book is available from the British Library.

Front cover design by Eduardo Rodriguez.

Contents

Preface — ix

1. Early Days
"They Became Alcoholica" — 1

2. Killing Is My Business... And Business Is Good!
"There was no clear thinking on anyone's part" — 15

3. Peace Sells... But Who's Buying?
"If she woke her up, she'd kill him" — 29

4. So Far, So Good... So What!
"I have an important business offer" — 48

5. Rust In Peace
"It was a joke how clean those guys were" — 66

6. Countdown To Extinction
"All working parts of this machine, keep it going" — 80

7. Youthanasia
"There was not a glass ceiling" — 95

8. Cryptic Writings
"Guys, girls, guys dressed up like girls" — 113

9. Risk
"Their opinion doesn't matter and neither does mine" — 128

10. The World Needs A Hero
"Put your head down and play real hard"   **141**

11. The System Has Failed
"Why don't you just leave me alone?"   **169**

12. United Abominations
"Maybe I'm from a bygone era"   **183**

13. Endgame
"I like that album more than the one I played on"   **210**

14. Thirteen
"I'm going to do a little Budgie part"   **231**

15. Super Collider
"You know I'm a very polarizing figure"   **243**

Discography / Videography   **265**

Credits   **272**

About The Author   **273**

Martin Popoff – A Comprehensive Bibliography   **274**

PREFACE

Crunchy, bitter, nasty, immoral and moral, uneasy and easy-drinking Megadeth... I've often said that all humanity can be summed up by The Damned or The Who but as life grinds on towards deth, I'd say all the ragged and joyous things of a community of lives, well, Megadeth embody that as much as those two bands I love even more.

Who cares what I think, but this is my introduction, so I'm gonna talk: Megadeth is chopped into three pieces for me. More on piece No. 3 later, but that one is in fact, very surprisingly, the piece that has sustained me in metal for the past bunch of years. Yes, Megadeth's voluminous and high quality production in the 2000s is some of my favourite metal music, and pretty much the only Megadeth I listen to these days, given all the nooks and crannies and the daunting playing, production and just the cool writer, both musically and lyrically, that Dave has grown into, or more accurately, proved was never any fluke.

In any event, pieces No. 1 and No. 2 represent the way I have consumed the music of Mustaine and his gathered supporting cast in my, ahem, youth, and that is growing with the band and loving the metal years up until halfway through **Youthanasia**. Then like many crusty old school fans, dismissing the band as compromised and done and assimilated into an everyman world come **Cryptic Writings** and the universally least loved album of the band's career, dagger to the 'deth, namely, **Risk**.

Now, funny thing is—and I'm gonna be *Almost Honest* here, like the hero of this weighty tome, Dave Mustaine, whose honesty is always refreshing and makes talking to him inspiring. I probably like **Cryptic Writings** more or at least equal to any of the first *three* Megadeth albums. I know, sacrilege, blah, blah, blah, but fact of the matter is, all three of those records I find a little creepy, squalid, depressing, hard on the ears, my perception being they are the work of guys who are a nasty piece of work.

Then again, to these ears, **Rust In Peace** and **Countdown To Extinction** are two of the greatest metal albums of all time, each admirable for different reasons. And I must thank the guys (specifically, that would be the classic Megadeth line-up) for making that happen because it happened at a time in my life where myself and many metalheads of a certain advanced vintage were giving up on metal. Possibly, the glory days of thrash were behind us. The UK quit caring way back in 1983 with the keeling-over of the glorious New Wave Of British Heavy Metal. Hair metal was good fun but now collapsing in on itself. I loved the Minneapolis scene and the Minutemen/Firehose axis, plus close by, Jane's Addiction and Faith No More.

Even more magical was grunge, especially Green River's second EP and lone album, the first EPs from Mudhoney and Soundgarden, plus **Bleach**. Grunge was dangerous metal magic, and never forget it. Lit. A. Fire.

But in the midst of this sea-change between huge commercial hard rock tides (Hollyrock to Seattle), was this thinking man's metal band who could think despite not seeing straight, who could craft and prog-rock and produce to exacting standards despite destructive drugging and drinking. This was the Megadeth that had me hooked, the Megadeth that I previously had warily admired with a, "Yeah, but I can't even listen to it because of that production" (yes, my main gripe with all of the first three Megadeth records).

Onto the modern era of Megadeth, and the best thing of all, it's opened the door for a jaded fifty-year-old angry metalhead to really get into and enjoy a catalogue of relatively recent albums, that otherwise I may not have given their due. What do I mean by this? Well, main thing, can you bloody envision how many CDs Tim, I and the boys were all getting for free during the run of our mag, *Brave Words & Bloody Knuckles*? We had that damn thing in print from '94 through to '08 and yes, there was piles and piles of stuff to listen to, enough to fill a 7" tall by 31" long wall of CDs, most with the jewel cases removed for tight packing. So even Megadeth albums got short shrift, and, as it turns out, through no fault of their own.

Why, you may ask? Well, it's because the albums you are to read about in the back half of this book, and the heroic heavies making them... this is some superb metal, perfected and crafted for the young end of my generation and arguably one whole generation younger. But, frankly, possibly, not the metalhead too much younger than that—the kids will have their own bands, and the portion of Megadeth's style that is traditional or rootsy, that's just gonna sound old to some of these Psyopus and Cattle Decapitation fans (I know, mature bands, but the point is, they are insanely heavy, something only unemployable kids raised on video games can process).

So yeah, writing this part of the book, much more than any pile of pages so far that I've done, has given me a shot of youth, just like having all the guys in Dave's band being just a bit younger than him, but, admirably on Dave's part, not much younger (Alice Cooper could use a bit of this attitude). In other words, I bet guys like Shawn Drover and Chris Broderick keep Mustaine on his toes, but they can also hold a meaningful conversation with the guy.

And what of Jr.? Love the guy, love his attitude, love the whole dynamic between him and Mustaine being able to live out their fates together. Man, just all these guys feel like buddies to me... their rocking out at such a high level of quality serves as a beacon toward how to grow old with piss and vinegar and maturity and fitness and, yes, a softening of old bullshit grudges.

So yeah, writing this portion... well, money can't buy the energy I've drawn from these records, especially **Endgame** and **Thirteen** but pretty much all of them to some degree. Fact is—and now we're really crossing into sacrilege (and I think I utter this nonsense elsewhere in the pages ahead)—I probably draw more value and enjoyment out of the recent days bank of albums than the old stuff, even if **Rust In Peace** and **Countdown** are probably the unassailable favourites of both myself and you, the kindly reader of this book.

And it's no secret why a lifelong metalhead who is long in the tooth such as I, can dig Dave and his universe as portrayed on **The World Needs A Hero** through **Super Collider**. First off, it's 'cos I've grown up with Dave and just appreciate the guy more all the time. Goes for Jr. too, actually. But it's more than that, really, deep into this idea again that Megadeth music is not exactly thrash or even progressive thrash, not exactly early definition US "power metal" (i.e. Metal Church and anything on Metal Blade through '86), not exactly hugely overlapping with the general generality of Dio, Priest or Accept, and not really very NWOBHM, even if I compare songs to that magic time quite often in the following pages. No, wrap all of this together and you get a very deliberate and relentlessly underscored deliberation of style that is uniquely Megadeth, hatched from the mind of the survivor that is Dave Mustaine. As James LoMenzo perceptively says in here, one of the great things about Dave is that he has kept Megadeth alive all by himself.

Let that sink in, because Dave's had to do a lot of shit to deal with all by himself, including a lot of goddamn growing up all by himself back to early childhood.

And so that's really about all I wanted to say here, I do believe. This part of my books—you know the drill by now after 40+ of them—is essentially an informal hello where I tell you what I really think, before the real work begins, the telling of the story, which I usually present with a certain detachment, letting it breathe through the words of the makers of all this art.

So that's it. I mean, thanks to everybody who's ever been in Megadeth. I suppose I'm closest to Dave Ellefson, and actually somewhat Dave Mustaine, and both Glen and Shawn Drover as well, but to a man, I've always enjoyed chatting with any of them. So without further adieu, here's a book on what I consider the three parts of art that comprise this now classic band of sustaining Mustaine.

Sorry, one final thing: my hope with this book is that if you're gonna snipe about, specifically, modern-day Megadeth, give the albums quite a few deep listens before you shoot your mouth off. Have good reason for it, because it's pretty hard to find fault with a lot of this catalogue—and yet people do all the time. So yeah, the hope... 1) that I'm turning folks onto these records, folks who are 40 to 55, and then, 2) that I'm actually writing a book that your 20 and 30 year old metalheads might read with the sentiment that I'm actually writing about bands and records for once that are somewhat in their orbit. I mean, hey, after two Sabbath books, two books on Rush, three Thin Lizzy books and four Deep Purple books... trust me, it's headbangingly invigorating to be looking at some hearty, heavy music that's not from my days with Evel Knievel, the Broad Street Bullies, clackers and fully legal firecrackers.

Martin Popoff
martinp@inforamp.net

1
EARLY DAYS
"They became Alcoholica"

Angry again. And again and again. That pretty much sums up the career of metal lightning rod Dave Mustaine and his mega-metal machine Megadeth. In fact, that's the story of heavy metal itself, and if there was ever a band that personified that ugly music, leached out its very essence and then lived it to the max, it would be Megadeth. Indeed every smack of naughtiness, from the sordid vagaries of Aerosmith, through the seamy underbelly of hair metal and grunge, just the bad reputation of California and what it does to people... it's all here in the corrupted lives and extreme redemption of the two Daves, as it is within the band they built, wrecked and wrecked again and then re-souped to the insane proportions it flexes now.

Dave Ellefson didn't start out quite as shoulder-chipped as his evil twin, but he soon got sucked into the swirl of Mustaine's orbit, as did the other comparatively innocent bystanders in the band.

Mega-Dave on the other hand, had lots to be metal about.

Born September 13, 1961 east of San Diego, California in La Mesa, Dave was part of a big family led by mother Emily and husband John, who, despite holding a good bank job, was a violent drinker who was particularly hard on Dave, his only son in a family with four kids. Despite his mother being Jewish, the kids were brought up Jehovah's Witness. Divorce would tear the family apart when Dave was but four years old; the break wouldn't sit well with John, who would turn stalker upon his family, forcing frightened move upon move, usually quickly and at night.

Dave's sanctuary was music, inspired first by his older sister Debbie who comforted Dave with the reassuring soft rock of Elton John and Cat Stevens. But adding to the anger within the broken home was the fact that they were now dirt-poor, with Emily cleaning houses to make ends meet. Music became increasingly important for Dave when at the age of eight, he acquired his first guitar, which was soon busted over his head by his sister, prompting a discouraged switch to sports. When Dave was 14, the family moved north to Stanton, Orange County, the southern outskirts of Los Angeles, to live with Dave's older sister Suzanne who had married a Bob Wilke, police officer.

Late '76, and now a budding metalhead, Dave left the home and rented his own apartment, beginning his short career as a low-level pot dealer while still going to high school, and, as the story goes, trading pot to his girlfriend Willow for records scoffed out of the store where she worked. By this point, it was a steady diet of Judas Priest, AC/DC, Black Sabbath, and later, Motörhead and Iron Maiden. Early '78, Dave had, had enough with high school and had decided to take another shot at playing the guitar, only this time, addressing, with a sneer, a sick music that had only recently been labelled heavy metal.

"Regardless of what I did with my career, I don't think my problems with my family would have been resolved," said Dave in 1986. "I did what I did because I wanted to do it. I didn't have any inhibitions or any kind of feelings towards what they thought. I lived with my mom for a long time and I just barely got to know my dad right before he died. After that, I was pretty confused over the whole thing, so I went my own way, away from my family. It was a big fight because they didn't really dig what I'm doing. It makes it weird, knowing the religious background that my family believes and what I'm professing in my music. I went to a private school for about two months. It wasn't my trip, because I've always been pretty well ahead of my grades and sitting in a class with religious people who say, 'Brother, can I have a pencil?' wasn't for me. I said to them, 'Fuck you, get your own pencil!' They didn't dig that. I've always gotten a kick out of defying authority."

"I don't know that what happened to me as a kid can drive anybody to do anything but kill their parents," quipped Dave, speaking with Sam Dunn. "You know? I'm not into patricide; I don't think that's a solution. I think good parenting is more important than revenge. For me, what drove me to want to play metal music was simply I just wanted to fit in. I wanted to be a part of things. Because I was a skinny redheaded kid with freckles. You know how we treat redheaded kids in school; we treat them like shit. And nobody dares do that to me now, but at the time they did it. And what could I do? I learned how to fight. So I spent a lot of my life fighting, but that don't make you good at guitar. In fact it slows you down because your fingers get slower. And I look at the main reason... I went to a party one time in Huntingdon Beach and I saw this guy playing. His name was John Tall, and he was a very unattractive guy, and in fact he almost looked like the dude in **Young Frankenstein**. And he stopped playing and the chicks were on him. And I thought, 'How is that possible?' I, at that point in my life, wasn't even as hideous looking as he was, so I figured the secret is guitar. And I got a guitar, and then I started getting chicks and I started meeting people, and guys would party and bring drugs and girls would spread their legs."

Mustaine's first band was Panic, consisting of Dave and Tom Queck on guitar, Pat Voeks on vocals, Bob Evans on bass and Mike Leftwych on drums. Dave says that two songs from this era would make it into his short stay within Metallica, namely *The Mechanix* and *Jump In The Fire*, with Panic also generating riffs that would weave their way into both his future bands, Metallica and later Megadeth. Although mainly a party band, Panic is most known for the fact that right after the band's first proper gig, both the band's soundman, Joe, and drummer Mike Leftwych were killed in a car accident.

"I was playing both *Hangar 18* and *Rust In Peace... Polaris* when I was in Panic," recalls Dave, musing on those days. "This was before Metallica, and *Rust In Peace* was actually called *Child Saint*. And the funny thing, Martin, I was listening to that famous radio station, KNAC. Junior and I were riding home one day, and Dave says, 'What the...?' And it was, oh my God, and the song ends and the guy goes, 'That was *Child Saint* by Child Saint.' And I was like, they even ripped off my name! Because I called it *Child Saint*. What happened was, is I went up with this guy who was playing drums with me at the time in Panic, to this house. It was a party, and there were some guys there that were playing, and they knew who I was and he asked me to kind of show them something. And I said okay, and 'This is one of my songs,' and they said, 'Do you mind if we play it?' And I said, 'If you can.' And so they played it a little bit, and next thing you know, they stole the fucking song. It was like, are you kidding? I wrote that. It was weird. It was very weird. That was my first experience having somebody record my stuff that I didn't expect them to record my stuff. You know, it's really different when you hear somebody recording your stuff."

"I would give Exodus some credit," continues Dave, asked if through Panic, or his first things with Metallica, if he in fact was the guy who invented thrash—not out of the question. "I've always said that I thought that if there really was a big five, that they would belong in it, and yeah, so I would say that. Did I invent it? No. You've got to think about who we were listening to before hand, and they were heavy metal, Priest and Diamond Head, and a lot of those other bands. Saxon was like a New Wave Of British Heavy Metal band, and I don't know if anybody really was doing that back when we first started doing it. The only people that we'd heard that were doing it were Anthrax on the East Coast, and there was us, and a couple bands in San Francisco. You know, I think, if you go back in time to a real good heavy metal band, they had double picking that was really fast and stuff like that. But I think the whole thrash and speed metal thing was upping the game for everybody."

So what would be the first couple of things Mustaine had written, where that subtle shift from speed metal to thrash might have been said to have taken place?

"That's kind of hard to say, because one of the first songs I ever wrote was *Rust In Peace... Polaris*, and it was pretty sped-up, and that spread out to different songs I wrote. You know, *Hangar 18* was another one I wrote at the very beginning, and *Jump In The Fire*. So I had a lot of really weird musical direction at the time. Because if you knew a kid that could write *Jump In The Fire* and *Hangar 18* and *Rust In Peace... Polaris*, as their first three songs, you would probably say, this is going to be very interesting to watch this play out. And it has been. But I never really thought about it, back when I was writing them. First thing, first song I wrote after I left Metallica was *Set The World Afire*, and that didn't show up until the third record. So there's no telling which song is first, and where it sits as far as importance is concerned."

So post-Panic, Mustaine answers an ad in The Recycler posted by an energy-mad young drummer named Lars Ulrich and without so much as an audition (Lars and James Hetfield would be satisfied with surreptitiously hearing Dave warm up), Mustaine was enlisted into the ranks of Metallica.

"I discovered a band called Budgie, and Budgie was one of the bands I mentioned when I talked to Lars when I auditioned for Metallica," recalls Mustaine. "I saw the ad in The Recycler said looking for somebody who was influenced by, I think it said Motörhead, Iron Maiden, and I said, yeah, I know those guys. And I said, 'Do you know Budgie?' and Lars was like, 'Fuck man, you know Budgie?' That's what he says. 'Yeah, I know Budgie. I mean I don't know them, but I know their music' and I really liked it because it was really obscure music from England. It was a three-piece band... you gotta really be good to be a three-piece and be heavy; it's really hard. You need that other guitar player, sometimes, to hold down the bottom when you go into a guitar solo, and usually that happens because you've got a crap bassist. Or your solos are pretty weak when you go into a solo, and there's no rhythm underneath it—it's because your solos are boring. When you have a three-piece that really works, you don't really notice when they go from rhythm to lead. The transition's effortless."

"But there wasn't a lot of metal out at the time," continues Dave, asked about his early influences. "You gotta remember it was just starting. In the beginning of the '80s, punk rock basically broke in the States the latter part of the '70s. So when the '80s came around it was... punk was at its height and disco was out and so was new wave. You remember new wave was like The Cars and stuff like that, and punk was Devo and metal was stuff that was coming over from England. To me, I thought AC/DC and UFO were really killer metal bands and I also liked stuff like Maiden."

Reaching back further, past the punk and the metal, to his very first experiences as a fan of music, Mustaine explains that, "Cat Stevens was one of the most successful singers of the '60s and '70s doing something that was folk-oriented. He was just radical for what he did. One of my favourite songs of his is *Father And Son*. You hear that one Harry Chapin song, that cradle song... *Cats In The Cradle*. That song is like a 1 on the scale of 10 compared to Cat Steven's *Father And Son* song. 'It's not time to make a change, just relax, take it easy. You are still young, that's your fault, so much you have to know. Find a girl, settle down, if you want you can marry. Look at me, I am old, but I am happy.' Except for the part... if he'd said, 'Look at me, I am old, and divorced and now happy...'"

"The Beatles were metal because they were junkies," continues Dave.

"The combination between Paul and John, their musical styles, both had fantastic lyrics but one sang bubble gum candy pop, la la la stuff, and the other one sang some really in-your-face political songs. And I think the two of them complimented each other; it was like the offset of something really acerbic and you put something in it and it's almost like a solvent and it neutralized the acidity of the things that Lennon was saying. Or it would give a bit more... some taste to what Paul was doing because his stuff was so chutes and ladders kiddieland stuff. And I think that just because you're a Beatle means you're exempt from making stupid decisions. Look at a couple of those things he did selling his publishing and the stuff with Michael Jackson. I'm not saying collaborating with him was stupid, but the whole way everything went down and their friendship and fake friendship and at war, and the buying and publishing and buying it back. If you listen to the difference between Lennon's stuff and some other people that came over from the British invasion... you've got the Stones and you've got the Who. Now the Stones, they had really cool stuff, too, but it was almost like out of the Big Four, they were one of them, but it was Beatles and Led Zeppelin, the Who and the Stones. That was the Big 4 out of England, I believe."

Asked who else was metal before there was metal, Mustaine figures, "I think Ted Nugent was. Not a lot of people give Ted credit. I think Ted was speed metal and thrash metal. He was great. I think that if you look at bands like Bob Seger, he could be considered that. Kiss definitely was a metal band, although they'd probably be labelled as a glam band. There's a lot of bands that I could say are metal. Pink Floyd had metal elements to it. The **Animals** record, there was some great songs on there."

"Growing up I played every song on every Led Zeppelin record," Dave told me in '97, cutting closer to the chase. "The guitar on it, Kiss and Ted Nugent, Montrose, Mott The Hoople, Bowie, even the Beatles. But it wasn't until I started hearing Iron Maiden, Def Leppard, Judas Priest, Budgie... UFO was one of my favourite bands, but the band that changed my world was AC/DC. As soon as I heard those guys I went, shit! It was **Let There Be Rock**. I can't honestly say I can remember it like it was yesterday, because, hell, I have enough trouble just remembering yesterday. But the point is it is so vivid in my mind when I first put it on, being young and impressionable, hearing that record; it totally changed my life. I know now that my playing has been accepted and that it's influenced a lot of people, but I don't think that would have happened if it wasn't for the New Wave Of British Heavy Metal."

Back in the land of the newer and nastier metal that had come upon us from California in 1982 forward, the story has been told many times before, so we shall be brief. But yes, Metallica with Dave in the band emphatically made their mark. Throughout roughly a year and a half reign of terror within the ranks, Metallica would record their legendary early demos, move from

LA to Los Angeles, and cross the country at the behest of one Jonny "Z" Zazula, who ran a heavy metal record store in Jersey called Rock 'n' Roll Heaven. Zazula and his wife Marsha would bet the ranch on Metallica, and create a record label out of thin air called Megaforce to make their records, signing Raven and Anthrax as well.

But, shockingly—and making him even more profoundly angry—Mustaine would be bounced unceremoniously out of Metallica, while in the midst of this eastern swing to seek their fame with Jonny and Marsha. Exacerbated by getting his eye scratched by falling rust while riding in the back of the truck with the gear, Mustaine showed himself to be a violent drunk, picking a fight with some people in a restaurant, and generally rubbing everybody the wrong way. Even on their way out east, the guys talk about playing demo tapes of prospective replacements while Dave slept in the back.

"They came to my house and then they became Alcoholica," remembers Jonny. "I had a little bar, with bottles of booze on it, and for somebody to drink if someone wanted a drink. And so they just took over my house, took the bottles, then left for the 18 Flea Market to meet Marsha. So my first day with them was, 'Oh my God, what did I do?' Because they were pretty crazy. Dave Mustaine got to the flea market but never made it inside. He was just standing outside with his long hair and his patches and everything, just throwing up in front of the place. And everybody knew they were from that band Metallica, so they were saying, 'What the fuck; who are these guys?' (laughs). And Dave was always… you never knew what you had with Dave. He was a man of many colours."

The rest of Metallica were already pretty sure Mustaine wouldn't be long for Metallica, already having gotten into verbal confrontations and actual fistfights with the red-headed firebrand. James remarks, partly in jest, that not only was Dave on a path toward killing himself, but possibly the whole band. One incident, before the band's move to San Francisco, ignited from a situation where Dave's pit bull (the guarder of the Mustaine's retail inventory) had put his paws up on Metallica bassist Ron McGovney's car. The oft-repeated tale is that Dave kicked the dog, but Mustaine says it was James that kicked the dog, resulting in Dave decking James, Ron jumping on Dave, Dave throwing Ron and then quitting the band and storming off. The next day, Dave asked to be reinstated and the guys just shrugged and said yes. But soon McGovney had, had enough. One day, Dave had been home alone at Ron's pad drinking and decided to pour a beer all over McGovney's bass, into the pick-ups. The next time Ron plugged in, he was the recipient of a powerful shock, prompting him to throw everybody out of the house—he would be out of the band within weeks.

On stage, every bit the extrovert as Lars was, Dave was actually the front man for Metallica in the early days, given Hetfield's shyness on stage. It was

Dave who stunned the band's moshing crowds with screeching, aggressive axe-mad speed, and it was Dave that exhorted them to go crazy and, in not so many words, help him invent thrash culture.

"I just remember Mustaine being intoxicated all the time," says Jim Florentine, "member" of New Jersey's metal appreciation clan, the Old Bridge Militia. "I remember, we were walking through the flea market and these guys were like, 'Look, we can't take care of him. We can't deal with him anymore.' It was like noon. And I guess that was right before he was thrown out of the band."

Unfortunately, Dave Mustaine wasn't destined to be a member of one of the many early thrash bands that got to enjoy the full hospitality of the Old Bridge Militia, partying at their houses out in the country, lapping up the insane fan appreciation at the shows. "No, I wasn't there long enough. I'm sure I would be welcomed into that circle, and I'm sure I was there in the beginning—I had to have been. There was no Old Bridge circle until we went out there. It was what it was. It was a bunch of kids that went to a flea market out in Old Bridge. We went out there and started that whole thing. I miss it. There were a lot of times back then that all that stuff was going on and I really wanted to be a part of it because I was part of it. You take me out of the mix and it wouldn't happen."

But Dave does remember with a shudder the hassles staying in the old Music Building, while doing those two legendary east coast shows logged with Metallica, April 8th and April 9th, before his ouster. "Anthrax, when I moved out there, we rehearsed right above them. If it wasn't for Danny Lilker, who was the bass player at the time, showing me a little mercy, I probably would have had an even worse time getting home. It was about the day before they let me go, Danny took me to his house and said, 'Hey bro, let me get you a shower' and bought me a slice of pizza, because we were starving. And the place we had, had no hot water and no shower, so you basically sponge-bathed in cold water in New York. Now in New York, you turn on the faucet and ice cubes come out. So imagine me trying to sponge bath myself and then trying to shave. I've got a full beard, I'm trying to shave in cold water. It hurt. I couldn't do it. So Danny showed me some mercy. I'll never forget him for that. That's one of the greatest things. We're not friends anymore; I guess he doesn't like the fact that I became a Christian, but that's okay."

"It was not nasty," clarifies original Anthrax vocalist Neil Turbin, talking about the Music Building, where his band saw Metallica play for the first time. "It was kind of like, if you have your office, Martin, and if it wasn't the most successful point in your career and you are starting out and you had an office somewhere, but you had to live in it. Let's say, it didn't have a shower and it didn't have a kitchen, and just no bedroom, and you just kind had to work it out. You had to use the public bathroom, and try to take a...

what do you call it, a Mexican bath or something? (laughs). A sponge bath; that's what they call it. You've got to take a sponge bath, and you've got to figure out a way to cook stuff, and we brought them some stuff in the room, to try and help them out. Scott was really buddy, buddy with them, trying to latch onto them, and so he really went... he had stuff that he could give them. And he was working an angle. He was buddy, buddy with them. I was friendly with the guys too, but whatever, I didn't have the money or the juice. I was just one of the guys in the band. So I was actually really close with Cliff Burton, and I liked him a lot, got along best with him. James had a little bit of ego. Mustaine was just totally hard to even... I was friendly with Mustaine, but he was kind of obnoxious, even back then. But Kirk, once he got in the band, Kirk was cool. And he was easy to get along with."

"I like Dave's stint in the band, because I thought the songwriting was different," continues Turbin. "I like that era. And then, as a person, I don't know (laughs), he was kind of hard to deal with back then."

But not, as the telling goes, always drinking. "No, not always, because they didn't have money. He just got out of control and he drank too much. And that's probably what he was doing with the other guys in Metallica, because he was out of the band. I think he was just obnoxious. I was around him when he was trying to get his way with me to borrow something of mine to wear onstage, my vest. And he tried to steal it, or not give it back. And I said, 'You've got two choices. You either give me back my leather jacket,' that has the sleeves torn off that I wore at the Paramount Theatre. I said to Dave, 'Either you give me back my jacket or I'll rip your arms off and beat you to death. And the jacket will fall off itself.' So he gave me back my jacket, but it was really hard to get it back. And that was actually the last time I talked to him."

Metallica proceeded to scrape up enough cash to send Dave home on the bus. Lars has said the whole process took no more than 45 minutes, from waking him up, to clearing the room of his stuff, to getting him down to the bus depot in the back of James' truck. Dave would be replaced by Kirk Hammett, heeding the call to leave Frisco rivals Exodus and hitch his star with Lars and James and Cliff. At best for Hammett, it was a lateral move, but Hammett didn't like the direction Exodus was going in and decided to take the chance.

"They sent David home because they didn't know what they were going to get," continues Jonny, who saw first-hand how Dave was bringing dark vibes to Metallica. "You didn't know if you were going to get a great Metallica record or just drunk, you know, fucking it up. So they brought in Kirk, which was great—that's on **Kill 'Em All**. The guy who produced the album with me had engineered Santana's earlier albums. And he was just mixing Kirk like Carlos Santana. And the problem was, I get there at the end of the album, after being broke from finalizing the recording, and James is all depressed.

And Lars has to speak to me and he says, 'Jonny, this isn't heavy enough.' So we went in and had James redo all the rhythms, with the big, big chunky sound he's famous for. Because at that point, the big test with us was, beat the demo. Can we be heavier and better sounding than the demo? Or people should just get the demo and not bother with the record. And we managed to come out flying. It was just a better sounding demo, and it has great playing by Kirk Hammett. He went out and blazed."

With Mustaine officially out of Metallica on April 11, 1983, the flash guitarist vowed revenge, promising to create the most dangerous heavy metal band of all time. But first he'd lick his wounds, returning to live with mom and getting a job as a telemarketer. No surprise this didn't last long, with Mustaine moving to Hollywood, forming a short-lived band called Fallen Angels until, one day, Dave Ellefson came into his life.

Ellefson had been practicing his *Runnin' With The Devil* one day in the apartment below Mustaine's. Hungover, Dave threw a potted plant off the balcony, which crashed into the air conditioner. Ellefson and his buddy Greg Handevidt decided then to go upstairs and try bum some cigarettes off of Mustaine, who told them that there was a store on the corner and slammed the door. Then they came back and asked Mustaine to bootleg some beer for them and Mustaine instantly warmed to the guys and they partied that night, talking about their rock heroes.

For a brief time, the three became an incarnation of Fallen Angels, along with Lawrence "Lor" Kane on vocals. Lawrence would soon be gone, but not before suggesting the name Megadeth. Once Lawrence was out, the trio latched onto a drummer called Dijon Carruthers and the first version of Megadeth was born.

Dijon would soon be out, replaced by Lee Raush. Dave, given lingering philosophical accents from his upbringing, was spooked by Raush's flirtation with Satanism and had soon decided they couldn't be in a band together. What sealed the deal was Lee himself coming to that realization, after playing through a gig in total pain from a foot injury and then deciding he'd had enough—he was going to search for the meaning of life.

Drummer-less again, Dave and Dave Jr. (Ellefson's soon to be instated perennial tag) auditioned one Gar Samuelson, a suggestion from the band's new and first manager, Jay Jones. Already a heroin addict, Gar nonetheless won the guys over with the fresh jazz sense he applied to Mustaine's already non-traditional yet uncompromisingly metallic songcraft. Unfortunately, Jones was, like Gar, a junkie but a dealer as well. Ergo, Megadeth was all too quick to enter the world of heroin and cocaine, skipping the slow build-up to such nasty habits, a metaphor for the music the band was making and the bad-ass vibes they peeled off at every modest career turn. Mustaine, one to enjoy the practice of vengeance, was doing everything wrong and everything right at the same time, at full speed.

At the guitar end of things, it was still just Dave, with Slayer's Kerry King winding up in the band for a few shows in the spring of '84. Slayer hadn't done much yet and Dave was impressed with Kerry's discipline and his abstention from drugs or alcohol. They became friends, but soon he was out of the band, back to try his luck with Slayer.

"The word 'megadeath' means mass annihilation," explained Dave to Ernie McKenzie in 1988, putting the record straight with respect to the naming of the band. "I first saw the word when I was living in California a few years ago, and the senator out there, Alan Cranston, had sent out a handbill that said, 'The arsenal of megadeath can't be gotten rid of no matter what the peace treaties come to.' I just fell in love with the term 'arsenal of megadeath.' I found out the term was used in reference to the body count after a nuclear war—it's a million deaths. That whole concept got to me, so I wrote a song called *Megadeth*, which really went after people and governments with too much authority—the people who can bring about megadeath. Believe it or not, I have no intention of trying to change the world. But I do want to try and make people aware of things that can have a major impact on their lives. Those things can be both good and bad, but they are things everyone should be made aware of. We're trying to deal with things that are a little deeper than what the average band does, but no one ever said we were an average band. There's so much going on in the world right now, kids need someone who can stay on top of things. We're not scared to tackle controversial subject and get people a little mad. That's what this band is really about. We're Megadeth, which means we can do whatever the fuck we want."

On March 9, 1984, Megadeth issued their first demo, with Dave tackling lead vocals as well as lead guitar. The demo, fronted with a crude drawing of the band's creepy mascot Vic Rattlehead, opened with *Last Rites/Loved To Death*, *Last Rites* being a typical innocent and pretty heavy metal intro (the pioneer in this was Accept with *Fast As A Shark*) the beauty of which was broken by the most ungodly of guitar riffs, ripping, complicated, seething with anger. *Loved To Death* then explodes and Dave has proven his brilliance at metal once again, laying down a track more sophisticated than anything on **Kill 'Em All**, up to the levels of **Ride The Lightning**, except not nearly as "likeable."

Speaking of Metallica, next up was *Mechanix*, formerly very early Mustaine-penned Metallica track *The Mechanix*, at this point re-engineered and famous as *The Four Horsemen* off of **Kill 'Em All**. Including this was vintage Mustaine, Dave reminding everybody that he was pretty damned important in Metallica, admittedly by all as the most talented guy in the band circa '82 and early '83. The demo ends with *The Skull Beneath The Skin*, another sophisticated construct, one that is so note-dense come riff time, it sounds like a combination of backwards recording and polyrhythm, yet it really is straight 4/4. The aggression, the anger, the revenge is palpable—this was the work of a man with much to prove, and poison was the cure.

"I had a terrible time singing and I still don't like it," reflects Dave, incrementally, on winding up as Megadeth's singer. "I don't think I'm very good at it, though people differ. A lot of people will say I have an original style. Yeah, I have an original style because I don't know how to sing. I guess what I tried to do in the beginning was tell a story with a melody. We had a guy that... we were pretty set on this guy. We were almost going to hire him; of course Megadeth would have been a five-piece. It didn't hurt Journey, except for the fact that the guy in Journey sang like a chick, and this guy looked like the dude from Journey, and he showed up with eyeliner on. I was like, 'Oh no.' He had two 12-packs of beer, and me and Dave Ellefson were living in his van at the time, so a guy who walked up with a couple 12-packs of beer, that's a party waiting to happen. So I said, 'Just wait until we're done drinking the beer, I'll handle this.' So I said, 'Yeah, that's the last... okay, you're fired.' And he wasn't very gracious, but who the hell's going to wear eyeliner to a Megadeth concert unless you're a girl?"

"So because we had such a hard time trying to find a vocalist, Dave Ellefson said, 'Why don't you sing?' Dave and I have been friends forever. Back then we barely knew each other. We'd only known each other a short period of time, and he didn't really know me very well so he didn't realize how scared shitless I was of singing. I'd talk between songs when I was in Metallica because James wouldn't talk. I didn't talk between songs because I aspired to be a front man. I looked over at him and he wasn't doing anything, and he was like, 'Say something' and I was going to go up to my mic and say, 'Say something, James' and then I looked at him and I saw some girls in the audience. And I started going, 'Hey,' you know the Mr. Microphone commercial, 'We'll be back to pick you up later.' But I guess for me, knowing that I had become a front man was when I started really watching people sing the lyrics I had written. You write something and you put pen to paper, the farthest thing from your mind is that one day people are going to be singing it, let alone in stadiums singing my songs."

"Finally, studio material from Megadeth," wrote friend of the author, Jim Powell, in the 'zine Grinder, which he shared with another buddy Dave Wright and Kevin Fisher. "After hearing how great they are on some live tapes which are floating around everywhere, I couldn't wait to hear them with a good recording. This demo was so great. I don't know how to describe it, but I'll try. The tape starts off with *Last Rites*, which is a classical intro. It then tears right into *Loved To Death*; it's the fastest song on the tape. *The Mechanix* is next, which is basically pretty similar to the version that's on the Metallica – **No Life 'Til Leather** demo. *Skull Beneath The Skin* ends this massacre in a real grinding manner. Dave Mustaine's raw vocals and guitar playing has definitely put Megadeth on top of the Power Metal scene. I highly recommend this tape to all whiplash inducers. Obtain at all costs, trades or deeds."

It's interesting to see Jim use the term "Power Metal," because the original (albeit loose) definition of the term described a certain technical form of metal that was often speedy but often mid-paced, tinged with the commercial but mostly what we used to call working man's metal or meat and potatoes metal. And if you think about it, calling this form of metal "powerful" made a lot of sense, given that the distinction was against everything else at the time, which would be '70s metal, NWOBHM, proto-hair metal and other forms of more melodic and even keyboardy hard rock. Megadeth, as represented by the demo, was indeed power metal, or even speed metal, very much in the wheelhouse of the first records by Metallica, Anthrax and Metal Church, not to mention much of the offerings from Brian Slagel and Metal Blade or Mike Varney through his guitar-charged Shrapnel imprint.

Next into the ranks of Megadeth was another non-singing guitarist, and then one Chris Poland. A friend of Gar's from back in Buffalo, as well as colluder with the notorious Jay Jones, Dave welcomed him into the band on the strength of his playing, sure, but also because he seemed pretty healthy and confident. Dave also liked the fact that he already had a practiced chemistry with Gar, having played in a jazz-fusion band with him for five years (Poland was 25 years old by this point, four years Mustaine's senior), having moved to LA in 1977 and forming The New Yorkers.

"My friend, Gary Samuelson joined the band," explains Chris. "And, you know, Gar said to me, 'I joined this band and I think you should join it. I think it's going to be really good.' The reason we liked it is that we came from a fusion background and then when he joined the band he felt like it was challenging enough for him to play, because he was totally into Tony Williams, Lenny White. Billy Cobham, drummers like that. Basically, I saw them play at the Water Club in San Pedro, and it was Megadeth three-piece, and I thought, these guys aren't going to make it three-piece. So I said, Gar, man, I want to get in this band. Because I wanted to play with Gar. I mean, I grew up playing with Gar."

"Dave's music isn't really metal," continues Chris. "I mean Dave's music is pretty freaking complicated and physically hard to play, and physically hard to make it look easy on stage, and still headbang and do all that stuff. So me and Gar were like, you know, this is not easy music to play, so let's do it. And believe it or not, they worked at a rehearsal studio in Hollywood at the time. Gar said, 'Listen, they're at Mars Studios. Why don't you just come down, rent a room, turn your stuff up to 12 and play guitar for an hour?' And that's what I did. I figured, I'll play some guitar and if they like it, they can come in and see if they want me. So I just rented a room down there and took all my stuff down and played. And about 20 minutes after I started playing, Dave knocked on my door and said, 'Hey, you wanna join Megadeth?' And I said, 'Yeah, that's why I'm here.'"

"I mean, when I think of Gar, Gar's the whole reason that we're talking right now, really," muses Chris. "Because he approached me and said let's do this thing, and it worked out, and I think the reason it worked out was because of Gar. It was because of the way he approached the drums as far as speed metal. How do you approach drums like that, and keep it sounding like yourself? I don't know, it's hard to describe. It's like I hear other people play it, but you also hear a lot of people play it the way Gar would play it. So he had a lot of influence on that type of music."

Soon rehearsing and playing live up and down California revolved around the scheduling of "getting well," dealing with "the heroin bitch," i.e. scoring heroin and then doing heroin. Dave was also not happy to see Metallica's career showing so much early promise, Lars, James, Kirk and Cliff moving from strength to strength almost gracefully, while Dave's second-place anger machine thrashed nasty with half the charisma as Metallica did. Megadeth was Metallica with edge, and at this point in the early evolution of thrash, Metallica's degree of edge was about all the punters could absorb without getting befuddled.

When it came time to do business, Megadeth took a shot at a deal with Enigma Records, but wound up with Combat, a scrappy metal indie with a reputation as bad as Megadeth's. But there was the possibility the band could have ended up on Elektra, the label that had just taken Metallica from Jonny Zazula.

"I had just started my job," says signer of Metallica, Michael Alago. "I was a young A&R person. Keep in mind, that music, at that point in time, was so fresh. And at that point in time, I think everybody was still listening to what I call the staples, like Iron Maiden and Judas Priest and Ozzy. And those were the things that were big, because after that signing, you have to remember that tons of bands were getting signed. So at the time, I wanted to sign Megadeth, on **Killing Is My Business... And Business Is Good!**. I even brought Dave to the Garden with me, when Metallica opened for Ozzy, and everybody was like, 'Why is Dave here with Alago?' I was just like, being Pollyanna, trying to make nice-nice. And everybody was cordial to each other, but after I had a number of meetings with Mustaine, he was like, 'You know Michael, I don't want to, yet again, be in their shadow.' So it never really worked out, but we stayed friends for a very, very long time. And I was always hanging around with Dave, especially when he was making **Peace Sells**, one of my all-time favourite records ever. But yes, he felt, 'You know, Michael, you're going to be so obsessed and you're going to be always with them.' And I guess in a way, I didn't blame him. But I was like a 23-year-old young and excited A&R person who just thought, you know what? I want to work with the best bands. And I thought Megadeth was fucking awesome.

But you know, you don't get everything you want. But that's okay too."

Turns out there would be ties to Metallica after all. Combat, with its hands in both punk and metal, was an imprint under the umbrella of Important Records, who were also all up into Megaforce, mighty homespun metal indie of the Jon and Marsha Zazula, nicer folks than those who schemed at Combat.

Megadeth's deal with Combat was typically onerous as any naively signed by desperate kids. Indeed, this band of bad news junkies barely paid attention to what they were signing, caught in enough trouble trying not to kill each other or hang onto girlfriends that could bring home groceries. Nonetheless the band had $8000 to record what would become **Killing Is My Business... And Business Is Good!**. Ensconced in Indigo Studios, which was initially constructed for the use of the Moody Blues, the band spent, as Dave quips, four grand on drugs and four grand on making the record. The drugs ran out in the first week and the band spent the rest of the time alternately dopesick and occasionally well. Manager Jay Jones was fired, and an engineer who had recently worked with Kiss was brought in to move things along. The band eventually weaseled another $4000 out of Combat and were able to finish the album.

2
KILLING IS MY BUSINESS...
AND BUSINESS IS GOOD!

"There was no clear thinking on anyone's part"

With **Killing Is My Business**, unleashed with a snarl in June of 1985, the band managed to capture a visceral vibe that frankly scared listeners. The record made **Kill 'Em All**, a better album, nonetheless seem tame by comparison, even if the production of all these demanding parts came off midrangey, ear-fatiguing, harsh. Fact is, the band were never happy with it, but it is no disaster. In essence, it was the exact sort of thing one expected to hear in the mid '80s, slapped with the Combat stamp of "it'll do." And although **Killing** would have been premiere product on Metal Blade or Shrapnel in the '80s, it wasn't quite as good as Metallica's **Kill 'Em All** debut from a two years previous. Nor was it as swell as Anthrax's **Fistful Of Metal**... from a year and a half ago. What's more, **Ride The Lightning**, issued nearly a year earlier, crapped on it from a height of several miles.

"It was basically not really anything that had been done yet," muses Poland, speaking the truth about the album's slightly off-kilter approach to speed metal. "So we were trying to just make it be what it was. Dave would come up with the parts and actually everybody would actually put their two cents in here or there, a harmony here, cut this part out there."

"I especially like the new remix," continues Poland, concerning the 2002 reissue. "I mean, that's just... man, making me look good! (laughs). But granted, we didn't have a big budget; we really didn't have our shit together for that record. But the performance and the playing on it is still the same performance and playing. So luckily they got it to sound better and it's a really great record. And now I enjoy that record."

"The philosophy is, you have your whole life to make your first record, and then after that you've got about nine months to follow them up," laughs Dave Ellefson, repeating a well-worn truism. "I thought **Killing Is My Business** had a lot of melody to it, that sort of got overlooked maybe because of lack of money; we weren't able to produce it that well."

Megadeth's first record opens the way the demo did, with an eerie piano track called *Last Rites* imploding amidst the smoke and flames of *Loved To Death*, a violent love song directed to Dave's obsession at the time, Diana Aragon. Track two, the title track, is a similarly obtuse, jazzy, yet catchy modern metal construct which bursts into a speedy bit to close things out. Again, it's not quite up to Metallica's standard, with Dave's punk predilection showing through. Lyrically, Dave says it's about the comic book **The Punisher**, particularly a hit man pulling off a whack job and then performing a second contracted hit, his own boss. As for the title, it came from where one might suspect, a slogan on a T-shirt the guys saw in a military surplus store.

"Metallica started in '80, but it was like a cookie cutter making the same cookie. I wanted to change things," said Dave in '97, looking back at the type of improvement he wanted to make over his firers. "So when I left, I didn't want to be seen like I was ripping them off. Not that they need another band in the universe ripping them off (laughs). But I wanted to try something different and a little more advanced. I'm not saying that we're more advanced than the next guy, but we wanted to do something more thrashier. You know, when there was speed metal, thrash metal, we were up there, we were some of the kings of that stuff. Now the genre has pretty much gone through so many different fusions into death, gore, grindcore, black, all these different types of metal. Back then they had just one category for it, before all these spawnings. I think it was easier to understand these things."

The Skull Beneath The Skin is another sophisticated grinder with many parts and personas. But the finesse welling up from Chris and Gar was somewhat lost due to the album's harsh tones. Mustaine puts some of the blame on manager Jay Jones, who was in there half producing with the band, Jones even suggesting the thrash version of *These Boots* for the album.

"Yes, the manager guy, Jay Jones, picked that, and he also picked *Superstitious*," says Poland. "He was a crazy guy, of course; that's the darkest story of all, but I won't go into that. But he's not alive anymore. He was kind of like a character/manager, manager/whatever, guy. He was a friend who did more than he had to do. He actually came out on the road with us once. He was crazier than all of us. But he had great ideas. If he wouldn't have been bitten by the drug thing, he would've been one of the best promoters that ever lived, because he had the knack for getting stuff done. He was a talker and a mover and shaker. He just couldn't get over that drug thing."

But Chris admits they were all hooked, just not to the same extent. "Everything... It was all heroin. I mean, everybody did cocaine too. But mostly, the drug that led everybody down the dark road was heroin."

But as mentioned, Jay up and died. "Yes, I think a couple years after I got sober. Probably 12, 13 years ago. But he was a great guy, he helped us before we even knew Dave. He helped me and Gar, in the fusion band we were in, booking us shows. And it wasn't until the Megadeth years that he seemed to go over the deep end."

But business got taken care of, and pretty much fairly. "Yes, we had a partnership," says Chris. "We split everything four ways, except the publishing. Originally, we had talked about splitting everything, even publishing, and Dave's attorney got him alone, and before we knew it, that's not what happened. And that's his business. That's his attorney's job, and I have no sour grapes about that. But again, basically, we had a partnership, that everybody got everything, and it was all four ways. We were all taken care of, our rent was paid, and it wasn't a terrible thing. It's just that we didn't have the same vision as Dave did. Especially me. I mean Dave Ellefson had Dave's vision. He wanted to do whatever Dave was doing. Me and Gar, I can't speak for Gar right now, but toward the end there, it was just being totally alcoholic drug addicts that couldn't lend any kind of sanity to any situation. There was no clear thinking on anyone's part. I look back at it now and it's a miracle we're not all dead. But, I think that's another thing that made those records what they are. I mean, we were as angry as that music sounds."

I had asked Dave, 25 years later, how he could have overlooked Gar's and Chris's heroin problems in the hiring of them into the band, drawing the analogy to the capable and ambitious Paul and Gene setting up shop with the likes of Ace and Peter.

"Because I really didn't figure it was that that bad at the time, Martin. I just figured, 'You do your own thing; I don't really care.' I didn't really know anything about it, and then one day Gar said, 'If you want to be great, you need to do heroin.' And we were struggling with the fact at the time that we had some people that were interested in us, but it just didn't... by this time we already had a record out. Because I wasn't really as interested in doing smack as the other guys were. And David was so innocent. I mean, Chris will tell you by his own admission in the press and everything, that we all had our addictions. But I don't know if there were many people who would have survived those years. Because we were just so out of control. I know that the drug use had contributed to Gar's liver problem, which ultimately cost him his life. I know that Poland is sober right now, thank God. I know that Ellefson is sober."

"You know, I've already explained how I do things," continues Dave. "That was really weird too. At the time it was almost bohemian to say that you were a junkie. Because everybody was doing cocaine, and cocaine was just such a juvenile drug, and there were so many, many, many types of it. You never got cocaine that tasted the same. But the heroin, it was pretty consistent. It was just one of those things where, you know, wherever you were, whenever you got it, just by the way it tasted, you knew what it was."

"You gotta remember, you've got to be a little open to the process," answers Dave, on the subject of merely even eating properly amidst the mayhem of those early years. "We're sick, everything is horrible, and you get well by taking the heroin, and then all of a sudden everything is normal. And you can eat, you're nice, you go out, you're congenial, you hang out with people, and then eating a cheeseburger is not such a big deal. Or granted, having a cheeseburger does not a great meal make, but you live. And David Ellefson and I were panhandling. There was a place that was right down from where we were living called Astro Burger, and I remember going in there, and always making sure I was asking for extra vegetables on my hamburger, so it's like, six inches of lettuce and tomatoes and shit (laughs). We had this manager Jay, right, and we would go to a place called Norm's, and Norm would have a meal that had salad, potato, steak and Jello cup, and all you can drink iced tea or some shit like that. And you know, looking at it now, the steak was kind of like one of those inserts for your insole, but at the time it was great. You could even eat the gristle (laughs)."

Back to the album, scrappy speed-metaller *Rattlehead* introduces us to ol' Vic Rattlehead, Megadeth's perennial mascot more smartly used than Maiden's Eddie, more grandly illustrated over the years, more sophisticated in his thinking, a political being no less. "Oh, that's all Dave's," notes Chris, referring to both any early drawings of Vic as well as the album cover's creepy "sculpture." "You know how Eddie was the guy for Iron Maiden? Well, Dave had Vic Rattlehead, the victim. And he hears no evil, because his ears are covered, and his eyes are covered, so he sees no evil, and his mouth's sewn shut. Basically he is our Eddie. And that's all Dave's artwork. He drew the very first T-shirt."

Mustaine famously hated the debut's album cover, but Poland says, "Hey man, I was happy with it. I had no qualms about it. And the second record was even better, and so, then they used that guy until the wheels fall off. But I wasn't interested in that. I was just more interested in trying to get my parts right when we made that first record."

Although if there's any actual Vic in *Rattlehead*, he only shows up at the end of the song, as a sort of Paul Baloff character bullying people into living for the metal. In fact, Vic emerges more meaningfully in *The Skull Beneath The Skin*. Even if the title was lifted from a book Mustaine spotted in a store, the lyric presents a Satanic human sacrifice, and as Chris alludes to, the poor victim becomes the Vic. This is very much in keeping with what happens to Eddie o'er the course of the Maiden covers—sure, he delivers some beatings, but over time he gets more than a few pieces lopped off his emaciated self.

Rattlehead is the fastest song on the album, and it was essentially all about the crowd throwing themselves into speed metal. It's actually a showcase for Poland; despite its rigidity, Chris gets to peel off fiery licks that Dave Ellefson said were possible because of a severed tendon Poland had in his hand that allowed him more reach that other mortals.

Confirms Chris, "Yeah, I do a lot of stuff with my pinkie, my ring finger and my FU finger, and my index finger is kind of messed up—I can't bend it. So there's a lot of weird stuff going on in the way I play. And a lot of guys, like guitar players here in LA, when I first moved out here, not unlike Mike

Albert, I met this guitarist, Bob, who was, 'You know what? If you didn't cut your finger, you wouldn't play the way you do.' And I was like, 'Well, OKAY.' But they told me I could never have it fixed, so I got what I got."

Chosen Ones is actually quite Metallica-esque of riff and substantial melody, not so speedy, with a lyric that Mustaine says was influenced by the killer rabbit bit from **Monty Python And The Holy Grail**. *Looking Down The Cross* finds Dave drawing upon his religious upbringing and imagining what Christ might have been thinking on the cross. As for *Mechanix*, well, this was the major tie to Metallica. As discussed, it was a Mustaine-penned Metallica staple in the formative years and showed up on the band's debut album as *The Four Horsemen*, with a considerably better lyric than Dave's gas station attendant sexual fantasy vignette.

"I didn't start playing guitar until I was 13," recalls Dave, asked about this one. "Early age for me would probably be around 15, and that's when I started writing. The first song I wrote—I'm pretty sure it—was *Jump In The Fire* or *Mechanix*. And after that was *Rust In Peace*, which was the third song I actually wrote. I wrote the music that went onto *Metal Militia* and *Phantom Lord* right after that, and then I started writing music that ended up on *Hangar 18*, parted ways with Metallica, took the songs that weren't recorded on *Kill 'Em All*, used those in Megadeth. The ones that were used in *Kill 'Em All*, there's no point in me recording them because they'd already done it, except for *Mechanix*, and that was such a gross departure from what the song actually was. We went into rehearsal one day and Lars wanted a slow part and I said okay. And I played *Sweet Home Alabama* and he went, 'Fuck that's great, man' and next thing you know it's in *Mechanix* and then *The Mechanix* is called *The Four Horsemen*. And so that's why I recorded *Mechanix*, because I thought, well, the other songs were really close to how they originally were. It wasn't like a protest or anything, I just wanted to play them the way it really was. So writing music for me at the beginning, I was pretty good at it right out of the gate. I got really fortunate with momentum from Metallica. But the first couple of songs I wrote… when I left Metallica, the first song I wrote after that was *Set The World Afire*, which didn't show up until the third record. Nothing comes out from me until it's time. I may have written it 20 years ago, but if it's not ready to be heard, you're not going to hear it. But it was like the last record. People are going, 'How much of this is old stuff and how much of this is new stuff?' Well it's a combination of both."

Of note, when the album was reissued in 2002 on CD, the original plastic-and-tinfoil sculpture done by Combat was replaced with an illustration truer to the band's original vision. As well, the remix makes it eminently more listenable, but there's another material change. The band's original thrash version of *These Boots*, written by Lee Hazlewood and popularized by Nancy Sinatra, had been deemed vile and offensive by Hazlewood, prompting a coerced cleaning up of the lyrics for the reissue... and a chiding from Mustaine in the liner notes.

But *These Boots* was controversial with the fans from the beginning, most considering a novelty track on such a bleak album, too much of a departure from the white knuckle sonic haranguing around it. But Dave was into it, first, because he recalled it making an impression with him as a kid, hearing it on the car radio on rides with his mom. Secondly, Mustaine could identify with the song's revenge theme. In any event, it was live on stage that the song won fans over. Ellefson would sit on a stool smoking a cigarette playing the bluesy intro on bass, and then Mustaine would come charging in and take over. All told, it was some light relief after so much grim progressive speed metal.

"Yeah, I forgot about that!," laughs Chris, on the live presentation of *These Boots*. "It's funny you say that. It's a barstool that we used to carry in the Ryder truck with us. He used to sit down and go 'ba-do do doom,' and I would do a little solo to it, and it was kind of cool." As for other live gimmicks used in his time with the band, Chris says, "Dave had this idea that he wanted pyramid cabinets, and so I think it was DeCuir cabinets; it was a big company out here in the early '80s. And he made these stands, so that all our cabinets, you know, you could stack four, three, two and one, and it looked pretty awesome. But Dave Ellefson had to play bass through a guitar cabinet, so that wasn't so happening. But it looked cool."

Touring for the album, summer of '85, found the band paired with rawer thrash machine Exciter, an Ottawa trio enjoying notoriety as an early Shrapnel Records signing. Explains Exciter guitarist John Ricci, "1985, we're touring the US, a seven week tour, coast to coast, Exciter and Megadeth. Megadeth, technically is our opening act, except for a few shows where we alternate headliner status, like some cities in the southern US where they were better liked than we were, so we would open. This went on to the whole seven weeks. We became very good friends."

But Chris Poland had got busted for trying to score heroin, so the band called a quick audible and hired a bit of a mystery man by the way of Mike Albert. Albert was emphatically no metalhead. Nor did he work, as is widely reported, with Captain Beefheart, playing at most, "a little slide." His credits were actually a late version of Zappa side band Ruben And The Jets, Latino act El Chicano, and the live rock backing band for Cheech & Chong!

But of course Mike wasn't doing any of that when Megadeth came calling, cowboy hats in hand... "Mustaine was told about me. In fact, I was playing in Huntington Beach in Southern California, and I was playing, actually, country. I had a country gig, and I was playing a lot of slide guitar. We did a lot of Allman Brothers and stuff like that, and I remember they came in, they introduced themselves to me, and they're sitting at a table right in front of me. I thought man, I know these guys are metal guys, rock guys. I didn't know who the hell they were, actually, but I'm up here playing country stuff, thinking I don't think it's going to fit. Oh well, I just thought, I'll never see them again. They're at the table staring at me with their arms crossed. It's like man, I said to the band, 'Can we at least do a heavy Allman Brothers song?' And they looked at me, and they looked at those guys, and they stuck out like a sore thumb. And they thought, what's going on, Mike? Who are these guys? But I think we did an Allman Brother song, and I looked down, and they were gone and I thought, oh well, there goes that one. There was a possibility. And then Dave called me the next day and said, 'Hey man, you blew the top of my head off. I've never seen anybody play like that. Would you be interested in being in my band?' And he gave me a cassette of the stuff, I brought him by the apartment, he played an acoustic guitar we had in the house to kind show me what they were doing, and a few days later, I went and learned pretty much the set. I spent like 12, 14 hours a day on it."

Albert was in the band's orbit due to his knowing Chris, Gar and manager Jay Jones, all, again, from the non-metal world.

"Gar was amazing, and he was one of the nicest guys," says Mike. "Everybody knows he was a fusion guy. But I knew him years prior when he was with Chris with The New Yorkers, and hung out with them, jammed with them. He was a Billy Cobham / Lenny White kind of guy, fusion guy. And he really interpreted... I mean, he really liked Hendrix and that stuff, but primarily him and Chris were into that style. And I saw him evolve. The first part of the tour, I remember when we started rehearsing for the first US tour, he was kind of a jazz guy, really didn't think he fit that much in the band. And I thought, man, didn't make sense, and then by the time we got back from the last city, we did like 30, 40 cities, we came back, and he was like amazing. He picked up the genre and he just sounded completely like a killer drummer I'd never heard before, in the style he was doing. And even Chris came to the rehearsal after we came back from the US tour. He hadn't seen us as a band for a while, and he saw Gar, and the first thing he said to Gar was, 'My God, I've never heard you sound so good. What the hell!' Gar just caught onto it, man. But the tour, and seeing the other bands play, it's just amazing to see how he accomplished so much. I mean, he was just amazing after that. He got it, and he was one of the best."

Adding a memory of Chris' and Gar's old band, the New Yorkers, Albert says that, "They had it back east, but when they came out to Los Angeles... I think back east it was called something else. But in LA, if you're called the New Yorkers you're one-of-a-kind (laughs). But they were amazing back then. I was pretty much one of the better guitar players with Eddie Van Halen; it was right before he had made it, and that's when Chris came in. And Eddie was the Pasadena guy, I was the Hendrix guy, down South in Pasadena, and then when Chris came in, it was like, now who does this guy think he is? And he was just like... I didn't know what the hell he was doing.

He was playing stuff that nobody on guitar really played. It was shocking (laughs). He was so good back then. I mean, even now he's amazing, but he was just as amazing when he was 19."

The other connection was manager Jay Jones. "I knew him even before they knew him," says Mike. "Jay was a character. But you gotta realize, Dave can say what he wants rapping Jay, but if it wasn't for Jay, Chris Poland and Gar Samuelson would never have got in there. Jay did have some clout back then, and he was a pretty intense guy. But as they say, he got caught up in that, and I think he was Mustaine's pusher back then. They kind of hid things from me. If they really had something to do underhanded, they would disappear. I knew something was up, but I was happy being in the band. I didn't care what they were doing, just didn't get involved with it. Jay was an intense guy, and he was a talker. I mean, he would promote them highly. He told me about them before I even knew what their name was, just that Gar and Chris got in this band with this guy who plays guitar really fast, this long-haired, red-haired individual. He promoted a lot of different things, even some stuff with the Circle Jerks back then. Chris got in with Circle Jerks, when he got thrown out of Megadeth. He was the bass player for them and did a tour with them."

"He was a talker," agrees Chris, plainly not comfortable talking about Jay Jones. "He could move in circles that you wouldn't think he could, but he did. And he was managing our band. We had a band called The New Yorkers, and at the same time he was managing Dave's band, Megadeth, and that's how I got involved in the project. And you know, he had a sad end, man, and it's not a story I want to tell. Because it was a personal family thing, and it's a dark story, and it's not something anybody needs to know about. But you know what? He was a friend, and I miss him. He also managed a bunch of punk bands. He got around and it wasn't drugs that killed him. No, he was basically stabbed to death. And that's all I'll say."

So now the Megadeth gig was Albert's. Talk about being chucked in the deep end... "Yeah, well, when Mustaine hit me up, people don't realize this, when I got in there, I had no clue what Megadeth was. The speed metal thing... I was into Deep Purple, I was into stuff like that, then Sabbath. When I first asked Dave, 'What kind of music is it, like Black Sabbath, this kind of thing? And he said, 'No, man, it's not anything like that. It's heavier. And I thought, what's heavier than Sabbath? He said, 'I can only explain that if you're driving 120 miles an hour into a brick wall, this is what you put on.' And when I listened to it, I thought, it is! It's end of the world music."

"So they were doing this new genre that was fresh out there," continues Albert. "I had no idea what speed metal or thrash metal was. I didn't even know what headbanging was. So I was thrown in with the wolves right there. I could play really fast, and Poland was a friend of mine, so we knew each other's playing. We used to hang out, we jammed together a million times.

And then when he got into Megadeth, he and Gar, all I heard was... they didn't know how to describe it. I thought it was like punk, a speed punk band. They didn't have any way how to categorize it. They were just doing it because they were making a few bucks off it. You know, they weren't really happy about it, they didn't talk about it or anything. But I heard they were making some money off of it, so I said sure, have him check me out."

Learning Megadeth music came quickly to Albert, being a session guy and all. "I still play like ten hours a day, and if I hear a style of music, if it's guitar, I'll learn it. And back then I was like a hired gun, and I still am, pretty much. I play guitar, so if anybody needs something, I can pretty much capture the feel and the licks, definitely, and the vibe of anything. I was kind of the go-to guy back then for that. And I think Chris knew that, so speed metal, I picked up pretty fast, although I didn't know what the hell I was doing. It didn't make sense to me."

And then this odd bunch hit the road. "Yeah, we were co-headlining with Exodus and with that band from Canada, Exciter. They were really nice guys. I really hit it off with them. And we did some shows with Death Angel, Dark Angel, Slayer, Anthrax, bands like that. I was just concerned with us, because I really got into it and pretty much focused on what we were doing. I didn't really think the other bands touched us. I think we flew to Washington DC, and then when we were back there, we rented a mobile home and just lived that way, not the easiest. You'd have an eight hour drive or whatever, if something wasn't really close. But there were days off, so we would just be travelling, which was a killer, but you gotta keep the money flowing in."

"Exodus, they were kind of distant with us," says Mike. "In fact, that's one of the guitar players I saw and was like man, he's really good. He'd be walking around with, I think a Pignose amp, and this guy would just be playing. Pretty intense. One of the better guitar players that I saw at that time. With Exodus, there was a bit more competition. With Exciter, I think they were a bit more down-to-earth because they're a Canadian band, and it was like that's great, because they didn't play a lot with us, like they wouldn't be in competition with us. And musically it was a different style of metal than what we were doing."

As for the drug scene, "It really wasn't as bad as people think. It was there, and they had it, and I really wasn't touching that. I wasn't into that. I was a drinker. But you know what? We had some stuff where the cops raided, they were coming to raid, people were calling the police, and something happened, and it was like that was the fastest we ever got out of a hotel. I mean, our road crew got us out in ten minutes, because somebody's running down the street calling for the police. So I thought that was it. I thought man, they're gonna search us. But we got away, you know?"

"They had a system worked out," explains Mike, on Megadeth's road deliveries of horse. "God, I hate to say this stuff, but they had it delivered somehow. I didn't want to be around that. I drink, but that was not my thing. I think they wanted a certain group of people... I was an outsider. You know, you're into that, and the other guys are into that, 'Oh, we've got to hide this from this guy; this guy doesn't like it. He has an attitude with it.' So I wasn't part of the family like they thought it was going to be."

But tough as nails, hard as metal, sick but sturdy, Megadeth could tough it through the shows. Heroin still had an effect however, says Albert. "It did. You could tell. Gar, especially. When Gar didn't have it, he was not happy. He was not a happy camper. He always played well, but you could see it on his face, that he was going through something. I was concentrating on my own parts, because I was playing something I'd never played before. We'd be on the tour bus, and I would be working on this stuff all day, even while travelling. Dave wouldn't pick up a guitar. And Dave would play live like he's playing 20 hours a day. It's his own style, which I really wasn't into. But his style of playing rhythm was just God-given. I'd never seen anybody play so fast, so precise, and he didn't pick up the guitar for days at a time. He would just go up there and play."

"One of the things that was cool was when we first met Metallica," recalls Mike, asked for any fond memories of his "40 to 50" shows with the band. "Kirk wouldn't show up, of course. I don't know what would've happened if he had showed up. But I know Dave, and I know that's one of his arch-enemies. Lars actually was a very nice guy, but one thing that turned me off, as we were hanging out, walking around, and we hit it off really good. We were talking like buddies for years and him and Dave are getting along, they were at the show, and I asked him, 'What do you think about Gar Samuelson?' I love Gar; Gar's not only a friend, but he's one of my favourite drummers. And Lars says, 'Oh, he's all right.' And you know what? After that, I didn't really talk to the guy. I wasn't really too happy with that, because, I mean, give credit where it's due. So that really got me. It was like, oh, come on. And especially after I heard him play. He was good, but he wasn't Gar, you know? But with Hetfield, him and Mustaine weren't friends at all back then. He would be like, 'Hey, tell Mustaine I'm here. Get me backstage.' He was like that. And I would tell Dave, and he would say, 'I don't want him back here.' So I would have to go tell him, 'You can't come back'."

Soon Mike was on his way out, by mutual agreement between himself and the boss. "We didn't really hit it off," figures Albert. "Me and Dave weren't like best friends. He was very moody. I know he said some bad things about me or whatever, but I don't want to get into that. A lot of it was because he knew that I really didn't care for his attitude, and I would let him know. And nobody else in the band would do that. I couldn't be quiet. He said I had a big mouth, and I did have a big mouth, because I want to be treated a certain way, and I saw what was happening. It was his band, and he needed people to be yes-men, and I wasn't, and that's what happened."

"He was perfect for Dave Mustaine," says Mike, asked about Ellefson. "Not only was he a peacemaker, he was just a mellow, down-to-earth guy. And he was a kid back then. He was Junior, he was little Dave, and he was a yes man for Dave. You know, 'Sit down, shut up, and do as I say,' and he would do it. He knew what he had. He was smart."

"We got into a lot of arguments," continues Albert. "When I came back from tour, I said I wanted money. I wanted money before I was gonna go into the studio with them. Because we came back, we didn't have any money after it all. All the money was gone, and those guys had their girlfriends or whatever they lived off of, and I had rent to pay. I said, 'You know, you wanna do this? I've gotta have money. You've got to talk to the record company. You gotta get a retainer; we need money to survive.'"

"And I refused to go rehearse with them for the new album. And Chris said, 'Hey man, let me back in the band, just give me some of Mike's gear, which is my gear, and you don't have to pay me. I'll just do it for free and you don't have to pay me. You don't have to. I'll do the album for free. I'm doing everything for free.' He just wanted back in the band and that was it. And I went to rehearsal, right previously, and Chris was with them in the band, and Dave had a major attitude then, because of course Chris would do it for free. 'I don't need you anymore.' And you know what, I was relieved, because it was just... I loved playing it, I really got into that genre of music, and I continued it after. Because I worked with one of the best guys in the genre, when I was there, and I got into it, and I tried to continue with it a bit, but it was tough. I just did my own stuff. I got offers. I was going to do a thing with the Chili Peppers and I had a fall-out with Anthony, the singer. And Alice Cooper, I had an offer with that, but after being on the road with those guys, I did not want to go on the road with anyone again unless it was my own band. I did a lot of sessions, I did a lot of TV and commercial stuff. But I didn't want to go back to that. It was so bad; you don't know what it's like. You're in another part of the country and you're with guys you just can't stand to be around."

A legal dispute arose as well. "Yeah, well, after the tour, we were working on the **Peace Sells** album. Dave had pretty much a lot of it written, but we collaborated on a lot of stuff as well, and he was supposed to give me some credit on it. I've told this before, but he was supposed to give me credit for the stuff that I wrote with him, and he called me up and said he was going to, and the attorney would call me. And this was after we had a fall-out. And I went, wow, that's great, a man of honour, that's cool. I guess he had been screwed over, so he was able to do it to me. And then he didn't call back, and then Capitol Records... I was going to try and sue Capitol Records. I didn't have anything written with him that I did write anything with them, so you know, I just wish it would've happened. I could've bought a couple houses."

Remarks Poland on the circumstances of his return to the fold, "You know what? I was kind of upset, because they did a T-shirt deal with, I don't know if it was Winterland or whatever, but it was only Dave Mustaine and Dave Ellefson on the contract. I was like, you told me and Gar that we were four members and whatnot, and I just got pissed and I said I'm not doing it. And then they came back. Dave said, 'Listen man, I don't want this guy my band. I want you my band.' And I said, 'You know what? I like being in the band, so let's try again'."

"A little bit here and there," says Poland on the extent to which he was involved with touring the first album. "We did some dates which were kind of frustrating, because you fly to New York and they give you a Marshall and a cabinet, and you wind up with what you wind up with, and it's like, ugh. But at that time I was not so... now I'm just so anal-retentive about tone and equipment and what I use and what I record with. At that time I was just kind of raw, trying to hack my way through it."

"But I know that Mike Albert helped them out, and he's a great player in his own right," says Chris, offering an assessment of Megadeth's mystery member. "When I first moved out to California in the late '70s, I saw him play shows where he sounded exactly like Hendrix. He could sound exactly like Santana. I mean, now, today, it's like, dude, that's not what you're about, man. Because I'm telling you, if you heard him play *Europa* (Santana classic from '76), if you closed your eyes, you would be like, man. So when he got into the metal thing, I was confused. He'd been in El Chicano and he played with other heavy guys. Mike Albert, he had tone, man, and when he joined Megadeth, he let all that go. I was like dude, you never should've... You should use that because you do it so well. But now he's still doing it, and I'm like, man, that's not what you're about. You're a blues guys, you're a classic rock guy. But he does what he wants to do, and I do what I want, so..."

"Yeah, Chris is back in Megadeth," said Dave, smoothing over the situation back in '86 speaking to legendary metal scribe Bernard Doe. "In fact, he was never really out of the band. It was just that he couldn't tour with us that first time. We talked to him as soon as we got back off the first tour and asked him if he'd gotten all his things straightened out. He said he had, so we got back together and commenced with part two of the Killing For A Living tour. You see, Chris is a really fucking outrageous guitar player, and he wouldn't stick with the band unless they were hot and happening. And since he comes from a more jazz-fusion type of interest, metal to him is kinda pathetic, because let's face it, listen to all the stuff that's out nowadays, it sounds like shit; it's all noise metal. When you have somebody that's that good and you're trying to say to him, 'Hey, look, there's a future in this stuff, there's money to be made, fun to have...' It's kinda hard to prove. But we managed to prove to him that it would work and he's now put everything that he was doing before out to pasture."

"Chris used to play with a bunch of bands at the same time all the time," continued Dave, "doing like session work, and that's what I meant when I said he was a session guitarist; he was playing with fucking everybody! I used to go along and see him jamming with all these other bands and I used to wonder to myself if he was gonna stick with Megadeth or move on to other things, and for a time, I didn't really know what was gonna happen. But we've proved to Chris that this band are gonna be a major success and we're not gonna be riding on the backs of Metallica and using them in every possible way to link us to success. We're making it on our own merits."

Noted Ellefson, years later, the band had always had a clear plan to extricate themselves from comparisons to Metallica: "I think probably Metallica—I would assume anyway—that once they made their guitar player change years ago, they just got on with it. They went on to be huge, and I watched Dave struggle with that whole thing. I think with Megadeth it was about finding our own identity, adding our own audience and not trying to take Metallica's audience, not trying to compete with them. It was as much about pushing our own band with our own fans and doing our own thing, regardless of how successful that was or wasn't going to be."

Aardschok's Gene Khoury caught the band in early 1986 at Irving Plaza, New York, as Megadeth finished doing their rounds for the **Killing Is My Business** album...

"Megadeth was finishing up a US tour and was interested in playing some of the newer material in front of the New York crowd," writes Khoury, reviewing the Overkill/Megadeth showdown. "Unfortunately, a large part of the crowd left and what little there was gave the band a dulled perception. Nonetheless, the band was the tightest that I have seen them in about five performances and the newer material was much more progressive in terms of musical complexity and band participation. The newer material included *Wake Up Dead*, *Devils Island*, *Mary Jane*, and *Looking Down The Cross*, all demonstrating the band's improved tightness of musical intensity. Older material like *The Mechanix*, *These Boots*, *Chosen Ones*, *Rattlehead*, *Loved To Death*, etc. once again highlighted the band's playing ability. It seems Dave has improved as a guitarist, taking in some fusion influences and meshing them with complex progressions and chords. The band has been building momentum to go into the studio to play with more intensity and aggressiveness so that the next LP shows off more variety and ultimately precise metal compositions. The band demonstrated they are ready to do exactly that as the live performance was quite enjoyable. The crowd was left in a haze when Dave and the boys left after a short 45 minute set. The reaction again was weak for a band which is deserving of a better reception, and in some ways, is owed a lot more by the metal world."

To close the chapter on Megadeth's abrasive first album, **Killing Is My Business** turned out to be one of the biggest sellers shady indie Combat ever hatched, but the album is the only Megadeth record not to break the

Top 200, despite selling more than 200,000 copies over time. Still, the haze-hatched Megadeth plan was to treat the album as somewhat of a demo, a demonstration, go indie, create a buzz toward landing a major deal more favourable than the one that might have arose from a three-song demo tape with a Mustaine-drawn Rattlehead cover. And that went pretty much as planned, not much different than what had happened to Metallica actually, even if Lars and James always seemed to be, infuriatingly, one step ahead.

3
PEACE SELLS... BUT WHO'S BUYING?
"If he woke her up, she'd kill him"

As a busy 1985 rolled into 1986, Megadeth had found themselves positioned on the scene as a band with scary talents as of yet unharnessed for mass consumption, or even full acceptance from a discerning metal underground. We've discussed the band's place in juxtaposition to Anthrax and Metallica, as one step behind, skilled but unformed, unfortunately an apt fit to their seedy label Combat.

Very much a comparative was Megadeth's career arc with that of Exodus, even if the germination was different. Exodus came up in parallel with Metallica, was somewhat stalled, but had now put together a creditable album in **Bonded By Blood** that was late to the game, emerging in April of '85 on micro-indie Torrid, associated with Combat. Exodus had lost a guitarist to Metallica, in Kirk Hammett, the replacement for Dave Mustaine. Megadeth, on the other hand, centred around its lightning rod ex-Metallica member Mustaine, embodied an Exodus-style buzz all within his fiery red-headed self, and then arrived late to the game, like Exodus, with an album with loose wheels and loose cannons. Long and short of it, Metallica and Anthrax were making metal for the deep, committed, extreme fan of the underground, but one could envision their records gaining converts from more mainstream metalheads, maybe even converting a few of the pliable to metal from the outside. But Exodus, Megadeth and even Slayer... well, you had to really love the stuff to put in the hours digesting their music.

Improbably, none of this seemed to matter. The mainstream record business wanted in.

"As we always see in our industry, the first one to the well usually gets to drink the choicest water," laughs David Ellefson, and of course he's referring to Metallica and their hooking up with Elektra. But Megadeth weren't far behind, reaching agreement with Capitol, not one of the lame majors by any stretch, like, say RCA (Scorpions) or London (ZZ Top, Y&T).

Continues Dave Jr., "So yes, certainly in this case, Metallica was the first horse through to the photo finish for sure. But what happened with that is that all of a sudden, the industry started looking around going, wow, there's something here. And so with us, with Metallica getting signed first to Megaforce, and of course Brian Slagel was already in the game, and was putting out his **Metal Massacre** records; that already inspired Armored Saint. So that really stirred the waters, and to some degree, Brian Slagel putting those **Metal Massacre** records out, that's of course Slayer, Metallica, Armored Saint. So to a large degree, he was the West Coast guy doing that and to some degree I kind of viewed Jonny Z as the East Coast guy doing that. So he was helping foster Anthrax, first signed Metallica. But again, first one in the water, all of a sudden, everybody else wants to jump in. I guess that's how I look at it."

"And so Metallica helped us all first get our own indie deals. Ours was with Combat, Anthrax was with Megaforce, Slayer, moving forward with Metal Blade, and they led the way. And then that same pattern repeated itself. Once Metallica signed with Elektra... and in fact Michael Alago, who signed Metallica, was courting us at one point to get signed to Elektra. And it's interesting because I think we were kind of questioning that, because it's like, you know, does this put us second fiddle to Metallica? What does this do? And it's interesting, because you question, where is their priority really going to be? Obviously Metallica is the big priority at Elektra. But I think what it did was, it certainly started to stir the waters for us."

"He's a fucking great guy!" says Chris Poland, remembering Michael Alago. "I remember him, man; he used to always come up, he wouldn't hug you, he would jump up on you and wrap his legs around your waist. He would always go after Junior. He was hot for Junior. But no, he was a great guy. I know there was something about Elektra, but I think, you know, we never took anything like that seriously, because we already had our label."

"Actually, I never had a problem with them, but Dave did," laughs Chris, concerning Combat Records. "There was a show we did... oh God, it wasn't L'Amour's, but some older theatre, and they took Dave offstage with one of those Vaudeville hooks. They didn't give us any food, but they gave Dave a bottle of fucking Seagram's Seven. Dave hasn't eaten anything, he's drinking Seagram's Seven, and he's telling the boss of Relativity off, on stage. And he's going off. It's like Dave, if he'd had a gun he would've started shooting at him. So they put this video screen down, and the only other person that broke that screen was Sid Vicious. But Dave fucking... God, he was trying to throw his guitar up into the audience, and he broke the fucking screen. And the next thing, there's a hook on him, and they're dragging him off stage. It's the craziest gig I ever did. Well, here's the problem. This is the biggest problem: Bad Brains opened. And that's a fucking big problem. You know, you better be on your fucking shit if the Bad Brains are opening back in that era. So we go on after them, and Dave's like halfway into a bottle of Seagram's. And the rest of us, we're not drinking fuckin' seltzer water. Then we did our thing, and Dave started... you know, I can't remember what the guy's name was—Steve Sinclair, I think it was. So he's telling Steve Sinclair off from the stage, for ten minutes. For ten minutes! Like, 'You fucking prick, mother...' And I was just like, holy shit. So we're done, and then Slayer came on. Yeah, Slayer was the headline act."

Asked about his relations with Slayer, as well as the other classic thrash bands Megadeth grew up with, Poland says, "The first time I played L'Amour's with Megadeth, I had known Kerry King because I'd worked at BC Rich, and sometimes I would work on his guitars and stuff. And I had this amp and it had no juice at all, man. Kerry had this Boss 10 band EQ, like Van Halen used to use, or I think he still does. Anyway, I said, 'Kerry, can I borrow that, man?' He said sure. So I mean, we had like a quasi-non-music relationship, with me working on his guitars and stuff, and he helped me out in New York one time, because I had the worst freaking rented amp. That always happens. I don't know how people do that. It's like you pull up and they're like, 'Yeah, here's a Twin Reverb; have fun with that.' And with Exodus, we did a New Year's Eve show, with I think Metallica headlining, Metal Church opened, then was us and then Exodus. And Exodus totally just tore us all a new butt, man. I couldn't watch our band play, but I watched everything else, and I'm like, man, that's gotta be the best metal band I've ever seen."

Continues Ellefson, on Megadeth's label upgrade, "Then Tim Karr, who signed us to Capitol Records, we did a show... I think it was in January of '86. Forgive me on the time on this, if it was somewhere in '86, we'd just recorded the **Peace Sells** record or we were about to go record, and we played a show at Irving Plaza. Our agent, Andy Summers, was like a cool indie agent, did a lot of punk rock stuff, Murphy's Law, I think, Bad Religion. I think he was even Green Day's agent at some point. So he really got the indie alternative types of music. And I think he saw our band as one of those kind of alternative... we weren't mainstream metal. The thrash thing was so out there, it was very alternative to what was happening in the mainstream, certainly MTV. And so he brought Tim Karr down to Irving Plaza to see the band and to meet us, and he loved it, and, 'Yeah man, I'm in.' And he came in and started bidding against Elektra. So yeah, our bidding war was basically Capitol against Elektra. And I think there might have been some interest from Atlantic Records, maybe even from MCA. I'm not exactly sure, but it seems like when one person jumps into the water, everyone follows."

So many similarities, the way all four of the big four moved on... "Right, so we're now all signed to these independent labels, and that's where the independent label guys are smart. Because they get in, they get a piece of you, and that's the idea. And so that's where they get their big reward, of course, is being sort of the broker who discovered the nugget of gold, that now he gets a piece of the gold forever (laughs), you know what I mean? And I don't know what everybody's deals are, but that was where to some degree, the indie guys... to be honest with you, Jonny Z, Brian Slagel, they certainly understood metal, as fans, and I'm not sure some of these other labels understood it as anything other than a business deal, and that can suck. And so, it's interesting, as I see from the outside looking in—and I don't know any of the details of the deals—but both Anthrax and Slayer started on these indies, and then Slayer with Def Jam, Anthrax, eventually with Island. But ours was definitely a straight vertical move right up to Capitol, straight off of an indie straight into a major label, and I'm not sure if some of these others were kind of imprints, because Island... even at that time, of course U2 was huge, but they didn't have a huge roster of artists, and they had very few bands that were huge."

Adds Mustaine, "I think Capitol, when they saw us, everybody wanted to sign the next Metallica. I wasn't the next Metallica. I *was* Metallica. And we fractured, and they went on and they did Metallica and I went on and I did something other than Metallica. But I still am Metallica. It's a part of me; it will always be a part of me. I will always belong in that band just like any of the guys were in Megadeth belong in the band. We just don't have a big enough stage to have 18 guys up there. But I know they all have their place here. We're not all friends. Most of us are, but not all of us."

Obviously, again, there's that pathology of needing to be a piece of Metallica, even if, to put it in perspective that Dave is somewhat missing there, Metallica went to do just a little more in their career than drinking their way through Savage and Diamond Head covers and the first few songs they wrote for **Kill 'Em All**. And as additional perspective, Dave could indeed do well to centre on the admirable career accomplishment of taking his band's thinking man's thrash very quickly to major label status.

Said Dave to Bernard Doe back in the day, when the ink on the contract was still fresh, "If it was good enough for the Beatles, then it's good enough for us! No, actually that's rather a sarcastic statement to make. I think the reason we went with Capitol is because they seem to be the smartest label out there right now. Even though they don't have three heavy metal bands that start with the letter 'M,' they at least have the integrity to give us everything we need. To direct our careers the way we see fit with their creative consultations and artistic advice. We do have direction control with this band, but it's not like we can do whatever we want. They have some say so too. We're a happy family now, we all work together, and we all have this one illegitimate bastard son called Megadeth and we all have to bring it up together. A lot of people think that a major label is a big monster, something to be feared, and a major means commerciality and stuff. And even know we're a wider, more acceptable band right now, we're not commercial in any sense—we haven't really changed. The songs are still the same, even though they've improved in productivity, quality and accessibility to the masses. We're still the same thrash band as when we started out and the next album is gonna be thrash too."

When Bernard asks Dave if the rumours are true, namely that Megadeth received $500,000 upon signing (other sources say $300,000), Dave says, "No, it wasn't as much as that. We can afford to eat now. Believe me, you really do need money to survive in this business. Now we're on Capitol, we have somewhere to live; we have this huge fucking three-bedroom apartment and the front room is like a football field and it's really good for the mind. You have no idea how stressed-out you can get when you don't take a shower for three or four days—you start hating your very existence. We used to live in our studio and all there was, was like a concrete box and there was this public toilet too, but it was filthy and it would get to the point where I would spend five minutes to set toilet paper down on the seat before I sat down—it was really that bad. We would walk over to the bar across the street to get a hamburger or something like that, and end up buying cigarettes and beer all day because we were so depressed with our existence and not having any money. So yeah, we're better off now, and are finally coming into our own. Believe me, with **Peace Sells**, this band is really on the point of breaking big right now."

The material that was to comprise **Peace Sells... But Who's Buying?** was put together, at a studio called The Music Grinder, without a major deal having been inked prior. Recording was a chore, because both Chris and Gar were unreliable due to their intensified heroin addictions. Dave and Dave Jr. slowly started to realize they were the two of the four members of the band serious about Megadeth, exacerbated by the opinion that Gar and Chris, as jazz musicians, kind of looked down their noses at metal. Nonetheless as they were completing the sessions, with Randy Burns, the deal with Karr and Capitol was completed. A remix with Paul Lani, at the behest of the label, was conducted and the album was all set for its September 19th, 1986 launch.

Of course, according to Dave, even the launch of the record didn't go smoothly. At the party to announce the record, a bar called Firefly at which the gimmick was an actual bar that you could light on fire, the band got into a full-on punch up as they were trying to leave. Chris' girlfriend Lana had commandeered the limo reserved for all of the girlfriends, which caused Mustaine to begin beating the crap out of Poland. Once the limo driver threatened to kick them all out of his car, the guys made up and celebrated by going downtown to score heroin.

"Oh, that was terrible, man," remembers Poland. "There were two limos. My girlfriend at the time, she was not to be stopped. And so I said, like, take one of the limos and go pick up for us. So she took a limo, Dave got mad, and I was sitting in the car, in the back of the limo, and I'm reaching for a cigarette, and Dave's telling me off, and he thought I was going to punch him, so he kicked me in the face. And I was like, 'What?! What the...' I got so mad, I just—you know, because he cut my lip—I just kept spitting blood at him. I was like, fuck you!"

The iconic cover art for the **Peace Sells** cover was deftly illustrated by Ed Repka. Along with the title—Mustaine lifted the idea from a Reader's

Digest article he saw called *Peace Would Sell But No One Would Buy It*—the art's representation of the UN with Vic splayed across a For Sale sign helped establish the image of Megadeth as a political band. This, along with Dave's gritty, snarling vocal style, continued roughshod production, the band's penchant for speed, and an overall youthful energy, had the band crossing over to the nascent hardcore crowd. In essence, Megadeth were a people's band, even activist, certainly boots on the ground, ear to the street, ready to rumble if there was a riot going on.

Mustaine explains the origins of the overtly orange cover art: "David Ellefson and myself and our agent at the time, a guy named Andy Summers, had got together in New York. We were in Manhattan, and actually across the street from the UN building. I don't know why we were there, but we were there. And we were talking about the album cover, and the fact that the first record was ruined by Combat, and how they ruined the artwork on that, didn't even do it, and just how important it was for me to get the artwork right this time. And we talked to this guy, this artist, Ed Repka. And Andy and David and I went out to go get ribs at a place called Wylie's, this rib joint—they had some franchises around Manhattan. So we went in there, and we just started talking. And over the course of the period of talking I said that I would like it to be the UN all bombed-out. And then somebody said this and somebody said that, and then we would have airplanes coming in, and a For Sale sign, and all these things, and it germinated from that meal with Andy Summers."

Then the illustration came in, and, "Of course we saw that, and it was pretty straight from the get-go. I wasn't really a big artist at the time, and you've got to remember, Martin, this was almost 25 years ago. And so I've learned a lot since then about artwork and T-shirts and album covers and stuff like that. But at the time, it was my first real proud moment. Because we had a lot of T-shirt artwork he had done. We basically got ideas from comic books and stuff like that, but as soon as that thing came out, it could become real. And that was the beginning. You know, we've had a lot of great success with it. We've had managers who've said they don't want Vic, he's been taken off of album covers, we've had the logo changed..."

Flip it over, and the back cover had the band looking quite pretty, even sporting a bit of make-up. "That makeup was because we had bags bad," said Dave, speaking with Metal Forces. "The scheduling on this band lately has been so incredible it's a wonder we're still alive. We've been playing one night and driving 900 miles, then playing the next night and driving another 900 miles and so it goes on. And after a while you begin to look like shit so you got to learn to look after yourself. Basically I think the reason they did something with covering up our bags and taking care of our hair is because although we're not pretty boys, we do have a marketable value to a female audience, and that's what thrash metal needs right now—more girls going to gigs. If more girls go, then more guys go and more money gets put into the whole market which means it's better for everybody concerned. It's a marketing ploy. OKAY, we're not gonna look like Poison, but we're still not gonna look like shit when we do album photos. Live, we go out and play like you see us now, but when it has to be for somebody who's mommy is gonna look at the back of the album, then we wanna look good. We're not trying to outsmart our fans, but trying to outsmart the industry that doesn't like it, and make the parents accept what the kids are listening to. We want to make it easier for us to spread our word and when we do make goals and open up doors, then it's gonna make it that much easier for the bands who want to follow us. And we don't get any problems from the PMRC, probably because we put a rating on our album without them telling us to do so. As far as the Bible Belt is concerned, well, they can burn as many of our albums as they want, because they gotta buy the album to burn it and they can only burn it once."

Once past the wrapper, the album opens with Dave singing the verse of *Wake Up Dead* pretty much immediately. That gesture in itself demonstrates that this was a band looking to connect, label deal spurring them on. The song itself was in the tradition of *Loved To Death*, a tale of sneaking around, a relationship gone violent, Dave well at home with the stirring up trouble.

"*Wake Up Dead* was written about me cheating on a girl I was living with because I needed a place to stay and I needed someone to feed me," notes Dave in his endearing manner, one that exudes from a man who at this advanced stage in his life just wants to get things off his chest, get the skeletons out of the closet so to speak, and set them dancing around for his personal amusement. "But the girl I really loved was the one I was cheating on, and thank God David Ellefson had a van. I would sneak downstairs into the parking lot of the apartment and I'd have sex with this girl and then I'd take those miniature bottles of vodka and splash that on my face and say I'd been out drinking with the boys and I'd come home. I mean, that's alcohol abuse right there. So I'd come up, and most of the time I would just flop in bed, but every once awhile I would have to do an encore performance and it was a little bit harder, if you know what I mean."

Chris Poland's take on it reveals more of the tale... "*Wake Up Dead* was about his girlfriend, Diane. He was living with this other girl, and he'd sneak out to see her, because he was so in love with her, and then he'd have to creep back in his house, like at 5:30 in the morning, and after he left at whatever time, and to go see her, and he knew if he woke her up, she'd kill him, because she was that kind of girl."

If the song was of a weird, unpredictable construct that characterized much of the debut, it was somehow nonetheless catchier, even if much of that came from the fake-out of the verse hitting the listener right between the eyes.

"Let's put it this way," articulates Ellefson, on why the record might have gained traction. "We went on tour and played the songs from **Peace Sells** before we recorded them, so we had a good idea which ones were going to work, so that was to our advantage to put the songs that are on the record, on this record. Then we got picked up by Capitol Records, and that became our first major label release. We had toured like three or four times before we'd recorded **Peace Sells** so we knew when we went in the studio what worked and what didn't, what people liked and what they weren't liking. So we had such a great pre-production of doing it live for three tours that it just came natural. And as far as those records go, man, they just stand the test of time, and every time I listen to them, I go, man, this is amazing stuff. And at the time you don't realize it. You're just playing and having fun and you don't realize that ten years from that day or even 20 years from that day, this stuff is still going to stand the test of time. I'm very proud of that stuff."

If the lead-off tracks on both of the first records relate to each other, so do the new record's second track and the first record's third. *The Conjuring* is a gritty thrasher, grinding at a catchy mid-paced tempo, but just as challenging, progressive and unconventional of structure as *Wake Up Dead*. Lyrically, Dave is back in the world of occult ritual.

Figures Chris, "Dave read Lovecraft; he got his ideas from a lot of stuff like that. And of course he kind of dabbled in the occult, so I think that's what *The Conjuring* was about. I mean, it was not like he was on the bus in the back conjuring Satan, but he had friends and girlfriends who knew about it, and he was kind of fascinated by it. So I think he drew from that too."

Next up was the album's ersatz title track, *Peace Sells* being the improbable hit single that would break the band. Its construct is almost stupid, plodding, like Kiss doing disco (or Ozzy doing disco—it's called *Crazy Train*!), or Kiss doing *Lick It Up*. In other words, it thumps, it's got spaces for easy breathing and digestion, and the end result is an underground anthem that benefits from a whiff of novelty, even a trace of humour. And yet the political lyric lent it some balancing gravitas, not to mention the idea, again, that Megadeth were a cut above merely extolling the virtues of moshing and metal. The song's traction was hugely enhanced by MTV using Ellefson's brilliant bass line as theme music on the show, stopping just short of the number of seconds it would take to have to pay the band a usage fee. Additionally, the song was the subject of the band's first production video, which, unsurprisingly, got lots of play on MTV when the station was at the height of its powers.

"*Peace Sells* was my first real educated song about where I was," recalls Mustaine. "Because by that point I had matured. Even though I was in my 20s already, I still was very much living a very self-centred and selfish life at the time because I was Dave Mustaine. If you didn't like me, that was okay, and if I didn't like you, that was not okay. And I had a lot of cleaning up to do, put it this way, once I got to grown-up land. And then you start to see people and you've got this weird feeling like you've just clogged their toilet and, 'Oh, I know that I did something to you... oooh, hey, can I talk to you?' Case in point, Brad Gillis. I just met Brad over the Seymour Duncan thing at NAMM, and I had to go apologize to him because I'd been saying that I didn't think he did a good job when he went out and played with Ozzy after Randy died. And he didn't even know about it and I was like (drops his jaw). If I didn't say anything, he wouldn't have known about it still. But at least I'm clean inside and I know I got right with that, and the dude's a great guitar player. I didn't say he couldn't play, I said he's more than capable of playing that stuff. And that's what kind of got me in trouble, because I said how I felt. You didn't have to ask me what I was thinking, because if you were in arm's distance, I told you."

As for Dave's politics, then and now, "I don't really think the political state of the United States has influenced me so much, so much as I know what our inalienable God-given rights are in the constitution as an American citizen and I know what is happening. Even right now in the administration that's in office right now, I know what's wrong. I don't know how to fix it because the way I believe in politics, I don't think anybody would do it. I think the politicians should work for free. I think if they're public servants then they should serve. I think the teachers and the cops should be paid more. Then you won't have corrupt cops and you'll have teachers that actually teach your kids. We have some of the dumbest kids in the world in our country. If you look at the scale in schools, we're not at the top any more, we're not even close. We used to be. People have always said I'm a political writer, and I'm not a political writer. I just write. How can you say *Trust* is about politics, unless you're retarded?"

Adds Ellefson, "*Peace Sells...* Dave and I—it was back in, I believe, January of 1986—we drove over to pick up our then drummer Gar Samuelson, and I remember it was kind of really rainy and Dave was just sitting there in silence in the car and he goes, you know, 'I've been thinking; what do you think about this, **Peace Sells... But Who's Buying**?' And I'm like, that's pretty cool! I didn't know what to say, but we got down to the studio and he picks up his guitar and he writes the riff and that was probably the quickest Megadeth song we'd ever written up to that point. It pretty much came together in one day, within one evening's rehearsal and that was it, it was done. And I remember the next day we were playing it, during the outro chorus, chiming in with the harmony, throwing this little vocal harmony on top and everybody is looking at me. They either think I'm completely losing my mind or they think it's really cool (laughs). And it was cool. Dave composed it, but it was one of those group moments where everything fell into place. It was like this song was there and it just had to come out."

Peace Sells got a bit of a jarring, disorienting video cooked up for it, one that nonetheless helped sell a lot of records. "It was pretty good," said Dave back in 1986. "But it was banned in England because there are strobes at the end, you know, flashes, where the scenes flashed back and forth from like war footage to a peace sign or dollar sign. And I guess the English authorities said that if you have a strobe light going on longer than 30 seconds, then it causes epileptic seizures. Now, I can't see anyone going into an epileptic seizure while watching one of our videos, but then again, who can, because you never know when the seizures are gonna happen."

Asked about what the follow-up video—for the track *Wake Up Dead*—was going to be like, Mustaine says, "Well, it's gonna have a little more of the band in the video. The first one had a lot of war footage and secular intellectual propaganda and shit like that. Stuff that goes right over the heads of your average listener until they see it. You know, stuff that they're controlled from not knowing that it even exists. There's riot scenes and people getting beaten with clubs for no reason—I mean, if you go to demonstrate against a cause that you don't believe in, then it doesn't mean you have to be shot or beaten; you should be able to protest in peace."

"**Peace Sells**, a lot of those songs... women and publishing is probably the things that break up more bands," laughs Dave Jr., back on the topic of day-to-day band existence. "And it's not the womens' fault, quite obviously. Well, there are a couple of things that cause tension in bands, and I say women, only because a lot of times people grow up and want to get married and have a life, and that changes the dynamic of the band. But the other thing is being in a room writing songs together. I don't think there's any two situations that are alike, like that. And that was always a very sore subject, in that group. To some degree, some bands have one writer—he writes, that's it, that's all there is to it. Sometimes that person writes, everybody gets a share, some sort of portion of that, and they feel good about that. Other times bands get together and they all write, they all throw ideas out, and all the money is split equally, and all the credit is split equally, that kind of thing. And I'd say my biggest involvement was on the **Peace Sells** record. Including the song *Peace Sells*, which was a tune, like I say, that was all put together in the band room, within about three or four hours."

On the personal side of the tracks however, Ellefson remembers the **Peace Sells** era as pretty squalid, a hand to mouth existence. "Dave and I had this way, that we would just sort of move in with you, but you didn't know we were moving in with you. So we went and ate all your food and ran up your phone bill, and do what musicians needed to do, write songs, and then we would leave. And that wasn't so pleasant for anybody. But those were our musician soup or survival moments, and those weren't a lot of fun, especially when people are chasing us out of their house. I remember with the **Peace Sells** album, just having some sleazy management, managers around, people trying to pack your nose with stuff to get you to be sort of inebriated so that you would then be reliant upon them; I had my days of dealing with that kind of stuff. And then having to read record contracts and not knowing what in the heck you were signing. Growing up in the Midwest, my dad always advised me, 'Don't ever sign anything without having an attorney look at it.' Probably at the end of the day, some attorney looked at it, but probably not as closely as they should have, or I should've let them, and then having to try get out of those deals years later, which could be very costly."

Back to *Peace Sells*, Chris Poland gives Gar credit, essentially, for the steps taken to send the track toward something useful in the mainstream world. "Especially on the second record, I really felt that Gar... on *Peace Sells*, Gar was like, 'You know what? This section's a little too long.' I think *Peace Sells* was actually seven minutes originally. Gar was saying we need to trim the fat on this tune. And Dave would listen when he knew it was the right thing to do. I mean, it was Dave's thing. We just kind of deciphered what he was trying to tell us and we would come up with our own parts, especially Gar, and then just take it from there. And all of a sudden the song would hone itself. Once you'd get there, it would be like, yeah, OKAY, that's it."

As for his own personal contribution... "Not really. I mean, you do not to get credit for... like there's certain little harmony parts that I thought sounded good in the solo guitar section on *Peace Sells*. But you don't get a writing credit for something like that. But as far as arrangements go, Gar helped. I can't remember if I helped or not. I tell you, it was a long time ago, but I do remember the day we were working on *Peace Sells*. We all felt it was too long, and Gar was the one who brought it up, said we should shorten it and edit it down, and we did. And it turned out to be the song that broke the band."

"*Devils Island* was inspired by the movie **Papillion**," says Chris Poland concerning the album's galloping fourth track, a bit of a forgotten Megadeth number. **Papillon** indeed was a movie that had quite an impact on folks growing up in the '70s, much like **The Exorcist**, **Serpico**, **Rollerball**, and TV fare like **Race With The Devil**—Dave would have been 12 when the hit film starring Steve McQueen and Dustin Hoffman was released.

Side two of the original vinyl opens with *Good Mourning/Black Friday*, and really, the impression is that Megadeth are still the unpredictable, obtuse, considerably untuneful collective of metalheads and jazzers that made the stand-offish debut so prickly.

"*Good Mourning* was one of those instrumentals I wrote," notes Dave on the layered and mournful intro to this grating thrasher. "I don't know where it came from. It was just a really sad piece of music I wrote," Poland adding that, "I remember we wanted to get a different reverb on *Good Mourning*, so we took the original guitar solo I did, and then sent it out into the drum room and put a mic all the way at the back of the room, and played it through the speaker, and re-recorded the reverb in the room. Instead of using like a digital reverb. Because they wanted it to have a certain sound."

The anger and aggression Megadeth was known for was present in spades within the gritted teeth delivery and deliverance of *Black Friday* (lyrically, a violent serial killer tale). And really, it was quite surprising we were getting music like this all up into a major label, especially when glam metal was all the rage, the gold and platinum albums beginning to drop in that realm with alarming regularity.

"It wasn't my style, brother," muses Dave, as to why he could never have jumped that bandwagon and gone hair metal. "It just wasn't my style. I don't fancy dressing up like a chick. I like chicks, I don't want to be one. There's enough guys out there that are sexually confused and they dress up like that, and it's like, 'Sorry. You're busy dressing up like that, I'll be fucking your girlfriend.'"

That sort of attitude was just part and parcel of the division growing every day between the commercially successful glam bands and the sullen, resentful camp busy inventing thrash and its evil younger brother, death metal.

"That's not folklore; that's real," says Dave talking to Sam Dunn about the division at the time. "Because the hair bands stood for glam. Anybody who really is worth their weight in metal, when they get out on stage, they're going to sweat. What are they gonna look like when that little Q-tip gets wet? They're going to look like a little wet cat, or in other words a wet pussy."

"Antidote implies that the hair metal bands were poison and that metal was, in some way, the remedy," counters Dave, asked if thrash was some sort of an antidote to glam. "I look at it more like metal's like a flea-bomb and glam is the fleas on the camel's balls. Glad that we were able to put an end to it in Los Angeles when we did, but bands that actually considered themselves glam weren't really glam. The bands we thought were glam, they wouldn't even identify themselves as glam. Because I thought W.A.S.P. was kind of like a glam band and I thought Mötley was a glam band, and they were. Face it. People will say W.A.S.P. is a metal band, and yeah, they've got some great songs and so on and so forth. I have nothing bad to say about W.A.S.P.. I'm not a tremendous fan of that music, and I've got nothing bad to say about Mötley either. I know those guys, we're friends. We're not swapping spit and kissing cousins and giving each other Christmas cards and that kind of crap, but I think there's some mutual respect between all of us, because when you survive this long and you become at the status where I'm at and where they're at, with the multi-platinum records and legendary status, the air's kind of thin where we're at. It's really easy for people who are down a couple thousand feet to look up and talk shit about you. You get used to it after a while."

"Looking at this as being an antithesis or being an antidote or something, I don't want to discredit the musicality of these bands that actually choose to have hair, because Rudy Sarzo was a guy that had hair, Randy Rhoads was a guy that had hair, Ozzy was a guy that had hair, Pantera was a hair band, Alice in Chains was a hair band. So if we go to what you're trying to ask, if it's a glam thing versus a thrash thing, I'm totally there. If it's a thing about hair, I got hair so I can't really... I'm not really a big fan of hair versus no hair."

Dunn poses to Dave the question of what a fan was getting out of a Megadeth show versus a Poison show... "Their chances of getting laid at a Poison show are better, because that's where the dumb chicks go. Especially the ones on stage. And then you've got people who come to metal bands and sometimes they'll walk away educated. There's a certain coolness to metal chicks. Just to know that my chick can beat up your chick, that's cool. You see girls that are metal chicks, there's a certain sex appeal to them, too, because they're the kind of girl that can load a firearm. I wouldn't mind tossing back a couple shots of Jack, if they need to go to grizzly, they can do it. The epitome of metal chick is Metal Sanaz. One of my friends, we've been friends for a couple years, and we just saw each other at the NAMM show. That's a chick that's like the epitome of a metal chick. Rita, Dimebag's ex—that's a metal chick. She's like metal chick royalty. I think that's something you can expect at a metal show versus going to a glam show, and bottom line is no matter how much you've got going on, all they need to do is just have Johnny Thong-Butt go by and he's going to take the chick from you."

Back to Megadeth's anti-glam record, next up is *Bad Omen*, a typically stilted, choppy, rhythmic track evocative musically of *Loved To Death*. Lyrically, it's yet another portrait of a Satanic ritual. Thinking back, it's interesting how more attention wasn't paid to Megadeth's regular occultism, but then again, pictures are worth a thousand words, and the **Peace Sells** cover, along with the album's biggest hit... if the public isn't smart enough to process two ideas, and one prevails, Megadeth was now a political band, albeit fired in the crucible of hardcore.

Novelty cover time, and to everyone's surprise, Megadeth prove themselves a convincing blues band, swinging their way through Willie Dixon's *I Ain't Superstitious*, pointlessly adding a punk thrash to the end.

"Well, Chris sounds a lot like Jeff Beck," explained Dave, to Metal Forces. "Plus we figured that, that song was so wimpy with Rod Stewart singing, Jeff Beck should have had somebody like Cronos singing on it. So we took that song and changed the lyrics around, made them a little more perverse like I did with *These Boots*, and we made the music and the lead as good as what Beck did."

One could argue that the inclusion of a vampy blues track was a ploy more suited to hair metal bands (or Van Halen), but it's also a known appeaser to major labels.

But Mustaine says the band had a good relationship with Capitol anyways. "I remember snorting coke off one of the executive's desks and them giving us champagne and a box full of Nike high-tops and this one dude was chewing on a cigar and had gold chains all around his neck and opens up this door and there's a mirror full of coke, and I'm like, 'We've arrived, David!' and he looks at me, yeah, high five. That's why you look at any of those pictures, man, we were in these rotten, holey blue jeans and disgusting, filthy, stained t-shirts, but goddamnit we had brand new shoes, because we got them from Capitol! They got us brand new Nikes! I think what they saw in us was they saw the answer. They saw something different. Something that could compete with Metallica but it also could compete with Guns N' Roses. Not that we were the same. Slash and I are friends and Slash was playing with me and at one point he was one of the guys we talked about having in Megadeth. Oddly enough, Slash came by the NAMM show a couple days ago and walked right up and said hello, and the whole place almost stopped because here's Slash, here's Dave, it's like a SALT talk summit meeting or something. And after he left, I went back to signing my stuff, and I looked around and there's all those people going (dropped jaw) because they didn't know that I knew him or that he knew me, and that we would even talk to each other. But I love the guy. I think he's great, and that's one of the cool things about Megadeth—we can play with anybody. We can get on stage with anybody. We have enough music with enough diversity in it that we can play with just about anybody."

"That was about the movie **Deer Hunter**," says Dave, addressing **Peace Sells**' Maiden-esque closer *My Last Words*, another quite forgotten Megadeth track, yet one that adds to the record's air of impregnability. In fact, it's probably Dave's most ambitious, poetic and imagistic lyrics to date, a harbinger of things to come as the band would grow and grow.

"*My Last Words* was written even before **Killing Is My Business**, I believe," notes Ellefson. "Because there were a bunch of songs on **Peace Sells** that weren't developed enough yet to put on the first record, which is probably good. So those songs had their best shot at coming to the light of day when they got to a major label, Capitol at that point. And there again, from a bass player's point of view, the bass line during the verse is just smokin'. There's no sitting still when you're in Megadeth."

Production-wise, the totality of **Peace Sells** ultimately wasn't much of an improvement over the debut. Or, as Chris Poland recalls, the production itself was fine, as was the first mix, but...

"Scott Menzies, who was basically our babysitter/attaché, the guy that kept us from getting in trouble, when he heard what Randy Burns did with **Peace Sells**, he looks at me and goes, 'I don't know who this band is' (laughs). We did a listening party at The Grinder, when it was still in existence, and I said, 'What do you mean?' And he says, 'You guys don't sound this good' (laugh). I just said, 'Well, that's why we get a guy like that to fucking record it.' Randy was already doing a lot of metal stuff; Brian Slagel and a lot of people used him for certain records. But then when he got a hold of us, he really honed in on it, because he new Gar was the right drummer, and he liked my playing, and he liked Dave's songs, and he knew Dave was Dave, you know, and he had to deal with that. But yeah, he did a great job on that."

"We did an original mix with Randy," continues Poland. "Anyway, Paul Lani did the second mix, and I remember we were on the road, and Dave had to fly back for a weekend to listen to the mix. Then he came back with the record, and I had already heard Randy's mix, and I said, 'This is slammin'.' He comes back with the mix, and it's like all of a sudden the drums are drenched in reverb—I mean totally drenched. And I looked at him, and it's like, 'Dude, you can't even hear the attack on the drums!' And he's like, 'Listen, man, this is it.' Well okay, man, that's it then."

"What had happened was, we were with Relativity, and then Capitol bought the record out from under them, and that's when Paul Lani came in. And obviously did a great job, from everybody else's perspective, you know, because the record is a huge record. But I didn't like the drums, man. It was like, come on, dude, turn that frickin' reverb off (laughs). Here's what it was: The Grinder was like an airplane hangar with a wood ceiling and wood floors. And they had mics that went back every like ten feet. And I had a feeling that he just got into these, you know, room reverb mics, and just said, yeah, I'm just gonna pump those. That's what I think happened. I wasn't there, but it's definitely not a Lexicon 480 or whatever."

Assessed Dave at the time, "I produced the album with a guy called Randy Burns this time and the production is like leaps and bounds better than the first record. You can hear the lead solos, you can hear the drums, you can hear everything. Everybody who's heard the album so far has been completely floored and for me, it's really flattering because I thought I'd never get out of the shadows of Metallica, what with them being so successful. Everyone seems to want to rub my nose in it and I tried not to let it bother me and kept on striving to make it. The album was recorded in Hollywood, Los Angeles, at a place called Music Grinder, and it recently had some huge acts there recording, like Jefferson Starship, Stevie Nicks, Pointer Sisters, George Benson and Missing Persons. So it's really a top-notch quality studio. Not that we were looking for that sound, but it's gratifying for us that we went to a studio that's producing such a quality work."

When Bernard Doe points out that Lars Ulrich sniffed that the place as more of a Top 40 studio, Dave couldn't help himself...

"The studio we recorded in is one of the second best recording studios in the whole of the West Coast. There's good studios on the East Coast too, but we didn't want to go to New York to do it. I mean, I don't have to fly to fucking Denmark so I can hang out with all my little hash-smoking pals to record an album and make it look like I can travel around the world; I go to where it is best. Lars just doesn't like Los Angeles because he's put down so many people there that they just wanna bust his fuckin' little head. Granted, Metallica are big, but he's made a lot of enemies because in the beginning they always used to say LA sucks, and LA's full of posers, and you know that stuff sticks. So I think he's just crumbing on Los Angeles anyway. I love the studio that we went to, The Music Grinder. Let's face it, when they put out four albums in a row and they're all No. 1 hits on Billboard, then you can't go wrong. Okay, the atmosphere might not be so perfect because you walk outside and it's Los Angeles; it's crowded, there's smog and stuff like that. But you're not there for outside; you're inside and you're recording in there. It doesn't matter what's on the outside of the wall—it matters what's inside your body, your head and in your soul."

"We toured with Alice Cooper, who I feel broke the band," says Chris Poland, concerning the live promotion of **Peace Sells** in February of '87. Alice was clean and sober on the comeback trail, playing his unapologetically heavy metal **Constrictor** album; in March, Megadeth hit the UK for a headlining tour, followed by dates in the US with Overkill and Necros.

"Actually, Janie Hoffman, who worked with MCA, she was a big part in getting us that tour," continues Poland, "and that tour broke the band. If we didn't do that tour, I think things would've been a lot slower. Because we faced full houses every night, playing with Alice Cooper. We also went out with King Diamond. They were a great band, great guitar tones live, great drummer. Of course he was a great performer."

In fact this author's first time seeing Megadeth, was at a club in Hull, Quebec, at which Megadeth played, but scheduled headliner King Diamond, did not.

"That's possible," recalls Poland. "He might not have come into Canada for whatever reason or restrictions, or maybe he just had a sore throat. But I'll tell you a story on the Alice Cooper tour, that you'd probably be able to figure out, eventually. He brings us on his bus, he sits us down and he says, 'Hey guys, I'm really happy you're on tour with us. Is there anything I can do for you that...' whatever. And we're all like, 'No, we just want to thank you for having us.' We were being on our best behaviour, and right before we leave, he says, 'Listen guys, you gotta be really careful out here. I know what you guys are up to and I'm just telling you that.' I can't remember exactly what he said, but we all just knew exactly what he was saying. Because he was sober. He was like, you guys are fucking crazy and you guys need to get your shit together (laughs). So that was a cool moment. And like I say, luckily we did."

But, as Dave writes in his autobiography, the road found Gar and Chris constantly seeking out hookers, mainly for food and the connections needed to "get well." Dave and Dave Jr. were not exempt from needing to get well themselves, and the whole tour began to revolve around the complicated plans needed to keep the band functioning from show to show, and not kill each other in the process.

"I remember this one gig, dude," regales Chris. "Dave and Gar are at odds, right? So Dave keeps spitting in the air, like really high, so that everybody could see that he's spitting on Gar. So Gar gets really mad, and he throws a drumstick at Dave's back, and it sticks in his... he had like some kind of studded guitar strap; I don't know if it was a bullet belt. It might've just been his strap, but it stuck in his back. And the audience thought that this was part of the show. So now they're going crazy, dude. They're like aargh!; they're screaming, right? And so we do our last boom, bang, all right, thank you. And then Dave takes this guitar and stuffs it into Gar's kick drum. So now, we're doing an encore, because they think we're magic or something, that we could throw drumsticks and have them stick in people's backs or whatever, and so the audience is... I don't know what they're thinking, you know? I just know what I saw."

"So me and Dave Ellefson come out. I'm tuned, he's tuned, we look at each other, Gar takes Dave's silver Flying V, like a freakin' paper airplane and just throws it in the air, and the whole thing happens in slow motion. Still to this day in my mind. I look at Ellefson, he looks at me, we look at the guitar, straight in the air, it hits the ground and breaks in half. So now our guitar tech, his name is Gadget—and that's a whole another story — Gadget gets a broom and mops and cleans it all up, and gives Dave back his white Flying V. And he says, 'I'm not playing this piece of shit — where's my guitar?' And Gadget goes, 'No, dude, Dave, you gotta play this.' So then he finds out when we get offstage that Gar broke his guitar. So now he takes a fuckin' tequila bottle and smashes it and he's trying to kill Gar with it. Yeah. So again, Scott Menzies, our attaché, whatever, he comes up, pushes Dave into the dressing room and closes the door. And I could hear from behind the door, Scott going, 'If you want to kill someone, kill me! Kill me right now!' So Dave calmed down, and somehow that all blew over. Things like that happened a lot. Eventually Dave was kind of like, you know, I just want some peons in here that I can tell what to do, and that's what happened."

"We had been through so much shit," continues Chris, "Me and Dave had lived like dogs in a rehearsal studio, birdbathing with cold water, walking two miles to get a beer at a bar. And then one day Dave Ellefson and Mustaine are coming to the back of the bus and saying, 'Hey, man, we're firing Gar. We want to know if you want to stay.' And I was like, 'What the fuck are you talking about? You're not gonna fire Gar! This is what we are, man. This is why we're here. Who are you gonna replace Gar with?' And I think the reason Dave fired Gar was because Gar was the only guy that could deal with Dave in a way that wasn't violent. Of course Ellefson never, you know, tussled with Dave. But I mean the kind of things Gar would do. We would be staying in the Winnebago, we're driving, we're all sick because we're all on you know what. And Gar always had a cigarette hanging out of his mouth. So he looks at Dave, and he's looking at a foldout of Metallica in Rip magazine, and he opens it up and goes to Dave, 'You know what, Dave? If you weren't such an asshole, you'd be in that band.' That's the kind of stuff Gar would do, man."

Poland was no church boy either. He's cagey on the drug stories, but offers, "I do remember one time, I can't remember what city it was, but I went to a bar, and we were stuck for two days, and the second night I was so bored, I just went to a bar and drank like a gallon of wine at a bar. And of course my per diems were wasted. And I came back, and for some reason I got in an argument with the guy at the hotel, and all of a sudden, there's like police dogs, police cars everywhere. I'm hiding behind a bush because they're trying to find me, because I threatened the guy at the hotel. And the next thing I know, you know, I have the keys to the RV. We used to have two Winnebagos and a Ryder truck, and Frank Papito, actually, when I did this, the other road manager quit. He says I can't work with this guy anymore. And you know, honestly, I hope I can be forgiven for all this stuff, but I was not in my right mind. Anyway, so I eluded the cops. I'm behind the bush, they go walking by with their dogs, and I'm like a statue hiding, not breathing, hoping they don't smell the alcohol on me, or the dogs, at least. So finally I get my keys, get in the Winnebago, puts the music on, get in my bunk. The next thing you know, Frank Papito, looks at me; he's leaning over my head, and Frank Papito has a glass eye, right? I never met the guy before. So he's leaning over me, and he looks at me, and I opened up my eyes, and he goes, 'You must be Chris.' And I go, 'Who the F are you, man?' And I look at his eye, and I'm like, dude, that guy has like an evil eye. And you can imagine how I felt. I was not feeling so hot, but then Frank took over managing us, and then some other stuff happened that I don't really want to talk about."

Poland does however admit to Dave's accusation of gear going missing to pay for heroin. "Gar never sold his gear, I don't think. But I mean, I would sell... like I got my backline. I was a member of the band, and we were given all this gear. And I never pawned anybody's gear but my own. It's not something I'm proud of. I know my daughter might read this in ten years, but you know, I would take my head, if I needed money, and then when it was time to rehearse for a tour and stuff... it's not like it's unheard of. I mean, I didn't pawn my cabinets. I always carried what I could carry, you know (laughs). I mean, I'm no Jimi Hendrix, but Hendrix did that shit too."

So Poland would soon be out of the band, but he still marvels about what came after. "You know what? The one thing that's incredible is the length of

Megadeth's career. I can't even count... I'm still awed by that, because even with all the lineup changes, even with all the years of drug and alcohol abuse, and just the whole craziness of the situation of going from new band members to new band members, to new management, new agencies, stuff in their personal lives, and the length of time that the band stayed together, that's all amazing. That's got to be Dave's force of will."

And not surprisingly, not only would Chris be absent from Megadeth's next and third album, but so would drummer Gar Samuelson. Reflects Poland, alluding in fact to an opportunity to rejoin two records forward, "The thing was, especially with me and Dave and Gar, and sometimes Dave Ellefson, we were all very headstrong with ideas. So it was hard with Dave, because it was like, 'I don't care about your ideas—it's my vision.' And I understand that—now. But then, it was kind of like, God, I wish I could approach it the way and say, 'Hey, let's try this, let's try that.' And I think that's what made me afraid for **Rust In Peace**, to re-join. Here I am on my own, I can do what I want, make changes, rearrange the song anytime I want. Do I want to go back and let Dave call the shots? And it was a hard decision to make, because financially, I would've been fine. I knew I wouldn't have had to have a day job. But artistically I didn't feel like it was the right thing to do."

4
So Far, So Good... So What!
"I have an important business offer"

Establishing a pattern, half of Megadeth would be replaced in time for the ramp-up to the band's otherwise "status quo" third album. First to be slated for removal was Gar, who had been getting more and more unreliable. One day, on the road in Detroit, a 21-year-old punk rock drummer called Chuck Behler offered to help set up the drums and that night, he hit the road with the band as their new roadie. As it turned out, he could sub for Gar in a pinch, with Dave soon beginning to realize that the band sounded better with Behler than with Gar, Mustaine appreciative of Chuck's more 4/4 approach to drumming.

"I can see why they would lean towards Chuck when they fired me and Gar," says Chris. "I don't know what he's doing now, but he was a great guy on the road. He was a friend too." Poland avows that Behler never actually subbed for Gar in the course of an actual live gig. "No, Gar was never incapacitated. But Chuck would sound check, because we would be out doing signings. I remember one time we did a signing in Chicago, and Jesus Christ, they brought us a case of beer and a bottle of tequila, so by the time we got out of there, it was like, now what do we do?"

Dave dismissed both Gar and Chris in the summer of '87, and for a guitarist, turning his sights toward Jay Reynolds, tall, blonde axe-slinger for promising Priest-style rockers Malice. The two Daves had in fact shown up on Malice's second and last album, **Licence To Kill**, providing background vocals on two tracks. However, Jay was also deep into drugs, of which he seemed to have easy supply—both a pro and a con to the con artist team of Dave and Dave Jr. But as it turned out, Reynolds was not up to the task of playing the complex and lightning-fast leads Megadeth had amassed in their past, or were still intent on firing off far into the future.

Enter one Jeff Young. "It was so weird, because this is how it always happens," explains Jeff, on winding up the next guitarist for Megadeth. "You hear these stories about how every door opens a window. I lived in a house... the band I was in before, and my manager and his partner, had a house with a studio and it, and during the time I lived at this house, everyone from Barry Brandt and Punky Meadows from Angel lived there, and Jay Reynolds from Malice rented a room there, and Jay and Dave Ellefson were friends. And I remember, months and months, meeting Ellefson long before the offer even came up. And Jay did give me some indication that they were having some problems with Chris, during the **Peace Sells** era, and they were thinking about changing him out. But at that point I was so close to a deal with my band, that I wasn't even entertaining the idea."

"But then by the time I had left this manager, who was a bit controlling, I split off from that band and moved out of the house, and months had passed by, and I didn't speak to this manager that I was living with. And one day I just decided on a reconciliatory gesture, and I took some four-tracks that I had been recording over to his house. He had since moved to an apartment, and was at that house no longer, and I went over and I played him some tracks, and we were catching up. And it was so weird, because the phone rang and it was Jay looking for me and my number, and Barry said, 'Jay, this is so bizarre, because I hadn't seen Jeff in probably four or five months but he's sitting right here right now,' and he hands the phone to me and Jay says, 'Jeff, can you come over to where I'm living now?' He had a house in Laurel Canyon, a guesthouse he was renting, and I said, 'Why, what's up?' And he said, I have an important business offer to discuss with you."

Continues Young, "He gave me directions and I went over. I don't know how long he had been in the band, but he was in the band and he was their new guitar player, and he hadn't heard Chris' stuff. Jay was a student, and I didn't reckon how he was going to pull that off, but he asked me, if he paid me 50 bucks an hour, if I would help him learn the rhythms, write the leads, and figure out Chris's stuff, and teach him, and that's how it was going to go. And they saw me trying to teach him this stuff. The guys were walking through the studio once in a while, you know, they would pop in and out, and they were comping Dave's guitars or doing something. They would hear me playing the stuff, and see Jay was struggling to play it, the stuff that I was helping him to write. So a few nights later, I had a voice message on my answering machine, and they were saying they wanted to meet me, and like I've said before, basically cut out the middleman."

"The whole reason I took the gig was because of Chris Poland's guitar playing," continues Jeff. "I played with Chris' brother Mark, in a band, right before I joined Megadeth. And I didn't know Chris. And it was just so ironic I ended up replacing Chris, because I had just played with his brother. And that's not any avenue on how I got the Megadeth gig. Like I say, that came through Jay Reynolds of Malice who was one of my guitar students, who they originally gave the gig to."

Picking up where the jazz-minded Poland had left off felt natural for Young. "We had similar influences. We both loved Beck and Holdsworth, so we had that common denominator. So it was really easy for me. And this is one of Mustaine's lies that he likes to say, that I wouldn't play Chris' solos the way Chris played them, which is the farthest from the truth. As soon as I finished tracking my stuff for **So Far, So Good... So What!**, I contacted

Capitol Records and I had them send the master tapes over to the studio, and I soloed all of Poland's tracks. I guarantee you I'm the only guitar player who did this. I soloed all his tracks, at normal speed, just by myself, and then with a click, and then I did it again at half speed. And I figure I did every solo that he ever did note for note, and that's how David enjoys taking the piss out of me in the press. But that's his stuff. But I have a box of approximately 15 tapes, which will eventually be heard, of Megadeth live shows, that will prove otherwise. Again, I took the gig because I loved **Peace Sells**; songwriting-wise I resonate with it. I think that album was better, but **So Far, So Good... So What!** has a certain power to it, and there's some great stuff on that. But I remember being a little disappointed with the material on the new album. Because the first thing I had heard that they gave me was **Peace Sells**."

"For me, my favourite, to be honest, Megadeth album, is **Peace Sells**, just because of the production," Young told me five years later, adding some extra detail to the story of recording his solos. "The reason I joined Megadeth was because I loved Chris Poland's playing, and the chance to step into his shoes and get the chance to learn his stuff under the microscope. And how I did it, as I told you, I went down the Capitol Records, and I requested the two-inch masters, and I soloed his tracks. I still have the cassettes of it right up in my bookcase. So I had Chris by himself, all his leads at full speed and then I had the engineer slow the two-inches down to half speed, which makes it a perfect octave, but lower. So I sat there with Chris Poland at as slow as you possibly could, and pored over every lick. So that was a big album for me, even though I'd never heard Megadeth, or, I hadn't really been exposed to The Big Four. I knew about Metallica, but I just never owned any of their albums; it just wasn't my frequency. But as soon as I heard **Peace Sells**, I liked the music because, again, they incorporate a lot of different aspects to their music. There's a lot of different influences far as the rhythms and where they're taking the riffs."

Jeff was brought on with only two weeks to go in the recording schedule, well after the songwriting for the upcoming album had been completed.

"The cool thing about Capitol, I mean, Megadeth had pretty much, at least as far as I could tell, carte blanche," explains Jeff. "They weren't really trying to break the band with a hit song. It was totally an underground, rising up, building a fan base through constant touring, thing. So musically, the album was already composed. I'm the only guitar player in the band that I don't think rehearsed with the band any amount of time before. You know, I literally heard *In My Darkest Hour* the day before I did the solo. Anything I did on the album was improv. I didn't have any pre-production time. The songs were written and some of the stuff was close to finished. And they would just get me every day... I went in the first day, the day before, Dave Mustaine gave me the tape of *Darkest Hour* and he said come back tomorrow, and I laid down a solo. And they gave me another song, and I came back the next day and I started camping out in the studio down on Melrose, and I started doing two or three things a day and learning the rhythms, and then go back in and do the rhythms later. So the cool thing about it was that it was really off-the-cuff and sort of out of the fire into the frying pan, so to speak."

"I didn't see them the whole time. They were never in the studio. Which was cool. They gave me carte blanche. The label gave them carte blanche and they gave me carte blanche and it worked out cool. Mustaine was never there. They'd hear what I did when it was done. The producer wasn't even there, Paul Lani. They left me and the second engineer whose name was Matt Freeman. He was their assistant, and he was punching me in and I played the stuff. I mean, there wasn't anything where they said, 'Do that over'."

Retelling the story five years later, Young says, "The first day, it started out, again, Mustaine and I met, we walked up and down Melrose, and he told me this, that and the other and gave me the tape. So the next day I go in and Paul Lani was there, Matt Freeman was there, and I stood in the back of the room, and I just remember (laughs), I turned my back to everyone and I just did that solo. I improvised. I did a few passes, and Paul Lani was freaking out. He had just come off the Alcatrazz' **Disturbing The Peace** album with Steve Vai, so he was really excited, and was like, 'This is great! I haven't had this much fun since working with Steve Vai!' And the solo came out great. We did that, and I think maybe the next solo, because I had already been working on writing that solo for *Hook In Mouth*, with Jay Reynolds. I already kind of had that worked out, so I think that was the next thing."

"To be honest, after that, Paul Lani disappeared," laughs Jeff. "And like I say, Mustaine was never in the studio any of those days. He like passed through once, I think, just started through; he was on a mission going somewhere. But Chuck would pass through the room, Junior would pass through the room, but no one was there. They left Matt Freeman, who was by all intents and purposes, he was like this second engineer, and their assistant. I don't know if he kind of grew into their assistant over that project or how all that went down, but I was showing up to the studio, and it was just a guitar tech, Matt Freeman and me. And they knew where I needed to do solos, and I was in there with the second engineer just punching in and we were doing what we wanted to do. We even edited (laughs)... to be honest, man, we cut out a bunch of *In My Darkness Hour*; there were a few more progressions in there, and Matt Freeman and I thought they went on too long, so we edited them out. And he never said nothing; he didn't act like he noticed, so... But again, Matt could've been punching drums in or working all along. I didn't know everyone's role, and how much knowledge he had at the time. But he was making the two-inch machine work and we were doing edits. You know, we cut tape—to edit *Darkest Hour* on two-inch, we cut inches out of that tape."

So Far, So Good... So What! was issued January 19, 1988, ahead of **...And Justice For All** by seven months. The band open the album with a fanfare much like Maiden's *The Ides Of March* before settling into a double-bass drum metal thrashing mad instrumental called *Into The Lungs Of Hell*, according to Mustaine at the time, "a whole instrumental piece where I do overhand and some really weird fretting—I'm using my thumb on one part of the fretting—it's quite intricate."

But it's *Set The Word Afire* that really gets the ball rolling, the long opening sequence giving way to a killer mid-paced groove and some solid singing from Dave, who is back reminding us of the evils of nuclear war, or the "arsenal of Megadeth," mega-death being one of the missives used to describe the body-melting madness of the atomic bomb. In Dave's words, it's about, "a post-Holocaust situation dealing with what it's gonna look like afterwards." If there's anger in the lyric, it might be because Mustaine apparently wrote the thing on a muffin wrapper whilst winding his way back from out east on the bus after being fired from Metallica.

"The first time you actually hear me shred on the album is at the end *of Set The World Afire*," remarks Jeff. "So that's a few minutes into the album. But I like the way there's kind of the half-time rhythm, that we're going into that E to F, and again, that progression right there is a perfect example. It's a Phrygian progression, E minor to F major—it's the flamenco progression that they're playing exactly right there, which lent itself... where I could do that kind of flamenco-esque lead. And I like how I did the tapping on the top of that solo; I didn't want it to sound like Van Halen, that typical *Eruption*-type of tapping, so I did it half-time against them playing faster. So I thought that came off kind of cool."

Jeff actually went on to distinguish himself in the flamenco field, playing all over the world with some of the best. "I've been into Paco de Lucia since I was 16; I heard the trio album of John McLaughlin, Al Di Meola and Paco De Lucia, **Passion, Grace And Fire**, and ever since I heard that album, I always loved flamenco. When I grew up in Ohio, there was nobody else to study with. So it wasn't really until I started touring around with Badi Assad and going to Spain and all over and playing Brazilian music, which has a big Latin feel as well, with her and the brothers, that I was really beginning to apply a lot of the techniques. Flamenco players have just the best right hand. I mean, for me, flamenco guitar because of the raspiness and the fret buzz that is there and the percussiveness, it's the closest thing to, I guess, distortion or that heavy sound, on an acoustic guitar."

Next, Megadeth kick it up a notch in the covers department, playing on Dave's modicum of punk cred but also his political predisposition by attacking *Anarchy In The UK* by the Sex Pistols. Initially Dave wanted to do

Problems, but the label found it to negative. Dave got his way covering the track years later, *Problems* showing up as the b-side to **Youthanasia**'s *A Tout Le Monde* and then on the **Hidden Treasures** rarities album of 1995.

"I think that song generalizes our viewpoint towards life," said Dave, talking with Metal Hammer's Dave Dickson in '88. "We feel we're the Sex Pistols of the '90s—we feel we have that kind of energy, that influence, that power. People right now think that we're a brash, obnoxious group, even though we are all nice guys at heart; the thing is, when we get together to play music, it gets kind of nasty."

"They were a band that we listened to, all four of us," added Ellefson. "We listened to them a lot when **Never Mind The Bollocks** came out and we still do. And Steve Jones has started to become a pretty good friend of me and Dave. He rode his Harley into the studio through the back door, and he had a broken arm at the time, because he had an accident or something. But he came in and played on the record. But he was really happy to do it and was happy with the way it turned out."

"I have a little more diversified music background than a lot of people know of, or a lot of people in our genre do," noted Dave, years later. "I grew up in Orange County and did a lot of surfing, so there were a lot of punk rock bands we listened to, anything from Devo to Split Enz to Dead Kennedys, and then the classics like Sex Pistols and American punk rock with Black Flag and Circle Jerks and so on and so forth. I'm not going to read down all the bands I could name just to look cool right now. Those are the only ones that were any good that I liked. And there were other ones like the Buzzcocks and the Dickies, but they weren't really in my playlist so to speak. I think a lot of it was the whole anti-authoritarian mentality. I don't think anybody during the '80s—which is when thrash really broke through the placenta into the world—I don't think anybody at that period looked at punk rock with any kind of favour. It was looked at with tremendous disdain. The people that liked thrash music were basically people who agreed along the same guidelines but weren't willing to shave their head. And I was very antiestablishment. I was very much into educating our fans about what our rights are and so on. Then after a while you kind of get tired of it. You can spend 24 hours a day trying to teach a pig to sing, and it doesn't work and it annoys the pig."

"So after a while you kind of realize that you sing for yourself, and if you like it then you've made yourself happy," muses Dave. "But if you're trying to teach somebody something in a song, that's kind of like Barney, you know what I mean? So I look at thrash metal as a tremendous way of escaping and telling people that I expect more as a citizen in this fine country that we live in. Just because I have long hair doesn't mean I'm stupid, by no means. A lot of the thrash had stupid lyrics. Nobody has a fucking pet dragon. Who wants to sing about dragons?"

If hair metal and thrash crowds didn't exactly see eye to eye, there was at least a little more crossover between Californians at punk gigs and at thrash shows.

"Yeah, believe it or not there were a lot of punk people. I think one thing that was really cool was crossing colour boundaries because there are a lot of brothers in the metal communities, and in fact one of the bands that kind of defied the whole metal mentality was a band called Hirax, that had a black dude named Cake in it, who had the most perfect metal afro ever. I think he should have fucking spray-painted it silver and gone out like a giant... big old metal fucking afro. Anyway. I liked the fact that we would go to concerts and you would see people that would show up that, granted, me being such an over-the-top sensationalist, when I would see somebody of colour I'd be like, 'Wow, look!' and just, 'Shut up, Dave, you're making it worse by drawing attention to one person being here instead of accepting him as a whole; you're singling him out.' So I had a lot of learning to do with watching the demographic of our audience change. Nowadays we see people coming into line and the guy's got a crusty moth-eaten Megadeth shirt and he's got a kid that's got his face all pierced up. And he's going, 'This is my kid, Dave. We got pregnant at a Megadeth concert.' And I look at the kid and I look at the dad and I'm going, 'I can tell.' You can tell the parents that party, still, because the kids, they're pretty liberal and they come to the shows, and it's great to see Megadeth transcending generations."

Recalls Young on *Anarchy In The UK*, "They already had it recorded, and I don't know if they did it because they knew they could get Steve Jones to come in, which he did, and played the rhythm track with a broken arm. And all he wanted in return was a little suction. In his words. He was just kidding. He rode his motorcycle into the studio and tracked the rhythm and he was probably there about an hour-and-a-half."

The pomp and circus pants of witchcraft horror story *Mary Jane* was next, this one being more of a production piece on an album that was produced so well, it actually sounds over-produced, and not in a good way. "Yeah, we did spend a lot of money," reflects Ellefson. "We spent a lot of money on it (laughs), and some top name, you know, engineers and producers worked on it. I don't know that it was ultimately what we should've done at the time, but that's all hindsight. Which then led to **Rust In Peace**. But **So Far, So Good**, Dave and I had to almost scramble to try to keep the band together at that point. Yet I still think that the record has some of Megadeth's best songs from the early days on it."

"*Mary Jane*, just for that album, is my favourite all-around piece," figures Jeff Young. "Because all the stuff from the beginning, and the very first solo that I played, I picked verbatim from a Chris Poland demo. So that was already there. That solo was composed, so I was in the space of figuring out all Chris' solos for **Peace Sells** and **Killing** at the time. And they were playing me the demos of *Mary Jane* and his solos. I'm sure you can see videos online of Chris playing *Mary Jane* with Megadeth—I'm sure he's doing that same solo. But in that middle section, I just tried to do something kind of Middle Eastern. So I love that tune." Of note, Young played some rhythm guitar on this one, as well as *Into The Lungs Of Hell*, *In My Darkest Hour* and *Hook In Mouth*.

"It's a song about a young girl who got exposed performing witchcraft to her father, and he buried her alive," Dave told Bernard Doe, just before the album launched. "This is a true story, and there's a place up in Jackson, Minnesota, which is where Dave Ellefson was born, where her grave is. But there's no records of her ever being born or dying, and to cut a long story short, there is an inscription on her tombstone which says, 'Beware my friends, as you pass by, as you are not as once I. As I am now, so you must be. Prepare my friends to follow me.' And it's pretty macabre when you think about it, the way it's beckoning you to the graveside. Actually, there's a few deaths that have been related to that. There was this guy—who Dave Ellefson knew—who went out and pissed on her grave and he was riding back in the car when it crashed and he died, but none of the other people in the car got hurt. Same thing happened to somebody else who knocked her tombstone over. We've also had some weird things happen when we played that song. In the studio, all the machines kept shutting off and the other night we were rehearsing when Dave blew up a brand-new speaker cabinet that cost an arm and a leg."

Over to side two of the original vinyl and we get *502*, this writer's fave track on the record, a classy, grinding rocker that is Mustaine's love letter to driving real fast—502 is police code for impaired driving, for which Dave was nabbed two years later. Although, as has happened elsewhere, an alternate meaning has Dave calling it, "a song about life on a tour bus, always driving and basically living in a tin can."

But it's *In My Darkest Hour* that would make the biggest impression on the headbanging populace. Launched as a single, the song failed to chart, but it quickly became a live staple. Dave's lyric, ostensibly inspired by the passing of Metallica bassist Cliff Burton, is actually yet another song about Dave's tumultuous relationship with Diana, with Dave placing himself in the role of beat-up and confused, dumbfounded, providing fast friend identification for any guy tormented by psychological games with the opposite sex. As well, Mustaine and the band make it easy for the fumbling fan to focus on Dave's bleak ruminations by getting out of the way, providing an almost welfare check metal soundtrack o'er which Dave mumbles his regrets.

"This is about being lonely and I'm sure everyone can relate to that," said Dave at the time, adding another layer. "It's like when we come back home off tour. At first not many of our friends know that we are home, so the first few days are really empty and it's quite scary to imagine what it's like to be always lonely in this big old fuckin' world without no one."

"*Darkest Hour* was my first solo," reiterates Jeff, adding to his earlier telling. "As I said, it was pretty much improvised, because Dave Mustaine took me for a little walk out on Melrose the night before and handed me a tape of the song, and I had never rehearsed with the band. I just got to hear like 60 seconds of that piece, to cut a solo to. So he's like, 'okay, here's the solo spot.' There was no singing or anything; there was just the rhythm, drums and bass, like a rough mix, and he goes, 'OK, I just want you to start soloing in 3-2-1, and then put a solo there. Take it home, and come back tomorrow and do it.' So I came back and you can imagine that, that was a nerve-racking experience, but it came off great. And that solo seems to be a fan favourite, although I also get a lot of comment about *Hook In Mouth*; I gotta say that a lot of kids comment on that solo when they write me on Facebook."

"We try make music that's a little more epic-orientated," described Dave at the time, "more panoramic, so you can actually see what's going on and listen to the music instead of some mindless trivia coming out of some guy's mouth and relentless, suffering masturbation on the fret board—we try and have songs that are a little bit simpler, that have a bit of melody to them, a song that has a meaning, a concept, that's about our personal life experience instead of having to sing about things that are never going to happen, a lot of fantasy and shit like that. We sing about stuff that happens to you too, that happens to all of us."

"You know what I thinks funny?" added Junior, chiming in. "That individually our parts in the songs are pretty complex, but when we get together and actually play the songs as a band, they're really memorable, hook-orientated songs. Instead of this, like Dave said, fret board masturbation where everybody's just flailing licks at all times, showing off their chops and nobody pulling back and giving each other space. A lot of these bands have good riffs, they have good melodies, it's just that their arrangements aren't right. That's where Dave is brilliant in the large part of our songwriting. I think the brilliance of this band—if you don't mind me being as arrogant as fuck for a second—is in the arrangements. Because arranging a song is just as important as the actual melodies and hooks that are in it. That's something that is definitely planned out. Right up to the time we track the song and the parts are changing. Usually in the past, Dave will come up with something and he'll show me and we'll work it out together. And I'll go, 'Fuck, Dave, yesterday you showed it to me and it was like this; now today it's different! Fucking make up your mind!' Right up until the day we record stuff, we change it."

"Simple bands don't dent the rock 'n' roll history books," mused Dave, staking a position for the band that he'd turn upside down and shake out for change a few years hence. "That's one of the reasons we're a little more elaborate in the way we approach our music. We pack every song with enough stuff to make four or five songs. That's the way to make an impact. When that rock history book is written, we want to have a whole chapter about us. We'll leave a footnote in the thrash metal section to other bands. I want people to know exactly what our intentions are. I want this band to be a legend. I want to open that history book up to where the legend section is and see my ugly mug staring out at everybody."

Noted Jeff Young back in '88, similarly lauding the vigorous musical workout Megadeth affords, "The difference between Megadeth and thrash is that we don't sound like a bunch of guitars and drums thrown in a blender. I don't see too many musical thrash bands. There are a few such as Testament that are really good. That's what I found appealing about this band before I joined; I listened and thought, 'Wow! Those guys are killers!' It's very challenging to play too. Before I was playing your basic Whitesnake, Dokken-type stuff, and in the rhythm you're falling asleep thinking, when will my solo come? In our songs, it's all out for everyone throughout the entire song. At the end of our set, the pace of playing the music makes you feel like you've just run a marathon. It's very physically demanding, you know, like your arms are about to fall off! There's no low moments, and if you break concentration for one second, a mistake is gonna happen so you've got to be clear-headed."

Interesting side note, in the same chat, Young had divulged that having Warlock as support have inspired a bit of a proposed side-project... "Doro Pesch and I will be working on a project sometime in the future, an EP or something. We'll just write some songs that we really like to play. Billy Sheehan will play bass and Tommy Lee from Mötley Crüe will play drums. Tommy is a great drummer, but he has never been given the chance to show what he can do. Megadeth are also changing management; we'll be going with the same management that has Bon Jovi and Mötley Crüe."

Back to the record, next up is *Liar*, which Dave uses to hurl a stream of insults at past axeman Chris Poland, Poland's biggest crime, apparently being the stealing of Dave's Echoplex (OK, more than that). Mustaine's vocal is a snarl of punk anger as he trash-talks Poland into dust, o'er top what is actually a catchy riff rocker that wouldn't be out of place on the gleaming **Countdown To Extinction** album. All told, it's a pretty funny song, with hints of hardcore Anthrax to it. "It's about some people we have dealt with in the past," said Dave, "some people we still deal with, and about some people we will be dealing with in the future. It just about sums up all the people who bullshit you in this business."

So Far, So Good ends with *Hook In Mouth*, a rant against the PMRC that starts with Dave singing laconically over a punky bass and drum riff before the song switches to half-time and an accessible riff fuels it. But like many a

Megadeth number, it's inclined to speed metal riffing, not thrash, but something from an earlier time.

"It's like the book **1984**, where you have this futuristic world where the government monitors everything you do," explains Dave. "And when somebody commits a crime, there's this person who works for the establishment who goes back through all the records and history books and deletes this person from ever existing. They would erase the record of their birth, their wedding and all that kind of stuff and that's what the song is about; they can make a person disappear and nobody would ever miss them. In the middle of the song, it spells out the word 'freedom': That's basically about the way the PMRC are taking our freedom. I mean, this is supposed to be America, the land of the free. We have freedom of press, freedom of speech, freedom of religion and all that kind of shit. And it doesn't mean nothing if they can tell us what we can and what we can't sing about."

So Far, So Good would go gold in a couple of years and platinum in ten. Fondness for the record within the band is thin on the ground, and most fans look at the album as transitional, many complaining of its "wet" sound. Indeed Mustaine was upset with the mix, questioning why Paul Lani had to take it clear across the country to upstate New York to deal with it at Bearsville. Dave eventually got fed up with Lani and handed it over to Michael Wagener, famous for his good sounds for Accept and Raven, but it was too little too late.

"He gets great guitar sounds," said Dave, spinning positive press on the situation. "Not to put any other band he's worked with down, but he's mainly a heavy metal producer and he's been doing bands like Poison and Stryper, stuff like that. When I called him up, he just got back from an eight week vacation, so his ears were fresh and he went, 'Yeah! I've been waiting to mix the heavy metal album of the century!' But that was before he heard the songs and then he was totally disappointed. Ha!"

"Yes, that was just mixing," recalls Wagener, concerning his brief association with the band. "As far as I know, the record was already being mixed in New York. I was wondering why they would only bring me in one song at a time, one tape of one song at a time, and later on I found out that somebody else was mixing the record in Europe, and I was just remixing it as it was going on, without him knowing that I was re-doing it, with out me knowing that it was already being done as we were doing it again. So that was a weird situation. That was a fairly bad time for them, in terms of drugs, I think. I would mix the song, they would come in for about ten minutes, go, 'OK, we like it, thanks, keep going.' The only input I got from the band was through Jeff Young, with whom I am still working today, on his stuff. I think Jeff was originally the guy who got me involved, because he liked what I did with guitars. Jeff is a brilliant guitar player. And for him, there came some input in terms of what he liked and whatnot, in the mix, but the other guys were in and out very quickly, and basically liked it. Told me they liked it and let me do my job."

Wrote Jim Farber in Rolling Stone, in a surprisingly favourable review, "On **So Far, So Good... So What!** Mustaine and stalwart bassist David Ellefson are joined by two new members—guitarist Jeff Young and drummer Chuck Behler—who prove as creatively belligerent as their predecessors. This is obvious right from the LP's opener, an instrumental that Young's serrated guitar riffs help turn into an overture to hell. From there things just get bloodier, but that doesn't mean all subtlety gets slaughtered in the process. The tricky tempo shifts in cuts like *Mary Jane* are carried off with deft rhythmic skill, and even what seems to be the band's most anarchic moment—the guitar and drum jam at the end of *502*—retains a sure sense of momentum."

Then it was time to hit the road, which, as Jeff Young laments, was where it all unravelled. "What I would say is that, and what I can say to all the Megadeth fans, is that I didn't play one show with that band where I had even so much as a drink or a smoke of anything. I played every show with that band 100% sober. And not one other member of the band ever played one show even 99% sober. And by the time Mustaine came off the stage every night, he was being carried. I mean, we played Oakland Coliseum, and I remember Metallica was standing there. James and Lars were there, and that was the first time, I think, they had seen Megadeth in a while, and we were opening for Dio and Dave was just ripped. And when you're doing an opening set, you've got 45 minutes to go out there and deliver the bang, pow, zap and get off. He went off into this ten-minute drunken rant and I just remember standing there and I'm thinking, this guy's old band fired him for just this very thing. And here he is, and they're standing there right side-stage watching him. And I was just embarrassed to be there, embarrassed to be part of it. It was a shame. I'm not trying to be a dick about it, but there's like 30,000 people out there and you are supposed to be happy because this is everything you ever dreamed about. It was nothing that you ever dreamed about."

And Young's impressions of Junior? Pretty similar to Mike Albert's. "I think his whole thing was about job security, and what he had to do to maintain that. And I wasn't willing to do that. I wanted to go through the music business on my music, if you know what I mean. So he was a yes man. I like Dave Ellefson. He's a cool guy. I mean, he's smart and he's the one who stayed in the band the longest; you've got to give him that. And he was more together than Mustaine, but in the same realm. I mean, they were trying to be the toxic twins like Perry and Tyler, and whoever before them."

As for drummer Chuck Behler, who, it is said, was more of a straight beat-keeper than Gar... "That's true. He's kinda got that whole Detroit vibe from up in that area where he grew up. The weirdest thing about Chuck, man, trip out on this, he moved John 5 out here. When I had John 5 on my radio show, he's like, 'Yeah, Jeff, I met you when I was 14. I'm from Detroit. Chuck moved me out.' Isn't that a trip, man? They're buddies from back in Detroit. The thing with me and Chuck is that for me, Gar was the best drummer in Megadeth. Because the whole thing that made Megadeth amazing left Megadeth when Chris and Gar left. Because it was like Mustaine's lack of technique, and bands that he was into, the New Wave Of British Heavy Metal and the Pistols and stuff, mashed up with what Gar and Chris did. Already, when they played together, it was the Mahavishnu, fusion-y, John MacLaughlin, Allan Holdsworth, Jeff Beck kind of thing. Which, they even did a Jeff Beck song on **Peace Sells**, right? *Ain't Superstitious*. That's a Jeff Beck tune, right? So that's what really made the Megadeth sound for me, and it kind of left. So there's a little bit of that missing on **So Far, So Good... So What!** for me. As I was getting the songs, I was thinking, you know, this is great, but it's definitely different from **Peace Sells**. which was way more fusion-like."

But Chuck could play Gar's licks no problem. "Yes, he played... first of all he had a killer sounding Sonor set, same drums AC/DC used to use. Mustaine hated them because they look like furniture—they were natural wood. But his drums live sounded killer. His problem was his tempo, because he was always on blow, so he was always rushing the tempos. And when you're playing in an arena... but a lot of bands do that live. They just have no self-control. When you're playing in an arena and you're playing music that's already that fast, and you're playing in a venue that sound like a giant dumpster, you gotta control your tempos, because it will help you sound better live. Plus the solos and the stuff I was doing was so fast already, to play it even faster was... You lose the breath. It's not only about the speed there, it's about the air. So you can't hold notes and do vibrato and stuff like that. So that would be my only thing. But he played the stuff great, and it was hard stuff to play. Chuck was cool."

There's animosity with Jeff at many things, but most sharply at the drug situation in the band, which, as we'll see shortly, caused a major career setback.

"There's a big deviation in the band and with Dave Mustaine, in all the interviews I've read over the years," sighs Jeff. "He wants to convince himself and rationalize the situation, and, you know, he bald-face lies about so many things. And I never—and I won't ever—stoop to that level. I was the one who was sober and giving my all, because that's what the fans deserved—that was my mindset. I remember sitting in Paris, staring out my window, looking at the Eiffel Tower, practicing so that I could be the best for that show that was coming up that night. On the other hand, Mustaine's like, 'You wanna see how fast I can score heroin?' And they did it, literally. They wouldn't get out of the car and it would be 30 seconds and they'd have it."

"They were getting parcels of heroin at every hotel, dude. I mean, it was out of control. The heroin was being sent inside cassettes for **So Far, So Good... So What!**. Their guy was sitting back in LA, taking the cassettes apart, taking the tapes out, putting the balloons in, and at every fuckin' hotel, you know, they'd be right at the desk, 'Did I get a parcel? We got a parcel?!' You know, The Breeders, that band The Breeders, which oddly enough, they're from Oakwood, Ohio, where I grew up, the next city over from Dayton, where I grew up, they got busted for that years later. So that whole thing, probably not the best way to be shipping your drugs around, via courier parcel companies anymore."

Did they shrink-wrapped them? "Yeah, he would put the balloons inside the cassette tape, screw the cassette tape back together, put the tape back in the box, shrink-wrap each individual tape, and send you a box of tapes, so there would actually be some legit cassettes in there. That's pretty scientific right there. That's Spinal Tap Mach four (laughs)."

Megadeth found themselves touring with the likes of Dio and Iron Maiden, before a self-destructive flameout scotched this promising version of the band. "He was the super-coolest," recalls Young, asked about the dearly departed Ronnie. "And since all this happened and he passed away, it brings it back. At that time, he was touring on **Dream Evil**, and our album was like No. 19 on the charts. He came in and congratulated us. He came backstage, and he was, as everyone says—I'm not saying anything new or revolutionary—but he was like a distinguished gentleman with a sense of humour. He always carried himself with class."

"Dio, I think it was the last night of the tour, and on that tour, Vinny Appice's drum riser would rise and he would do the drum solo, and they had all the fog and a bunch of lasers. So Vinny, on the last night, Craig Goldy and Megadeth, we and his pyrotechnics guy... every night Ronnie would come out of there was a big explosion at the end of the drum solo, and they break into *Rainbow In The Dark*. The drum solo I think was in the middle of *Rainbow In The Dark*, and he would disappear. And when he came back out, through the back, from underneath the drums, this night, he got on the drum riser, and he went all the way up, and we were all, 'Leave him up there!' And the guy left him up there for like a good portion of the last portion of the song, and everybody in the set, we were all laughing, it was hilarious. He had a good laugh with that as well. The final crack-up was, when he came through the end of his drum solo, they had rigged a dummy with the same clothes that Vinny was wearing, and he rigged it somehow that a concussion mortar would go off, and the dummy propelled up toward the mic stand and landed right next to Dio. So he looks at the thing, and he looks back at the drum riser, quite entertaining. Those are the highlights of touring I remember."

On the other hand, when I talked to Jeff years earlier about Maiden, Young was sort of ripping on the guys for not being all that sociable, except for Bruce. But after meeting Steve Harris' daughter, he's become a bit more understanding.

"Bruce Dickinson was cool as shit, and all the other guys never said a word of hello or hi. But Megadeth ripped a lot of their style from Iron Maiden. So I don't know what the vibe was there. But Bruce was always in our dressing room. The best thing about him was he could imitate different singers. Like he could do Plant, Dio; he would just have us cracking up imitating other singers. And he was spot-on. He did about five or six different singers, and your mouth would've been on the floor."

"But yeah, you know, I've had Lauren Harris on my radio show, and she's talked about it on the show. She's been here and hung out and we've gone out to lunch together, and I can't imagine. She's the example... you know, there are so many fucked-up kids that come out of showbiz families and music families, and she's the prototype of how it should be done. I don't know what they did, because I know he had to tour and he couldn't always be there, and we talked about that, but that's the kind of kid you want to raise if you're a musician. She's a fine upstanding young lady. And I know from talking to her that her dad was painfully shy. So the Maiden cats were a little... I mean, it happened so fast, because Guns N' Roses were on that tour, and Axl did something and they got fired, and we just came on real quick. And I forget how many... It was the **Seventh Son Of The Seventh Son** where they had the white stage. Which was cool, because every stage you play on is black. So for a change of pace, that was really, really cool, to be able to play on that stage."

It meant a lot, given the level of fandom in Megadeth for the band. "For sure. I mean, **Killers**, I covered *Murders In The Rue Morgue* and learned it note for note for note for note. And all that stuff from the very first album on, that's what I grew up with. We were like Iron Maiden junkies. Even though they didn't talk to us at the time, you know, I think again they're all gentleman in that band. I know that Steve is painfully shy; Lauren's talked about it. Because she said he said, 'I was afraid you were going to end up like me,' being painfully shy. So it's different with each band that you're hanging with. And also there was a lot of drugs around Megadeth, and maybe they didn't think that was cool. I sure didn't think it was cool. So they didn't really speak to us that much or whatever, but I wouldn't if I was them either."

Then it all blew up. "Yeah, yeah, right at the end, or pretty near the end. We were still doing some live gigs. Doug Thaler and Doc McGhee flew out to Pennsylvania, and we played like a headline gig. It was like a day off, when we were touring with Dio. We would do headlining gigs at various clubs, and I remember this club was wild, and we killed it that night. It was like probably one of our best shows. They signed us. At the time they had only

Bon Jovi and Mötley Crüe. So we were the next band that Doc McGhee signed. But then again, after the Monsters Of Rock went down and we bailed off that tour, much to my chagrin, because there were five more dates after Castle Donington. All the drugs were going down, and at that point it was not cool. And so they dropped us. But I just tried to stay out of that, because I was so new in the project. I was just trying to be neutral—in this situation that was all over the map (laughs)."

"But playing Monsters Of Rock at Castle Donington was my last gig with them," continues Jeff. "Which sucked, because like I say, there were like five shows on that tour, and Testament had to take over so Ellefson could go into rehab. Both of them did. And they made up the little fib that the bass player hurt his wrist, which was bullshit. And it always made me wonder about Dave's latest claim when his wrist was bugging him. And whether that was real or a conjuring, if you will."

"I consider standing still and being able to play without making mistakes possibly an advantage," quips Jeff, answering to charges from Mustaine that he had never been happy with Young's stage demeanour. "And wearing your guitar higher because it keeps you from getting carpal tunnel, especially when you do wide stretches the way I do. When you're doing Chris Poland and Allan Holdsworth and Jeff Young-type stretches, you don't wear your guitar like flesh, unless you want to get... But Dave is all about that. He's all about cartoon characters. To me, he's not really a musician; I hate to say that. It's more, you know, a guy who poses for a magazine with a practicing unit... there's this practicing unit he's endorsing. You don't need to be making grimaces when you're advertising that. It's a little bit of a pose to me. And the thing about the way he made me dress, and the and tight jeans and the high tops... he makes comments about my hair and whatnot, and even the Megadeth comic book had some slag about that. Which I take as a form of compliment. Because I figured someone had to be around to draw the girls in for them. If I was him, I'd be more worried about the pants he was making us all wear."

"He talked about it once in a while, but I mean, it's probably more in the press," continues Young, asked if he was witness to much of Dave's long-boiling regrets over what had happened with Metallica. "A lot of that stuff was still kind of bubbling under, maybe because it was so fresh. He was out for revenge, and he was on the ascent at that time, to get back whatever he had perceived that he had lost. If you want my personal opinion, I think it's a lot imagined. I think his songwriting was fine, and as great as it is, my problem with Dave is he can't share credit with any of the musicians that have ever played with him. Not just me, but... and the whole thing with Metallica, I think Megadeth's music for me, is more progressive, more chops-oriented, and I prefer that. As I always told him back then, I said it then and I'll say it now: I like Megadeth's music better than Metallica's. I think

Metallica is a little bit more primitive and Neanderthal, if you will, tribal. And that's all cool and I love that stuff, but there's just something about Megadeth that's a little more progressive, in the architecture of the music. Which he, obviously, had to bring some aspect when he was in Metallica."

"So that's his bag, and it's a drag that you have that and you can't just be satisfied with that," muses Young, echoing a sentiment I've always felt when talking to Dave and coming away surprised at how he'll denigrate his own accomplishments in comparisons with Metallica's, especially at the commercial end of things. "Because he doesn't need to. It doesn't matter whether you're No. 1 or No. 2, this, that or the other. Megadeth has achieved all its own stuff. I mean, **So Far, So Good... So What!** was the first thrash album to crack the Top 20 before Metallica did. So he has plenty to be proud of. He has plenty of recognition that he's done all on his own, without dissing out everyone else around him."

"There's no secret what went down in the press a few years ago, when my guitar student brought me, 20 years after the fact... and everyone saw the **Behind The Music**, the original one, before he edited myself and James LaMenzo out of it, in the remaster. I kept it cool when VH1 came to Florida to do the **Behind The Music**. I tried to be a gentleman about everything, but when he comes out... and I've seen him do it with Friedman saying he's singing people's solos to him. And to me, he wasn't in the studio when I recorded at all. And when I say at all, I mean period. So I don't understand why 20 years after the fact—and I haven't read his book, but my publicist reads every biography and she's mentioned a couple things that are in it..."

"I don't know, he's a pathological liar at this point. And it's kind of a drag, because it just detracts from allowing the fans to enjoy the music. Because they don't give a shit about any of that drama. But when a kid brings me a magazine 22 years after the fact, and the solos were the very solos we're talking about right now. There's a reason the kids like *In My Darkest Hour* or the solo in *Hook In Mouth* or whatever, and there's a reason why the other guitar players attempt to play Chris' and my solos the way they are. So just give each person who's served you and helped put you where you are, their due. Especially Marty—I mean, he said a lot of derogatory stuff about Friedman. He's a great player, who's gone to Japan and done amazing things. He's created a very unique career for himself, and it's just like, give everyone a high five that came through your thing. That's my problem with Megadeth, and that's the only thing that takes a bit of the pleasure out of it. Which is, that's exactly what he wants to do."

"I just want to look back, as we're looking back 25 years later, and enjoy it, without 25 years later having to read somewhere in Guitar World magazine that he's saying, 'Well, I sang Jeff's solos to him.' It puts everything in an awkward light. And I saw him say that with Marty. I thought to myself—and it was in the same magazine—I raised my eyebrow, and I said, the cat he doesn't even know we use those types of scales. I just didn't believe that he's singing Marty's solos; it's just too peculiar. And then you know, he went and turned around and did it with me. It's just, you know, odd. It's not about the music at that point. It's about ego."

"Dave's his own worst enemy, dude. He's a douchebag," continues Young, clearly grappling with a haphazard stacking of the positives against the negatives. "That's what it boils down to. All the Metallica thing, how he shamed himself in the Metallica movie, like crying like a baby, all that stuff. He should've just been a man long ago, just grow up, stop partying, just concentrate on your shit, man. And worry about yourself. Don't worry about what Metallica is doing, don't worry about the other musicians who played with you, just honour them, don't rip them off. What he went through with Junior and their lawsuit and stuff, it's ridiculous. You're bandmates; you just treat people fair financially, and you play with them as long as you can, and you make it work as long as you can, and you just be a human being from there. He doesn't know how to do that. That's my problem with him, and I'll never say anything different. I mean, as long as he acts like a clown, I'm going to bat him over the head whenever I get a chance."

And the point must be made. Megadeth was, and is, a great institution. Dave started it, he held it together, his vision lived on past all this drama, and he's got multiple gold and platinum albums to show for it—millions of votes, or "high fives" from the fans.

"Exactly! He carved his own niche, and he should have just been secure with that. Every kid dreams of being in that place. And again, it's character. He's done it, but he lost the respect of a lot of people along the way because character is how you treat people, and it's how you move through life. What I'll say about this, Hetfield I admire. I played pool with him one night; I've only met him briefly. But I like the way he carries himself. He tries... I mean, sometimes he'll mention Mustaine or even joke about him, but he just doesn't acknowledge him. And that's what I've tried to do. But at this point people now, people are curious. I just came out with new music, and I'm dropping more stuff, so people are gonna be asking. So it's a delicate thing, where I want to honour the history. The album is a classic album, and it was a classic experience to be a part of. But again, when you're with someone like that, it's funny how even after all the years, he does his best to try to take the fun out of it for everyone else but himself."

5
RUST IN PEACE

"It was a joke, how clean those guys were"

Dave's Megadeth circus to date had found some considerable extreme metal success despite roadblocks and stumbles all along the way. The band's foundation was built with the help of two jazzers. Then there was a guitarist picked out of a country band. Next axeman, Jeff Young, was noticed whilst coaching the guy they had picked, Jay Reynolds. On the drum stool, the band's runaway roadie slowly just took the gig from one of the original jazzers whose heroin nods and psychological wars with the band's also heroin-addled leader had him slowly sliding off his perch.

Fortunately, as every band has at some point, Megadeth was about to build what would be known as their classic lineup. Flash guitarist Marty Friedman was every bit as good as his two (three?) predecessors, but he was the first guy into the role who came up from metal and metal alone. Friedman had been inspired to pick up the guitar like many a' metalhead, by witnessing Kiss in their mid-'70s prime. Working his way up through Deuce then top-flight Shrapnel recording artists Hawaii, Marty landed with Jason Becker in the land of shred, turning heads with Cacophony, who issued two albums, also on Shrapnel, **Speed Metal Symphony** in 1987 and **Go Off!** the following year.

Having dissolved that act, Friedman tried out for Megadeth. It is said that Dave was disconcerted with Friedman's visual presentation, but after stamping upon him the appropriate image, he was in, joining in the band in February of 1990.

"We wanted to make the changes as comfortably and as inconspicuously as possible," recalls Mustaine, corroborating the tale. "Nick was in the band long before Marty was. He came in and brought fresh air to us. It took us so long to find Marty and we weren't going to get him because his hair was two different colours. We just looked at him and we thought, that's not what we want at all. The three of us were at our managers office and we listened to Marty's solo CD and we went, 'Holy shit, this guy wants to join this band'!"

"I think my guitar playing fits the metal realm in that I play really aggressively and really hard," muses Friedman, on what got him into Megadeth at the perfectly congruent age of 27 years old. "When I play there is no doubt that I mean what I'm playing. I think that is common in heavy metal. For example, if you're talking about jazz or light pop or a lot of kinds of music, the guitar player, even if they're really good and technically wonderful and can do all kinds of things, they just play with this light kind of wussy touch, for lack of a better term. And I think whatever kind of music I'm playing I play with this kind of authority, so to speak, and I think that's a real heavy metal thing and that came from me growing up loving heavy metal."

At the drum end of things, Megadeth was soon to acquire the services of Nick Menza, born in Germany July 23, 1964 and thus also the perfect age to join the tribe. Menza, who had been pounding the drums since he was two, joined the band by the same route Chuck Behler did: he became Megadeth drummer's drum tech. When Behler faltered, the classically trained Menza was an easy fill-in, having played many styles of music all his life, as well as having appeared on one album with his band Rhoads, called **Into The Future**. His first show with the band was in Bradford, England May 12, 1988, but it wasn't until later that he would become the band's official rhythm machine.

Megadeth was in dire straights at this point, having blown off promising dates on the Monsters Of Rock tour in '88 due to the drug habits of the band, as well as an Australian tour. But as will be the pattern for years to come, Mustaine pulled himself out of the fire, dragging with him Junior, his partner in crime, in construction of what would be the band's superlative work, **Rust In Peace**.

The album, produced by Mike Clink, and recorded at Rumbo Recorders, and the first to be distributed by the band's label, Capitol (making it a pure major label issue, essentially), hit the racks on September 24, 1990 to instant acclaim.

"We were very hungry, when we made that record," laughs Ellefson. "I mean not literally; well, maybe we were. We felt like we had a lot of ground that we needed to regain, that maybe we had lost over the couple years between **So Far, So Good... So What!** and **Rust In Peace**. It was, we saw an opening, and we just went in and we seized it."

Lost is right—the band had basically fallen off the radar, not touring in 1989 and most of 1990, although granted, into 1990, there was an epic album being made, one that would vault the band into a spot between Metallica up above and Slayer nipping at Mustaine's heels.

That swaggering and electric record, a little something called **Rust In Peace**, opens with a showcase of musicianship and heavy metal might called *Holy Wars... The Punishment Due*. The song's ambitious messaging matched its construction, matched the messaging of the political album art as well. This was a Megadeth on fire, the frenzy captured by Clink's killer sound palette. Megadeth finally had a hi-fidelity record on its hands.

Explains Mustaine on this mega-classic, "*Holy Wars* was a song that I wrote... I woke up in Dublin, Ireland and the night before I was in Antrim and had been drinking Guinness. And some guy in the audience was selling

Megadeth T-shirts, bootleg T-shirts, and I said, 'Go get the stuff.' I'm not against people, if they want to be part of our team, earning money with us, if they want to work with us. But taking from us is taking from our families and it's hurting our band and hurting our ability to take our music to the masses. So I don't support bootleg merchandise at all; I don't appreciate it at all. It doesn't have anything to do with me not having enough money. It has to do with, first off, the merchandise is usually shit, and second off, the people who are usually doing it are sneaky bastards."

"But in this case, it was totally unrelated to what I just described. In this case it was someone selling T-shirts for the cause. And I thought, well what the hell is the cause? And I'm already like two Guinness pints into this thing. And they say if you draw a happy face in the foam in the top of the Guinness, you'll have a drinking partner for the night. So I'm drawing smiley faces in there and I'm getting absolutely tanked. And I asked this Irish guy... and I'm part Irish. I'm a little different than most American Irish people when I go to Ireland. When American Irish people go there they go, 'Oh, I'm Irish, I'm part Irish!' And the real Irish people don't give a fuck. They don't want to hear about you being a sliver Irish. But because we have a lot of fans there, and I'm of Irish ancestry, they're glad for the fact I have some heritage from there."

"So I get away with it a little bit that I think I kind of was being a little bit too nosy when I was there. And I asked the guy what the cause was about. And he made it sound so, so beautiful. It was so eloquently described. All he said was, 'It's the Protestants and the Catholics. They have a problem with each other and they both think their religion is better than the other. And it's basically just prejudiced religion.' And I went, 'Oh, that's simple.' He didn't say that they're bombing each other, killing one another, that they're throwing Molotov cocktails at cars and children are dying and innocent people are getting killed all the time and all the things that are involved with it. And I didn't even know what side of the cause he's fighting for."

"So I get up onstage, and I said, 'This one's for the cause. Give Ireland back to the Irish. Anarchy in Ireland.' Now Paul fucking McCartney can say, 'Give Ireland back to the Irish.' Dave Mustaine can't. So I say that and that's the last thing I remember. And the next morning I go out for breakfast and David Ellefson won't talk to me and I said, 'What's your problem?' And he says, 'There were three fucking bomb threats last night and they had to clear the venue three times with dogs, come in there sniffing for bombs, because of you and your fucking IRA statement.' And I said, 'What IRA statement?' He said, 'Give Ireland back to the Irish. This one's for the cause.' And I went, 'What?!' And I couldn't believe I'd done that."

"So we get to Nottingham Rock City and it was in England and I just put pen to paper and everything just came out. And the most important part for me was that killing for religion is something I don't understand. And then the other relevant part of it was fools like me who cross the seas, come from a foreign land, and then ask the sheep, the followers, for their beliefs. And I asked the guy, and instead of just being the entertainer, playing my songs and shutting up, I said something I shouldn't have talked about. And that's one of our most popular songs. The second half of the song, *Punishment Due*, is about a comic, **The Punisher**. The first part is about Antrim."

"*Holy Wars* had a whole bunch of guitar solos," recalls Friedman, "and I did them and I was unhappy with them all and Mike Clink was producing and saying, 'Oh, that's fine! Keep it, it's great, it's wonderful!' And I really wasn't happy with them, especially since it was my first album on a major label. I wanted to be totally 100% stoked on it. But also, since I was the new guy in the band, I really didn't have a whole lot of say. If the producer likes the solo, it's pretty much there. But I fucking got on their nerves. Every day I was in there I was like, 'I've got to redo that *Holy Wars* solo—it sucks.' And eventually I did, and got my own way, and it was fine (laughs)."

As for his new bandmate Nick Menza, "Great drummer," says Marty. "We were all about chemistry, really. Great chemistry, the four of us, musically, as far as I was concerned, a great band. Great front end, great drummer, great guitar player and great bass player. And the sum of those four parts together was more powerful than any one member, I believe. And I think that's what the fans responded to. Nick Menza, great guy, I haven't heard from him in a long time. Hope he's doing well."

Holy Wars was of a Megadeth type that eschewed the band's confused punk chaos, and at the same time, took their awkward jazziness of the past and put it to more sensible heavy metal use. This was high-minded Megadeth moving through time with authority. And Mike Clink, having previously worked with Metallica and the important (yet over-rated) **Appetite For Destruction** album by Guns N' Roses, managed to bring out all of the subtleties in the performances by this crack band.

"That song had, I think, the most edits I've ever seen in a song," says Friedman of track No. 2, *Hangar 18*, arguably the catchiest headbang on the record despite the working over of it. "I mean, that song changed form so many times. By the time we got it done, the whole floor of the studio was full of two-inch tape. It really started off to be much longer than that and got hacked up and came to be what it was, just by being chopped up so much. It really was an experience in editing. That was before ProTools. There were a lot of computers being used at the time, but not the way they are used now for editing. There was actually physical tape all over the floor and I remember I had to come in to cut guitars and I remember them having to clean up the floor because there was so much tape on it. It was insane. Most of the songs were like that, but *Hangar 18* in particular. I had that visual memory of a lot of tape. Everything we ever did, when I was in the band anyway, was done that way. We learned them all after the fact. You would relearn everything after the record got done and then you would go on tour."

Take No Prisoners, lyrically concerning prisoners of war, was an example of Megadeth mastering and harnessing the energy found within the band's Poland-era material. There's a lot of thrash, rhythmic breaks, transitions one wouldn't expect, and it all adds up to a gnarliness that links the band to its sordid past.

"Just a lot of playing on that record," recalls Menza. "That's why it says lead drums on there, because we pretty much just took charge of that whole record. We were playing on ten the whole way through. That's just a lot of fun to play those songs. I'm not going to say that I don't miss that because I do. So **Rest In Peace** is probably one of my favourites probably because it's the most progressive."

Five Magics demonstrates the new band's sense of complex melody, and it also allows for a signature bass walk from Dave Jr. The song is based on the Lyndon Hardy fantasy novel from 1980 called **Master Of The Five Magics**.

Ellefson is back laying it down for the intro on ode to heroin, *Poison Was The Cure*, which is another note-dense thrasher, rendered mercifully short, but once more supporting the record's bid for integrity amongst old school Megadeth fans.

"*Poison Was The Cure* was the first solo I did for Megadeth coming into the studio," recalls Marty. "And to get one under your belt, so everybody knows what kind of thing you're going to do... but I remember Dave Jerden was in the studio for like one day, and he was just way too rock 'n' roll for us (laughs). We were really into perfection and nailing stuff like a machine, and he was like, 'Oh, close enough for rock 'n' roll. Let's go.' And we totally weren't into that at the time. Sometimes there's a place for that, but Megadeth certainly wasn't that place, especially at that point in time."

A surprising statement, given the band's notoriously druggy past... "Yeah, I've never really been a big fan of doing drugs, when you're a professional," counters Marty. "I don't really like that too much. But when I joined Megadeth everybody was straight as an arrow. It was a joke, how clean those guys were. I was impressed. Because I didn't really know Megadeth well. I had heard rumours that they were druggies and in and out of rehab and stuff, and then when I joined the band, it was like, these guys were straighter than I was. They were on it. Totally impressed. Obviously down the line, things went in and out of control. That whole drug thing just sucks so bad, but I can't be around it. At some point there has be some sort of balance and moderation. When we did the tour with Aerosmith, Megadeth and Aerosmith, in America... now, as a rock fan, myself, that is supposed to be like the dream tour of your life, parties, massive rock god touring. You get all geared up for that, and you go on the actual tour, and it's a bunch of AA meetings and nannies and babysitters and baby blankets and a bunch of counsellors, and just so much crap, that... oh my God. Of course the shows rocked and everything, but everything that you've got posters on your wall as a kid as a rock fan, and all of your fantasies, it could not be farther from the truth. It was like, 'This is Megadeth and Aerosmith touring the United States?! Fuck me runnin''. Man, it was tough."

"But I haven't used drugs since I was in high school," continues Friedman. "You know, everybody's got their own demons they have to deal with, and I'd say Dave held it together pretty good considering his desire to use drugs or whatever. I think he did a pretty damn good job. It's a Catch-22. Some people perform... well, they don't perform better, or they have that personality they've got to have, I don't understand it. I mean, I can tell you this though, when everybody was full-on tight as an arrow, tight and straight, there was no one who could touch us. We were shit-hot. I was fairly proud to be in that band at many points in the career."

Back to the hair metal-killing **Rust In Peace** — remember where we are in rock history — next up was *Lucretia*, a chunky, catchy, rhythmic mid-pacer sophisticated of rhythm (and lyrically, about an intense visit to a fortune-teller), followed by *Tornado Of Souls*, yet another track with Metallica-esque magnetism, especially come chorus time.

Notes Marty, "That seems to be one of the tunes if I do a guitar clinic or seminar, people always ask me to play the guitar solo in that one. I guess it's a long solo; maybe that's why. That's when I really felt like I was in the band, when we were cutting that and I nailed the solo. Mustaine came in, and he hadn't heard me playing any of it. He just came in and listened to it when it was done and he didn't say anything. He just shook my hand and he had this looks on his face just like, dude, right on. And I was like, pretty cool. But to me, I was much happier with some of the other work I had done on **Rust In Peace**, but I guess that's the one that stuck to most people."

"It's one of the songs from the **Rust In Peace** sessions that Nick Menza, Dave and myself, worked relentlessly for months putting that record together," adds Ellefson. "And when we went into the studio, Marty Friedman had just joined the band, and because he had just joined recently, most of his contributions were in the guitar solos. And I remember sitting down waiting for Marty to really deliver the goods. And every day I would come into the studio and listen to his new solos and go wow, this guy is good! Then when I heard *Tornado Of Souls*, I had goose bumps and I just looked at Marty and went, 'That is fucking incredible.' It is definitely one of my favourite Marty solos."

Junior's back and prominent yet again, leading us through *Dawn Patrol* with a naked bass line while Dave talks a low vocal concerning environmental Armageddon. Nick's there but not Marty, on this bit of stoner rock amidst the flash-rocking thrash.

The album closes with *Rust In Peace... Polaris*, a second song with ellipses, as if to make up for the fact that **Rust In Peace** is the first album title without three dots. The track is a prog metal gallop extraordinaire, with all sorts of hotshot riffing over the top of a Menza double bass drum groove, all the while Mustaine growing into his skin as a vocalist as he exhorts mankind to improve the damn place.

"I thought that was going to be the song that broke us into the mainstream of the world," muses Marty. "I thought that was the best riff that we had, and Mike Clink also thought so. And Mike Clink, at that time had just finished **Appetite For Destruction** from Guns N' Roses, and it was the biggest rock album of all time as far as I was concerned. And when he thought we were going to be huge because of that riff in *Rust In Peace*, I got all excited because I agreed. And it turned out to be a sleeper and nobody really picked up on it. But I always thought it was a classic Megadeth riff."

All told, **Rust In Peace** represents a crystalline moment in time that Dave Mustaine would do well to appreciate. Snug in the middle of his near lifelong resentment at being fired from Metallica and Metallica's stratospheric success, in 1990, many a' discerning metalhead would have found themselves proclaiming Megadeth to be a better band than Metallica. Additionally, there wasn't a lot of difference for this brief moment in terms of commercial success, given that Metallica hadn't smashed the bank yet with the self-titled "black album." Megadeth were sitting with gold records for each of their directly two previous albums, and certification of **Rust In Peace** as gold was more or less a formality, the album reaching that status inside of four months. Granted, Metallica had a few golds and platinums by this point and **Justice** had even hit double platinum already. But still, both bands were "successful," even if a striving Dave didn't think Megadeth were successful enough.

More importantly, however, many smart fans of this stuff would have said at that time that **Rust In Peace** was cooler than Metallica's current record **...And Justice For All**, and what's more, many would plump for it—and indeed the band's next, **Countdown To Extinction**—over the smash **Metallica** album as well. That's a lot of vindication for Mustaine right there, and many Megadeth fans were confused that the guy couldn't enjoy the praise and goodly reputation for what it was.

Rust In Peace would rise to No. 23 on the Billboard charts and be certified platinum on December 23, 1994, thanks to the slingshot effect of the even more successful **Countdown To Extinction**. The album would garner a Grammy nomination at the 33rd Grammys, adding a second nomination for *Hanger 18* the following year.

Wrote Entertainment Weekly's Jim Farber, in a welcome (and smart) mainstream review, "The band has found a way to keep its brutality inventive. On **Rust In Peace**, its fourth album, Megadeth is still coming up with new inflections amid the blitzkrieg rhythms and lightning-fast leads.

To aid in that pursuit, the group has two new members (lead guitarist Marty Friedman and drummer Nick Menza), both of whom prove as creatively abusive as their forebears. They help the group's new music dent its way into your memory without ever resorting to conventional hooks. Sheer velocity, combined with dexterity, is the draw here. The band members make their triple-timed rhythms seem effortless, and no matter how thick their guitar chords, they still manage to make them swing. That's true even in tracks like *Five Magics*, with its sudden, risky tempo changes. The rich guitar chords hold things together at all times, allowing for such unexpected breakouts as a bass volley in *Tornado Of Souls* and a drum flourish in the title song. Numbers like this should hit hard with the slam-dance crowd. But even for more demure listeners the album offers a helpful twist on an old lesson: Here, at least, speed doesn't kill—it thrills."

Adds Rolling Stone's Robert Palmer, "It's difficult to isolate new guitarist Marty Friedman's individual contributions within the helter-skelter of pummelling riffs and pyrotechnic leads, but the strong contributions of new drummer Nick Menza are readily apparent. Earlier Megadeth drummers tended to rumble down below like John Bonham on amphetamines, powering the music but cluttering it too. Menza, son of famed jazz saxophonist Don Menza, has the requisite power but also displays a sense of restraint, a mature use of space and texture that lifts the crunching guitar riffs right off the ground, making the entire band swing like mad. And bassist Dave Ellefson hasn't wasted those years off the road; his playing is spectacular and innovative throughout. This is one thrash metal band that jazzbos can get into, provided the snarl of Mustaine's lead vocals and the sustained level of anger and intensity don't send them running for the door."

Megadeth, immediately upon the record's triumphant release, found themselves hitting the tour trail, highlights being the Clash Of The Titans package to be sure, but also dates with Judas Priest, who were out trying to prove how they could compete for maniacal metalness with the young whippersnappers upsetting the social order. Wielding the creditable **Painkiller** album, Priest variously took on as backup Pantera, Sepultura, Testament and Mustaine & Co, a game bunch that frankly were supporting better records that the doddering Brits could manage by this post-**Ram It Down** point.

"I'm a huge Priest fan," says Friedman, "so of course when were touring with Priest, I'm plugging the members for exactly the kind of information you and I are talking about here. 'So tell me about the recording of *Hot Rockin*'.' You know what I mean? That kind of detail. And they were more than happy to share that stuff. Very friendly. I used to hangout with K.K. and asking those kinds of things, and I'm sure he answered them very friendly. There was a very friendly kind of camaraderie. Rob was very friendly; they all were. At the time, they had an American drummer, Scott, and I think he's younger than the rest of the guys, and American, so I kind of saw him as... it must've be kind of tough to assimilate. Obviously on stage it was no problem, but he probably had a hard time. He seemed to be alone a lot of the time. Which I can understand. What do you talk about? The other guys probably have grandkids and stuff. But that's a pro for you. You gotta just jump into any situation and rock it out."

As to the contours of Marty's fandom, "I love **Sin After Sin** and **Stained Class**. I didn't really like the real early stuff, because the sound was too primitive. I couldn't get into that production, but the songs were great, *Tyrant* and all that. **Sin After Sin** I just love. *Dissident Aggressor*, bitchin' song. Even their shitty albums like **Point Of Entry** had good stuff. I always stuck up for the Priest when they tried to go commercial (laughs)."

Clash Of The Titans found Megadeth hooking up with Slayer, Testament and Suicidal Tendencies for a swing through Europe, September and October of 1990, and then North American dates, with Slayer, Anthrax and Alice In Chains. The significance of Clash Of The Titans has been ossifying for years around the idea that it was thrash metal's finest moment, the peak before a list to the side.

"Yeah, it was packed," recalls Dave Jr. "That definitely was the apex. I definitely remember, as we were on that tour, seeing what was happening on MTV, because Queensryche was starting to be popular, with *Silent Lucidity* and videos like that, and the grunge thing was starting to happen with Alice in Chains. I just remember on the tour, every night we were pretty full, if not sold-out arenas, and what I thought was interesting—Metallica was able to do this on their own, where it took the combined effort of the three of us, plus a support band, who, at that time didn't really bring a lot of people into the building. But it really took the combined efforts of the three of us to sell out these arenas. But it dawned on me, especially as we were writing music at that time which would then become **Countdown To Extinction**, there was a real synergy in our group, and we could just feel that, oh man, we're a really good thrash band, but there's a whole lot more to our band going on here. And I was the one really pushing to be aware of that. You know, Dave was writing, as always, a great hook writer, wrote great hooks, and even though he was never really considered a singer, so to speak, he was always really good at writing good vocal melodies, and just had melody in his mind. Especially as a singer, for a guy who wasn't a formally trained singer, he was a very melodic vocalist. And of course Marty was just this ace in the hole that we had, and we really inspired him to bring everything he's got to the table."

"And so I felt like, when we were on Clash Of The Titans, I just remember so clearly thinking, this is never going to get any bigger than this," continues Ellefson. "This is it. This is the pinnacle, and it's huge, and it's great, but we need to now not retreat backwards. We really need to press forward big time right now. And then that became **Countdown To Extinction**, and that record sold twice as much as **Rust In Peace**, because it was embraced by MTV and it was embraced by the mainstream! The mainstream is finally ready for a band who cut its teeth on thrash, to become a mainstream metal band. And conversely I saw Slayer, kind of just do the same thing again, and they, all of a sudden, to some degree, maybe just stayed the same or even went backwards for a few years. And of course the irony of that, because they didn't alter or do anything different, they are probably the reigning champions now (laughs). They probably sell more records, they play probably to more people each night, as their own headline, under Slayer, than probably any of the rest of them, quite honestly. I mean, besides Metallica. But then again, they've got some other things. They've got the original line-up, and there are some internal things that never changed with Slayer, and ultimately fans always like that as well."

But at the time, Slayer and Megadeth weren't quite getting along. "It did run smoothly," says Ellefson, however, asked about the bigger picture. "I think, for some reason, between our band and Slayer, of which I had nothing to do with, there were al these rubs (laughs), which I had nothing to do with; those are pretty well documented at that time, anyway. But yeah, the deal was, for us, we always let Slayer play after us. Because it was a rotating lineup, and that was one of the first things that we did, to make sure that there were no... to get rid of egos. No one is a headliner, we're all headliners, and we'll rotate the slot. So we just put it in our thing that we always played before Slayer. So of course, the night Slayer opened, then Anthrax would follow them, and then we were the closer. And then other nights, Anthrax would open, then it would be us, and then it would be Slayer that would close. So there was always this... it felt like a good flow to the music. Because every band was very different. The energies of the shows were very different, and that just seemed like a good flow to the evening, to have it run like that."

"And that's the way it worked all through the entire tour. That way we got equal billing, equal times to open, and to be the closer. And I've got to tell you, being the closer wasn't always the best position to be in, because you've got to consider, kids have been there for hours thrashing the shit out of themselves and being in mosh pits, and sometimes the middle slot was the best place to be. Because sometimes you get the best energy from the crowd."

"Clash Of The Titans, I believe, was the precursor to the Big Four," figures Mustaine, offering his reminisces more than a decade down the line, lines on his face. "And although I think that the Clash Of The Titans would be much different now, I still think that the fans deserved that. They deserved to see the best of the best on the same stage, and I think there's been such a peculiar relationship with all of us for so long because we were the Big Four.

I mean we *are* the Big Four. There's none bigger than the four of us in the States. You've got different types of music, but in metal? It's us! The four of us! I think right now is the beginning of a second wave and that, if done right, if everybody can keep themselves out of pine boxes, we're gonna be okay."

The presence of Alice in Chains on the bill, however, seemed to pose some sort of bellwether question that the tide might be shifting.

"They were getting pelted with garbage every night and they were getting all kinds of stuff thrown at them," continues Dave, snickering at the ebb and flow of the music business as only he can, caring and not caring at the same time. "I thought it was kind of sad because I liked Layne. I actually helped him a little bit when he was trying to get sober, and I like Jerry a lot. I just watched that crazy TV show with the bass player on it, with the rehab thing, and oh god, what a mess. And then the drummer, I don't know him very well, but when we toured together he seemed like a pretty reasonable guy. It was fun to have him around. I like their music, although it's certainly not what I would listen to if I was trying to relax."

But them's fighting words, this idea that grunge could kill thrash. Hair metal, maybe, as is the popular conceit, but not thrash, spits Dave. "That's horse shit. Grunge can't replace thrash. First off, most grunge guitar players are wankers, and most thrash guitar players are four, five, sometimes maybe even ten times more talented than most grunge players. Now you do have certain people who can play guitar that play in a grunge band and that have really limited themselves. Like I was saying Kenny G, being a friend of ours, his son is a metal guitar player. That's how we met him, and my manager manages him. The funny thing is, though, Kenny G's son Max, what you hear of him, it's nothing like he can play. He's a monster. Take me, Chris Broderick, Marty Freidman, Yngwie, roll us all together, make it sound good, make it something you want to hear, that's him. He can do anything. He's a monster. Now he has to do what he has to do because that's where his niche is."

"It was just during the time when that record blew up," figures Sean Kinney, drummer for Alice in Chains, alluding to a case of coincidence more than anything, concerning his band winding up on Clash Of The Titans. "We were one of those bands that had the luxury of being able to play, and we would play with anybody. Poison and Warrant getting in a fight over hair products or something in Portland, and we had to be home in Seattle on a break. We were on tour for two days and we get a call like hey, we need somebody to play down there. At the arenas. Oh. So we jump in a van, we rent a van and jump in with our gear and we go down there. So we did that and next thing you know we're out with Megadeth, and we're out in Europe, and we're out, you know, on the Clash Of The Titans. That's a rough crowd, but we powered through it every day and made a lot of friends."

"We were just excited to play," continues Sean. "I can't say people didn't throw shit at us. We'd just throw it right back. It was fun and the guys from

Slayer, you'd think they're evil, they're the coolest guys. We're really good friends to this day. We made great friends and you learn a lot on tour. You get three bands who are revolving headlining and we were the standard opening act. You'd see the same crowd reacts differently to each band, and you'd learn a lot. All the big touring and... you know people have riders with elaborate shit on it. So you learn, oh, that's weird, we're never going to do that. You learn a lot; we pay a lot of attention trying to keep it relatively simple. We're pretty humble guys. We don't take it for granted and we're just pretty honoured to do that. The one thing you can't make happen is people liking your music and they pass it on."

"We were certainly all really stoked to be there and doing it," figures Anthrax's Scott Ian. "It definitely was, at the time, it definitely was the apex. Yet, at the same time, we put the period on the end of the sentence, I think, for that... let's say it was not necessarily a decade, but let's say from '83 to '91. I think the Clash Of The Titans tour kind of closed the book on that chapter. Because, you know, you take three of the bands, three of the four bands anyway, and you put us out together playing a pretty massive tour, and we sold out Madison Square Garden. That obviously had never happened before with this kind of underground music, as they say. So yeah, everyone, we loved being there, everyone got along great. Well, us and Slayer and us and Megadeth did, but Slayer and Megadeth weren't getting along so well. But it was an amazing time, to be able to look and see, 'Hey, look what we've accomplished.' We are becoming what we've always wanted to be. We love Iron Maiden, and now we're playing the same place that Iron Maiden plays. It was just amazing to us."

"This is where the metal bands got the grunge thing before the fans did," muses Seattle journalist and DJ Jeff Gilbert. "And look at what Soundgarden did. They went out on the road with Guns N' Roses. It was, 'How can we take this to a bigger audience?' I had this conversation with Kirk Hammett from Metallica. Those guys loved the grunge stuff. They were on it way before anybody else. In fact Kirk Hammett joined Sub Pop's singles club, where he wanted all the music that came out of Sub Pop to be sent to him immediately. This was their way of acknowledging it and wanting to promote it, because it was never polarized, and metal did a lot to help grunge in that regard. Alice in Chains on Clash Of The Titans, on first look you're going, 'No, that doesn't work at all.' But then when you saw it and heard it you went, 'Okay, this makes perfect sense.' It's funny because I had all those Alice in Chains glam pictures, and I was a real good friend with Dave Mustaine at the time, and I went down to the venue to do an interview with Dave for Guitar World, and I took those pictures with me. He had them photocopied and smeared all over the arena. And he loved that picture. He put it up everywhere. He had his whole road crew go over the entire venue, in the bathrooms, on the walls, anywhere he could stick a photocopy. So I came back later and I'm walking down the hallway, and I see Layne, and I go, 'Hey man,' and he goes, 'Hey!' because he knew that I was the one who gave those pictures. It was all good-natured ribbing."

"From a band point of view on the tour, we all loved them," continues Scott Ian, when I asked him about Alice in Chains. "They got that tour... my memory is a little hazy on this, but I seem to remember that the band was going to get the tour. I think Pantera was kind of like in the league to get on that tour, initially. And then it was actually Dave Mustaine who had brought in Alice in Chains, because I think Alice had opened for them, and Dave brought in an Alice record, the first album, and said everyone should check this out. It was at one of these Clash Of The Titans meetings, where me and Jonny Z, Dave and his manager, and usually Tom or Kerry and their manager, Rick Sales, and it was Dave who brought up Alice in Chains, and everybody took copies the record, and within the next week, I think everyone made that decision to take them as the opening band because everyone loved it so much."

But crowd reaction? "Not good," laughs Scott. "Yeah, I mean they were really thrown to the lion's den. You can even ask Jerry this. I've talked to him at length about this over the years, but I think it was one of the formative things that helped make that band become what they became, because they had it really, really hard. They were out in front of ten to 15,000 people, hating them, every night, throwing as much as they could get their hands on, at them. And never once did Alice, did they ever cut their set short; never once did they let it get them. They stood on stage and they did their thing, and I think they garnered a lot of respect. And within a couple of months, when *Man In The Box* started to break big, you know that every single person who was throwing full beer cups at them went out and bought the record."

Asked if there was a sense that Clash Of The Titans was one of many examples of purist metal bands helping to break grunge metal bands, but then that was not reciprocated later on when grunge was king, Ellefson says, "That's an interesting take on it. I wouldn't even say that the grunge movement, as much as it may have had a metal influence to it, in some way, they were clearly not metal bands. If anything, they were very alternative, dirty, even heavy, and even kind of metallic, and kind of Black Sabbath-heavy, as it may have been, but it never had the real sharp precision that metal had. And I think that's what really differentiates the metal thing from all other genres of music, is that it's really just a sharp, hard-edged, metallic sound. It started with maybe Scorpions, Accept, Judas Priest, and it really was refined in the thrash thing, where the tempos were bumped up, the recording processes become more high fidelity, and then even Pantera can be part of that. So I think probably for grunge, grunge got probably a nice entré nous through metal, but I think as soon as they got a chance to establish themselves, you're right, they did not reciprocate. Just like we... Alice Cooper took us on tour with him. That didn't mean we were a shock rock gore band. We weren't going to start wearing makeup and cutting heads off babies. But Alice Cooper was kind enough to entré nous us into the mainstream, even though we were really there to establish our own identity."

6
COUNTDOWN TO EXTINCTION

"All working parts of this machine, keep it going"

After **Rust In Peace** and its high profile tour cycle, there was a sense that Megadeth were now big business. "Megadeth were pretty far along," explains DJ Will, working in A&R for Capitol at the time, "because they had, had two Capitol releases under the belt at the time, with **Peace Sells** and **So Far, So Good... So What!**. And I think the department was really focused on... when the time came to put out a new Megadeth record, every department was all on the same page. Everything was in sync. Another situation where you had a sort of laissez-faire attitude; you know, if it ain't broken, don't fix it. It's Megadeth—if you get a single, it's going to be not 100% commercially viable, but at the same time, Dave has written very many... the label wouldn't ask him to write a hit single, or to collaborate with some rock 'n' roll version of Diane Warren, to craft something that is going to be hooky, poppy, and straight, exclusively for radio. I think when we would have our weekly meetings, it would be a collective roundtable of all the artists on the roster. Everyone would go through what the status is on each one, every A&R rep would go through their acts, and we would talk about them as a whole, everything from promotional materials to tour support, release dates, artwork, conversations with the artist, if they are unhappy or happy about something. So everything was sort of like, 'Okay, there's this band; what's going on with them?' Blah, blah, blah."

"It was important to have a continual progression," continues Will, "because **Rust In Peace** did so well, with *Hangar 18*, and MTV was playing the videos. We were getting a lot of airplay with either *Lucretia* or *Holy Wars*, which was the main single at that time. So there was a lot of strong momentum, plus a huge tour, and the sales were really going through the roof. I think it went gold relatively quick, and so the important thing was from **Rust In Peace** to **Countdown**, all working parts of this machine, keep it going. Off the top of my head, I don't recall the producer from **Rust In Peace** to **Countdown**, but I would say this: it was definitely the next step, where they had another strong song with *Symphony Of Destruction*. So it was, 'Keep it going, don't mess it up, don't interfere.' It was a great time, a great time for Megadeth."

As for the level of drug use he might have been aware of... "Here and there, here and there. There were shakeups. I would say there was some friction between members, but it was eventually smoothed over; not of a lot of things went into the press, and not a lot of things were, 'Oh, right now they're breaking up!' There was a lot of static, a lot of friction, but things were kept together by management and the label."

"For **Countdown To Extinction**, we started writing songs when we were on Clash Of the Titans," recalls Ellefson. "And as a group, we saw sort of an end of an era, and the dawn of a new one, which I think we helped create. And we made a conscious decision to write our songs sort of in a new direction, and to really capitalize on a lot of the good qualities that we had, like rhythm, melody and song structure."

"It was a totally different time period," seconds Mustaine. "The '80s, you could pretty much do what you want, and in the '90s, you saw the invention of sobriety police. Bands would take them out, and if you were caught drinking or partying or anything like that, you pretty much were labelled and ostracized and singled out as a pariah. You were a bad guy. Since when can you not have sex, drugs and rock 'n' roll if you're in a business that the sub-title is 'Sex, Drugs, and Rock 'n' Roll'? For me, I'm a much different person right now. I'm in a monogamous relationship and I'm divorced, which is a sad situation, but we're friends, which is great, and I've got two great kids out of it and I'm in a business right now where, me being a Christian in a heavy metal band, a lot of people think that's impossible. Well it's not impossible. I don't push it on people. I think that's what makes people hate that, is when they push it on people. It's kind of like when a guy newly gets sober and he says, 'You can't drink around me.' Well unless you plan on tying me down and French kissing me, if you're having a beer and I don't drink, there shouldn't be a problem, right? So yeah, I look at the way things are progressing with us with the music business in the '80s compared to the '90s, there was a self-policing that took place."

And Capitol was more involved as well. "Yes, I think what happened was there were so many bands that were crashing and burning that it left the labels holding the bag so many times that they just had to answer... when you have the year-end corporate meetings and you're saying where's the pig bleeding from? They find out where the holes are and usually what it is, is the signing of an untalented A&R personnel. They find a band they like that's got one good song, they sign them, and then about a year later they realize they made a mistake. The thing is most bands, the guys have about a year-and-a-half between their first record and their second record to write that. Now what the people don't take into consideration, they had their whole life to write that first record. Try and write a second record in a year-and-a-half. You can't. Everybody has a song that's part of their makeup. That's why they say 'vibes.' We all have a vibration that we oscillate at that makes us feel good or bad. Some people like to vibrate really high, some people like to vibrate really low. That's why people are mellow or high-strung. And for me, certain music just vibrates or resonates with my being differently. When I started playing music, I didn't want to play heavy stuff just to disturb people; I play music because it resonates with my being at all different levels during the course of the day."

Adds Scott Greer, international marketing at Capitol, "I worked with Megadeth on the **Countdown To Extinction** record and records prior and after, and I mean, the thing you could say is that vocally, at least from a Mustaine perspective, he can get into more melodic avenues of singing and can be a little bit more commercial and radio-friendly. That's the difference between, say, Lamb Of God and those bands. Lamb Of God was uncompromising, and it wasn't about radio and video play. It was about this real and raw musical quality. It's authentic. And so you're marketing it different than you would market a Megadeth or Metallica. Maybe it's more akin to Pantera, to a certain extent. But that did have some radio."

"So I was doing international marketing at the time," continues Scott, "when they were sort of breaking out, when it really was going to a commercial standpoint across Europe, Japan, parts of Asia. And I remember at that time Megadeth had a very strong relationship with the label. We all went down to their rehearsal for that arena tour they were going on. They did a private performance for us. But there was that very strong relationship with that label. So you did have that strong label interaction. From an A&R perspective, they contributed. But I think they did what they wanted to, and I think at the time they wanted to make a more commercial record. They probably felt that at the time."

Greer has also talked about being impressed with the band's ambitions of "world domination," an enthusiasm that carried over to Capitol, who were really trying hard to make Megadeth the biggest metal band on the planet. And by the time Megadeth were playing their comfortably musical card called **Countdown To Extinction**, Metallica had already busted their career wide open with their decidedly more accessible "black album." And here was Megadeth making very much the same move, leaching out much of the band's past in thrash and writing more economically and tunefully.

"I don't want to talk about Metallica badly," says Dave, talking to Sam Dunn diplomatically many years later. "Even in comparing records, I don't feel that I have the right to say what they did or did not do right or wrong. I don't know what they did. I can tell you from my perspective, at the time when the black record came out, it was a period where heavy metal in itself was starting to really... it was starting to disintegrate. We weren't getting the places that we used to play, insurance was flipping out on tour buses and drug use, and there were all kinds of problems with underage people travelling, and there were more and more things coming down. And actually cleaning up the music business, but in effect, really hurting it because there were so many miscreants in the music business that you give them some guidelines to live by, and a lot of them can't live up to it. They equate trying to live a legal lifestyle—to a degree—as being handcuffed. For me, I can do whatever I want without breaking the law and have a pretty good time. I think that there's a lot of people out there, they think when you get into a band, if there's a sober person in it then the party's over. For me, it wasn't that the party was over, the party had just started."

"Grunge metal was, I believe in a large part, responsible for the death of the rock star," answers Mustaine, asked by Dunn if grunge's meteoric rise in 1991 had something to do with convulsive changes in thrash. "Granted Axl Rose's behaviour was less than exemplary for someone who deserved the kind of accolades he was getting, and the hero worship he had, I think it just put gas on the fire. If anything, Axl is kind of suffering the same kind of self-righteous entitlement that Mike Tyson has. And I loved watching Tyson fight. I loved watching Axl play. But somebody needed to tell those guys, 'No. No, you're not doing this. Get on stage, get in the ring, stop biting people, stop making people wait. Go do your job'."

Amusingly, Dave says the nu-metal trend years later was harder to hack than the romance with grunge when hair metal died 'round about 1990.

"Nu-metal came out and you've got a bunch of talentless guitar players that have detuned their guitar so you can't hear that they can't play. It's real easy when you're strumming a guitar and you don't hear the strings, you just hear something that sounds like somebody's playing a zipper. It's like, well, what the hell are you doing? For me, when guitar players started getting away from guitar solos, it's like, okay, now everybody can do it. The reason these guys don't play guitar solos is because it isn't cool? Wrong. It's because you can't do it, you puss. That's why."

Max Norman would be picked to produce Megadeth's paramount **Countdown To Extinction** record, and the results, crafted and constructed over four months in early 1992 at The Enterprise in Burbank, would be exquisite. In fact, arguably, **Countdown** was the highest fidelity metal production to date from anybody, especially in the world of extreme metal, even if Megadeth's songs this time around were decidedly not very extreme, save for Dave's vocals of acquired taste.

The album opened with *Skin O' My Teeth*, which demonstrated the band's new penchant for pregnant pauses, use of spaces, airtight riffing and songsmithing extraordinaire. Lyrically, this one is quintessential self-deprecating Dave, Mustaine matter-of-factly riffing on suicide attempts that fail because they just didn't get enough elbow grease put into them.

Skin O' My Teeth was issued as the third single from the record (October 5th in the UK, three months later in the US), but it is lead proposition *Symphony Of Destruction* that did most the heavy lifting for the band as they marched the record toward double platinum. *Symphony Of Destruction* is simply irresistible. It's as much AC/DC as it is *Peace Sells*, a distant relative of which it shares a few tricks. Lyrically it ain't much, but what's there sets the stage for Mustaine's later heavy interest in shadow governments, the power behind the puppets.

"That was another edit-fest like *Hangar 18*," remarks Friedman, who proceeds to undermine the track's creativity. "It's a fun song to play live. That was our biggest quote unquote hit. I think that pattern of songwriting found its way into so many other Megadeth songs. If you were to delve into the details of Megadeth songs, you could see the songwriting pattern of *Symphony* in like ten or 15 other songs, after and before."

"That was probably the best band experience because things are great when times are good," continues Marty, speaking generally. "And I remember times were good. I remember taking limos across the street and getting the report and the record is No. 2 now and you just went double platinum and you're going to do this and you're going to Lear jet this and major TV that and MTV. Everything was just happening beyond according to plan. We were just a thrash band kicking ass, and all of a sudden we were like huge. It was the happiest time. That was probably the hardest record to record because it was done by perfectionists, three perfectionists, Mustaine, Max Norman and myself. And we had just gotten into recording stuff on computer, so you could see how accurate you were. And it got into competition to see who could make stuff more perfect. And it's painful because it's very unforgiving. There's not a single thing that's out of sync on that record."

"The writing of the songs for **Countdown To Extinction** happened in two sessions and *Symphony* came out of the second one," offers Ellefson. "We were working at a rehearsal studio in North Hollywood. We worked for a while and then we would run outside and shoot hoops, play Pig or whatever. And after about 20 minutes we would come back inside and write songs. Right as we came in... when Dave picks up the guitar is usually the moment of brilliance when a whole new riff would come up, and that's when *Symphony* happened. And I just remember how it developed between the stops and the riffs and then the ascending bass line during the chorus, and again, that was just one of those magical songs that came together really quickly. When it happened, we just felt there was greatness that was going to come from that song."

"So that was one of those magical moments where a song just falls out on the floor," continues Ellefson, "and then, boom, right? You know when it happens. *Symphony Of Destruction* was like that. We were like, ha! Get done shooting some hoops, go into the room and pick up the guitar, and bam, the tune is born. Spontaneous moment. **Countdown To Extinction** was the period where there was just great group camaraderie. I mean, we came off the **Rust In Peace** tour, which was very long, a lot of hard work, came off of that Clash Of The Titans tour feeling very triumphant. It was just like wow, we've turned the corner, and I felt at that moment, coming off of that, that was really the biggest pinnacle of what thrash metal was going to be. And I felt that as we went into the **Countdown** record, especially with the talents of Marty Friedman and just the rambunctiousness of Nick Menza and just seeing what kind of writer that Dave was coming into, being more than just only a thrash metal writer. I saw that as an opportunity to, let's expand this and make it even more open. Don't lose what we've got, but let's see where we can go with this. And to me **Countdown To Extinction** was creatively one of the coolest records, because I think it was really a good environment for writing. We'd wake up, we'd call each other, we'd go over to Dave's house, I'd show him some lyrics to *High Speed Dirt*, we'd go to rehearsal and work on riffs, and everyone was bringing the best to the table. And I think as an artist, whether you're a member of a band or whether you are the artist, having those platforms to create cannot be shut down. To be inspired, to raise up, you can see when those moments happen, when it was the right lineup and the right chemistry and the whole thing was greater than the sum of all its parts. And that's what we, as fans, look to—and that's why that was my favourite album."

Mustaine has said that the *Symphony Of Destruction* lyric came to him after a particularly lucky stroke of inspiration as he drove down Riverside Drive in Toluca Lake suffering from a headache. The political lyric was written down on a receipt for sushi, with the story growing into a video featuring a political assassination, too hot for much MTV play.

"First thing I remember is that we used to joke around that metal titles must absolutely have the word 'of' in it," chuckles Friedman. "And come to think of it, the whole first side of *Countdown*, everything pretty much has 'of' in the title. Yet, I don't have any particular recollections of the songs, one by one, other than fucking great lineup. You know, it was a great side A of any record, and side B wasn't bad either. But I think I was really happy with the way that all came out. And on tour, I think we did some shows with Metallica on **Countdown**, over in Europe. Constant touring; it was awesome. I've only the best memories of that. We even played Rock In Rio on **Countdown**."

"We kind of took a new attitude," said Ellefson to Metal Hammer, back in '92, at that point unveiling band's new more commercial sound. "I think that we have always been playing music very similar to this, only this time we've slow down a lot of the stuff so that you can actually hear it! I think that it's every bit as progressive and has as much attitude as our previous records, but it was actually a lot harder to play this stuff slower. It's a new technique for us, to slow a couple of the numbers down and lock into some heavy grooves. On the demo that we did for *Symphony Of Destruction*, the song was a little bit faster. It wasn't until we were in the studio to record the song properly that we really messed around with the tempos on all the songs to make sure that they were all in the pocket, as they say."

"I used to go about it the wrong way before," seconded Mustaine. "I used to write music that was complicated for the sake of being complicated and unless you play guitar, you know what it sounds like? It sounds like you got fucking hornets in your head! You know, you can't figure out what I'm doing. I'd lost sight of everything. So this time, we're coming back full circle. 'A dog always returns to his vomit' as the Bible says, and we're playing music that we like! You know what? *Symphony Of Destruction* was written in a couple of days—it was one of the simplest songs that I've ever written and it comes across as one of the most acceptable as far as people liking it goes. I realize that you need personal instant gratification, you know, P.I.G. That's me, I'm a P.I.G.!"

"We had fun this time," continued Mustaine. "This is the first time that I've been really tuned into the project from beginning to end and really sat and made my opinions known to everybody. On the last record, I was just freshly sober. I'd just kicked heroin and freebasing and I was still kinda working the bugs out of my brain. It's almost been two years since I've done smack or crack and I feel really good! Before we were setting out to plant our flag and reclaim our territory and show everybody that we didn't sell out and this time it's like, you know, if you think that we've sold out, then fuck you. But if people think that, well, that's okay, because you know what? The record's still gonna sell, and we're still gonna tour and we're gonna have fun while we do it. It's the first time that I've made a record from beginning to end that I cherish every single note of."

"Before it was like combat, now it's more like comrade," Mustaine quipped, in conversation with Dave Ling. "Nick and Marty's names are on the credits too. You get more out of people if they worked on something; if you have stock in a company, you work harder. I'm not to say that we've become the metamorphosis of Zeppelin, because a few of 'em are still alive, but we've come a long way. A lot of that has to do with the fact that we still have group therapy meetings where we sit and air things; it's not like going to see a shrink or anything. It's a forum where we can say if anything's bothering us."

Added Dave Ellefson, "Yeah, we have these weekly meetings where we have a drug and alcohol counsellor at. There's a half-dozen bands like Mötley Crüe, Ratt and Poison who are falling by the wayside because the more successful they got, the more they failed to get along together. We're doing almost the total opposite! We were strung-out on drugs and had no money but we weren't that bothered about things. Now that we're starting to get some success, we're pulling our ship together even more. We're like the total Marines of metal!"

Symphony Of Destruction got the full metal jacket treatment in the UK, issued as a limited edition 7" on coloured vinyl in die-cut sleeve, as a 7" picture disc, as a 12" with large poster, and as a CD in die-cut sleeve, with a variety of non-LP bonus tracks across the set, most notable being non-LP track *Breakpoint* which perhaps sounded too much like *Holy Wars... The Punishment Due* to be included on **Countdown**. *Breakpoint* was used on the **Super Mario Bros.** soundtrack and also would show up on **Hidden Treasures**.

Architecture Of Aggression, more of a grim slow-boil thrasher and one of the under-heralded tracks on the album was inspired by the first Iraqi war (Operation Desert Storm) as well as a book about the Nazi war machine called **The Architecture Of Aggression**. Its abstract lyric can be read as a straight carry-forward of the themes behind *Symphony Of Destruction*. Musically, there are a lot of those artful riffy transitions we heard all over **Rust In Peace**, but at a leisurely pace.

Next up is *Foreclosure Of A Dream* which, despite being left fairly universal, was inspired by the foreclosure of Ellefson's parents' family farm back in Hartland, Minnesota. A theme throughout Megadeth albums so far, throughout '80s hardcore, throughout Ed Repka's artwork for the band, is the recessionary effects of the Republican administrations of Reagan and Bush the first. As we look back and glorify Reagan—and even Clinton, a Democrat—we easily forget how recession always seemed to be close at hand or in full swing, with the farm crisis being a very real subset of it.

Musically the track is quite mellow, although it gets loud for the chorus. Friedman has said that getting the acoustic guitar parts down were excruciating, as the band, as well as a demanding Max Norman, searched for tones that they could live with.

"In the '70s, there was a boom period where farmers were starting to make a lot of money," explained Ellefson, to Hit Parader, "and the banks had approved loans for farmers to buy the machinery and land. Farmers were told they could take a loans for 30 years and do things to really make their businesses boom. And then in the '80s, they were foreclosed upon. It was about the American dream being turned into the American nightmare. Suddenly they said, 'We need the money back! Pay or we're going to take back the land and everything that you put up for collateral.' That was how the foreclosure came down. And a lot of people that had farms and their families, for years, lost everything. The irony is here in the heartland, where it's a family-oriented kind of culture, people were folding under the pressure—divorces, suicide, infidelity—all kinds of things because of the foreclosure of the dream. It's like the savings and loan scandal. It's really hard to base your whole life on your job. The foreclosure of a dream is when it comes time to retire and collect the benefits which are rightfully yours, because you were told they would be yours, but all of a sudden you're let go. That happened to my father."

Sweating Bullets is practically a swing track, a light-hearted combination of *Peace Sells* and Alice Cooper's *No More Mr. Nice Guy*, which Megadeth would naturally cover. Again, meet Dave the wreck, and this time, more specifically not the failed suicide but the schizophrenic prone to it, although on the less traumatic end, Dave says it's a song about "living inside (his) head." *Sweating Bullets* was issued as the record's third single, six months after the release of the source album, reaching No. 29 on the charts, aided by the music video which portrays Dave in an insane asylum. The maxi-single included a number of live tracks and something called Gristle Mix applied to the world-beater of the album, *Symphony Of Destruction*.

On *This Was My Life*, Dave's tormented love adversary is actually examining his head as he's lying in bed. Dave talks about this track being about his intense six year relationship that resulted in him wanting to either kill himself or her, the actual lyric being a rumination on the deed done, namely the latter. At the music end, Marty says that the song was the first the band finished right through to mix, the guys understandably being thrilled with the results as they listened to it at Dave's house.

Next up is the album's title track and, again, surprisingly, the song's forward-thinking animal rights messaging originated with the band's drummer, not Mustaine. The smart lyric floats over the top of a mournful melody forged in mid-metal, bonus being a couple of different Priest-like twin leads.

"I remember Nick Menza coming to me with the lyrics for that song," explains Mustaine, 'and then about a week later seeing the same exact story in, I think it was Time magazine, and I thought, 'You little fucker!' (laughs). So he plagiarized Time magazine, I think. So I reworked the lyrics so they would be flowing and semantically correct and have some kind of continuity to it. And I get all these letters from people all the time, (in crying voice), 'God, I'm so glad you love the animals!' And I feel like writing back and saying, 'Yeah, with the proper spices, those fuckers taste good, don't they?' But what the song is about is really a dreadful topic. In Texas they have a lot of ranches, as well as in other mid and southern states, where they take these exotic animals, and they just let them out of the cages and these pussy hunters just shoot them a few feet away from the cage. And you know, in reality they've bagged the animal, but they didn't go to the Serengeti jungle to do it."

High Speed Dirt is another catchy mid-paced metaller, with tight riffing and a nice groove from Menza, who takes the band in and out of half-time. "**Countdown** is a cool record," muses Menza. "There are no mistakes on that record. Pretty much everything was gone over, tuned; all the parts were just nailed and that album is real concise and under high scrutiny when we were making it. My drum sound on that record is really good too. It's got a really tight, tight sound and good tones on everything. I remember it took me seven days and I was done with my drum tracks and I was really pleased with everything on there. Cool songs, and like I say that was our biggest record. That was the hoopla heyday."

"*High Speed Dirt*, there's a little blues solo in the middle of it—a lot of people mention that," notes Friedman. "And that was a scratch guitar. There was just a hole in there, and it was not a real guitar, just a guitar to play the scratch track, and there was a hole in there, and I just played something in there and they kept it. In Megadeth, guitar-wise, it's just one big long song, is the way I see it (laughs). It's all good—a really good song. But there wasn't a whole heck of a lot of variation. It just seemed like one, big, long, ass-kicking song, which was cool. Altogether, those three albums—just one long ass-kicking song."

High Speed Dirt is the band's ode to skydiving, a sport of which the guys indeed partook. To make the lyric more metal, there are some imaginings of what happens when the parachute fails to open. Mustaine has said that just like fast driving, skydiving is one of those things he's tried to use to keep him away from drugs. Amusingly, Marty Friedman was reluctant to do it, but said he would if the album went platinum. **Countdown** duly went double platinum and he kept his word. As for Dave, his first solo flight was filmed for a segment of MTV's Headbanger's Ball, VJ Riki Rachtman presiding.

Nearing the end of the record we get *Psychotron*, a chunky, rhythmic rocker, again, quite mainstream and relaxed, riddled with spaces like the *Peace Sells* blueprint that helped get the band here. The lyric was inspired by comic book character Deathlok but also an article Dave had read about the Russians experimenting on a brainwashing device called a Lida machine. As a harbinger of things to come, Dave's interviews at the time seemed to have him believing tales of the supposed outlandish and covert uses of the microchip technology, leading him down the path to the various new world order-type ideas he believes in now.

Second to last, *Captive Honor* has Dave telling scary tales of beatings and rapings in jail, over another upscale riff rocker of vaguely doomy proportions. Says Dave, "*Captive Honor*'s about a guy who goes to prison and he gets butt-fucked the moment he walks inside the door. And you know the strange thing? It's that stuff like that really happens! That was one of Junior's songs."

Closing the album, *Ashes In Your Mouth* is a considerably proggy-minded tale of war with all kinds of harmony work and rhythmic contortions that intensify as the band marches toward the conclusion of this fine album.

But the debate was on whether the new high-rent Megadeth served as much purpose as the grim, hungry-for-everything headbangers the band once were. Despite the record vaulting to No. 2 on Billboard (kept from the top, much to Dave's grim chagrin, by Billy Ray Cyrus), many fans found the meticulous detailing of the thing not metal enough.

Wrote Rolling Stone's Karen Csengeri, "While **Countdown** echoes the band's earlier work thematically, it's stylistically disappointing: The music, which is considerably more subdued than anything Megadeth has ever done, sounds formulaic; the musicianship is pedestrian; and the album as a whole seems to have been written for marketability rather than merit. Nothing on the album compares with the brilliance of either *Holy Wars... The Punishment Due* or *Hangar 18*, on **Rust In Peace**. The only song that even begins to approximate the drive of earlier albums is *Ashes In Your Mouth*. Put simply, **Countdown** just does not measure up. Even though it was never as technically advanced as Slayer, Megadeth, from its inception, was in the vanguard of metal bands. What attracted its fans were the passion, energy and variety of its music. All of these qualities have been watered down on **Countdown To Extinction**. This smoother, mellower sound may attract a wider audience, but original fans should quite rightly feel let down."

Touring for **Countdown** didn't begin in earnest until September of '92, first with Megadeth as part of a Monsters Of Rock package in mainland Europe and then, with Pantera, into the UK and back into Europe through October. November through February found the band back in North America (variously, Stone Temple Pilots and Suicidal Tendencies as support), with the Eugene, Oregon stop on February 17th being marred by Mustaine's Valium overdose, which prompted the cancellation of an extensive Japan leg.

The rest of '93 was light, with the band playing select dates in June and July (highlight being a Milton Keynes Bowl stand with Diamond Head and Metallica) before a massive regrouping would take place along with plans for the follow-up to the wildly successful record at hand. Latter part of '93 is in fact where Aerosmith kicks the band off of their **Get A Grip** tour, replacement being much more agreeable and abiding southern hair rockers Jackyl.

Dave explained to Rip magazine's Steffan Chirazi that the whole Valium crisis began with getting sick, which led to throat problems and a cycle of codeine and alcohol.

"I have vodka and 7-Up, which was my favourite drink in the old days. My wife pointed out that I stank of alcohol, and she didn't like the smell, so in my addict mind, I thought, 'She can't smell Valiums.' I bought a jar of 500 of them. I was reaching the stage where I knew I'd have to go and get some serious help—not just drying out, detoxing and going right back out on the road, but going someplace where they were going to look inside my head, heart and soul, and tell me what it is that drives me to keep on relapsing. There was never anyone to give us reality checks. No one really told us that the pace was too gruelling. Everybody kept saying, 'Well, this is what Metallica did,' and so on. But we're not like Metallica. We are not like anybody else."

"We were in Canada, and I was eating Valiums by the handful, these 5mg yellow ones. I was drinking cognac again too. I was off to the races. One day I was in the back of the bus and I'd just taken my Valiums. There's a big bed in the back of it, so my wife, son and I can sleep, and it's all mirrored back there. I'm trying to hide these Valiums behind the VCR, forgetting there's mirrors everywhere. My wife asked me, 'What's this behind the VCR?' I grabbed them and told her, 'Look, I'm tired of this. I got Valiums because you didn't like the smell of alcohol. I don't like touring anymore. I don't like my agent. I don't like my manager, my band or anything.' I dumped all the Valiums down the toilet except for 36, which I threw into a basket with washcloths in it."

"The next morning we flew back to California, and I ate them all in a day. I should've died, but God's kept me around for some reason. I think it's so I can share these experiences with other people going through the same stuff. I went to the hospital, and the doctor was trying to detox me. What does he shoot me up with? More Valium! I ended up dripping blood from everywhere. My wife came in and found me slumped on the toilet, bleeding. I was dying. I knew I was being over-medicated. I knew I had to get out of there."

"So we flew to Phoenix. I don't remember getting on or off the plane, driving to this place or anything. Eight days later I finally realized where I was. They said the morning after I got to the hospital they'd taken me to the emergency room because I was dying. I stayed at this place for seven weeks. I told my manager that I didn't know if I wanted to play music again, and I sure the fuck didn't wanna play right then. I was seriously thinking of retiring. I started thinking, 'Is it time to quit?' I thought of my wife and of my son growing up with a dead father. So I went to this place, and I really had to get honest, which was very painful. But I kept thinking about the fact that I was doing this for myself, my wife and my son. If I continued to play, great."

"I didn't know if I wanted to play with Megadeth anymore. I was trying to commit suicide when I overdosed on the Valiums because I was tired. I lost the will to live. No one was hearing what I was saying—my agent, my manager—the relationship with my band had gone to shit, and I didn't want to play anymore. I lost the fun of playing. My heart wasn't in it. Going out to Arizona, I got my power back. I don't want anybody else's power; I want my power!"

Also in 1993, on a lighter note, Dave Mustaine, who years earlier had dreamed of having Sean Harris on as lead vocalist in Megadeth, guested on Diamond Head's **Death And Progress** album. Notes Diamond Head guitarist Brian Tatler, "I think I first met Dave Mustaine when Megadeth were touring, possibly in 1991, and we got invited backstage, and I met him then, and he seemed really nice and intelligent, and we talked about doing stuff. At that point, yeah, we were doing the **Death And Progress** album, and we invited him to play on it, or mix a track. I think he offered to mix or produce it, I don't recall. Do what he could. With time constraints, we ended up sending over two songs to him and his producer, over in California, and he mixed

Truckin' and played on it. And then he sent it back and it was fantastic, so it just got included straight on the album."

While **Countdown To Extinction** had tongues wagging and Megadeth rocking on top of the world, exiled guitarist Chris Poland had followed up his **Return To Metalopolis** shred album with a major label proposition. The self-titled Damn The Machine album, issued through A&M Records on June 8, 1993, was a thoughtful prog metal proposition not unlike the work of Fates Warning from that era.

"Actually, Janie Hoffman had a really big hand in that," explains Chris, referring to the influential publicist now married to Eddie Van Halen. "She was somebody in the music business for a long time, and she managed me and then we became like a couple, and she really worked hard with us and we worked hard, because she was working with us, and we didn't want to embarrass her."

"Basically she got a hold of A&M, and we had Bryan Huttenhower come down, and then he brought the vice president down who signed The Doors. They were like yeah, we dig it, let's do it. And the biggest thing that happened, my biggest heartbreak, since I've been... you know, I won't get in this position anymore because I don't open the window that wide anymore, but Al Cafaro basically sat me down at a table, with all these hidden doors, and we're having this crazy dinner, and people are walking out of these doors, like when it closes, you can't even tell it's a door, and guys in tuxedos are giving us food, and he goes, 'We know you're a three record band, we're gonna go to the wall for you guys, we're gonna make you the next Rush.' And I said to myself, finally I found a fucking home."

"And about six months later, I can't remember the guy's name, but he was the guy that signed really big bands and slept with really big rock star women, but he walks up to me in the parking lot, and he goes, 'Chris, no matter what happens, I want you to know you guys made a great record.' And that's when I knew I was fucked (laughs). So when it finally happened, they gave us... Janie was smart enough to get a guarantee for a second record budget, and they just gave it to us."

That record never came out, but in the quixotic and exotic debut, we're left with a pretty cool prog metal document, borne of an era when grunge had every metal property on the planet questioning their identities.

"The thing was, I should've never agreed with it when Bryan Huttenhower said, 'You gotta make it a live record,' reflects Chris, smart and skilled at rock enough to zero in on what might have improved **Damn The Machine**'s chances in the market. "I should've said no, we're not making a fucking live record. We're gonna get a good producer in here with us and do overdubs and we'll stack the guitars like everyone else does. That's what we should've done, because it would've been twice as big. But instead it was this kind of obscure, weird-sounding record. Yeah, the playing was great and everything, and the songs were good and the lyrics were incredible. But you know what? We should've made a record like everybody else was making, because nobody was making live records then. That was the Achilles' heel on that project."

At exactly the same time Chris was confusing the metal world with **Damn The Machine**, Megadeth returned with a high profile single song called *Angry Again*, cooked up for the **Last Action Hero** movie soundtrack. Dave, back out after a stint in rehab, has said that at the time, he was angry about a whole lot of things, not the least of which was an intervention of the classic kind, where the miscreant is called on the carpet for his recent wrongs.

"We'd been in off the road for awhile," recalls Marty, "and we hadn't seen each other for a month or so. We went into this tiny studio in the middle of the desert in Arizona and cut *Angry Again* and got a Grammy nomination for it and I thought it was a cool song."

Confirms Ellefson on this commercially successful thumping rocker good enough to get Wayne Isham video treatment, "*Angry Again*, we were on a break toward the end of the **Countdown** tour, and we went out to Phoenix to record that song and it was the last session that was ever recorded in this old dilapidated recording studio on 64th Street and Lincoln, right in the heart of Paradise Valley, which is a beautiful old money part of town. There's like a fire department there or something because they mowed the studio down after we recorded there. And I remember going in and setting up and putting that song together within an afternoon. That night we were tracking drums. I remember Max Norman beating on the console to get the knobs to work; it was shorting out all the time. So again, that song came together very quick; it had a singleness of purpose, which was to be on the **Last Action Hero** soundtrack and I remember sitting there listening to the mix thinking, you know, this is probably the best bass tone we've ever had on a Megadeth record."

Adds Mustaine, "Basically, after talking with our producer Max Norman, who I have a wonderful relationship with, I rewrote the song. When I got to the studio, the band built the song in an hour—this is after one of our old agents told us songs couldn't be written on demand! Initially, the recording was meant to start while I was in the treatment center, and I told my manager that if anyone could put it back, he could. I said, 'Don't you guys fuckin' get me? Me, the person, is more important than the band right now.' I couldn't have just left and recorded without finishing my treatment. That would've been like getting chemotherapy and leaving before the last treatment. These days, there are no more snap decisions. I take my time over things and plan them out. Every time I walk through the fire, I become stronger and stronger. I know that my next drug and my next drink are right around the corner, and it's whether I have the mental and physical defences against it. It's really important that I put my priorities in order. My recovery's first, then my family, then it's music."

"There's a lot of kind of euphoric career moments," reflects Dave Ellefson, looking back on what most Megadeth watchers now agree is the band's most accomplished album, if not the most fiery and excitement-inducing.

"Probably the biggest one is... **Countdown To Extinction** is the biggest selling record in my career—that's sold probably four million records now. But when they shipped one million records, Capitol Records... and that was back in the day where they used to basically give you platinum and gold records based on what they shipped, versus now, they base it on what you actually SoundScan, which is the accurate record of what you actually sold. But I remember that we were rehearsing for the tour in Los Angeles at The Soundstage, and Entertainment Tonight came down, and it was big stuff; it was like real mainstream showbiz kind of stuff. And the president of the record label came, and he handed us all these platinum records. The record had only been out like a week, and it was just, you know, it was euphoric. Because leading up to that point, it was obviously, I don't know, ten, 12, probably ten years anyway, of very, very hard work, a lot of starving, a lot of just... a life that most people are not willing to make the sacrifice to live. So certainly for me and Dave Mustaine, we were high-fiving each other like, 'Holy cow, can you believe this?'"

7
YOUTHANASIA
"There was not a glass ceiling"

So yes, Megadeth, not that they could know it yet, had finally submitted. And sure, Dave Mustaine would maintain his insatiable competitive streak moving forward, his large chip, but it would never get any better than this. And yet what Megadeth had achieved in the wake of **Countdown To Extinction** was pretty remarkable. Indeed despite Mustaine's lack of healthy perspective, with **Rust** and **Countdown**, Megadeth, in the eyes of many fans, had actually bested nemesis Metallica. What's more, this was no mere critical triumph: the band was now a gleaming platinum rock 'n' roll machine.

Classic lineup firing on all cylinders, after manic touring, it became time for the much lauded follow-up to **Countdown**, and that's just what **Youthanasia** was: son of **Countdown** and nothing like the four before it, the first record in the band's career to rock, ride and roll somewhat similarly to the album before it.

"**Youthanasia** was pretty insane," begins fan-fave drummer Nick Menza, "just because we built a studio and then recorded it right as we were done building, in Arizona. We basically got a warehouse out in the middle of nowhere, in the ghetto in Phoenix, and made a studio inside of it. Max had built a studio that was modular so he could take it apart and bring it back to LA and set it up there. We built all these rooms and then we recorded it, and it was just fuckin' hot out there, man. Coming out of the drum room, it was like a 25 degree difference. I kept it about 70 degrees in my drum room and coming out of there into like 115, 120 degree heat, it was just like 'ugh,' a big shock to your system. And then you go into the control room and it's like 68 degrees. And we kept having problems with gear shutting down because it was too hot. Unreal. But that record, we did live. Everyone played live at the same time. We didn't really do it like drums first, then bass, then guitars. The rhythm tracks were all played at once and most of those songs are first takes. There's maybe a couple of them we played twice. We had like a two songs rule, two times through. If we didn't get it the first time or by the second time, then we wouldn't play it again that day, because then it's like going through the motions and it loses that spontaneity."

"I thought it was a good sounding record but I don't think we had a strong enough one tune to break us to where we wanted to go," adds Marty Friedman. "That was after we had the double platinum record, so we were definitely rock stars at the time and we thought that we were rock stars and anything that we played would just immediately go triple platinum. So we just played the stuff that we thought was arena rock and it was really, really good, but we didn't have the one great breakout single that would have pushed us home. There's a lot of great music on there but we didn't have the one breakout single where you could just drop the needle and know that it was a hit."

Indeed nothing broke out like *Symphony Of Destruction*, but it wasn't for lack of trying. If anything, the sum total of **Youthanasia** was seen as a slight but detectable further rounding of the edges off the Megadeth sound.

Fact is, Megadeth were cognizant of the fact that thrash in the purest sense could be limiting, not only commercially but creatively.

"You know, it's interesting," reflects Dave Ellefson, "I saw this as a scene, as a movement, because of course around us there were bands like Nuclear Assault, Destruction, a community of bands that were going to just kind of do that one thing forever. That's all they were ever going to do. And I always felt in our band—and I certainly thought Anthrax do it as well, the transitions—I think that all of us were good musicians, good players, and we learned to play more than just three chord punk, and we learned to do more than just one or two Judas Priest songs. We were very well-versed players, we had roots and depth that went down much deeper than the music we were playing and writing at that time, and I think that part of the development for all of us... I certainly felt that with our band, that there was not a glass ceiling. I felt almost like, the only one that could put the glass ceiling there was us. Which for me, was why I always encouraged everybody, and was always optimistic about, let's bust through that. Why would you limit yourself? Just as a species, it runs contrary to what we're designed to do. We're designed to be forward thinking, we're designed to be trying to reach for the highest possible goal, or anything that we can. It's just how we're wired. And so just to keep yourself in this small box is ultimately to whither and die."

Glass ceiling to be sure, but the latest round of thrash albums had pushed that ceiling pretty high. Was thrash riding on the coattails of all metal doing well in the late '80s, particularly hair metal?

"Well, I think as it pertains to the mainstream outlets like MTV, or maybe major labels, and maybe to some degree even radio, there might be a shred of argument in that," laughs Ellefson. "Because ultimately, the media outlets are always looking for what's the next thing, what can we sink our teeth into next? And to some degree, you want that, because the media can then perpetuate your art and your craft and what you're doing and help to make it more popular. But you have to be careful that you don't do that only for the fame in itself, that you have to have something solid that is genuine and authentic, and if they take that up and blow that up, then at least you've done it the right way. To just go out and seek fame and fortune is putting the cart before the horse. And so I think all of us in thrash were very protective of what we were doing, to the degree that we didn't want to just blow it out and sell it out. That bands got popular—I think that's a cool thing. Like Clash Of The Titans, we were all on... what, our fourth album, you know what I mean? So what's really cool about that was we all earned our stripes, and we weren't overnight sensations, so that even the mainstream media outlets were getting tiresome of pop glam metal, that all of a sudden, it did become interesting to them."

"Also, The Headbangers Ball became a legitimate two-hour show every Saturday night as opposed to, in 1986, when we did the **Peace Sells** album, I think it was a half hour from noon to 12:30 (laughs). You know what I mean? It actually became something to be taken seriously and it became a lifestyle, and so I think some of the glam fans, who in their heart of hearts, maybe they wanted to rock a little harder? And a lot of them did come over and become friends of thrash. They toned their hair down a little bit and traded their spandex for blue jeans, and they came to the concerts, and yeah, they still liked hair metal, but at the end of the day, who doesn't like a good bone-crushing riff like *Symphony Of Destruction* or *Enter Sandman* or something like that?"

But thrash was definitely changing, especially the popular face of it, first with the **Metallica** album, then **Countdown** and now even more so with **Youthanasia**. "I remember sitting with Juan from Abattoir," chuckles Ellefson, "well now, Agent Steel, listening to anything from Sabbath to Judas Priest. And you listen to it, and if Judas Priest was just sped up another 50 or 60 beats per minute, some of it would have been thrash metal, you know what I mean? Because the riffs were great, the playing was great. Yeah, it had a much older organic sound to it, whereas thrash, it was definitely an elitist movement for sure. It's like, if you were into thrash, it was like everything had to be harder and faster. I'll never forget Kerry King, every time I talked to him, he would always reference Tom Hunting from Exodus as the fastest drummer on the planet. And that became almost his benchmark of, 'Tom is the fastest, and if you're not that fast you suck' (laughs). So fast became a benchmark of whether it was credible or not."

And obviously, the massive success of "the black album" would have to be called the greatest stake through the heart of that kind of thinking...

"Well, again, Metallica I think should always be credited with breaking down doors and doing things for the thrash movement," agrees Ellefson. "Metallica broke down doors on such a huge level; it's almost like having a new president in office (laughs). They were able to make changes and make things happen that never would've happened before. To a large degree, they became a spokesperson for an entire genre, even though they weren't the fastest band, and they certainly weren't the thrashiest band. But they were definitely the biggest band. So I think by the time of the black album, personally, I admired how with that band, every record was new, was fresh, was forward-thinking, almost to the point where you had to listen to it a couple times to make sure you're hearing what you are hearing. Hearing them go to **Ride The Lightning** was a major step from **Kill 'Em All**; **Master Of Puppets** became, to me, like hi-fi speed metal almost, and **then ...And Justice For All** was very, very progressive, and then by the time the black album came..."

"So I think to some degree, our band was on a similar trajectory," continues Ellefson. "Again, we're on Clash Of The Titans, looking around going, this is a huge, huge, monumental tour, this is a celebration of really all that we've accomplished. And yet to me, I saw it as the pinnacle. And quite honestly, there's never been anything as big as that ever, in my opinion. And yet at the same time, we were starting to turn some corners because it felt intuitively like it was the right thing to do. And I think that was sort of a maturity for us, which was to say that, you know, we've done all of this, we've taken over these beachheads, we've conquered this ground and we've done all this; now we have to go inland, and to continue to sort of build the kingdom here. And I think at that time, we were doing that."

"Metallica that had just released the black album, and I remember even going down to see them at the Forum, and I just remember sitting in the Forum going, these are all the same fans that come to our concert, except that it's five times as many out here, you know what I mean? (laughs). And I was going, why don't they come to our concert, you know? Because this is it. This is our tribe. For some reason they all come out to see Metallica, 20, 25% of them come to see us, and yet I felt good that we're in the studio recording **Countdown To Extinction** going you know, we're doing our own thing, and it's really cool, and it's still different, and we retained our own identity. All of us in our lives and in our professions and just whatever it is we do, you almost need like that mentor band that comes out and says— you know the Michael Jordans, the Wayne Gretzkys—and Metallica is one of them. They're one of them that you go, this is so uber-huge, and this is how big and how huge it can ultimately be. And so to some degree, whether you like the black album or not, definitely in metal, you had to admire that wow, these guys have really captured the genie in the bottle."

"Let's put it this way. I think the bands that rose to the top, ultimately, the thing that we had, because I'm going to throw us in there, is we were able to write a song. And that was even more apparent to me many years later when we started doing some acoustic shows, and all of a sudden, it's been said that a great song, if you can play a song on an acoustic guitar and it sounds good, it's a great song. And I think ultimately that's what you can do: if you can cherry-pick the bands and the hits and the songs out of that. I mean, you play everything from *Symphony Of Destruction* to *She Wolf* on acoustic guitar, and it's still a great song. You play *Enter Sandman* on an acoustic, and maybe even *Welcome Home (Sanitarium)*; those are still great songs, and I think that ultimately is what set us apart. At the end of the day, these are songs that are going to stand the test of time, and *Symphony Of Destruction* gets played on classic rock radio stations now. Which is just really a testament to that. And I think the bands that didn't do that, or that just wasn't in their vocabulary to write those kinds of songs, they, of course, did not get that reward from that either."

Megadeth would indeed gather just reward for the songwriting skills demonstrated on **Youthanasia**. Issued on November 1, 1994 (and a week earlier in the UK), the album would reach platinum inside of a couple months, although rising no further over the years.

"As is standard Megadeth ways, we've done a little play on words," noted Ellefson in our fledgling magazine Brave Words & Bloody Knuckles, back in issue No. 4. "In the past, there have been themes of war and political situations. This time, with the exception of the title track, there isn't much of that. They are all much more personal rather than political. They're talking about things we've individually been through, different stuff we think about, different philosophies we have. It was great for me because I don't do good at making up lyrics. I do much better when I can write something that I've already been through or can truly feel from first-hand experience."

"Being No. 1 is a funny thing," muses Ellefson, having been No. 2 with **Countdown** and at the time of release looking at a metal world abuzz at Pantera's No. 1 placement for their shocking and apocalyptic **Far Beyond Driven**. "If you release a record when there's nothing else out there, it's easy to become No. 1. And just being No. 1 from the outside looking in may be cool, but there are other things that are more important. I'm not discrediting the Pantera guys because they've been working nonstop and they deserve everything that they're getting. However, for me personally, I think it's more than having a No. 1 record. We were No. 2, but who cares? It's all about having a great record."

Asked about **Youthanasia**'s artwork, Dave Jr. says that, "Hugh Syme did the cover artwork, a fellow Canadian of yours. The photos that world-famous photographer Avedon have done, will be the group shots on the inside booklets of both the CD and the tape. For us, it was a real honour. Here's a guy who took pictures of JFK, the Beatles, Bob Dylan, all the greats, and the list goes on and on. When we were standing in front of his camera lens, it was a pretty heavy experience. It all came about when we were brainstorming on some ideas a couple of months ago, about who we wanted to work on this record. Someone brought up the idea that instead of using one of the more common rock photographers, to really get someone from a completely different photography style."

Of note, the cover art, which features babies being hung up on a clothesline, was essentially "banned" in Malaysia and Indonesia. It's a striking image, and one that supported Megadeth's pessimistic life philosophy, of a pretty vacant world of problems, bodies and anarchy in the UK.

Once past the amusing wrap, and the swank pictures of Megadeth hamming it up with their air guitars, **Youthanasia** opens with a song that fully demonstrated the band's solidifying and clarifying attitude toward thrashing with levity, hook and decreased velocities. *Reckoning Day* was a catchy, rumbling rocker built to bulldoze arenas. Its opening riff is legion and genius of construct, the memorable music giving way to a vicious and artful Mustaine lyric about the man's favourite subject, revenge.

Train Of Consequences is more of the same warm, mid-speed thrash, although it's somewhat poisoned by a challenging, sour vocal melody, arguably a flaw. But then again, the track does burn into the memory circuits.

Train Of Consequences was issued as the first single from the album, reaching No. 29, helped by its loopy production video, which got regular MTV play. The CD maxi-single for the song included album track *Black Curtains*, three live songs, but most usefully, a kick-ass riff rocker called *Crown Of Worms*, a rarity lent NWOBHM magic through Dave co-writing it with Diamond Head's Sean Harris. The song was made widely available on the remastered reissue of previous record **Countdown To Extinction**. In the UK, on its December 28th release date, the punters could buy this as a numbered, laser-etched 12" maxi-single or as a clear vinyl 7" with "free giant sticker." Impressively, full page ads for the single in the UK also included, "Internet users, don't miss Megadeth Arizona" followed by a couple of URLs—and this is in December of 1994! Additionally, the album was available in Britain on blue vinyl.

Train Of Consequences is most definitely a chugger of a song where one can get a sense of the band's ensemble playing. "**Youthanasia**, we wrote a lot of that together as a band, jamming, in a rehearsal environment and then playing it live," says Ellefson. "We had obviously a big success with **Countdown To Extinction**, and we saw that, that opened a lot of doors for us, kind of stylistically, so we just sort of kept following in that same path, on **Youthanasia**."

"Joe Elliott said one time that he couldn't stand listening to Def Leppard's first record unless he was drunk," said Mustaine back in '94, talking to Metal Hammer's Jerry Ewing about his increased attention to singing during the **Youthanasia** sessions. "And I used to think, 'What a prat!' I love that first album! But now I know what he was saying. I don't have to be drunk to listen to any of our records, but I do understand his embarrassment towards what he's done before and how he's developed as a singer. I was very young when I did **Killing Is My Business**, and I only sang on it because the dickhead that came to sing for us turned up wearing eyeliner and carrying a sixpack! It was like, 'Hey, thanks for the beer, see you later!' Now I'm finally comfortable with singing."

On the subject of the band evolving past their previous tagged status of "state of the art speed metal," Mustaine sneers, "That came from some dickhead from New York who used to courier us drugs out on the road! He was sitting at home smoking joints going, 'State Of The Art Speed Metal! I got it!' We never were speed metal. We're Megadeth. If we say we're anything more specific than a metal band, we're limiting ourselves. Face it, you can go all the way from Slayer to Crowded House and find similarities. Granted, one plays faster than the other, but at the end of the day, it's still the same stuff. I guarantee you this, though; when people hear this album, more bands are gonna have the courage to play songs like this. Bruce Dickinson left Iron Maiden to do what he really wanted. I've always felt that we should be doing it. I just didn't have the balls to do it before now."

Next up on **Youthanasia** is *Addicted To Chaos*, which is even more laid-back and introspective than its two predecessors, framed upon an almost sobbing, melancholic riff which gives way to a chorus just as grey of days. Quipped Dave to Jerry Ewing, "My life is so volatile in the first place, it's hard enough for me to live it, let alone explain it to anyone else. I was gonna fucking quit when I left Metallica! When I got put in rehab in 1988, I was ready to quit. After we left the Aerosmith tour last year, I was gonna quit. I figured I'd be doing time after I killed somebody—no names mentioned, but I'm sure you could speculate! But I look at it like this: nothing feels as good as playing music with these guys. I've done just about every drug and every sexual position, been to just about every country in the world, and nothing feels as good to me as being with my family and my bandmates. If the world ended today, I could say that I love my wife and my son, I love my bandmates, and we made the best fucking record that's out right now. Unfortunately, no one else would know that if the world ended today... Well, *you* would!"

"Things are actually great right now," seconded Ellefson, speaking just before the launch of the album. "Things have actually been great for the last year; they really have. We took the last three months of 1993 off from the band and the music. We just took some time out to get firmly planted on the ground. Dave and I both moved out here to Arizona. We had begun discussing when we'd record the new album and that's when Max Norman began building the studio out here. Even though we weren't making music, we were still making a whole other set of decisions for Megadeth. We were reorganizing the band back in Arizona. I was nervous about the drug thing, but earlier this week we had a management seminar where someone came in from the outside who helped us rebuild companies and corporations. He came to take a look where we were at and help us get rid of some of the self-sabotaging behaviours we have. I know people reading this are probably going to go, 'What the fuck?! They're a band. Why are they doing that?' But it's weird because most bands have troubles and they either succeed or fail over things that have to do with money, personalities and things like that; it has nothing to do with the music."

"I'm just starting to see a lot of the ideal-type of band situation that I've always envisioned," continued Junior. "All four of us are now taking part in the decision-making for the band. All four of us are involved in the writing. We're finally hanging out and liking each other's company. And that's a hard point for any group to get at. Let's face it, from the beginning, Dave has been the self-appointed leader of the band because there wasn't one, and he's got a tough job. Being the leader is definitely not a popularity contest. Now, he admits that he's moved from being the leader to more of the spokesperson for the band. So he's kind of put himself in the position that still isn't the most popular to be in. It's pretty cool right now. The way we all work, it's a lot more fun, there's a lot less stress, and I think we're a lot more productive and creative."

"With Megadeth, we've lived to the hilt the whole time," mused Ellefson, a couple issues later in our mag. "It's not like we're going to hit an age when all of a sudden we're going to have a midlife crisis and snort all of the drugs we're supposed to and play as heavy as we should have when we were young and all that kind of shit. We got to the point where we asked the question, 'Do we evolve or do we stay here at the comfort zone because we know what to do?' We decided, fuck it, let's roll the dice and try some shit we've never done before. For us, we've done exactly what we wanted to do all along. As we grow older, we're just moving along. We've already made **Killing Is My Business** and **Rust In Peace**. We don't need to go back and we're not insecure about moving forward. The arrangements of these songs may be simpler, but the parts are every bit as complex as they've been. Now we sing in three minutes what used to take seven or eight minutes, because the songs are much more to the point."

Youthanasia'a best foot forward as a single, *A Tout Le Monde*, comes next. It's a sturdy song and somewhat of a ballad, albeit a dirgy, death-shrouded one with a leaden *Balls To The Wall* plod to it along with some choice Judas Priest-styled twin leads. The song was issued as the record's second single, in February of '95, the US CD version including the band's cover of the Sex Pistols' *Problems* and a gem of a non-LP track called *New World Order*, redone years later on the band's **Thirteen** album, but possibly even more high fidelity and gorgeously appointed right here, with the classic lineup. The plush video cooked up for the track was considered too pro-suicide for MTV, who wound up banning it from their airwaves, Dave's very convincing rebuttals of their interpretation of the song notwithstanding.

The song is, in fact, part and parcel of Dave's connection to the city of Toronto... "We have our relationship with Toronto that supersedes the amount of people who show up here for shows. I have friends who play on the Leafs, plus I got a fantastic song. *A Toute Le Monde* came from this city because I met a French Canadian girl who I fell in love with and had a relationship with who would coo French in my ear. And I liked the way that sounds; I like the Beatles song that does that—*Michelle*—and that's where *A Tout Le Monde* came from and I will never forget this city."

Elysian Fields is next, continuing to support the album's mid-paced vibe, along with its recurring Accept grooves and the propensity toward melody come chorus time. *The Killing Road* is one of the record's hidden gems, this one heavy, catchy and choppy like the best material from the more spirited and purposed **Countdown** record. As well, there's one of those endearing, self-deprecating, autobiographical choruses from the band's chief sneerer.

"We've been through hell and high water," says Mustaine, who has indeed lived that chorus hard and harsh. "But that's all part of the creative process and it's necessary for us to have credibility towards the people we sing to. David Coverdale putting on those leather pants and spiked wristbands, going out and singing every night, then slipping into his Giorgio Armani suits at the end of the day. I want to bitch-slap that guy. I'm so close to the ground that sometimes I'm face down in the gutter and people are looking down on me. I have the credibility to do that stuff because I've been there and I came from the street. I lived on my own since I was 15. It's kind of hard because it seems that I've had a cushy life as society keeps degenerating deeper. Trying to be No. 1 by boasting about hardships is not the reason I talk about it. I try to give some identification to people who have the same problems. The facts don't matter; the feelings are what matters and that's what's spun in the tale of our music. It's not about the things that took place, but the feelings we're relating to them."

"The fans are all that matters, not the industry and not making the money," continues Mustaine. "To understand is much more important than to be understood. With us singing about what we do, we're saying, 'Hey, we can identify with you. We're not so removed because of the success, that we don't give a shit about you anymore.' I wouldn't even be alive without them giving me the energy and the will to carry on. We live for each other. They're the heartbeat that keeps us alive and we're the mind that tells the heart to keep working."

Next up is *Blood Of Heroes* which again finds the band in hypnotic groove mode, Menza laying down a simple 1-and-4 AC/DC beat over which rhythm guitars form a dirge of soldierly march, sophistication added for the pre-chorus and chorus, the latter, essentially the verse riff but with **Youthanasia**'s trademark melodic vocal smeared over the top. It's a favourite of Friedman's, who speaks fondly of the string arrangement and the fact that he performed the solo with wah-wah.

"We trimmed a lot of the fat this time," noted Friedman at the time. "We made sure that everything that went down on there was correct for that particular song and had a meaning and a purpose. We took off a lot of self-indulgent crap. I feel much more aggressive about this record. It's much more crushing, with a lot more impact. Over the years, we've learned how to get more impact out of our music. It's kind of a consummation of everything we've learned over the past couple of years. There wasn't too much I could do at the time of **Rust**. I got into the studio and blew some solos on an album. I couldn't really make exact comments about the vibe though. When it came time to do that world tour and we began playing that record, it started to become a band. Having completed an entire cycle of touring and recording, it was time to kick ass."

"I think that this album is the album we've always wanted to make," noted Ellefson during the same full group sit-down, getting at **Youthanasia**'s warmer, more organic vibe versus that of **Countdown**. "This is the album we've been working our whole lives to make, which is a good feeling to have. Some of our earlier records, we would walk out of the studio saying, 'It's okay, but we didn't have time to do it better.' Either we didn't have the money or the time, so you do the best you can, catch it on the fly and then release it. That's what people consider raw. What are mistakes are to us, is raw to the listener. But doing away with the mistakes, which we tried to do on **Countdown** through technology, we ended up losing the rawness. With this record, we did away with losing mistakes by just being prepared and being able to get the stuff right in the first place. We went just far enough to improve Megadeth, but we didn't go as far to change our direction. It's a good feeling to know that we've come this far doing things our way and not having to compromise. It isn't so much that every idea is used, but every idea is heard. That way everyone can bring their ideas to the table and can have a fair shot. That's the mentality that we set out to have. As we make more records together, it starts become an intuitive nature to know what's needed. Now that this is the third record that this lineup has made, we're all feeling a lot more comfortable musically and personally."

"This album is a lot warmer than the last one," said Dave, different chat, talking to Drew Masters about the album's thick, inviting sound. "The other day I was listening to a radio station and they played a block of Megadeth songs. A couple of the songs were off of **Countdown** and I was just cringing on the bass sound. The last album's tones had a real sharp point on them, and it was very brilliant sounding. But a lot of that was because of the faster music, and whenever you play a lot faster, the music has to be brighter to be heard. With this album, there are some fast songs, but the slower ones are played at the proper tempo and sound better. We were able to fatten up the overall sound of the record to make it a little warmer sounding. Max Norman designed the studio on his computer on CAD, an architectural designing program, and he hired a crew of construction people to come out and build these modular rooms inside of a warehouse in Phoenix. Once we're done with the mixing, he's going to dismantle it and bring it back to Los Angeles and set it up there."

The mature and level-headed band dynamic during the making of **Youthanasia** represented a far cry from the days scraping together the early Megadeth albums, as Mustaine recalls... "During those years, Gar and Chris were junkies. We would have to pull over on the side of the road, take our equipment truck into the fuckin' ghettos and score heroin with all our gear. All it takes is one guy who is high with a gun and all our gear is gone. They didn't have any vision. Chris even stole my guitars. With the second lineup, I could see how there would be some things spoken about me. I was having internal terrorism from my group from the beginning and if someone came in at the wrong time, they were going to see an angry person. They didn't see the beauty of making the record and all the success that went with **Peace Sells** going gold. Usually my attitude was affected by two guys who didn't give a fuck about anything and were screwing Junior and I."

"With the second lineup, you've got Chris Behler who would be sitting in the back of the bus freebasing and none of us knew about it. He could have lit the bus on fire and we all could have died. You've got Jeff Young secretly hitting on my fiancée at the time. Needless to say, there was a little bit of anger and attitude around. I think from the beginning, Marty and Nick were probably a bit tainted by some of the past stuff that was going on. They set their own pace and standards on how to live their lives and have their careers. Nick doesn't have to play Chuck's parts. He plays drums to those songs now. They never really were Chuck's parts and they never really were Gar's parts. It was Megadeth music. When you remove the personality and you play your ass off to the song, it becomes your song too. I was just in Los Angeles talking to somebody who played me back an interview that I did in 1986 and I was saying the same thing eight years ago that I'm saying today. Which for me was incredible because it shows that I haven't deviated one iota from my path of pure integrity when it came down to delivering music to our fans."

Moving toward the latter third of the well-reasoned and capably executed **Youthanasia** record, there's *Family Tree*, a lesser known and lesser discussed stadium rocker framed on a simple Ellefson bass groove. Lyrically, Mustaine tackles child abuse, poetically, obliquely, commendably. *Family Tree* gives way to the album's uniquely ponderous title track, a near heavy metal ballad about throwing away a generation. Friedman has likened his solo on this to an Irish jig, but indicates that it is the rich meld and melt of rhythm guitars that makes the track.

I Thought I Knew It All is back to the record's trunk vibe, its smoke-choked Accept plod down a near doom pathway, Mustaine again connecting directly with a near eulogy of regret. Friedman recalls how the chorus to the track was written by himself and Nick Menza at Nick's house in North

Hollywood, with Nick suggesting for inspiration, a Gipsy Kings song.

Second to last, *Black Curtains* is pure sluggish doom metal with a horror-filled lyric to match, while album closer *Victory*, written spontaneously in the studio in under half an hour, is framed somewhat like the song *Peace Sells*, namely jarring rhythm guitars and spit lyrics set against pummelling bass guitar.

"It's been five years and it's funny," reflected Nick at the time, on the copacetic band relations that helped make **Youthansia** such a cohesive album, song credits to all four members, as discussed, much of it played live in the studio as a group. "Looking back on it, it seems like yesterday. But when I think of all the things that have transpired, Dave has always reminded me of one thing: remember where you were. And I often think about that. I hear so many people complain and it really doesn't matter what your job is or what you do; there'll always be someone you don't like and something that you don't want to do. Megadeth is really an exception to the rule. We can do whatever we want. It's come to my attention that from where I came in and where I am now is definitely night and day. This is what I've been waiting for. **Youthanasia** is it and I'm very proud and there's a lot of me on it. I'm confident to say that this is not only Dave Mustaine's band, but it's my band too. And Dave's cool with that."

"I've seen a lot of changes," continues Menza, asked about Mustaine and his position in the band. "Mostly it's open-mindedness and being able to take some control away from him. It was him handing it over to us and knowing that we are competent enough to handle it. In the past, there was no trust. You couldn't leave these other guys alone because they didn't have the same vision, the same focus with the same interest. I think we've come to a point now that everyone thinks the same thing. Maybe not at the same time, but we're all looking in the same direction. This is our band and this is what we do and it's a good feeling. I've always wanted to come to this point and it has been a process until this point. This album is the biggest collaboration from all four of us. Dave and I have had a number of confrontations over the years and that's why I'm still here. It was apparent to me that the 'yes man' attitude was not the way to do things. At first I was intimidated by Dave. I felt threatened and insecure. I felt I had to be a certain way that he wanted me to be. That got me into more trouble than simply disagreeing with him. At this point, we've come to a level of trust and respect. All yes men are expendable. I'm here to make objective decisions. We've become closer friends; granted we're business partners. You've got the business, the band and friendships and that's one of the most difficult things to separate. I've taken the attitude now that I'm in this band. I can't even fathom joining another band or starting a new band from scratch to try and come up to the level where we are at. We've done shit that I've never dreamed of doing. Some of the things we've done are milestones in our life and I'll never forget them and I know we're headed for greener pastures right now. It's a really rewarding feeling to be part of."

Seconds Ellefson on the new collaborative Mustaine, "In the past whenever someone would come in with a song, we'd have very specific ways as to how the parts should be played. On this record, say when Dave came in with the song, rather than him saying play this or that, he'd give us a whole lot more freedom to do what we thought was right and good for Megadeth. When someone takes off the harness and lets you be yourself, it's quite a relief. I think we came up with much more creative parts and it really takes away the restraints and fears we used to have as a band."

Sure it would get worse later, but there were already grumbles around the fan base that **Youthanasia**, as utilitarian as it was, was a step too far in terms of melody and the slowing of the tempos. **Countdown**, to be sure, was accepted with open arms much like the black album was, but **Youthanasia** was considered somewhat more of the same, maybe too much more, a serving of **Afterburner** after **Eliminator** as it were, or **Defenders Of The Faith** not making much more of a statement on the heels of **Screaming For Vengeance**.

Still, there was much to like from the new album, again, with the pleasure circuits getting hit with instant gratification, even if the all too accessible joys of the album tended to wear off with increased consideration.

"The talk of Led Zeppelin-style jamming in the studio led us to expect a looser, live sound—one which has scarcely materialized," wrote Kerrang!'s Jason Arnopp. "Only the songwriting method seems to have undergone a little ironing. Megadeth 1994 are less about manic riff showcases and more about free-flowing songs. There's thankfully none of the extended guitar-break marathons that tainted *Hangar 18*, for example, and none of the Daffy Duckisms of *Sweating Bullets*. The ratio between hard riffs and strong melody lines may have started tipping in the latter's favour, but Mustaine has undeniably learned how to write an emotionally biting hook. On first listen, Megadeth's sixth album is a disappointment. What you *don't* know, however, is that these 12 songs have secretly booked into your Brain Hotel. By the fifth listen, they're chucking televisions out of the windows."

Jerry Ewing, writing for Metal Hammer, is even more positive about the record, calling **Youthanasia**, "a powerful tour de force that finally realizes Megadeth's true potential to the max. It rocks furiously, yet with a controlled, underlying power that lends it an air of something altogether far more dangerous. And throughout it all, sneer ever present, Mustaine is there, delivering like he's never delivered before. From the opening bombast of *Reckoning Day* to the final rumble of the decidedly dark *Victory*, **Youthanasia** charges out at you, knocking you senseless. It is the most powerfully cohesive work from the band; and the most surprising of all, in place of Mustaine's normally snarling whine, comes a vocal delivery that's as impressive as the music it adheres to. Adding weight and melody, Mustaine has undoubtedly attained a class many thought him incapable of. Only really on the title track itself is there any trace of the sneering growl of yesteryear. Musically, the power, the chops and the rhythmic twists are all still there, but the awesome melody that runs throughout the lifeblood of **Youthanasia**, combined with its solidly heavy power, suggests that if this is Megadeth's trump card today, the ace in their packs still awaits."

Certainly, with **Youthanasia**, Megadeth had put their house in order, as Mustaine explains, performing a sort of deep-cleaning, from management issues through to family life.

"If you are going to live through someone else's opinion, then that means your very selfless," mused Mustaine, offering his unique form of positivity, edged with the negative. "A very famous man once said, 'Don't believe anything you read and only half of what you see.' It's easy to hop on the bandwagon and pigeonhole someone. It was politically correct to be a Metallica fan and not a Megadeth fan, and that was how it was for a long time because we had a cold war going on. There was no activity; it was a standoff. Based on my relationship with those guys and how I was fired, I was very bitter. I did recognize that I contributed to me getting fired. When I came to terms with that, we all made amends, everything is cool and the ice is starting to melt. People are saying that it's not so uncool to be a Megadeth fan. A lot of them are kicking themselves and saying, 'We fucked up; we've overlooked some wonderful music.' A lot of people don't like the things that I say because I say the things that they know are right. I have the guts and the balls to talk about these things."

"Upon getting this lineup, the band congealed and we started noticing the outsiders who were using us," continues Dave, divulging the intensity of the house-cleaning at this juncture. "I was so removed from reality that I had no idea everybody had their dick up my ass at the same time. We changed our management, our agent, our attorney, our accountant, all our crew. We had one more thing to look at and everything would be fresh. That was the record contract, and we have been currently negotiating with our record company to try and change that. We don't want their money, we want our money. We don't want their respect, we want our respect. I just want to be treated fairly. When people think that I'm difficult to work with, then they've probably rubbed me the wrong way or I'd given them shit because I caught them not doing their job. We don't champion for mediocrity, we don't settle for second. We all know what our roles are and what our positions are and that we can do it. When I left the studio, these guys did their own parts. That would've never happened with the previous administration. Today, it's a completely new regime."

"Right now my priority is 100% dedication to this crew. Ultimately, my first priority is my worship, then it's my family, then it's the band. If things aren't in that line, then I can't give myself to the band. If I'm not right with my Creator, that I can't stay sober. If I can't stay sober, then I can't be a family man. If my family's fucked then I'm not going to want to play music. That's what lead to my overdose—my family life had fallen apart. This band is a blessing to me right now and that's why we're here in person and not on the phone."

Megadeth would open the tour campaign for **Youthanasia** in style, playing Chile on November 29, 1994, followed by seven dates through Argentina and Brazil. Into '95, the band would play solid from January through to September, first in North America through February 25th with Corrosion of Conformity as support, then into Europe for two months followed by two Israeli dates and then Japan in the latter half of May (May also marked the release of the **Evolver: The Making Of Youthanasia** video). From there it was mostly North American dates (with Flotsam & Jetsam, Korn and Fear Factory), with the tour winding up once again in South America, closing out in Argentina on September 9th.

And that would be it until the middle of 1997, the band taking its second long break away, but this time, for Dave to whip together a punk rock side-project with Lee Ving called MD 45, with a record to boot called **The Craving**.

As well, what began as a bonus EP of Megadeth rarities for the UK market—as part of the limited edition version of **Youthanasia**—became a short, stand-alone, odd's 'n' sods album of eight tracks called **Hidden Treasures**, issued in the US and Japan on July 18th, 1995.

A quick look at the high quality, quick-paced record in its entirety... Opener *No More Mr. Nice Guy*, a cover of the Alice Cooper classic for the **Shocker** soundtrack, was in fact a surprise hit for the band in the UK back in late 1989. The song was chosen specifically by the film's director Wes Craven, and Dave did indeed feel a little uncomfortable doing it, given its commercial vibe, along with the fact that the producer they had to work with was notorious hair metal maven Desmond Child, who, Dave says, was forced against his wishes to rough up the tune Megadeth-style.

Breakpoint is a choice original from the **Countdown** sessions that nonetheless was used on **Super Mario Bros.**—it was left off the record, figures Friedman, possibly because it was a bit frantic and **Rust**-inflected to fit the vibe of the rest of the album.

Go To Hell was another great original, this one slated for **Bill & Ted's Bogus Journey**—the song represents Marty Friedman's first credit and as a second trivia note, the prayer text is recited by Dave Ellefson's wife, Julie Foley, who Ellefson married in April of '94. Of note, *Breakpoint* and *Go To Hell* were also the two bonus tracks on the Japanese version of **Countdown To Extinction**.

Angry Again and *99 Ways To Die* further demonstrate the band's songwriting bench strength, the former, a one-off recording during a reconvening after the **Countdown** tour, showing up on the **Last Action Hero** soundtrack, the latter on **The Beavis And Butthead Experience** from November of '93.

Up in the sequence, there's the band's tight, efficient yet one-take version of *Paranoid*, which was a highlight on the **Nativity In Black** tribute album from October of '94. *Paranoid* won the band a Grammy nomination for Best Metal Performance in 1995, with the full album achieving gold certification in 2000. Next there's a cover of the Sex Pistols' *Problems*, which was previously unreleased, and *Diadems* (from January '95's **Tales Of The Crypt Presents Demon Night**), a dark and progressive power ballad from the **Youthanasia** sessions, constructed somewhat along the lines of Metallica's *One*.

"I think that we've proven that even when we do some tracks, like a one-off, we're pretty tight," mused Dave. "Like *Angry Again*, that was our biggest song on radio. And that song, my God, I had just crawled out of a drug rehab and into the studio. And *99 Ways To Die* was quite good. And *Paranoid* we did that same session. We were doing *99 Ways To Die* and somebody said the **N.I.B.** record was coming out, did we want to do something? We listened to every record Sabbath ever did, and just about when the song was pretty much at the deciding factor stage, they would go into one of their infamous jazz fusion breaks or classical round things—you know, I guess the devil likes classical, and we weren't into it. And *Paranoid*, I thought, God, this is so obvious, why didn't we do this in the first place? It took four or five hours of listening to all these records on studio time when we could have been working."

"It's good to kind of lay low between projects," Dave told me with a chuckle back in 1996, on press duties for his sanity project away from the Mega-machine, his MD.45 album, **The Craving**, issued December 2nd of that year. "If I did not, there'd be no spontaneity. It would be pretty much rehearsed lines. There are a lot of people in the past who are infamous for planting shills out in the audience when I do press conferences, with rehearsed questions. I'm not one to believe in that theory. The people out there asking questions deserve their questions asked, rather than publicity stunts. I'm saying this has happened in the past. Not so much now. But then again there are so many people in the business who are so brand new to it. They have one song that gets pumped on radio to the point where it's exhausted and then they're burnt."

"I don't know if there are many Dave Mustaines in the world," continues Dave, reflective before we got to the record, "but I think right now the music industry is pretty much like a giant ocean liner. No matter how hard you pull on the wheel, it's going to take awhile for it to circle around. But it is coming back around, with Slayer and Metallica and Megadeth, Pantera, and some of the other bands that are in our genre doing the things that they're doing. Some bands are drastically changing, some are doing exactly the same, some are going back to their roots. The door's pretty much wide open for us to do what we want right now. I believe we're going to do what the Megadeth fan expects us to do, and that's deliver a good record and not take any unnecessary risks on their behalf."

And MD.45? "I believe what that did for me, it gave me the opportunity to... Instead of changing a heavy metal institution and making it something alternative, it gave me the opportunity to get some songs out that weren't necessarily to the Megadeth format. I think it's a little bit fairer to our following, not trying to dupe them by putting out
stuff that's not Megadeth-type songs and saying, 'Hey, you like the name Megadeth; you're going to like the music.' I think they like Megadeth music, and just because the band has a reputable name, it doesn't mean that everything we do is always going to be great."

Hence MD.45, a collaboration with Fear singer Lee Ving, a project that actually began three years earlier as The Beverly Killbillies. Joining the prime perpetrators were Kelly Lemieux on bass and Jimmy DeGrasso, soon to be a Megadeth member, on drums.

"That was just a record we kind of made old school, like almost punk rock-style," explains Jimmy. "We went in and blasted that thing out in a couple... God, in a couple of weeks. We went and did a couple of preproduction days, and Dave had a bunch of licks, some rough songs, and we just meshed them out, and just blasted the thing really fast; it was fun. We were down in the desert, and we'd be out mountain biking all morning, and record all day, do the same thing over and over again; it was fun. Lee Ving, he's truly a character, that guy. I haven't seen him in years; I liked him a lot."

And he was the punk rock side of the equation, then? "Oh definitely," laughs DeGrasso. "Him and Kelly Lemieux, the bass player. I'd just got done with Suicidal Tendencies, went back to Alice Cooper, ran into Dave, and it was like, 'Hey, you wanna do this record?' And I said yeah, sure. So I just came out of the Suicidal Tendencies thing, so I had a lot of punk rock left from that. Dave just wanted to do something different. Megadeth, they were doing records with producers and they were spending three and four months, things like that, so he just wanted to do something fast and have it a little bit more relaxed. And he had different ideas that weren't right for a Megadeth record. I'm just guessing, but I think that was the general vibe of it, just something to do different from what you normally get boxed into doing."

"Basically what I wanted to do was go back to my roots with the New Wave Of British Heavy Metal," explains Mustaine, "and I really liked Lee Ving as a singer, whether he sung in punk or with his country band, or when he did little stints on TV. Whatever, any time I saw him do anything, I was impressed. And that charismatic energy from Lee, coupled with my ability to play and so on, made things very explosive. It could be unpredictable, and no one would know what's going on, what to expect. So I wanted to get back to my roots. This is going to sound really bold, but Lee reminds me a lot of Ian Gillan, not so much as with singing talent but just the kind of vibrato, and he sounds a lot like Tygers Of Pan Tang and Venom and Tank and Raven and Budgie. I wanted to go back to stuff that was simple like that with a really deep, strong-sounding voice."

Asked if he'd consider touring **The Craving**, Mustaine figured, "You know, I don't really know. We would love to play. Obviously Lee and Jimmy and Kelly and myself have a very unique chemistry. But I truly believe my priority right now is Megadeth. If the fans like MD.45, if it becomes bigger than Megadeth, then 'Der' (laughs). Then my priority will be MD.45. You see, Megadeth right now is so successful that it can kind of take time between projects, and our following will wait. I don't know how long they'll wait. But I know we continue to deliver consistent material. There's never any long lapses in-between records, and if I had to take a month, a week, ten days or whatever to hit a couple key select cities, then I know that Dave and Marty and Nick would understand. I'd say, 'Hey, guys, I'm going to go do my little side thing for, you know, a few shows or a few countries or a few months,' they'd go, 'Cool man, good luck!'"

Never happened, and flash forward a year, Dave was of a slightly more dismissive disposition o'er the whole MD.45 episode...

"It was a necessary time for me, because I was feeling kind of alienated from the band for my own reasons—and by my own doing. And if the opportunity came up to do it again, I probably would wait. Because there are some songs that were made on that record that would have really been great done by this band. And obviously right now, Megadeth is my priority, and it always has been. I don't think that I'll ever do anything like that again. I may, but right at this moment, I'm not going to."

8
CRYPTIC WRITINGS

"Guys, girls, guys dressed up like girls"

No real reason Megadeth should have been on a decline in the mid-'90s other than "the troubles," and that would be Megadave's rather than anything to do with the fighting Irish. Well, that's not fair because those of us who were there in the journalism world can tell you just how utterly under siege heavy metal was. In other words, sales of records across the heavy metal board were on a dramatic decline, bombarded from shifting tastes toward industrial, hard alternative, gooey alternative, grunge in its mature phase, electronica of various forms, and then toward the end of the decade, nu metal.

It is in this environment that Megadeth returned from their longest gap away with **Cryptic Writings**, an album placed specifically and accurately on the trajectory from **Rust** through **Countdown** and **Youthanasia**, and now this, the band's most mainstreamy and easy-on-the-ears record yet.

"Yeah, we've demoed up our new record," Dave told me during these dog days, referring to the upcoming **Cryptic Writings**. "I think with some of the changes in the genre of music we've been doing, there might be a little shifting in the poles (laughs). What we want to do is continue to deliver music to our following that they can count on. And one thing you know for sure that when we play a song, there's going to be a pretty good rhythm section to it, there's going to be clever lyrics, and more than likely there's going to be an unbelievable guitar solo on it. And the rhythm section with Dave and Nick, those guys are definitely pretty tight."

Continuing with the uneasy talk of change—and the preparing of me, the press, the people, for that change—when asked about the next plateau for the band, Dave quips that, "Well, I can honestly tell you this: we aren't going to have a group body-piercing. So I don't know if there's going to be any surprises. To my knowledge, the first time that I actually saw all these guys, we were all tattoo-free. So I don't know that we're going to be slick and hip and cool like everyone else is, you know, sticking metal through every piece of meat they've got on their body. But I think that when you put headphones on your ears, it doesn't really matter what we look like; it's how we play like. And I can tell you that our playing has improved, because you know, practise makes perfect. There are some definite heavy songs. I was in Italy and I saw a picture of a wolf up on the side of a building that was carved in stone, nursing some babies, human babies, and it gave me a great song concept.

And there's some stuff on there that's reminiscent of *Bad Omen*, some stuff like *Ashes In Your Mouth*, stuff like *Crown Of Worms*."

Will it be heavy, a nasty return to form? Will it bite? That's exactly what I asked, and Dave wasn't going to outright lie to me about it, although... "Well, we don't have a resentment for the music industry. The most important thing obviously is our own listening tastes first, and delivering to the fans. Now if we write a song that we really love but the fans will think we're out of our minds, then we won't release it. We'll keep it for our own personal use, and pray that the cleaning woman doesn't take it or something. But my tastes are pretty much those of the audience, the friends and fans that have been with us for all these years. You know, face it, right now, heavy metal needs a good shot in the arm. And we're that shot."

"We were discussing producers yesterday," continued Dave. "The tapes have been completely demoed. We've got all the material we've been thinking of recording. And you know, obviously as serendipitous and spontaneous as I am, no one can keep me from writing a song on the spot. We do know that we'll be doing drum tracks in New York, and we'll be doing guitar, bass, vocals and all other overdubs either in North America or uh, the rest of the world (laughs). We're not doing anything right now, because it's just too bloody hot."

Turns out that **Cryptic Writings** would be recorded when it's too bloody hot, at The Tracking Room in Nashville with song doctor and session guitarist Dan Huff producing, an odd choice, but a known and skilled industry insider. Out on June 17th of '97, **Cryptics Writings** wouldn't look like a Megadeth album, lacking the conservatively heavy metal logo the band had used since their second album, and lacking any spottings of Vic Rattlehead. This was a Megadeth trying hard, not to be trendy, but to be less part of the heavy metal ghetto. Essentially, becoming a rock band but, commendably, not leaping into any currently hot style of radio-accepted hardness. If anything, by going rock, the band would be positioning themselves as older school even than thrash, right?

But what emerged as the cover art for **Cryptic Writings** was essentially a case of plan B. "I don't think there's ever been an album title that was the title when it came down to it," explains Dave. "**Cryptic Writings** was supposed to be called **Needles And Pins** and we had this really foxy model we picked out who was supposed to be on the cover naked and her parts were air-brushed out so you couldn't see any nipples or pubes or anything, and she's supposed to be holding a voodoo doll. We get it back and it looks like Bjork, right? And I don't have anything against her, I just don't think she's worthy of being on my cover. This is that whole Hugh Syme story. Now Hugh is great, he's a great artist, but he's an artist and artists get on a tangent. And you know what? I'm paying you to do something, you fucking do it. And I don't give a shit what your reason is or what your vision is—do the work the way I want it. And I respect Hugh tremendously, I think he's a fantastic artist but it's a shame the picture didn't turn out the way we wanted it to and if it ever came up again, yeah I would use him again. You know, I don't consider my relationship with Hugh to be bad right now. I mean, he may hate my guts, I don't know. Do I care? I don't really like people going around hating me."

Anyhow, the fresh approach seemed to be working. Opening track *Trust* was issued as an advance single, and it quickly became the band's most successful single ever, hitting No. 5 on the Billboard Mainstream Rock Tracks chart. MTV played it liberally, and in January of '98, it was nominated for a Grammy, with Metallica also part of the pack, for *Bleeding Me*, that band even more publicly dealing with an identity crisis in an era populated with shorter hair but more tattoos and piercings (according to Dave). Befitting the times, both bands lost out to Tool.

The song cuts deep emotionally, Mustaine delivering bitterly an admittedly autobiographical lyric about relationship breakdown based on mutual mistrust. Musically the track crawls to full volume on tribal drums and strings, a mournful riff taking over upon a bed of puffy production even rounder and warmer than that afforded **Youthanasia**. It's squarely a chugging heavy metal song, but again, extremely musical, even if the song's verse riff, roughed up and with heavier attendant parts, could hold its own on **Countdown**.

"We were very flattered," said Dave of the Grammy situation, where ten years ago, you'd probably get a Johnny Rotten answer. "It's nice to be recognized by our community, as a nominee, and it's exciting for us again to potentially win the Grammy and if anything, this is a really wonderful time for all hard rock and heavy metal fans."

"I don't think the same thing is happening to Megadeth that's happened to Metallica," continued Dave, asked by me to compare career and creative paths that seemed similar at the time and still do today. "I think that we're two totally different animals. And what they've chosen to do is something that they're comfortable with, and we are not comfortable with going that route. I don't think it's my place to be saying what's right or wrong with either band, and by making comparisons, obviously, somebody's going to come out superior. I would rather just say that we don't wanna go the route that they have."

An alternate (not alternative!) version of *Trust* was issued, on which the extensive chorus was sung in Spanish, resulting in a mouthful of phrasing for Dave who does an admirable job with the challenge. This was used as a bonus track on the Latin American edition of the album; years later, the idea would be reprised for a Spanish version of *Promises* from **The World Needs A Hero**. The CD single of *Trust* includes album track *A Secret Place* as well as live versions of *Tornado Of Souls* and *A Tout Le Monde*. As a final note, the classical break enclosed (played by the Nashville String Orchestra) was something from a track of Marty's called *Absolution*, which was demoed for both **Countdown** and **Youthanasia**.

Next up is *Almost Honest*, lyrical concept fully conjoined to that of *Trust*, music even more light and airy, with a chorus that is blatantly melodic. There's weird sound effects, some acoustic guitar, different vocal textures, and lots of wide-open spaced for Junior to chug on the fat strings.

"There's a continuum of melody with this band now, and it's gotten better and better for the person who is not like a blood and guts kind of heavy metal fan," qualified Mustaine. "You know, we are appealing... we are gaining more appeal to different people, especially the female audience, which is something that we haven't really delved into very much in the past. And it's obvious, if you're at the concerts now, if you go to Megadeth concerts, before it used to look like a military recruiting lineup, and now it's definitely looking more like a regular concert—guys, girls, guys dressed up like girls (laughs)."

Almost Honest was launched as the record's second single, and it dutifully acted that way, rising to No. 8 on the same Billboard sub-chart. But this accessible one-two punch wasn't enough to take the album platinum, **Cryptic Writings** sitting at around 800,000 copies in the US, good for the middling reviews it got from press and fans, but hey, very impressively, the five Megadeth albums before it are all platinum, with the last to reach that plateau being **So Far So Good... So What!** in 1998.

"It hasn't hit platinum,' confirmed Ellefson, speaking only a few months post-release. "Usually, in Canada, its proportionate, about 10% of what it is in the United States. If it's gold there, it's gold here, that kind of thing. So at this point, getting too caught up in the status of it kind of takes away from what we are here to do, which is perform and talk to the media if you will, and sort of raise the whole awareness of what we're doing, and what our songs are about and touring and everything; so that's the focus right now. And then maybe at the end of this whole thing we'll kick back and see what it did all around the world, you know (laughs)."

"First of all, thank you—that's a compliment," laughs Ellefson, at my assessment of the organic, bass-rich sound quality of the album. "You know, I think in the early days, our records always forced us to try to live up to a really high expectation live, and we weren't always able to pull that off, and we got a lot of criticism about it, like on our first couple of tours. Now the lineup, as it stands right now, we've had together for quite a few years, we've made several records together, and there's like a chemistry happening right now. And it takes quite a long time for that to really come together. We always try to use the latest technology that's available for making records, and we've always tried to use people that were as adept at applying that technology in a way that's musical. You know, I don't think there's anything wrong with using high-tech to make good music, and good recordings. We play on the stuff, so it doesn't really matter. In fact, if anything, what's happened right now, due to the advent of lower-priced home recording equipment, independent record labels and the Internet, to a large degree, almost anybody can make a record now. And what's happened is the quality control of music in the world has suffered. I mean, it used to be that you had to actually deliver the goods in order for a record company to get behind you, sink some money into you and jump through hoops and really make a commitment. And you had to be good, because they're obviously sinking a lot into you. So you have to deliver the goods. And we just live in a much different era now, however, because Megadeth grew up with that old school philosophy; we've also maintained that. And everybody in our camp really has that kind of work ethic to make the best quality records that we can."

Next up is *Use The Man*, a tale of heroin overdose, in which the victim dies after his very first hit of the drug that demonized Megadeth as much as any band, short of those that suffered deaths from it. Dave talks of visiting the guy's place and seeing vestiges of the goals he had, the life he planned to lead. Also trotted out as a single (and reaching No. 18), *Use The Man* is set to a musical track that is a tried and true Megadeth conceit, namely the dark and epic ballad, with acoustic guitars, heavy parts, interesting rhythms, surges and swells, and in this case, a pile of innovative and obscure string arrangements, presumably by the Nashville String Orchestra, who is not credited on the album. Interestingly, the song is prefaced by a clip from The Searchers' hit *Needles And Pins*, which, as mentioned, Mustaine also considered using as the title of the album. On the remaster, this intro was removed.

Mastermind is a funky heavy metal rocker on which Junior gets to shine. The riff however is prime **Countdown**-era Megadeth, even if with this production, the comparison is obscured.

Says Mustaine, "*Mastermind* is a song describing a metaphor. Well, I don't even know if it's a metaphor. But the song is about the human mind being one of the most powerful computers, and it's talking about this person who is brainwashing people and treating them as though they are living drives, basically. So it's very interesting." And musically, says Dave, the song is part of a record that, like a quilt-work, represents them all...

"**Cryptic Writings** is probably best summed up as a discography of all the records that this lineup has made. You have elements from **Rust In Peace**. People say **Rust In Peace** is so great. Well, *The Disintegrators*, *She-Wolf*, *Vortex* and *FFF* are all very à la **Rust In Peace**. So, that addresses that issue. **Countdown To Extinction** is a very melodic record that still has heavy metal elements. *Have Cool, Will Travel*, *A Secret Place* and *Mastermind*, and there's another one on there, and *Sin*—these are all songs that are very similar to the **Countdown To Extinction** era. And then you've got songs that are very much like the **Youthanasia** period—*I'll Get Even*, *Use The Man*, *Almost Honest* and *Trust*. But the thing is, granted, we've gone backwards in time and evaluated each one of those eras and done a musical offering from each one of those periods, but we've raised the level of credibility of each one of those songs to where we're at right now. A lot of personal demons were exorcised with this record. We have been able to cast out the naysayers and prove to them that, you know, we're still here. And it has been two against one for the longest time. And you know, it's not like that anymore."

And speaking of *The Disintegrators*, that one is next, and it's a compact, old school thrasher that would fit, unshaven and punked, on any of the first three records. Lyrically, Dave was inspired by being caught in traffic, late for rehearsal, and then coming up with a scenario in which a biker gang rolls into town and wrecks everything.

I'll Get Even ("about one of my favourite topics: revenge," says Dave) is laid back to the point of bluesy, contemplative, for the most part, not even heavy metal. Dave sings as quietly as he ever has, but it doesn't present him as a bona fide singer, given the spoken style. In effect, Dave as singer is best experienced in the melodic chorus of this track and elsewhere over the trinity of similar albums of which this is the second. Mustaine amusingly blames second gen Bad Company vocalist Brian Howe for the tempering, tampering and tamping of *I'll Get Even* (at manager Bud Prager's behest) Howe getting a quarter of the songwriting credit for his troubles.

Speaking of credits, *Sin* features the first of two co-credits on the album for drummer Nick Menza, who gleefully pounds away on a meaty groove all through this cool party rocker at the snarling heavy metal end of that spectrum.

"That record was very cool because I got probably my best drum sound that I've gotten, playing with that band," reflects Nick. "That was all natural drums, no samples or any crap like that. And the sound on it was just slamming. It just got better each time, being in the studio."

As for the album as a whole, specifically stylistically, "I think it was OK," says Nick. "But it was something I didn't think we should have pushed so far into. It was more management and Dave saying, hey, we need to be more mainstream. And we should have been thinking hey, we're Megadeth—we should always be heavy and stick to what we do and not try to become a pickle, you know? It's like once you become a pickle, you can't go back to be the cucumber. I didn't feel 100% to go going into that area. But it's like hey, you know what? You know what you're doing. You've been doing this long enough. It was more about, look how long we've been in the business and we're still not really doing that great. Our biggest peak time-wise was right around **Countdown**. We sold the most records on **Countdown**, like 2.5 million in the US and that was our biggest time, when we were making a lot of money and we were touring a lot and everything was good. And then we just started to slack off—down, down, down—and towards the end there, we were barely making ends meet. Doing this tour and trying to break even, it was tough and people get attitudes. David had a son and then he had a daughter on the way and he was under a lot of pressure."

As for an assessment of his experience writing with the band, Nick calls it, "Pretty good. They would never let me write a song solely by myself. I would either be collaborating or helping him complete something he had already started. I never really saw anybody write a whole song by themselves in that situation. It was kind of stifling and it kept me down. I wanted to do more and write more stuff. It's the end-all side of bands. One guy is always doing everything."

"Dave wasn't really open to getting songs," continues Nick. "You had to pick the right time to present anything to him and towards the end it was like, just give it to the management and let them sort it out. It was like, wait a minute (laughs), aren't we in a band here? He didn't want to listen to any of my music really, or anyone's for that matter. I just found it disheartening and it gave me no motivation. It was like, dude, I mean, I presented a song I have on my solo record a couple times to him. And he would say, 'Don't try to fucking pass this song off on me again.' He goes, 'This song is crap, and it will never make it and it will never amount to anything.' And I said, 'Dude, you're crazy and you know what? I take that as a big compliment,' and I walked away with my headphones and my little mini-disc player. I'm like, God, I can't believe this guy. So that was the first song I recorded for **Life After Deth**, *Next To You*. And I said, 'You know what? This is a hit song. Period. And I'm putting it on my record.' So that was like him saying, yeah, I'm jealous and I hate you."

A Secret Place is a strong **Youthanasia**-styled track with Egypto melodies out of Zeppelin, Purple and Rainbow. It is the third song from the album to be subjected to a video and fully the fourth to chart as a single, reaching No. 19. Lyrically, the song is about climbing inside one's head, but the video (in which the band is never shown, either acting or performing) is spun from *The Incident At Owl Creek Bridge*, a short story from 1891 by Ambrose Bierce.

"I think that the lyrics on this record are really not much different from anything in the past," says Dave, asked about the potentially quite autobiographical sketch painted all over *A Secret Place*. "They're still very personal to me. However it's not dealing so much with what I see in society, as much as it is with myself. Someone had said something to me that my lyrics aren't provocative anymore. And I thought, well, dur, you just must be perfect, because if you don't have problems with trust or honesty, you just must be visiting this planet, you know? And so the songs are obviously about stuff that happens to us."

Have Cool, Will Travel is an artfully constructed song with Accept-like

Youthanasia power chording spiced with more note-dense **Countdown** bits, not to mention harmonica and melodic singing come chorus time. And then up into the last quarter of the album, things heat up for *She-Wolf*, the thrashiest thing on the record, a choppy bit of work poisoned with the typical heavy metal lyric about an evil woman archetype, in this case, says Dave, the ex-wife of a friend.

As the album rocks fairly hard towards closing time there's *Vortex*, yet another sturdy rocker that could have fit on **Youthanasia**, and a song that was in fact demoed up for that record, with Marty re-performing the solo he did on the demo note for note.

Nick Menza's final credit on **Cryptic Writings**, for last track *FFF*, would also be his final flourish for the band, Menza long gone by the time the next Megadeth record would surface two years down the line.

"I'm not ashamed of it and I'm not upset about it," says Menza, asked if there were any regrets toward ending his time with the band. "That was a great learning period for me, and experience, songwriting. He was a really good teacher for me. I learned a lot of stuff from him, what to do and what not to do. Basically in that situation I couldn't go any farther. There wasn't much more room for me to expand in the band. I was fired, and Dave said I left because I was unhappy or whatever. But he fired me over the phone. I left to go have a surgery done on my knee, which was just a routine thing. I was out for maybe seven to ten days until they took of the staples and I was fine. It was just a little cyst I had removed on my tendon on my right knee."

So it was an excuse to have rid of you.

"Yeah, basically that was part of it—it gave him the green light and he said, 'OK, we're letting you go.' And I'm like, 'Letting me go? That's pretty funny, man; don't joke around.' And he says, 'I don't think you're hearing me clearly.' He was really cold and brash about it over the phone. And it's like, God, man, you think you know somebody for ten years or 12 years..."

"I'd say attitude," continues Menza, asked what the problem was. "My attitude suffered because I just didn't want to hear his bullshit anymore. We butted heads a lot of the time, Dave and I, because I was telling him exactly what was on my mind. And he respected me for that, that at least I could tell the truth. I was the only one in the band who ever really stood up for shit that was being done. It was like, wait a minute, that's not right. And he'd be like, 'Well, what are you talking about? No one else is complaining about it.' And I would say, 'Well, nobody else has any balls in this band (laughs).' And when I was fired, nobody said anything about it. It was like they were all afraid for their jobs."

"It's like, come on, grow some balls and have some personality, grow a spine, will ya? And it just left me as the bad guy all the time. Whenever I would say anything. I mean, David would do insane stuff. He would play jokes on those guys and tell them, 'Here's the artwork, it's done.' And they would go 'Oh yeah, love that!' And meanwhile, he had just told me two minutes before, 'Look at this! It's crap, this thing sucks!' And those guys would say, 'That's cool!' And I would be like, God, you guys, you just dug yourself into a ditch. And I just felt I was his right-hand guy and he would never fire me. I really had no fear of that. And then when he did, I was just like, wow, I guess I wasn't his right-hand guy (laughs). And I see him now, and he's got a bunch of yes men around him which enables him to be controlling and manipulative. It's his band. I totally never had a problem with that."

"The thing that bummed me, I was writing songs," says Menza. "I had a lot of music I submitted to them that just got shot down, and it's like, who's to say what song is going to be a hit song and what's not? It's like, if we gave full attention to all my music like we gave attention to Dave's music... they're all contender-type songs, depending on what kind of treatment you do on them and what the nucleus and formula is of the songs. It's like, man, any song can be a hit. And we would like just fall right in on his stuff. He would write something and boom, we would be right there playing it. It's like, if I had that in my band... which I'm starting to have now. It's cool to be writing something, and then have players come in and just rip on your stuff and just play it, and all of a sudden you've got a song going on. That's why I say I'm going to split everything equally. I want other guys to contribute to making my band happen and that's what makes real bands—all guys equal; they're there because they do what they do best."

Asked how it all played out financially, if by the end of that run he and the other guys felt they were taken care of, Nick says, "I've got a house in Studio City, a pretty nice one, pretty big, like a quarter acre and all those guys moved up to Phoenix. So that was one thing that kind of vibed Dave. He's like, well, you are not being the team player. And I'm like, dude, there's no way I'm moving to Arizona. Just no way. I can't live out there. It's too hot. There's just dirt everywhere and rocks. And he goes, 'Well, move to Scottsdale where we're at.' And I'm like, you know what? Sorry. When it comes time to work, I'll come out there and stay wherever I need to stay to rehearse and that's it. It's like, those guys all moved within five minutes of each other. Dave bought a house and then they moved to within five minutes of where he was. And I'm thinking, what a bunch of yes men. And then as soon as I started doing some solo things like saying, hey, I'm going to put out a solo record, that was a problem for him. And I submitted all those songs a couple of times to Dave and he just wasn't open to it. He's like, you'd really be shooting yourself in the foot if you didn't play those for Bud or Mike, our managers at the time. And I'm like, you know what? I don't have to play anything for anybody. I can put out a solo record and they don't have a piece of it. They manage Megadeth. They don't manage Nick Menza. I manage Nick Menza."

"I had a couple of people making inquiries about me," says Nick, about where he potentially might have ended up after such a high-profile gig as the classic lineup of Megadeth. "It was all newer bands. I actually was going to go try out for Ozzy, because someone had called me from his management and asked if I was interested in the drum position and I said sure. When Ozzy found out that I was from Megadeth, he said I don't want to have anything to do with him. Because he, I guess, hates Dave and Dave hates Ozzy and he basically just blackballed me and didn't want me around. And Sharon was like, 'Oh, but he's really good and he knows all the songs' and he's like, 'I don't care, I don't want to hear about it.' And I was like, damn, man. And then when Korn lost their drummer, they were asking about me. And I said sure, I'm interested in Korn, no problem. And that didn't happen. They got Puffy, who was with Faith No More and was playing with Ozzy at the time. He's playing drums with them. And since then, I'm getting ready to go try out for Limp Bizkit on guitar. I sent them a package and everything and they're actually interested. They're having this worldwide search, like guitar auditions at Guitar Center. It's just a big publicity thing, you know. This big hype he's got going. Fred Durst is pretty smart. My stuff was on his desk. Actually Phil from Motörhead got my stuff to their manager. I know all those songs, no problem. There's not a whole lot of guitar going on in their stuff."

But before we can visualize, jaw on floor, Nick Menza playing guitar for Limp Bizkit, there's still work to do with Megadeth, taking **Cryptic Writings** to the masses, albeit mostly on a smaller scale than previous.

"We started the tour off in the United States," Mustaine told me at the time, recounting the trip to that point, namely January of '98. "We played in Phoenix, and then went straight over to Europe then straight over here, and did some festivals and some very small clubs, and then we came back to the United States again, and then after that we went over to Japan, and then down to South America, and we're doing United States again. We're going to be taking a break off during February and start again in March through April, and then during the summer we're going to be probably doing some of the Ozzfest dates.

"The focus is the tour, the live show," added Junior. "We're always changing our set list. We're working on new things. If we spent much time working on writing songs on the road, it really takes away from our focus on the live show. So it's kind of like one thing at a time. I think the show tonight will be a complete surprise, because we haven't toured yet up here on this record (laughs). We play a lot of material off **Cryptic Writings**, but we also play a lot of the older songs because we have a lot of fans from all the different eras of Megadeth. So our focus is basically give the people what they want. So we've listened to the requests that people have given us for songs, and we try to play 'em all."

Plumping for the album, Mustaine says, "I can tell you right now, the critical acclaim for **Cryptic Writings** is the best we've seen so far, more so than **Rust In Peace**. **Rust In Peace** is a record for music aficionados. The people that listen to **Cryptic Writings**... we were eagerly anticipating a bad review, because we thought it was a fluke, that no one was saying anything negative about it, and then finally when the first bad review came in, it was like, thank you! It's over; now we don't have to wait anymore. You know, because the next thing you know, fucking Tipper Gore is going to be saying, these Meger-dude guys are okay, you know? Then it's all over. Then we're really done."

But at this point, basically inside the guts of the **Cryptic Writings** tour, the band was far from done, at least from the perspective of maintaining what would become regarded as the band's classic lineup.

"We're secretly married; no one knows that," quipped Mustaine, asked about the state of his relationship with Ellefson, Junior adding in all seriousness that, "Probably away from the actual working in the band, Dave and I, I don't know, we hang out quite a bit. I don't know how much Dave hangs out with Nick and Marty. When we're off the clock, so to speak, we get off the stage, we rap, we travel, we spent a lot of time together anyway because we travel. I think personally, my view on it is, when I first met up with Dave, he had the vision of what Megadeth was going to be, and regardless of what it looks like from the outside, most bands have one or two people that are the leaders of the group, and in our case, Dave is that guy. And for me, I see so many bands get into so much trouble, and it's probably even happened... it has happened in our band, where everybody tries to force their vision into it. I mean, we all contribute to the band, no doubt about that. There's definitely four contributions, at any given time. But when you've got something good that's working, I think it's—my view on it is—it's for me to just basically align myself with what works. And the vision that he's had for the last however many years has been working really well. So that to me is kind of the ultimate in teamwork, is that what's the best for the group, as opposed to what's best for any of the individuals."

"And I think that's probably the thing in the past, with previous lineups, that didn't work. There wasn't a group unity. There was like me and Dave and there were two other guys. Now it's not like that. Now there's four guys in Megadeth. Because Nick and Marty, I think, adopted that same attitude when they came in. It's like they came on board to what was already happening, as opposed to trying to come in and change it, like, 'OK, I'm here now' (laughs). It's teamwork, really, is what it is."

"We've pretty much lost touch with most of them," continues Ellefson, asked about the Mega-members shed along the way. "I mean, they know where we are (laughs), because we come through town and play concerts and stuff. So if it seems that it's kind of just... There is an animosity there, but that was yesterday, and this is today, and I don't think any of us would like intentionally go seeking each other out trying to find each other. It was what it was and it's over—we've all moved on to new things."

"Jeff Young is in Dayton, Ohio talking crap about us to this day," adds Mustaine. "Any interview that he does, whether it's radio or press, he has to talk negatively about us. And I think, see, I think he's a fabulous guitar player, and I would really wish he would move forward. Chuck Behler, I don't know where he's at. Gar Samuelson, we were in Greece, and I was reading a little tiny fanzine in Greece, and poor Gar, he's probably thinking, they'll never see this. And he's talking smack about us again, and I read it, and I just went, you know, their accounts of what happened, and you know obviously, there's two sides to every story, and then there's the third side which is the truth. I mean, I'm not blameless. I know that I caused a lot of problems, and I'm responsible for those, and I'll take responsibility for them, but the way that these two boys have recalled what happens, they must've been in a totally different band. Now, Chris Poland, we see him when we're in Santa Monica. He's just a really straight-up dude, just an extremely wasted talent, because he's so fabulous. But he's a little bit insane, and I think that was part of the beauty of his playing, was that he was insane. But unfortunately to be in this business, you need to be somewhat sane. There's another guy named Mike Albert that disappeared. There was another guy named Jay Reynolds, that we don't know where he's at. And anybody before then was basically just mileposts on our journey."

Dave and religion.. there's a whole book there to be sure, but as it stood in 1998... "I'm not on a religious quest,' dismissed Mustaine. "I think for me, the whole religious thing, you know, for the most part, a lot of chicks don't want to hear about politics. And a lot of dudes don't want to hear about God or family. So me getting all religio, or all politico, I alienate people. People want to know, you know, who we're sleeping with, what kind of drugs or alcohol we're taking, and basically, you know, how big our dicks are. And that kind of stuff is kind of personal too (laughs). But we need to pretty much live the rock 'n' roll lifestyle, and let people know that this is a rock band. Yeah, we do, do that. We do still party. Even though we're not still using substances, we still have more fun than most people do that do use substances. And for me right now, where I think, my belief is that, you know, you go through life and harm as little amount as people as possible, and you have the best time."

And you take care of business, hands-on all the way. "Hands, feet, lips, everything on. There's nothing that goes by this band that we don't know about. We are so on top of this business, because we are just so in love with the process of how this band has blossomed. And there's really not much that goes by us. I mean, every once in a while something will slip through the cracks, like some really exciting news someone will hear before us. And then again, there's something we hear before someone else, and they want us to act like we haven't heard it yet. No kidding? A Grammy nomination! Wow! So this is our first Grammy nomination? Well, yeah, not including the other five."

"One of the things we learned right away was that 'Trust me' meant 'Fuck you,'" continues Dave, with a laugh. "And that stuck with us the longest time, until we finally found... I mean, it probably isn't until the last two or three years that we actually felt that we could trust certain people. We've got a fabulous lawyer who takes really good care of us, who has our best interests at heart. Everybody at this firm just loves you, just loves our dirty drawers. Our agent, we've been with for years and years and years, but unfortunately there was a period where we fired him because we were betrayed by someone who blamed him for something that he didn't do, and the person that we did trust ended up being shit personified. And now it's like, you know, everything that we have in our camp, I don't think there's anything that isn't acceptable to us right now in our field. Now granted, there are some things we would like to improve on, but everything is totally acceptable right now."

Adds Junior, "Like Dave just said, for us, the whole thing, it's a labour of love. It's a passion for us, and all sides of it, not just the music, but the business end of it. And you learn how to do stuff after you fuck stuff up a lot, and people have made off with your money and you didn't know it until after the fact. So after that, after that happens a lot, you sort of start paying closer attention. But there again, it's like teamwork. It's like everybody has to kind of be double-checking everybody else."

"Growing babies," says Mustaine, asked what the guys are into at this point, besides running the band efficiently. "For me, it's still martial arts, and my son is into hockey, and I started teaching him how to skate. I mean, I'm not a great skater, and I only played hockey for a little while, but he loves it. And my hobby right now is collecting hockey jerseys for him, while I'm on the road. And I'm going back to college right now. I am taking business management. I'm probably almost at the end of my first year, and my grade average, I think, is 3.86, still. 4.0 is straight As. And the counsellor I had said that if you have a 4.0, you don't got a life. So I'm glad I've got less than 4.0. And then (directed at the author) I'm gonna write books about heavy metal (laughs)."

"I spend a lot of time mostly just with my family, just doing personal things," adds Ellefson. "I do some authoring, this column that I have, and that's kind of fun for me, for some reason. I listen to music and I play music for fun. It seems like that's my life. It's my hobby, it's a passion, it's what I do, obviously with the band and everything. You know what I listen to now that I get a kick out of? I go back and listen to those Beatles albums. I just, personally... I like feel-good music. I don't have to think about it, I don't want to have to dissect it. So sometimes I sit in my hotel room and play acoustic guitar to Beatles songs. It's simple. There's no wonder everybody liked them, because it's just so easy to listen to. Actually, someone was saying that about *Almost Honest*, that it has these Beatle-esque hooks. And I thought that was a compliment. I didn't personally write that song, but I was like whoa, that's cool, that they're thinking about our music in that way. Because that's the beauty of it. Music should have a good feeling to it, and not... you don't have to put on your fucking thinking hat to listen to it and dissect it."

With **Cryptic Writings**, it certainly wasn't just Ellefson that was thinking this way, but also the boss as well as manager Bud Prager. It's also no secret that Marty had evolved into quite the pop guy, which we'll talk about a bit more next chapter. In any event, Megadeth at this point was a band searching for a place in the music industry, perhaps feeling a bit obsolete, looking for footing through a deliberate type of positioning, as more of a traditional heavy metal band and less about thrash and all its visual and lyrical trappings.

"Well, that's flattering that they would even say that, cite us as an influence, anybody, period," says Dave, told that all manner of new metal band now cite Megadeth as a major inspiration, especially those playing the hot metal of the day, which in '98, for want of a better term, was Swedish melodic death metal. "I think with these new bands, they have a type of musical freedom and a lot of that has come from bands who went out there and broke the rules and didn't care. And I count myself in that, although I don't know how many rules I broke (laughs). But you've got to have somebody go out there who isn't going to champion mediocrity, but is going to protect the scene by delivering performances of consistent quality and not be walked on. Because when Joe Q. Promoter Man takes advantage of somebody that's in a show, to screw over a big band, what are they going to do to the smaller bands, the newer bands? They're going to get it even harder."

"I think most metal bands suck," continues Mustaine, "because they can't play and they can't sing, and play the same riffs over and over, and they need a shower. I think most of them, you know, they're on this pseudo-Satan, just thrill ride that is so stupid. It's like, I mean, so you can't play, and you become a Satanist, and all of a sudden you get imaginary power. And I understand. I was there and I did that stuff when I was a kid. It's like those extenda-penis condoms. You go to those condoms with the three-inch extension on the end of it, and all of a sudden you're a man. Well I'll tell you, it may look, for all practical purpose and intent, from a hundred yards away like you're really something, but when you look at it closer... you see that on closer inspection that it's just a façade. And I think a lot of these groups that are out there are just horseshit. Just terrible, a waste of vinyl."

And you know Dave was talking very much about the exploding black metal scene there, along with the deluge of bands from that genre that lean towards thrash or black or, ahem, blackened thrash. This is tied up in Dave's sometimes glowing, sometimes waning religious centreing, but also in a realization that he was now proposing an album like **Cryptic Writings** at a point in history when the ersatz genre he was always going to be associated with was doing so many exciting things in a place way heavier than Megadeth had ever been.

Asked what he is digging, then, out there, Mustaine is cautious, going on to betray himself as becoming out of touch. "I said it joking, in Metal Edge, in America, I said I like the Spice Girls, Prodigy, Metallica, Veruca Salt and someone else. And they printed it. So I have to be a little more serious, because I got a bunch of dumb asses coming up and saying, 'Do you really like the Spice Girls?' I mean, I like about this much of them. But I think if there was a record that I would say really had an effect on me this last year, in 1997, it would probably have been the **BBC Sessions** by Led Zeppelin. And we heard a couple other records that were really interesting for us, but if I listened to more than one song in a row, it sounded like the same song over and over. Obviously, we liked what we heard from Life Of Agony, or they wouldn't be supporting us. Contrary to popular belief, I thought **Load** was an okay record. It did really good for us, in a lot of places—it's fuelled the controversy."

And what of your own music? What are you most proud of there, so far (so good)? "From the whole catalogue? There are certain riffs that we have that we've created that without a doubt, the core of the Megadeth sound... pedaling down to down-picking in *In My Darkest Hour*—that's come back in with *Sin* and it's also evident in *Almost Honest* and *Angry Again*. And that's the stuff the kids just love. But for me, there's no one particular song that's more important than another one. It's those parts where it locks down like that, where people just love it. I love some of the parts in *Sweating Bullets*. Especially the fact that now that I'm enjoying being a front man again... there was a time when I was dreading it going out there, because everything I said was taken wrong. 'Boo, fuckin' Dave's off on another tirade. Now he's saying too much.' It's like shut up already. And then the other day... part of the reason I haven't talked too much during concerts lately is because, you know, I just don't want to talk. Most front guys are full of bullshit. 'Come on, give me fuckin' attitude!' Here's your attitude."

9
RISK

"Their opinion doesn't matter and neither does mine"

Touring for **Cryptic Writings** went rock solid from June of '97 through to June of '98, when on the 9th of that month, in Santa Cruz, California, Nick Menza drummed his last dance with the band. The very next night, Jimmy DeGrasso took over, and the band moved toward a string of Ozzfest dates through the summer of '98 followed by South American and Japanese swings to finish out the year.

November 23rd in Tokyo, the band whipped out a cover of every metalhead's favourite Cheap Trick song... "That's the song I wanted to write when I first picked up a guitar: Cheap Trick - *Auf Weidersehen*," recalls Marty Friedman. "You know what? If you ask me what my high point was of the whole time in Megadeth, it would be playing that song live in Japan. We played that song live and it was like, OK, I can die now. It was the ultimate. We worked it out in the dressing room and we played it at the end of the gig."

The first half of 1999 was taken up with trying to prop up the band's declining fortunes, which had now been on a continual slide since the critical triumph that was **Rust In Peace** and the commercial and critical triumph that was **Countdown To Extinction**.

The recording of what was to become **Risk** took place once again with Dan Huff presiding as producer, the band putting the thing together from January 4th to April 22nd at Masterfonics Inc., The Tracking Room, in Nashville, with the mix taking place April 23rd to May 21st of that year. And the title? that comes partially from advice proffered from Lars Ulrich to Dave to take more risks with Megadeth's music, as relations continued to thaw, more rapidly with Lars, not so fast with James.

On July 22nd of 1999, original Megadeth drummer Gar Samuelson died at the age of 41 in Orange City, Florida, cause of death, liver failure. Next was cremation, after which Gar's ashes were scattered into the Atlantic ocean. Playing the high-profile Woodstock '99 gig three days later, Megadeth, headlining the west stage on the final night, dedicated to Gar their performance of *Peace Sells*. As a side note, on the resultant 2CD **Woodstock 1999** album, Megadeth would be represented by recent relative obscurity *A Secret Place*.

"Man, Gar had all kinds of problems," recalls ex-band mate and ex-Megadether Chris Poland. "Actually, there was something... he smoked so many cigarettes that the doctor... that's the cause of death. He had emphysema and his liver was bad from drinking, because he never stopped drinking. So it was a lot of everything. His liver was like... well, let's just say, that's what it was."

What did he end up doing for work after Megadeth?

"He had his own studio. He built a studio in Florida, had a band; he used to record other bands. Always writing music. He was a really, really good songwriter. As I said, we wrote a lot of the songs we played in a fusion band called The New Yorkers, that we were in years before we met Dave. So really good songwriter too. Awesome drummer. I mean, we were crazy. All of us were kind of crazy then, so it was fun. We all had a chip on our shoulder and Dave had the biggest chip because of Metallica. You know, he was our leader, man. It was actually good that way. I learned a lot from Dave on how to keep a band together. We just followed his lead, really. I thought, for the conditions, you think about it now, when you're sober, how did you get anything done? But, you know, most people aren't sober. Most people have a drink when they get home at night, or have three drinks, or sometimes get drunk on the weekend. So I think about it now—we used to drink a lot and we would get stuff done. But people drinking get stuff done all the time. I mean, look at Hemingway. I just look back and think that it was meant to be. He invented a style of music that still stands the test of time. I wish what they woulda done was, I wish it would have stayed in that vein rather than getting more and more, I guess, accessible to the public. Recently, I was lucky enough to do a solo on the song *Purified* by Lamb Of God, and it was just like a kick in the butt, man, to remind me that there are still bands out there that are really cutting-edge. They reminded me of Megadeth on the first two records, except better. And they're better than we were, better players, and it was a lot of fun to do it, and it's just good to know that Dave, myself and Gar and Dave Ellefson influenced bands enough to make them play better than we could play that stuff, you know?"

And speaking of Ellefson, "He was the nice guy, in a word (laughs); that's how he was always described: Dave Ellefson, the nice guy! He was a great bass player. He was the perfect bass player, great performer, and he was the positive... You know, he does have the positive outlook—let's get this done. He was that guy. Not that they needed anybody to tell them how to get stuff done, but Dave Ellefson was always there to push things forward too."

Was he the cleanest of everybody?

"To begin with, he was. But in the end, I mean, everybody... once you start with that shit, it slowly takes over your life. It took over everybody's life, and luckily we all got sober."

As with **Cryptic Writings**, when it came to the cover art of **Risk**, all of the heavy metal visuals from the past were placed aside, with the creepy cat and mouse visuals cooked up for the project actually being pretty cool.

Inside the record however was music that was even lighter and more rock than last time out, and laced with industrial and other trendy recording appointments that made the fans upchuck.

"Well, I don't think there is that much of a difference," ventured Mustaine at the time, our interview this time taking place three weeks prior to the album's August 30, 1999 release date. "But I guess being involved with it, I guess you can't see the forest through the trees. But I imagine for somebody who is on the outside, it will be a little bit easier to imagine and pass judgment on and say it's a departure. For me, the band has just progressed along the same lines from when we started with **Countdown To Extinction**. Although **Cryptic Writings** and **Youthanasia** could have been flip-flopped, because of the melody and stuff, I think when we went from **Countdown To Extinction** to **Youthanasia**, the transition was an enormous step. **Cryptic Writings** was absolutely perfect for its time and space. But if **Cryptic Writings** would have come out before **Youthanasia**, it would have been an absolute perfect progression within the last four records. For us right now, **Risk** is probably the best timed record we've ever done as we're not over-shooting where our space and time is in history right now? And we're not playing it safe."

An interesting perspective and not altogether off-base, there, as Dave twins the previous two albums, I suppose a bit too closely. Indeed, his curious statement seems almost designed to plump for **Cryptic Writings** as a heavier record than **Youthanasia**. The tacit message a conspiracy theorist might derive from that is that with **Risk** arriving in a matter of days, Dave is preparing the fans to hate only the current record and forget their distaste for the last one.

Still, as evidenced on **Risk** opener *Insomnia*, the talk of progression is more apt, with **Risk**'s initial salvo sounding like a textured and trendy take on **Cryptic**'s more middle of the road moments. And yes, there's a pile of production here, to the point where one is almost surprised it's merely Nashville's old school Dan Huff back for a repeat performance.

"I think when you work on a song, you never know where it's going to end up," says Dave. "You don't know everything that's going to be on it. You just build with it. I would be dishonest if I said that I knew, yes, there is going to be this and that on a specific track, because you never really know. In fact, when you build a home, you have an idea of what it's going to look like, but you never know all the little nuances. For me to come up with some horseshit and say I knew where everything was going to be, I would just keep pretending that I was more than I am."

"I think the classic Megadeth sound is still there," continues Dave, addressing the song *Insomnia*, which Marty credits pretty much to Mustaine entirely, also indicating that it was one of the last things recorded for the album. "It's just that now it's the center of everything rather than being the totality. If you look at the stuff that is going on with the guitar riff in the middle where it's a synthesized guitar chord, well I still played a guitar chord, only I played it into a computer, and then we used the guitar chord modulating down, in a chromatic pattern during the verse riff. And some of the stuff that is going on in the middle... it's the guitar sound being almost like an underwater sound. Again, it's my guitars, my amps, but being played into a computer. The core sound is still there, it's just the way the signal has been processed."

Lyrically, the song is essentially autobiographical, revolving around what happens when drugs and booze screw with your sleep patterns. As for the modern sounds all over it, Dave admitted to being influenced by the industrial metal and techno sounds usurping metal's place in the popular imagination at the time, and wanting to get in on some of that action.

Prince Of Darkness is a heavier, more sinister track, but it's also chock full of production appointments to the point of belaboured. But it's pretty much modern-day pummelling Megadeth, locating a nice groove, even if the *Sympathy For The Devil*-themed lyric is a bit naff, Dave qualifying, however, that a deeper reading of it refers more so to his own personal demons. Given its metallic directness, the track felt good as a show opener for much of the **Risk** touring cycle.

"Yes, actually we took longer to record this record than any record so far," responds Dave, asked about all the details and arranging. "When we did **Cryptic Writings**, we got to Nashville in September, actually started in October, and finished some time around the end of December. With all the holidays in there, we had short weeks and we weren't working weekends. I believe we were done at the end of December or the beginning of January, and we were just doing stuff like television mixes, different mixes with vocals up and vocals down. With this one, we did our last concert December 31st, started the record January 3rd, and at the very first, we had a meet-and-greet fanfare for our fan club, and by the 3rd we were in Nashville and rockin'. We finished I think May 14th. And after that it was more of the production stuff behind the scenes, like going to Portland, Maine to have it mastered, do single mixes and so on."

Next up is a named intro called *Enter The Arena* which gives way to *Crush 'Em*, a song that was an advance track, and a controversial one at that, given its disco bass line, its sports theme and its arena rock chorus. What had the base even more up in arms is the radical alternative mix of the thing, Friedman sympathising, lamenting that the band threw too many ideas into it and listened to too many opinions of what it could and should be.

"*Crush 'Em* and *Insomnia* are the main ones," explained Dave, concerning different mixes. "When you and I say alternate mixes, I think of something different from what is on the record. That could just be an edited radio version or the really short radio version. And then there is alternative mixes, and we've got really successful with this first track on alternative radio in America. With our last record, we were the most rejected at alternative radio, and this time we are the most added."

By this, Dave is referring to *Crush 'Em* which was issued as a single four months ahead of the album, initially on the soundtrack to **Universal Soldier: The Return**. The song was intended as a hockey anthem, but it was general enough to get picked up in wrestling circles as well. Mustaine, a big Phoenix Coyotes fan, had offered the song to the team but didn't get very far. Silver lining, it got picked up for limited but general use by the NHL, and also the NFL and the UFC. As it turned out, Mustaine's plan to write something that would replace Gary Glitter's highly annoying *Rock And Roll Part 2* and the like scored a favourable result, additionally reaching No. 6 on the Billboard Mainstream Rock chart. Interestingly, the "crush 'em" mob chants were recorded at a fan fair in Phoenix, Dave leading his Mega-charges in the art of backing vocals while he held a DAT recorder up to his loyal throng.

Breadline also caused furrowed brows amongst the ranks of the faithful, being a relaxed and regular rocker with a shockingly melodic chorus, but one that all would have to admit, sticks in the brain but good. Lyrically, it's very much about poverty, with Mustaine relating how he and Dave Jr. used to drive past the soup kitchens, realizing that if the band didn't take off soon, they'd be in their own breadline but quick.

Marty Friedman, who co-writes on *Breadline* and in fact most of the album, fully admits that he had no problem with the poppier direction of the band at this point, in fact very much driving that side of it.

"I think my playing is really melodic because as well as being a heavy metal fan growing up and stuff, I'm a pop fan first and foremost," explains Freidman. "I'm really a great fan of pop songs and pop music. So that influence is something I don't think Dave had very much of. I think he is the most traditional heavy metaller that you can come up with. And I think I added an element, a massive pop mentality. So it's basically a real pop thing."

Asked to assess the band's two quote unquote pop records, after which, shockingly, he would be making his exit from the band, Marty figures that he was "relatively" happy with his final two records with Megadeth.

"I'm into reinventing myself and growing. And I am so totally not into repeating anything that's been done, especially that's been done to death and done 15 years ago (laughs). I had no intention of going back there. I mean, it's been done, and it's been done well and right on, it's 2001. So I might have been relatively happier with those two albums but I wanted to commit more to a wider direction, and more new things in the music. I wanted a bigger sound. I wanted it to be more intense. I mean, if I wanted something to be heavy, I wanted it to be so fucking heavy that you just wanted to kill yourself after hearing it. And if I wanted it to be pop, I wanted it to be the sappiest love ballad this side of the Backstreet Boys. I didn't want to do things half-heartedly and say, well, let's try to lighten up for these people, but keep it fast for these people. And I think Mustaine was trying to compromise somewhat to please me and to please a lot of people."

"But what was probably in his heart is that he just goes into default thrash metal mode," continues Marty, at this point speaking from his mini-empire in new hometown, Tokyo, right downtown! "That's his thing and that's what he does best and that's where he feels most natural and God bless him, let him keep doing that. That's what he is really meant to do and everything else is really, really a strain. And rather than us straining, me trying to grow one way and he going completely another way, the relationship became musically toxic, so to speak. It hadn't occurred in the new material, but I knew what was going to happen. I saw the writing on the wall one time when Dave said, 'Come on man, let's write a new album. I want it to be somewhere between Cacophony and **Rust In Peace**.' And like, I love both of those records, I really do, but the thought of even going there, it kind of burned me inside. It was like, fuck man, look at Metallica. Metallica is such a wonderful example of people showing the world that just because you're a heavy metal musician, it doesn't mean you have to just be playing all this thrash crap. It's like, they crossed over to everybody. I'm so impressed by what they did and they kept their dignity doing it. I really look up to them in a big way. I didn't want to copy them, but I wanted to keep growing the way they did. They grew in massive proportions each step they took. And when I heard, let's go back to copy this and copy that and do some of this old stuff we did before, I knew there was no way I could do it."

Unlike Nick Menza, Friedman's problem wasn't not being let in on the songwriting. The flash guitarist is in on seven of the **Risk** tracks.

"No, I wrote plenty," says Marty. "I wrote a lot of stuff; it's just that the stuff that I was writing... I wrote stuff that was full-on really poppy and really heavy and all points in-between. And the stuff that got on there was probably the stuff that fit the whole band at the time. I didn't have any complaints about the songwriting at all. It's just the stuff that wound up getting chosen of mine. I don't know, as I said, I always wanted to be more extreme, one way or the other. The middle ground just didn't appeal to me very much. My whole thing was that I was trying to get as far away as possible from the traditional sound that Megadeth had done, and done very well, but I wanted to get away from that. But for some reason there always had to be an element of that thrashy sound, that fast guitar picking sound. And I never thought that stuff translated live, especially where we were playing and where we wanted to play, those venues. Nobody does it and there's a reason nobody does it and it's because it sounds like shit. The stuff sounds great when you're in a small club and it's 1984 and people are just getting blown away by fast guitar like that. But I just thought it had been done so well in the past. God, I love heavy metal and all that New Wave Of British Heavy Metal—Raven, Angel Witch—but that has no relevance to anything I want to do now. It's in me, I grew up with that stuff, so it's definitely in my musicality but I don't make any reference to that when I'm trying to come up with a new song."

Breadline in particular had a role in Marty's impending departure from the band. Having played what he thought was his best solo on his favourite song on the album and then gone home, he later returned to hear the mixes, at which point he found that Dave had wiped his solo and done his own, the consensus being that Marty's solo was too happy.

That's neither here nor there as pertains to the band's identity crisis however, one that had acutely been plaguing Megadeth doppel-headbangers Metallica at this juncture in time as well. "I was never very good at double bass," deadpans Dave, when I told him about Lars Ulrich and his observation that as he played more of this general rock stuff, his double bass skills had suffered. My point was wondering whether there were intensifying parallels between the two bands and the accessible types of music they were playing in the late '90s.

"I think it's flattering to think that we are similar to them, although I know that's not what you are saying. For us to see a similarity would be pretty bold on our part because they have been so successful. For us, when we take into consideration how many musical styles are out there, and take into consideration also that our own personal satisfaction is really important... obviously we have to appease the fans. But you know, if we keep making the same record over and over again, it's not going to be necessary to make a new record. Well just put a new cover on an old one. So, I don't think the fans are stupid, and the ones that are not really fans in the first place, those are the ones that are going to say, 'Hey, we don't like this stuff.' People that are fair weather fans are the ones that like the flavour of the month. You know, if you're really into hardcore stuff and you don't like our new direction, man, that is so cool. That is okay by me, and I don't really care. I remember listening to Zeppelin **IV**, and I remember listening to **In Through The Out Door**; they are two totally different types of records, but they're still Led Zeppelin and I'm still a fan. And even *Hot Dog* to me, even though for the life of me I couldn't understand why they put that song on the record, I've grown to like it. You know, when you're a fan of a band, you're a fan of the band. You're not one of these people who say, 'Oh, you suck now.' They're all entitled to their opinion. Their opinion doesn't matter and neither does mine. Thank you for your support, but if you don't like us any more, that's fine."

"There's nothing that I have been listening to that has inspired me for this particular record," continued Dave. "There is stuff we did listen to during the creative process. But although we listened to it, it really did not influence the songs. There's a lot of music out right now that is really great, a lot of new metal bands, a lot of classic bands, even some of the dinosaur bands that came out of ancient history and are out touring. Even though their new stuff sucks, their classic hits are great. I think music in general, given that, that is what I've chosen for my career, I have to be well versed and brushed up on it. I need to be up on what I'm doing. I need to know what is out there and keep open ears on the competition. It perhaps kind of puts the odds in your favour a little bit."

Brushing up on Alice or not, *The Doctor Is Calling* has a distinct Alice Cooper vibe being a classy, creepy ballad, layered with cool textures and some middle eastern Zeppelin melodies, as well as spoken bits which again, remind one of Alice and his conversational style. *I'll Be There* is another melodic track with a bit of a psychedelic grunge vibe inside of the melody. All told, the track supports this idea of the band getting ambitious with their arrangements and Mustaine looking for emotional connections of a more mature sort, Dave coming up with what is one of Marty's favourite vocals on the album, Friedman also calling out the chorus of *Ecstasy*. Dave particularly appreciates the lyric on this one, which he pairs with *In My Darkest Hour*, both concerning the subject of loyalty, but this one written as a message directly to the fans.

"I don't know that it is southern rock so much," says Dave of *Wanderlust*, one of the rich and dark horses of the record, Megadeth addressing a style that fits well, although I can't help but hearing Bon Jovi's *Wanted Dead Or Alive* in it. "When I think of southern rock, I think of the Allman Brothers, the Outlaws, Skynyrd. Those are bands that I respect but I don't really like or listen to. I think that Lynyrd Skynyrd has some fantastic guitar. It's just not stuff I would listen to if I had a choice. I think what we tried to accomplish with that song was our version of **The Good, The Bad And The Ugly**. Clint Eastwood was very influential on my whole life. I watched all his movies growing up. It's all about how the young guns are always trying to take on the fastest gun, how they continue to try and track this person down, and they want a gun fight because he's the fastest. And how many people inevitably die trying to get a reputation. This has happened with a lot of the newer bands that have come around trying to out-heavy us or out-speed us, and stuff like that. The same thing happened when it was the very beginning with the big four, us and Metallica and Slayer and Anthrax. Everyone went after their particular target so to speak. Any one of us four they would try to take on. And the four of us are still here, although we've all gone to our different degrees of success. The bands that came after us in the beginning have all fallen by the wayside."

Still, harping on the southern rock of it all, *Wanderlust* even includes a sped-up rave bit, before settling back into its sturdy stadium rock chorus, as well as choice acoustic guitar picking a desperado tune. These are all southern rock tropes and they amusingly can be mapped within this oddball yet worthy track.

And **Risk** stays poppy, and, paradoxically if you are Megadeth, risky, with *Ecstasy*, which is something like an uptempo ballad, like dark Tom Petty, but again, digging into the guts of human connectivity, Dave writing about a girl who knows the relationship isn't going to work, but that it's a buzz worth continuing for as long as it lasts.

"I think it's the same thing I've been writing about for the past four records," notes Mustaine. "But I think by moving away from death and insanity and politics and war, I've been able to reach more people. Because unless you are a soldier, or fucking insane, or dead, those songs don't really strike a chord with you. For the most part, the politicking in the world, most people are just so over it, you know? And it's so sad, because voting is the way you decide your future. And politics have become so corrupt that even to sing about it anymore is just like, you're wasting your time. People just don't want to hear about it anymore. They want to hear about how to get through the day, and have as much fun as they can, and find Mrs. Right or Mrs. Right Now, and have a good time with their friends."

Asked how roles have changed in the band on **Risk**, Dave says, "It's funny that you say that, because I played more guitar on this record than I have in about five or six records. The last record that I played this much on was probably **Rust In Peace**. And that is because after we cut our basic rhythm tracks, Marty Friedman went home and I continued playing and playing and playing and playing, until it was time for him to come back out. And by the time he came back out, we recognized that all the stuff that he was supposed to have done, was done, except for his solos, and some really tasty kind of texturing parts."

Next up is *Seven* (as in the deadly sins), a minimalist yet brisk rocker with a kind of Gene Simmons riff—the song's original title was *Hornet Fuck* and then *Anti-Hero*. By vibe, it's somewhat AC/DC-tilted, but of construct, it's a weirdly modest party rocker, and a song that Marty says is the least-produced on the album. "You know, we were in Japan and I came up with the riff," notes Mustaine. "And we were just goofing around and all of a sudden everybody who was working with our staff just kind of stopped and listened, and I knew we were onto something. And actually the very beginning of the riff of the song where it sounds like it's coming from a little tiny amplifier? The amplifier was inside of a box of cigarettes. There was a plug in the top of the cigarettes, and then a hole where it comes out the opposite side to go to another amp and to go into the console. And there's a speaker about two inches in the front of this amp. We set up a microphone and we we're shaking the cigarette pack in front of the microphone to get that sort of oscillating sound."

Seven is a simple song, and, perceptively, simplicity is something Marty

Friedman in particular noticed worked best in a live environment, as opposed to the wall-of-sound thrash of **Rust In Peace**. "Yeah, and people don't appreciate it and the people that do appreciate it, wouldn't be there. It's just something that was done wonderfully before and there's no reason, for me anyway, to do it again. If others want to do it, that's great. It was one of those things where I said I can't really support this anymore. It's not a fight that I want to spend my life fighting, holding up the flag for traditional heavy metal."

Marty is appreciative of new drummer Jimmy DeGrasso and his performance on this track. However, DeGrasso wasn't exactly digging making his first record with Megadeth.

"When we were doing **Risk**, I was like cringing," says Jimmy. "I was like, oh, really? The songs are not good. But I'd only joined the band like four or five months earlier, so I couldn't really say anything—because I had to respect what they wanted to do. Because Dave and the other two guys had been in the band obviously longer. But I had basically zero interest in doing **Risk**."

As for producer Dan Huff, "You know, I thought he seemed like a nice enough guy. He's a musician. He was good at corralling the band. I thought he was sort of conservative. I thought he should've let the band maybe out of its box a bit more. But I thought he did a good job. I mean, come the end of the day, the album sounds good; I think sonically it's a good record. I just think some of the songs I just don't care for. I think there are a couple good songs, but there a lot of songs I prefer to never hear again. On **Risk**, there was a song called *The Doctor Is Calling*, which was a really slow song, and wasn't a difficult song to play, but I just like interesting grooves. Sometimes I like slow, moodier grooves. I thought that was a good drum track."

Things get ambitious for the record's closing pair *Time: The Beginning* and *Time: The End*. "Pretty much it's about my race with time, and trying to stay ahead of the obvious hourglass of my life," says Mustaine. "Because I think a lot of us in the world, especially now, are trying to conquer aging. I mean, I'm comfortable where I'm at with my life and my age and everything like that. And you see these people who are like 40 and 50 years old and they wear like kids clothes and they'll hang out at young places. I watched this movie **Varsity Blues**, and the funniest thing in that was this dude who showed up at this high school party, and one of the guys who was actually on the high school team said, 'Put this hat on' and then he said, 'I'm going to hit this guy right in the nuts' or the stomach or something, baseball bat right between the legs. It was because he was out of place. And I think that what the song *Time: The Beginning* is about, is, hey, I know that time is sneaking up on me; it's sneaking up on everybody. And then *Time: The End* is where time and I are face-to-face and what is going to happen."

Yet oddly, *Time: The End* is one of the most uptempo, cooler pieces on the record, blessed with an irresistible and almost sublime riff that keeps coming back, despite strong competition from a panoramic and passionate chorus where time, specifically Cronos, the Greek god of time, seems to be winning. Great track, and one of the better examples this side of **Countdown**, of Megadeth writing high quality accessible metal songs that aren't thrash.

Touring for **Risk** found the band filling in all of the latter half of 1999, highlight being a European jaunt supporting Iron Maiden. On the US west coat in January of 2000, Megadeth would play their last show with Marty Friedman on guitar, at Seattle's Moore Theater on January 14th.

It's no surprise to the band's drummer Jimmy DeGrasso, that Marty's replacement, Al Pitrelli, was ready to go two nights later, at the famed Commodore Ballroom in Vancouver, notably a large club, reflecting Megadeth's declining fortunes at this point.

"Marty's got a strange approach to the guitar," chuckles DeGrasso, asked to compare the two. "He's got something that's a little bit out to the left, but Marty's an awesome guitar player and a really nice guy. And Al, he's the ultimate gunslinger. That's what he is. He's one of the best guitar players I know. He could play anything. I mean, he could walk into any situation. That guy could pick up any stick with a string on it and make it sound good. It's unbelievable. Like I saw him play one night. He was in the Bay Area one night, and he was just filling in for Blue Öyster Cult. I said, 'When did you start playing with them?' He said, 'Oh, I'm just filling in, because their bass player's sick.' And I go to the gig, and backstage before the gig, his Les Paul broke. They just got done gluing his Les Paul headstock on (laughs). Later he was trading solos with Buck, and I'm thinking... but Al, he's a natural, and then he sits down and start playing organ. And it's like, 'When did you learn to play keyboards?' 'Oh, about a week ago.' He's just one of those guys."

"I don't know what to say,' said Friedman, with a laugh, reflecting on his departure a few months after the fact. "But I've got to tell you, I really wish them the best. I know that they wanted to do a real back to the real nuts and bolts Megadeth. And compared to the stuff that I was writing, I'm sure that is exactly what they did do (laughs). But I tell you, as I said, if you listen to **Risk**, the heaviest stuff on that is stuff that I wrote, as well as the lightest stuff. And I wanted to make the heavier stuff heavier and the lighter stuff lighter. I mean, if it's going to be heavy, let's just make it sick heavy. If it's going to be pop... you're not going to get the chicks if it's still got all this distorted guitar in there. And I think he probably had more on the line than I did when it comes to committing to something because he is the front man in the group and it is maybe riskier for him to change his image that much. But I was ready to go full-on into the pop realm and just piss off a whole lot of people."

"I can't even compare those records," continues Friedman. "I've always liked all of them. I guess **Cryptic Writings** was the one where I thought we had the most hope to build in a direction that would at least please me. I don't know about the other guys. But I think **Cryptic** showed the most promise. But I may have to agree with all the fans and say that the best record of all the time that I was in the band anyway is **Rust In Peace**, just for sheer excitement and chemistry. It was more like a test than anything else. Nick hadn't recorded anything with the band and I hadn't either. It was like two very new guys. Nobody knew each other and what we were going to do, so everybody was just playing their ass off and it was done really traditionally. It wasn't recorded with a lot of effects or anything, just straight-ahead, balls-out dry. It had a great impact and it was a good representative record of what we were doing at the time. But you can't repeat that again. It wouldn't nearly be as good."

But now up into **Risk**, despite very sincere and real creative differences, there was that recurring cloak of bad vibes and negativity that seems to shroud the band, on and off, but on enough to cause that sort of reputation, a nagging realization in the heavy metal community that Megadeth's closet was filling up with skeletons.

"That's kind of another reason why I didn't want to be around that environment," agrees Marty. "I don't want to get into it, but I don't like negativity. It's funnier now that I'm not in the band (laughs), but when I heard that kind of stuff when I was in the band it was like oh, come on."

Reflecting back on Dave Ellefson's role in Megadeth, Marty figures that, "I think without Dave Ellefson in the band, there would have been no Megadeth. Ellefson has just been the perfect band member, but not just for Megadeth, but I think for any band. I think if you've got somebody like Dave Ellefson in the band, you're going to do well. Because he's the kind of guy you can always count on to play well and do what it takes to get the band to the next level. Just being the diplomat of the band. Just wherever he goes, he's going to represent the band well and just be a good inter-band relationship-type guy. When you're living with each other for ten years, 24 hours a day, you need a guy like that, that has a good brain and knows how to deal with people and just a good friend kind of guy and a perfect player for the music we were doing, and always learning new stuff."

"I'll tell you a funny story if you have time," continues Friedman. "During the end of days of when I was in the band, there was this Japanese pop singer. I'm way into Japanese pop music, and I was playing this Japanese pop singer's music and I was jamming to it with this guitar in the back of the bus. Dave Ellefson picks up the bass and he starts jamming this stuff, and it's like really interesting music, totally avant-garde techno pop, but really upbeat and poppy sounding, and I'm showing him these odd chord changes in this song and we're going over it and we're jamming and getting really into it and there were a couple of other people in the back of the bus. And

Mustaine walks into the back lounge where we're jamming this stuff, and I mean, you kind of have to hear this pop music to get the full effect. Imagine the gayest pop that you can possibly imagine with a chick singer whose voice is like 70 octaves higher than anybody, and we're just jamming along to this. And Mustaine walks into the back lounge and he looks at the two of us like, what the fuck are you guys doing?! Just the look on his face was worth like a million bucks. I think he was worried that I was writing this new tune and showing it to Dave. But I think the writing was on the wall. But you know, he knew what he wanted his band to sound like and I can't fault him for that. I don't have a problem with that at all. If I had a heavy metal band and all of a sudden the guitar player is playing all this disco, I'm surely not going to be too pleased about it."

So... as we close the book on Megadeth's first (second?) phase, as longstanding fans, looking in at what we know about the psychology of Dave Mustaine, do we think Dave was pleased that **Risk** had garnered Megadeth a gold record?

If the answer is yes, I'm sure it was a bittersweet sentiment accompanied by a crooked smile. If there was any degree of satisfaction having reached that plateau, surely for a sourpuss like Dave, pretty much all he could make out half-blind through the snowstorm was that fully the previous six Megadeth albums—an incredible stretch of fortune for an, ahem, uncompromising metal band—had done shiny platinum or even bloody better.

What must've stuck in the craw even worse however, was that the band's loyal fans—many now as mad at Metallica as Dave perennially was—had come to the realization that in these non-metal times, they couldn't count on Dave and Dave Jr. either to fly the tattered flag like the stout-of-heart Slayer, the punk rocking Anthrax, or the army of brash upstarts invading our shores from Sweden, or the Next Four, or, or, or...

Megadeth had, alas, risen through the fecund period that was thrash in its adolescence and by the close of the decade fallen hard. Representing that fall, **Risk** was a befuddled risk as well as an equally ill-executed flight to safety—and it pleased no one, or at least no one that would matter in Dave's life as he would begin to see clearly post-Friedman. However, this tale does not end badly. In fact, as the '90s gave way to the '00s and 9/11, Dave would kill his band to rise again, madder 'n hell at geopolitics but, after a few fits and starts, arriving at a Zen-like peace forged within the purest of metals, recreating, as it were, a new and fully metallic Megadeth situated at the eye of the tornado.

10
THE WORLD NEEDS A HERO
"Put your head down and play real hard"

After the abuse Dave Mustaine and his hurtin' Megadeth took for their eighth record, 1999's anaemic **Risk**—and with none of those big commercial rewards the band were supposed to cull, presumably by selling CDs to girls—it was time to pause, reflect, and maybe, just maybe, kick some ass and take names.

One rock 'n' roll symbol of that pause is the dissemination of a greatest hits album, a document that tends to send a signal to the fans that one era is over, long live whatever the hell their band of brothers do next. Unfortunately, a greatest hits album also often means contractual obligation and in Megadeth's case, that's what was going on, with the band now off the fabled, stable major and onto exciting new start-up Sanctuary, domain of Rod Smallwood and by extension the strong man's Iron Maiden empire.

"The new record is finished, but the next record that will probably be released will be the greatest hits record," said Dave in my next sit-down with the larger-than-life ginger, this time backstage at Toronto's Molson Amphitheater, August of 2000, Mustaine explaining that the actual next studio record was intended for Capitol release, along with what would become **Capitol Punishment: The Megadeth Years**.

"We had a contract with Capitol and my word is very important to me, my integrity and my honour, and I finished my contractual obligation with Capitol, gave them the record, and then we were done. And then we went back to them and said we want the record back (laughs). And they said OK, because the relationship has been productive but it's been very difficult with a lot of different presidents there. Some were great, some were not. Oddly enough, the guy that is there now was gracious enough to let us go. We just have to give them a couple of songs and they get the greatest hits record and we get our freedom. And the sad thing is we're going to miss a lot of people that have been there with us forever. You know, when you take on a new job, it's like marrying into a family and you've got stepkids. You know, you want to love them, but you are also saying, 'You little fuckers.' And we've always been the red-headed stepchildren with all these new presidents that come in. And consequently we're not the only ones who have had to suffer with administration change after administration change. With all due respect to all the presidents who have been there, they're all fine, professional people and I think they've all done really well for us helping us get to where we're at. But the time has come to make a change and we're grateful to Capitol that they are willing to let us go."

"We're talking to some people now," continued Dave, who was not yet signed to a new label at the point of our chat back in the dog days of summer 2000. "We're almost at the definitive moment with a couple of people where we're going to tell them yea or nay. Some of the people we talked to, they would say no, or we would say no, or it was a mutual not interested. And some of them were really interested and they didn't have the kind of money we were looking for. And some of the people had the kind of money we were looking for but they didn't have the wherewithal to take a band of our stature. You really have to know what you are dealing with, with a platinum act."

Dave's plan was, in fact, to call the next studio album **Capitol Punishment**, bringing up the question, er, what did the brass at Capitol think of that idea? (Cooler heads ultimately prevailed, Mustaine going with the curious **The World Needs A Hero** instead).

"We actually asked Roy Lott, the president of Capitol before we had named the record, if that was okay with him, because we wanted his good graces on it. And then I decided I didn't want to call it **Capitol Punishment** anymore. When we turned in the record, you see, we didn't think they were going to let us go. We thought we would turn it in and they would say, 'Hey, this is a great record' blah, blah, blah. And I believe it's a really good record, but Capitol is trying to reposition themselves in the urban pop market and a little happy band called Megadeth from Arizona really doesn't fit into the pop world. So they were okay with it. And in fact they are calling the greatest hits record **Capitol Punishment** after we said we didn't want to call our studio album that anymore. And the whole purpose wasn't about Capitol punishing us, like that guy Graham Parker who called his record *Mercury Poisoning*. It's not a dig at the record label; it's that the music was punishment during our Capitol years. We feel we've had a really good run. 20 years in the music industry for me is a long time and we've been with Capitol like 15 years or something. And they've really helped us out, but now is the time that they are really going to shine because they are primarily a catalogue-type label and I think they're really going to help us with the sales of our catalogue."

As a taster toward where the band might be going on the follow-up to **Risk**, Megadeth included two new tracks on the hits pack. Said Dave of *Kill The King* and *Dread & The Fugitive Mind*, "They are from the same session as the new studio album. There was only one session. We just went in and hammered it out from beginning to end."

Kill The King (it being the title of a classic Rainbow song would not have been lost on Dave)is a choppy, rhythmic, monotone mid-paced thrasher with a melodic pre-chorus and an urgently metal chorus, certainly nothing like anything from the past two records other than *She-Wolf*. *Dread & The Fugitive Mind* on the other hand is an exactor knife of a stop-starter every bit as good as the best tracks on **Countdown**. Here, the heavier song is not in fact the best; rather, it's Dave as a consummate "less is more" songwriter that wins the day.

"Although they did say we could use them on our new record," explained Dave at the time, "I think that that's a little peculiar with them having the rights to them and us putting them on the new record and then that new record company having to send money back to Capitol. It's a very clever business ploy but I don't know if we're going to do that. I don't know if we have to do that because we have some more songs left over."

Ultimately what happened is that Dave split the difference and included *Dread*—wisely played, as, again, it's the far superior track.

Before, however, any of this occurrence of a corrective new album would happen, Megadeth would follow up their contribution of *Paranoid* to the **Nativity In Black** Sabbath tribute, with the much more interesting choice of *Never Say Die* for **Nativity In Black II**, issued on June 6, 2000. Both performances breathed fire, and both selections made perfect sense for Megadeth, given Sabbath's mostly domineer canon. As well, during this transitional period, Megadeth found themselves doing a shed tour called Maximum Rock, through the summer of 2000 with, of all bands, Mötley Crüe.

"I can't get into that," says Mustaine, asked about problems that occurred with Anthrax along the way. "That's none of my business. Mötley Crüe is headlining this tour and they decided to make it a Megadeth/Mötley Crüe package and that is something you would have to take up with them. I know the truth and my feelings towards the whole thing. Whether it ever becomes public or not or what is in the public is the actual truth, you know, I'm not going to go on record and say anything. We have no comment. I think if anybody wants Mötley Crüe's reasoning for doing it, they need to look in Nikki's press release. And you know that whatever the reason is or was, five of my friends aren't out here right now."

But why tour with the Crue? "Did you ever see their audience? Did you ever see all those tits out there? (laughs). No, just kidding. One of the things is that the money was really good. And you know, when we play in T.O., we're at the fucking Warehouse every time. You know, this is a great opportunity for us to play the Molson Amphitheatre. We had to think, do we want to sit at home this summer? Or do we want to go with Mötley Crüe and play in sheds? And we can pick up new fans too because it's a different audience. I'll tell you what, the girls that are there to see Mötley Crüe, they say the difference between us and them, some of them are like, 'Ick!' and some of them are like, 'Yeah baby!' And I'm digging that a lot of the Mötley Crüe fans that are guys are going, 'Who are these Megger-deth guys? They're pretty heavy!' A lot of people don't know who we are."

"But don't kid yourself. Mötley Crüe does not sound like us. They are louder here because they have the P.A. clamped, which is part of the game that you play when you are the headliner. And they've got girls up on stage who are really, really terrific people and I think they are foxes. And I know them backstage without their costumes on and everything. And they've got the pyro and bombs and glitter and snow that comes from the ceiling and stuff. And personally, I mean, I like some of the Mötley Crüe songs—not all of them but I know some of them. And I think Vince is a very up-front kind of guy. He'll tell you what he's thinking. I guess he hand-picked us. He wanted to play with us for awhile. I'm flattered about that. But you have to remember, they were fucking enormous. And the reason we agreed to do this is because it's very similar to the Guns N' Roses/Metallica package, a glam band and a metal band."

Essentially, all this was happening because of the concurrent success of the Poison packages going out at the time, probably the biggest chunk of evidence that glam could make any sort of comeback... "Oh man, Mötley Crüe should be on the Poison tour, no doubt about it, because that's their type of audience. And I think that we probably should have been on the Iron Maiden tour, but I don't think it would have been appropriate for us to support Iron Maiden in the states, because we are bigger than they are here. And I don't think that they would have felt that it would have been prudent for them to support us."

Meanwhile, Dave was breaking in on stage a new guitarist called Al Pitrelli. "It's very similar to how me and Marty worked," says Dave, always game to play up the new hire. "I play with a lot of hate and Al plays with a lot of love. I'm not a technician. I'll hit bad notes and not give a shit because I don't care. I play with feelings and it's not about being perfect every night. Granted, I wish I was better that I could be perfect every night. And I get really close but I hit a couple of clams every once in awhile. And then you have to deal with the idiots yelling, 'Hey, fuck you,' and they're holding up their shirts with you-know-who on it. And it's like, you know what? I get a paycheck from those guys so it doesn't matter. All you're doing is going, 'Hey, remember these guys? They're paying for your new house!' You know? Stupid cunts."

As for highlights from being out with LA's bad boys (who was worse is up for debate!), "Uh, this is the first time that a band we've been on tour with has jumped into the audience and beat up one of our fans. Nikki and Vince jumped into the audience in Mexico City and beat up one of our fans. And I don't know if he asked for it or not."

Not anything to do with Vince being hit with a bolt then? "No, and you know what? That's really sad. Because you know, I'm not really close with Vince but he goes out there and he tries really hard to do his thing and he has his own personal demons, and being hit with a foreign object that is solid and in the face. I've been hit before and I don't appreciate it. It makes me think what the fuck is wrong with you people? I wouldn't go see a AC/DC or Led Zeppelin or Page/Plant for that matter and throw something at them. I think a lot of it has to do with the fact that some people are very anti-Motley or anti-Megadeth and they come to the concert to see one or the other and they don't want to tolerate the other band. I mean, look at Woodstock in the '60s. You had Joan Baez and Jimi Hendrix. How much farther extreme can you get? You're looking at one girl by herself playing a guitar and then you're looking at guy who has about four hundred of himself going on in his head."

Squelching rumours that Megadeth's days on the Motley tour were numbered... "As far as us leaving the tour, that's news to me. I wouldn't know. I mean, us leaving the tour. Us getting kicked off the tour? Maybe. That could be a scoop and we can be going home tonight, I don't know (laughs) . And that would be something to ask Mötley Crüe."

Have you complained about anything? "No, I think we put our heads down and we've worked our asses off."

There's no reason they should kick you off, then? "There's probably plenty of reasons (laughs). But if we're going home, I don't know about it."

Back in the world of shiny silver, **Capitol Punishment** emerged on October 24, 2000 and indeed was a standard hits pack, but with the two aggressive new tracks leading the proceedings. Lyrics to every song were also included, as was a hidden track called *Capitol Punishment* which was a sound effects-laden medley/remix of sorts, sampling a bunch of Megadeth hits. The CD has sold over 200,000 copies but is currently out of print. Still, somewhat robust numbers like that indeed demonstrate the business case for compilations, even if the dedicated fan pays them little attention because they already have all—or in this case most—of the music.

More importantly, six months later, Megadeth revealed their new nastier selves with the previously alluded to **The World Needs A Hero**, issued May 15th of 2001. On the cover, there it was, Megadeth's time-honoured spiky metal logo as well as abused and abusive band mascot Vic Rattlehead, who is pictured crawling out of what one supposes is a Megadeth fan.

When asked a few months later how the band patched up since-soured relations with legendary cover artist Hugh Syme (of Rush fame), faithful bassist and sturdy mid-Westerner Dave Ellefson says, "I think that's our new management's doing, because in the course of things, how they happened, Marty leaving the band, Al Pitrelli coming in, us writing the songs, recording the record, turned it into Capitol, and asked for the record back... which they did. They took two songs, *Dread & The Fugitive Mind* and *Kill The King*, off the record, we finished up the summer tour, cleaned house, got new management, and got a new record label, Sanctuary Records and consequently went back into the studio to record a couple more songs and ended up recording several more songs to complete the record. And

Sanctuary really wanted the record; they wanted it to be a really heavy record and actually I think it was somebody at the record company who wanted to have Vic back on the cover again, our mascot. And to answer your question now (laughs), our manager, he had loved the work that Hugh Syme had done in the past, especially with Megadeth. So that was where we put the whole thing back together again."

True to how ex-guitarist Marty Friedman characterized Dave's thought process, when I told Dave I wasn't too enamoured with **Risk**, Mustaine makes peace, as he does so well, but usually with a bit of an edge.

"You know what? That's okay. Your opinion doesn't matter and neither does mine. The thing we tried to do with that album is tap into some musical outlets that we hadn't done before. And if this new record we're putting out is my last, which I hope it isn't, if it is, I didn't want to go out like a punk. I wanted to say that I had explored all the musical avenues that were inside of me. With MD.45, I got to get a lot of my harder punk crap out of my veins, and with **Risk** I got out a lot of the music that has been hanging around with me for years and years. And you know, now it's a clean slate and we went back to just put your head down and play real hard."

"The basic tracking was done at A&M Studios in California in Hollywood, and it's no longer called A&M now," continues Dave, explaining the birthing of **The World Needs A Hero**. "It was bought by the Henson Muppet company, whatever. It's like Muppet rock now (laughs). and we did the overdubs at The Salt Mine in Mesa, Arizona and we did the mixing at a place called Scream in Studio City, California."

So the band had moved on past Dann Huff and song-central Nashville, where they had crafted two records in a row, the "Fall" in the subtitle to the first book of our potent pairing.

"We're done with that whole thing," says Dave. "I mean, we love the people in Nashville, Tennessee and I think that Jeff Balding and Dan Huff are terrific people. We just kind of lost sight of what Megadeth's core charter is. This is a metal band, a hard rock band. It's not an alternative band and it's not pop. Granted, we're not an ugly band into babies on swords and shit like that like a lot of these wankers are. But we've got to do what we do, which is put your head down and hammer it out."

"I'll tell you this," figures six-stringer Friedman, at this point gone but understanding where Dave wanted to go with **The World Needs A Hero**. "If **Risk** would have gone multi-platinum and our heaviest stuff would have been our calling card, it might have been different. But the record went gold, which is respectable or whatever, but it didn't change anybody's lives or anything. It made it all the easier for Dave to go into what he does most comfortably, which is play kick-ass metal. There are very few who can do it as well as he does. It really comes natural and that's his bag. He does it great. I think his new album is as much of a risk as he wanted to take. So with the mediocre success of **Risk**, it made it all the easier for him to go, OK, I'm going to make this heavy record next time. But I never thought the heavy stuff he wrote was very heavy. I think the popular heavy rock today is so much heavier than the stuff that Megadeth was writing. Even our remotely heaviest stuff wasn't even close. Like, why even bother competing with that? But as far as heavy rocks goes, you can needle-drop on about 20 different heavy albums that are so incredibly heavy. But you know, we defined heavy differently. He defines heavy as being fast and busy and I define it as stuff that just makes your throat go dry when you hear it."

And it really was this creative musical quandary that was at the heart of Friedman leaving, not any problems with Dave being a difficult "rock star."

"You know, I love rock star stuff," affirms Friedman. "Especially for a lead singer. I think the lead singer should be the ultimate rock star. I'm way into rock star stuff and I hope he continues to be a rock star (laughs) because that's what I am and am born to be. People don't like that term rock star, but tough, I can't do anything else. I think there's nothing wrong with that. But I think his behaviour turns off a lot of people, a lot of people with the potential to help the band, career and all that. And that sort of turned me off. But it wasn't the deciding factor in me leaving the band or anything. But that kind of behaviour was a little bit detrimental. The negativity especially. I'm an extremely positive person, really into, let's have a good time, let's party. So the negativity was kind of toxic to me. The thing is, what counteracted that is that I know that David is a good guy, and he's always been a good friend to me. He would be the kind of guy that I would want to have as my friend. So I was very forgiving to that rock star stuff because I thought hey man, we are rock stars! So whatever, you know what I mean? You can do that shit. But I always knew he was a good guy and he was never uncool to me so I had no problems with him. It was really only the music that made me want to leave the band. And you'll hear it. When you hear my new stuff you'll get the whole picture (laughs)."

"I can honestly tell you that it's back to what Megadeth is," promised Dave, describing to me **The World Needs A Hero**, at the time of our next chat, finished but unreleased. "It's just what we are. If you look at the first record, there's a lot of really fast stuff on it and there's a lot of really emotional stuff on it. I mean, it's not 200 miles an hour like a lot of people think it's going to be. It's probably more along lines of **Rust In Peace** and **Countdown** than anything else."

Assessing the catalogue at this juncture, Mustaine figures, "You know, I hear **Youthanasia** some times and I think there are things on there I would have done differently. I would have sped some of the tempos up. Max Norman, who you see in the **Evolver** video, is counting the BPM, telling us how fast the songs should be. And I never let anybody pick the tempos of the songs—I always did that. But you see, being an alcoholic, in my alcoholic thinking, more is better. So when we had the success of **Countdown**, Max helped, so let's let Max help more! And I used more of his ideas. And granted, he's a great producer, but that album backfired on us because people don't want to hear all those songs at 120 beats per minute. He said that's the formula for rock radio, 120 beats per minute. And I couldn't have made a bigger mistake than believing that. But for me, I gotta just do what I do. And that's why on this new record there's stuff that's fast, there's stuff that's slow, there's stuff that is extremely heavy, there's a nine minute song on it, there's stuff that has like an Irish violin on it. I just got this whole cross-sampling of all this stuff in my head because I think it's what my fans want to hear. Not what we have to do (shaking and hitting the **Risk** CD) to get on MTV and radio. Now consequently the manager who was working with me on this record... I have two managers with ESP; the band doesn't work with the other guy anymore because of this situation that happened with this record. I still respect and admire him very much, but the other band members don't want anything to do with him so in honouring the band's relationship with each other, he's not involved with our business any more."

But Dave doesn't blame Capitol for what happened with **Risk**. "No, they did really good, but I think what happened was if you would have put the record out with just my name on it or anybody else's name on it, it would have been enormous. But because the word Megadeth was on there, it turned people off. It turned our fans off. And I'm cool with that, because we had great success with it in a lot of foreign countries. It was huge. In America, it did OK, it didn't do great. In Europe it did OK, but not great. What is great?"

Fact is, Dave's right about the label's support of **Risk**. Sure, the band delivered the type of toned-down record any major label could get behind, but get behind it they did, advertising it to the fullest, making sure the band was well pushed into press duties, all told, working with Dave and the crew to put in front of as many people as possible. The problem was, the late '90s were a bad time for anybody who looked or sounded metal, and simply turning down your metal wasn't enough in a world swirled by alternative and hard alternative and whatever you want to call what came after grunge.

Instantly, once inside **The World Needs A Hero**, one notices the crunchier sound picture Dave wanted to re-paint, here in not only a new (last) decade or new (dead) century, but new millennium. Indeed, opener *Disconnect* sounds like a mid-intensity **Countdown** track, pushed face-forward through a plaintive display of guitar, vocals, bass and drums. Lyrically, Dave has said that the track is about "living a double life," the divide between the public self and the private self, and how when things go south, we disconnect.

"Bill Kennedy co-produced it," continues Mustaine, asked about the record's sonic qualities, Megadeth, in this writer's opinion, having never again faltered in this area since the under-water knob job soaking **So Far,**

So Good... So What!

"He did an unbelievable job of recording the record. The sounds are really, really, for me, nothing like **Risk** and **Cryptic Writings**. I mean, there are some moments on **Cryptic Writings** that really capture Megadeth's power, and the songwriting was really developed for me. I learned a lot about songwriting and formulas and stuff like that which I used in **Risk**. But **Risk**'s tone is really, really far away from what Megadeth is about. I think a lot of that had to do with the fact also that Marty Friedman wanted to put his signature sound onto **Risk** where he was—obvious unbeknownst to me but obvious to the rest of the world—signalling his departure, because of his desire to play another type of music. It's evident on the record. You know, we wanted to keep harmony in the band by allowing certain things to happen, concessions and so on, and I guess we didn't make a big enough concession. And Marty, there's no replacing Marty Friedman. We've now got Al Pitrelli, and I want him to be the best Al he can be, but he's not forced into being a Marty Friedman or a Jeff Young or a Chris Poland or anyone for that matter."

Next up is the title track, on which Dave continues to add to his bank of anti-government rants, warnings and salvos against those who rule, nefariously, secretly, in collusion, a rabbit hole and topic and consideration that take up more and more of Dave's brain power as the years wear on. Dave's no Ted Nugent or Alex Jones, but what those two seem to be consumed with every waking hour... it's like catnip to an addictive personality.

The track is another crunchy rocker, no surprise, says Jimmy Degrasso, drummer on a Megadeth record for the second and last time. "The band was trying to blatantly write to get radio airplay on **Risk**, and then on **World Needs A Hero**, the band was ready to try to win metal fans back. It's pretty simple. Real simple. With **Risk**, I think the band collectively was not happy with the result. Personally, the record didn't thrill me. I didn't think it was that good as a whole. But I will say that a lot of people who never liked Megadeth, like that record. You know what I'm saying? Because I remember, a friend of mine, you know, saying I've never really been a Megadeth fan. And I understand; I'm not offended. But he says, 'I really love that song, *Breadline.*' So, you know, it's weird, because when you do a record that's that far of a left turn, some people really do dig it. So it was weird; a lot of it was just weird. It's just an odd record (laughs). That's all I can say about it. It was just odd. There were some bright spots on it, but the whole thing was just odd."

"But **World Needs A Hero** for the most part, was a good record," continues Jimmy. "I thought sonically it was good record, I thought it was well-produced, by Bill, I thought a lot of the songs were good. We did a track called *Kill The King*; I thought that was a good track. *Disconnect, Moto Psycho*,

1000 Times Goodbye... I think it could've been tweaked a little bit more. I think we were a little bit rushed. If we had another couple of weeks, I think we could've just tweaked it a little bit. But for the most part, it came out pretty good. We were on such tight deadlines with everything, where we toured, and then OK, we have to go, you've got two months to write a record, and then get back on tour. It is not quite like that anymore. I was reading a book, I think it was about Aerosmith, and they were saying, you know, back in the '70s, they had to tour all year and get two records out. It's like, how the heck do you do that? (laughs). Because I mean, creatively, that's the problem. When you're a band... what's the saying? You've got your whole life to write your first record, and then your second record, you've got like six months. And that's where, let's face it, a lot of bands go dry. The well just goes dry. You can write that song over and over again, and sometimes it doesn't lead to anything new either."

I asked Jimmy if there was anything identifiable about his drumming style, what drummers might say he tends to do more of or less of. "I don't know. I was talking to Damon Johnson (band mate in Alice Cooper) about this one time. He said, 'You know, I can't really pinpoint your style. You have a little bit of everything, and I can't say what it is. It's like, you hear the jazz, you hear the jazz influences, but it's done in a rock way.' And I think, I don't know, you have to ask the people I play with. Because I can't tell you myself. I just play the way I play. I don't really think about it. I just know how I approach songs and how I think they should be done. Ask any musician, what's your sound, what's your style, it's really hard to say, because I just do what I do. With Megadeth, you're playing more with guitars as opposed to bass, because it's a heavily guitar-driven and drum-driven band, so you play with the guitar players. So I would play more with Dave Mustaine, because I listen to him all the time, more than anybody—the rhythms and stuff, that's what dictates the drum parts."

As pertains the concept of calling the song and record, somewhat oddly, **The World Needs A Hero**, Ellefson explains that, "We were in Japan eating dinner with the promoter, Mr. Udo. He takes us out to this wonderful dinner, usually toward the end of the tour, where you cook this steak on this hot rock in the middle of this table. It's incredible, and Mr. Udo is an icon in the business and we pretty much hang on every word he says and we have these wonderful conversations. And anyway, the conversation that night over dinner, we were talking about musicians falling from grace over drugs, and all these people who at the pinnacle of their careers, just fell from grace, even through their own stupidity or saying and doing the wrong things. And he says to Dave, 'Dave, the world needs a hero.' And the air... you could just hear the words lingering out there in the air as he said it. And Dave kept that and proceeded to write some words. So that's where it came from and also the conversation surrounding that was important as well. Because if you think about it, any human, that old saying, everybody gets their 15 minutes of fame, and that's pretty much the way it is for any human that you try to make an icon out of. You can't be all things to all people all the time. Eventually you're going to fall."

The concept is open to additional interpretation however, with Mustaine decrying the lack of heroes on the world stage as well as the lack of iconic figures in hard rock and metal, given the casual Fridays dress code of bands through the '90s, specifically admiring the image and effect both Priest and Maiden had on metal fans.

There's an immediate bare-bones quality to the production afforded **The World Needs A Hero**, but it's still bright and impactful, really accentuating the rhythmic aspect of the record, which is what road rage song (and lead single from the record) *Moto Psycho* is all about, the bed tracks evoking those time-honoured choppy percussive structures most memorable, perhaps, on **Rust In Peace**.

Says Ellefson, "The production, you know, it's funny... our earlier records have a real vibe and attitude about them; that came partly from our inexperience and also because we didn't have enough money. If you are like most bands you get it together as best you can in order, so you jump in the studio and you bang it out until your funds run out and then it's done whether you want it to be or not (laughs). And that wasn't the case with this record. But there was certainly that attitude of let's get in and nail it. Man, we were ripping out drum and guitar and bass tracks in a couple of days. The entire album went quickly, and that was cool. And that was the fire, the honesty in the band members to get it right as opposed to money dictating it, which is a cool place to be. And as far as the producing with Dave, originally it started out to be a co-production as all Megadeth records have been—Dave and fill in the blank—and we hooked up with Bill Kennedy. He actually flew out from L.A. and we met him at the Phoenix airport and had a quick sandwich and a couple of Starbucks and the next thing you know, we're booking studio time a half-hour later. It was like, OK, this guy's it, let's go."

"And it was like, we the band know what we want and Dave has always been at the helm steering the ship even with the other producers who we've worked with. Dave's always been the spokesman for the band creatively and in the studio, and really Dave being the producer, it just kind of developed that way. Because as we were going, we realized that Bill Kennedy was an excellent engineer. But with this team, Dave and Bill Kennedy, Dave was really starting to do more and more and more of the work musically because, I don't know, it was needed for him to step up to the plate and do it and he did. So Dave sort of unknowingly walked into the producer's chair. And I think he did a fantastic job and it's cool that the whole thing is now in-house."

"The first record, the intention was there," Ellefson told me, charting the trip from the beginning right up 'til **The World Needs A Hero**. "We just didn't have all of the components and people in place and the finances from the label, and even the label at that point, to make it happen. So we really didn't hit our stride until the second record, **Peace Sells**. And even with that, once you're on a major label, it doesn't mean the thing is going to sell. Fortunately, people were interested in what we were doing and so we had a hit record. Even though you have a hit record, it doesn't mean your third record is going to be a hit either. So every time... that old saying 'you're only as good as your last gig' is true. I think the **Rust In Peace** record was the one that really helped us regain our turf. That was about us putting our flag in the dirt and this is who we are, this is what we stand for. That was a milestone record for us and it set the stage for **Countdown To Extinction**. That was the beginning of us really broadening our horizons as a band as far as songwriting and melodies and everything. And once we got to **Cryptic Writings**, it was the same thing. That again was about, times have changed, music has changed, and that record was to show that we are every bit as much Megadeth as we ever have been, but this is how much better we've gotten."

"And now it's kind of the same with **The World Needs A Hero**," continues Junior. "Which is funny, if you notice, it's like every other record is like a real defining moment for Megadeth—it really is. Every other record is the one. And I hope it's kind of a testimony to our willingness to stand up for who we are and not get pushed around in that sense, but also to show that we are willing to keep growing and moving forward and keep trying some new things."

"**Risk** was Megadeth going as far out on a limb as far as developing our melodies, as far as we've ever gone," says Ellefson, warily tackling the delicate topic. "Heavy metal was at a very precarious time when we made **Risk**. Pretty much all the industry insiders were saying it's dead, it's done, it's over, don't even utter that phrase in your sentences or you'll be killed (laughs). And obviously Megadeth is pretty much a metal band. Fortunately we're metal with a combination of other types of music, so we were able to make a record like **Risk** and pull it off and in my opinion, do very well with it. After doing that though, when we started writing songs for **The World Needs A Hero**, we started writing them out on tour, which is where most Megadeth songs develop actually, at least the riffs and concepts. When we started writing those songs, we were in a major transition. We knew we were coming up on our last record for Capitol Records, which was our domestic label at the time. Our guitar player Marty Friedman had just announced that he wanted to leave the band. We had, had some outside songwriting influence from one of our managers, Bud Prager, who is listed on a lot of the songwriting credits on **Risk**, and so all of a sudden there was this major disruption going on in our camp, and I think that is what fuelled **The World Needs A Hero**. It was very much a conscious effort to not do anything that anybody from the outside would ever influence us to do."

"Which for us, in itself was a challenge, because for **Risk**, **Cryptic Writings** and **Youthanasia**, we wanted to become somewhat pliable to listen to producers and management and people and our record label, people who have had experience in the business to help guide us in our career. We did not want to be that pig-headed that we couldn't be guided (laughs), because that could be the kiss of death too. This record was all about, you know what? Let's go back to doing what we did when we were a brand new band. And there's kind of a shoot-from-the-hip naiveté that gets lost the longer you go on in this business. And I think that is the essence of what we tried to capture with this record. I think it's very heavy. Musically it's heavy, production-wise its heavy. I look at **The World Needs A Hero** as the best of the best that Megadeth has ever done."

Back to the tracks, *1000 Times Goodbye* is yet another groovy, mid-paced metal monster, with Dave in self-deprecating mode, allowing a love interest to feed him cliché lines throughout that set the rube up for the inevitable break-up, until the character in the song hears "I love you like a brother" and click, has had enough. A highlight of this song is Jimmy and his drum sound, DeGrasso getting to fire off some simple but effective fills. Did the man on the throne ever wish he was represented more robustly in the songwriting credits?

"No, not really, and the reason being, I think, when you join a band like that, you kind of... I mean, I was involved to some degree. I have songwriting credits on a few things. I was involved to some degree, but I don't want to come in and start writing songs. When Dave asked me to join the band, I wanted to join the band as Megadeth. I didn't want to come in and change it. I wanted it to be what it was. And I think to do that, it was going to be the bulk of the material should be written by the person that was there. Because that was the sound of the band. So no, my forté with that was, give me some riffs and I'll try to make up some good drum parts that kind of work with the riffs, or give me a song, and if I'm more coming into parts, I can contribute—but I didn't want to do writing. Like for example, when I was in Y&T, I would write songs. But for Megadeth, I just thought Megadeth should be that, what it was. I didn't want to come in and start throwing my ideas around. Because the Megadeth, at that time, had a particular sound."

"You have to listen to your public," muses Ellefson, realizing at the time that the fans very much had in mind what the Megadeth sound should and shouldn't be. "And everybody's a critic; it's just that some people have typewriters (laughs), or word processors I should say. And they have their authority to put the opinion out to the masses. And that definitely influences people. **Risk** actually was critically a pretty well-received record and there were a lot of new fans we picked up along the way. Trust me, I stand behind **Risk**; it was fun. Because anytime we did anything that sounded reminiscent of previous Megadeth records, we tried to improve upon it. And that's hard. I mean, when you have as many records as we have, one of the biggest challenges is to just not repeat yourself. Because I can think of about three or four bands right off the top of my head whose names I won't mention who have basically made the same record over and over most of their career. And that's fun for a while but then people will start looking for something new. And that's something I think you can never fault Megadeth for. We've never just retreaded the same old tire and delivered it back out to the people. We've always pushed ourselves to make something new. So even though some of our fans maybe want to hear an earlier style of Megadeth, there's also a whole other part of our fan base; they love the anticipation of a new Megadeth record because they know there will be something new and cutting edge on it."

Burning Bridges is a dark, gothic metallic epic with prog metal touches, quiet bits and elements of pummelling thrash. Mustaine sings savagely and ruefully, perfect for the artful lyric about painting oneself into a corner, burning bridges, as it were. And then it's into what can pretty much be described as a power ballad, *Promises*, co-written by Dave with Pitrelli, being replete with string arrangements. *Promises* was issued in a Spanish version as well, partially so, Dave singing the choruses in Spanish. Lyrically, the track is about relationships that are difficult to maintain given current social mores, be they same sex, Protestant/Catholic, inter-racial, and how they might have to simmer on hold until the afterlife.

With *Recipe For Hate... Warhorse*, we're back into classic Megadeth, from Dave singing (and talking) spitefully about his favourite topic, revenge (evidently directed at Capitol), to Junior getting to display his bass parts up-front in the mix, to the point where the verses consist of Dave's ruminations over bass and the sparest of drum parts.

"Bill Kennedy is a great engineer," begins Ellefson, asked about the bass sound on the record. "I mean, he knows how to get huge rock tones. For the bass, I think we had about six different amplifiers all with different tone settings and combinations. The closest we've ever gotten to getting that intense with bass tones and the variety was on **Cryptic Writings**, which also has some pretty gnarly bass tones on it. I always thought the bass... and I'm really lucky with that, because Dave will always invite the bass to the forefront of a song at any given time, whether it be an intro or a breakdown in the middle of the song. And it's nice, because the bass doesn't just linger in the back somewhere. It's a very dominant part of a Megadeth song. That's the cool thing about being in Megadeth. Everybody gets their time to shine, their moment in the spotlight."

But that only goes so far. Ellefson, for his part, is pretty much content not to be a big part of the songwriting process. "Yeah, I mean, songwriting can be credited or divvied up any number of ways. I think there is a certain sound I bring to the band, first of all. Because most Megadeth songs originate with Dave and a guitar riff. And where they develop from there is usually contingent on the drums and bass parts and all of the other things—melodies and solos unfold from there. And for me, one of the things that I'm best at is being the resident historian in the band, the fact-checker. When we're sitting in a room putting a song together, I'll remember some riff from some soundcheck in Raleigh, N.C.. 'Remember that riff that went guh-guh-guh?' It'll be, 'Oh yeah right! Can we try that one here?' That's usually what I'd bring to the table. My mind kind of works like a tape recorder in that way, being able to hear little bits and parts. I'll also spent a lot of time cataloguing. We've got DAT tape after DAT tape after cassette tape of all different soundchecks and dressing room tapes from around the world and I catalogue and compile and put all that stuff together. And especially on **The World Needs A Hero**, that was my contribution. From day one I've always been a team player, so whatever I can bring to the team and make it better is my philosophy."

Asked about Bill Kennedy's background, Ellefson says that, "He did some work with Trent Reznor in the past, and I think that name right there kind of sold us on some stuff. Trent had even done a remix of *Symphony Of Destruction* a few years back and Trent is known for his attitude and style. I can't remember some of the other stuff, but he was playing some of it in the studio as he was putting some tones together, in a way to convince us, 'Look, guys, this is what I'm shooting for. I know this seems like a lot of work now, but this is the end result.' And he would put on a CD of some band that he had done, maybe this baby band that had this incredibly huge sound and it was like, whoa! You know what you're doing—go for it."

"Our mission is so strong and pure right now," mused Junior, on the nature of Megadeth's press duties for the album. "For the next week we're going to do everything we can possibly do, and this has been going on for the last year-and-a-half, on just this record, what we can do that is in our control, to make the best record we can. And just lay it on the line in the interviews that we do, really just lay the whole thing out, as far as all things Megadeth goes—and a week from now, it's completely out of our hands. And that's kind of where you're at. Then it's up to the public whether they like it or not."

"I don't think there are any other plans for me," says Ellefson, when I asked him if his "how to" book on the music business was still in print. "Right now it is all about solidarity in the camp. As far as the writings of books, I had never set out to be an author; it's just that one day I woke up and said, you know what? This needs to be said. And it required me to be an author in order to do it (laughs). So that is the way that happened and obviously it was many years ago. But right now this is the focus and it has to be, in order for us to complete our mission, and everyone has to be on the same page."

Back to **The World Needs A Hero**, *Losing My Senses* is very much a **Risk**-type track, thumping along in that psychedelic zone some grunge gets up to. The chorus is rich and complicated, as is the lyric, which looks at regret and mortality. The keyboard melody in the break appears to be a lift from UFO's *Long Gone* but it's brief, giving way to a jammy solo section, textures everywhere... this is a late-period Marty Friedman song if there ever was, or something Rush mighta stuck on **Test For Echo**.

Dread & The Fugitive Mind we've discussed, but now as it sits deep in the sequence of the album's tracks, it's very much immediate and punchy like the album's heaviest songs, as well as blessed with a groovy section and gobs of traditional metal melody that might be called Schenker-esque come chorus time. It was the second single and last single from the record after *Moto Psycho*, the latter receiving video treatment as well as use in the video game **Heavy Metal: Geomatrix**.

Silent Scorn is an instrumental featuring Herb Alpert's trumpet player, Bob Findlay. At times the brief track sounds like Metallica's *The Unforgiven*, both evoking Clint Eastwood, a hero of Dave's. An additional inspiration was an instance whereby Dave had been on his way to Cabo San Lucas and had a bull charge at their vehicle. *Silent Scorn* was used as outro music in a live setting, as can be heard on the **Rude Awakening** live CD.

Second to last on the record is *Return To Hangar*, which Mustaine calls, "a lyrical reprise to *Hangar 18* from **Rust In Peace**. Because I thought back, we were going through the Bahamas, and I thought, God it would be interesting, everybody is always saying they love **Rust In Peace** and I'm thinking, with us returning to our roots on this record, it would be really symbolic if we return to *Hangar 18* and saw what had happened. So the lyric is about a situation where you come back and the song is about all these aliens being in cryogenic chambers being served by military intelligence. And this time we come back and see that there has been an insurrection by the aliens and they've broken out and hung all the military intelligence. One line in particular says they are suspended by their broken necks. I'm trying to not say, 'Oh, they hung them.' But I think anybody with imagination will know that that's what it means."

The track features a blistering thrash outro, on which Jimmy pounds away forcefully, providing a foundation o'er which Mustaine and Pitrelli trade lighting-fast licks. Given its lyrical grist, the song was inserted into the live set directly following *Hangar 18*, creating a concept piece of sorts.

The World Needs A Hero closes with the curious *When*. At the beginning of its nine minute heft, Dave mutters through gritted teeth a familiar tale of love gone poisoned. Eventually a conventional—and very familiar—metal structure takes hold, one very much similar to Diamond

Head's *Am I Evil?*.

In fact, Dave planned the track as an homage to that song and its writer Brian Tatler, telling a story of coincidence in the process, how upon coming up with the idea, he walked into the studio and there was a phone call for him, out of the blue, from none other than Tatler.

The two actually wound up conceiving of a project together, one that never came to fruition.

"We stayed in touch," says Tatler, having already executed a brief collaboration with Mustaine for Diamond Head's **Death And Progress** album back in '93. "And then at some point, I think in 2001... he'd done that solo project, MD.45, and I think he was going with the idea of doing a similar thing outside of Megadeth, and he thought myself and him should write it. And so we began that process, where I would send material to Dave, and he would send it back, and he'd say, 'I really like this and I really like that and it should be more of this.' And so we went along for six months or so doing that, and he seemed ultra-busy to me. You know, I got bits and bobs on, but he would either be on tour or in the studio, and it seemed to me he didn't have a lot of time to commit to this project. And then eventually he had that problem where he hurt his arm. Slept on it funny or something. I forget was it was called, but his left hand was kind of frozen or something, and he pretty much disbanded Megadeth, I think. Sold his amps and guitars and everything, so he was pretty serious. And he had to admit to me that the project we had been working on was going to have to... you know, he can't do it; he can't go through with it. He wasn't mentally in the right place. So I just said, well, that's life, nothing ventured. And to be fair, it did give me a kick to work on material, and some of that material probably ended up on the next two Diamond Head records, at least as a skeleton to start a new song from."

"*Mine All Mine* is definitely one of the riffs I came up with, from that project," continues Tatler, prompted to point out traces of the collaboration. "*Broken Pieces* was another one; *Feel No Pain* was one of those riffs. So I would just keep storing all this material away, and then when it comes time to write for a Diamond Head record, I would sift through this stuff, and go, 'That's good, that's good, that's good,' and I think some of that was reused, definitely. You know, I don't throw anything away (laughs)."

"But it was all music," continues Brian, meaning no vocals from Dave yet. "Just musical ideas getting toward arrangement, I suppose. But he was all for putting vocals on later; he was starting to come up with ideas and concepts for lyrics, but no, I never saw any of that. Musically, I think he had it in mind that it should be like early Diamond Head, and really early Megadeth. I think that was where he was coming from. But that's hard to do really, for me. I don't like repeating myself. I can understand, yeah, keep the tempos up and make it exciting, but I couldn't write another *Am I Evil?*. I couldn't write another *Lightning To The Nations*. That was of its time. Whatever my brain was doing at 19, you know, in 1979, it's not doing that now (laughs). It's hard turning that on."

"At the moment no," said Dave, when I asked him if we'd see any sort of side-project from him. "I'm just trying to piece together the remaining songs we need to do to finish the record. I'm open to stuff but it can't interfere with my main priority which is Megadeth. If there was something really stupendous like there was a Metallica reunion or Jimmy Page said, 'Dave, I want to work with you,' I'd say, OK boys, you know what? I'll be back in a couple of days. But I just heard Jimmy hurt his back and actually went home. And as far as the Metallica thing, you know, I talked with Lars recently and he invited me up to his house to hang out. That's quite a considerable development for our relationship from where the public perceives us. It's really uncomfortable when someone walks up to me and they go, 'Dude, Metallica sucks.' And I'm like, you know what? Don't say that to me. Because you would probably walk right up to them and say, 'Dude, Megadeth sucks!' I don't need to hear that stuff. If you're coming up to meet me for the first time, it's your one chance, don't bring it up."

Remembering the track *When* in conversation with writer Jeb Wright touched off a spot of reflection at the tortured path so far and so redolent in the lyric to this emotional album closer.

"Like I said in the song *When*, I've been through stuff most people would die just watching. We continue to be victorious, no matter what the adversity, whether it be the industry at a given time, or the fan base at a given time, or what music is popular, or economic challenges, or misinterpretation of things we say during a song, or on stage; we always come out on top. Sometimes you're right and sometimes you're wrong and if you're man enough to apologize when you do wrong then the fans will forgive you. It's not about how many things you do right in this business; it's about how many things you don't do wrong."

"It was pretty toxic," continues Dave, on the self-destructive past that numerous times almost squelched the band's career victories. "But a lot of that had to do with how I was brought up. My mom and dad divorced at an early age, when I was four. My mom moved out when I was 15 and that was in 1976, so that would be like a ten-year-old living on his own today. Growing up, being homeless and having to panhandle for food, the only comfort I found was in a bottle, or in some other form. After my life started to turn around there was still a big black hole inside of me. Yeah, sure I could eat and I had money and a roof over my head but I still had to find something to fill that hole. Sometimes people use a significant other, or sometimes it is a substance and sometimes, like people talk about in the 12 Step fellowships, it is a power greater than yourself. For me, I think that having that spiritual fulfillment is what has helped turn my life around. A lot of people confuse religion for spirituality. I heard it summed up real simple: religion is for people who are afraid of going to hell and spirituality is for people like me, who've been there."

"I think that life, in general, is a series of challenges," continues Dave, "and that you just try to stay in the center of the herd. When the lions attack in the Serengeti, they don't run into the middle of the herd and get the strongest animal, they look for the stragglers. They look for the weak and the sick. As long as you stay in the center of the herd, you're pretty safe. For me, I liken it to this: if you get into this business for the money and the fame, then you're not doing it because you love to do it. I did it because I loved to play the guitar and that is why we persevered, because when the money and the fame weren't there, the music was still there."

"I try to share my life story with our fans. There is an old, ancient saying—I guess that is being redundant saying 'old' and 'ancient'—what I meant to say is that there is an ancient Oriental saying that says, 'A smart man learns from his own mistakes, while a wise man learns from the mistakes of others.' I think that is part of what being a dad is all about; showing the child the mistakes not to make. It is not all about telling them what to do, but also showing them what not to do."

The World Needs A Hero maintained Dave's place in the middle of the pack, failing to set the world afire sales-wise. But then again, metal was still in a tough place after its near dismissal from public consciousness for most of the '90s. The album entered the charts at No. 16 and by '05, had sold an estimated 219,000 copies in the US. If gold was a disappointment last time out, one can only wonder what selling half as much must have done to the band's sense of themselves.

Of note, the Japanese issue got a bonus track, a maudlin near hair metal ballad called *Coming Home*, which subsequently saw wider exposure on the forthcoming live album **Rude Awakening**. The coming home of which Dave speaks is "to Arizona," and yes, quite possibly, this is the softest, quietest Megadeth track ever, yer first clue perhaps being the pervasive sawing of a violin.

Concurrent with the release of **The World Needs A Hero**, Marty Friedman, still living in Scottsdale, Arizona at this point (i.e. not yet king shredder of Tokyo), was putting together...

"Red Dye No. 2. Yeah, it's a dream project I've been working on for almost a year now. It's almost impossible to describe the music except to say that it sounds like crossing Aqua with the Ramones and add a heavy dose of Marty Friedman guitar in there, you might get close to it. There's a female vocalist, myself, and another guy who does a lot of the sequences and loops. It's very electronica-based. Its ultra-futuristic bubblegum cheerleader pop with heavy metal guitar in it. We've been re-cutting and re-cutting our demos so that it is practically radio quality right now. It could be released as it is right now as a demo really; we're just listening right now to what record company people have to say, A&R people, and we're taking their input before letting a lot of people hear this stuff. We're listening to the advice of a lot of people we respect, and we're adding this and adding that and we just shot a promo video a week-and-a-half ago and we are editing that and getting a big package together. We're hopefully going to make a big impact rather than just let it trickle out."

"I wish I was up to a lot more with him," Marty told me, with respect to past band-mate Jason Becker. "Obviously you know that his health condition is very bad. He has ALS which is Lou Gehrig's disease, which is a degenerative muscle disorder. Anyway, he's had it for a long time and most people don't even live as long as he has. Due to his incredible spirit and his will to live he's managed to survive. And hopefully with the research that's been going on, there will be a cure for it some day. And somebody put together a tribute album for him and I laid down a track for that. As well, Trent Gardner is doing a record right now and I was asked to play lead guitar on it. I heard that Terry Bozzio was playing on it and I thought it would be a great opportunity to play the really insane guitar that I think lot of guitar freaks have been complaining that I haven't been playing for a long time. Give them something to chew on. I don't know, they might like the Red Dye No. 2 stuff but Trent Gardner's music is ultra-progressive, way-out progressive chops music. I would never entertain the thought of playing that stuff live (laughs)."

"I'm actually working on music for a solo album," continued Friedman, alluding to what turned out to be 2002's **Music For Speeding**. "That is stuff that I've been working on for a long time. I'm doing it at my own leisure in my own studio. But the main thing I'm really working on is Red Dye No. 2. That's probably the next thing anybody is going to hear from me. I'm so computer-illiterate that there isn't even any website for this other than fan sites. We've been keeping it pretty quiet. We played at the Viper Room in L.A. and we did a gig here in Phoenix where we shot our video, but we've kept it pretty low profile. There are three of us in kind of the main part of the band and there is someone else who kind of spins DJ-type stuff and we have a backup band that we will use for live. But the basic core of the band is three people and two of us live here in Phoenix and one of us lives in L.A."

Flash forward two years into mid-2003 and Marty was actually sharing concert dates with a Megadeth guitarist that preceded him, namely Chris Poland.

"The tour came together through Steve Bauer and Andy Somers," explains Chris, who, unlike the missing-in-action Chuck Beehler and the deceased Gar Samuleson, seemed to have landed on his feet, his fire for creating complex music still burning. "Steve came up with the first idea and Andy took it. Basically, since we're all play different types of music than we're normally known for—me known for the Megadeth records I made, Marty as well—I'm playing a jazz fusion thing with fretless bass and Kofi Baker on drums, who is a total fusion drummer. Alex Skolnick, who was in Testament, went to Berkeley and got his degree in jazz guitar and now he basically turns old standard heavy metal tunes into jazz tunes. And as you're listening to it, you're going, wow, this guy's really good, until you realize it's a Scorpions song, but he's playing it like Howard Roberts. And Marty, instead of doing the Megadeth thing, is doing more of a rock instrumental thing, which he's always wanted to do. It's just kind of our evolution, so we're calling the whole tour Guitar Evolution."

"We're going out for a month so far; we're going to do the West Coast and then try get some gigs in the Chicago, Detroit area and then go to the top of the East Coast to the bottom of the East Coast, probably come back to Texas, then come home. My band is Robert Pagliari on bass and Kofi Baker, Ginger Baker's son, on drums, all instrumental. Marty's band... Dave Ellefson's going to be playing bass, so they might do a couple of Megadeth songs, and the last drummer for Megadeth is going to be the drummer too. This is separate sets. My band is called Ohm. And then Alex Skolnick Trio, that band is opening, three band set, and then Marty is coming out with the Marty Friedman Band—maybe we might get together to do a song."

"The only difference I know of is that we may have had different influences," continues Poland, contrasting his guitar style with that of Friedman's. "My influences were Hendrix, Beck, Page, Clapton, when I was just growing up and then I totally had blinders on and all I could see was John McLaughlin for like ten years. There's a lot of Jan Hammer in my playing and that's probably the only difference in that I have a little bit different background. I'm not sure what Marty listens to, but I know he was in Cacophony, so I know he's very progressive anyway. But as far as stylistically, I would think Marty is more of what he's doing now, more of a rock guy. Where I've always been more of a blues, kinda fusion guy. I have a very, very big blues... like when I was a kid, I was totally into blues. I wore out two different records just listening to Hendrix's studio version of *Red House*, trying to learn that, trying to make it part of me. I enjoyed B.B. King, Albert King, people like that. But I was more into like Eric Clapton, Cream, Hendrix and Beck doing stuff like *Cause We've Ended As Lovers*. Those songs were more the staple of where I draw from. Maybe they're Marty's too, because we never really sat down and spoke."

As for Chris's line of work post-Megadeth, "I manage a rehearsal studio downtown, that I helped build. It's called Downtown Rehearsal. I manage a couple hundred rooms; I'm here right now. It's a great job for me because I do my stuff I have to do in the morning and then I just take an hour lunch, play guitar and work on stuff. Then I come back at night and rehearse the band. So I'm always around music, which is a good thing."

Back in Megadeth's world as it existed mid-2001, the band threw themselves back on the tour trail. Previous to the album launch, the band executed an unplugged tour of small venues in the US and Canada, but right at launch, it was off to Europe in June, supporting AC/DC, followed by Japan and southeast Asia in July and August—Malaysia was cancelled due to censorship.

The attacks of September 11, 2001 cast a pall of uncertainty over an extensive US tour, supported by Iced Earth and Endo, although the band managed to play the very next night after the attacks, at the Commodore Ballroom in Vancouver. Following month, October 16th marked the video release of the illuminating **Behind The Music** documentary done on the band.

Speaking with Mustaine at length on October 9th as the band came through Toronto, Dave explained how and why the band had gone back to their roots with respect to song selection in the late '01 live set.

"A lot of the credit for that goes to Al Pitrelli, because when he came in—and this is Al saying this, because I know a lot of the fans have resentment for me and my confidence and the way I speak about the band—he said, 'Man, I'm in one of the greatest heavy metal bands of all time and let's just be Megadeth.' And I said, fuck yeah, baby, because I'm looking over and I see a guy in white pants and now I look over and see a guy in blue jeans with his Les Paul down at his knees kicking ass—it's like it's kind of changed. It's kind of like Michael J. Fox, **Back To The Future**, you know what I mean?"

"So all we did, basically, is go back through the catalogue," continues Dave. "I had to teach him everything live that Marty was doing. Because when Marty left, we were really doing a Megadeth-lite concert. I mean, there were some heavy staples in there that needed to be played, but for the most part it was songs that were kind of questionable. Because I was trying to keep band harmony, we were usually leaning more towards the songs Marty would want to play. And Marty is a great player and he's going to be successful at whatever he does; I don't know the degree of it but, but to be a good leader you have to have band harmony. And when Al came in and said, 'Let's just be Megadeth,' I'm like yeah! And the record label said, 'Do me in favour and put Vic back on the cover.' And I went yeah!"

"So everything is lining up and I'm doing the things I like doing. You know, we were out on tour one time on Ozzfest and there were these two really big dudes and they were putting their hands on top of their heads and doing pirouettes and shit during *Symphony Of Destruction* and I'm not afraid of anybody. I don't care how big they are. If I want to fight someone, I'll fight them. And I'm looking at these two guys and I'm thinking you know what, I feel like putting down my guitar on the stage and walking out into the audience and kicking the shit out of these two guys right now, right here. And I should have known right then that they were sending me a message.

But you know what, all I did was I took it personal. And thank God I have friends like you and Tim (Henderson) and people like that who in their apparent anger were able to reach me because I was lost, you know?"

What's left to do? Have you accomplished most of your goals?

"Well, it's no secret I'm rich," says Dave. "That's one of the things that happened with being a rock star. I can live the rest of my life very meagerly and never have to work again. Do I have enough money? Nobody ever has enough money."

But is a record like **The World Needs A Hero** an exercise in something you perhaps crave or want back, and that's the respect of your fans?

"The one thing that I like is being with our fans and them not feeling like they're a class below me. Because all I have to do is think back a few years to being in school when I had to get lunch tickets because I was that poor. And I think that's part of why I stopped wanting to sing *Anarchy* live. How can I sing *Anarchy* when I'm driving around in a Mercedes? I'm a fraud. Then I thought, you know what? Fuck that! I worked my ass off for that and the fans believe in me, and I stand up for them, and what I may own in a material way, I've taken it in the chops from people, you know? So we added *Anarchy* back into the set list. Now, I don't think it's the right thing to be playing right now, given the current situation in America. The American people need to come together as do all the other nations to fight this fucking very worn-out subject right now which I don't want to get into. It's very pertinent, but it's also very, very unrelated to what we're talking about. Some of the other songs too, we'd listen to them and we would say we've got to add this one and we've got to add that one. And we're planning on doing a live record down in South America and we want to play 40 songs. And we're going to put two songs in there that people are going to hate. We're going to put *Secret Place* in there because it was a No. 5 hit in America and we're going to put *I'll Be There* in there because *I'll Be There* was a song written specifically for South America. They sing soccer songs down there; they sing soccer songs in Europe."

"November 16 and 17 we're going to be in Buenos Aires, Argentina recording a live record," continued Dave, on a visit that was not to be. "It's going to be 40 songs, so it will probably be a triple disc. And they're going to do a movie around it and all that crap too. So it's going to be a live DVD thing too. I mean, they're not going to show everything that goes on, because I don't want them watching me wake up in bed like some of these dumb rock videos where you see some guy crawling out of bed and going out on stage. But I want them to see the madness and the beauty of the Argentine people and how they like the music."

"But to get back to your original question, how we picked the songs, we picked songs that we thought the fans would like. The next song we're working on is actually *Take No Prisoners* but it's kind of hard to keep adding old material because at the same time we're preparing for the next studio record. The good thing is that playing all this old stuff is affecting the way the new stuff is coming out. I talked with the other members of the band and said what we have to do this time is not tell anybody what the record is going to sound like. Because when we said we're going back to our roots, a lot of people misinterpreted me saying 'going,' being an adverb, to being 'we are at our roots.' And we weren't 'at our roots;' we were going there. And it's a much-often used analogy by me. It's like turning one of those big cruise ships around. You turn the wheel all the way and it takes forever. It takes a while for us to get turned around but I think we're turned around right now in the right direction and we're getting back to the point."

An interesting admission from an honest Mustaine. Of course, it's a statement that speaks to the man's artistic integrity: it's not that he couldn't write songs that are back to the roots immediately, it's that he doesn't want to. Mustaine is still writing for himself and that will always result in a number of different heats and intensities on a Megadeth album, critical backlash be damned. And yet...

"Our credibility, you know, I was the leader, I was *a* leader, for the metal community," sighs Dave, who, arguably, couldn't be knowing that he would soon in fact return to a purity of metal intent that has not wavered to this day. "And for whatever reason, things happened and I kind of went in a different direction, and I guess watching what happened with my previous band and watching what was happening to us, I made a choice. Do I want to be big or do I want to stay small and have my credibility? And I made a choice and said, you know, I want to be successful. But then the success was much more difficult than I ever imagined and the flak that I took wasn't worth it. So I said you know what, fuck it, I'd rather be playing small clubs because we're playing music that's not really popular and have people that love me because I'm Dave Mustaine, rather than have fair weather fans that will be here today because my song's on the radio, and tomorrow, they won't be there, they don't even know who the guys in the band are."

But maybe the old fans were fair weather fans too, who left when it got too mid-paced and commercial... "Maybe, but I'm not going to judge them. Everyone has their views and why they do the things that they do. I think that this whole... I'm not going to say like I metamorphosized because that's a 25 cent word, but just going back to what makes me feel good when I pick up the guitar. Because when I pick up the guitar... I mean, Jeff Beck used to say that he makes his guitar cry or some stuff like that, and I like to make my guitar puke. I like to beat the hell out of it. And I can do things with guitars and sing at the same time that most people can't. And I wasn't challenging myself anymore. It's kind of like being Michael Jordan and not trying to do anything exciting anymore."

"You can still be very creative," reflects Dave, on balancing experimentation with staying metal or thrash. "What I learned going into the progression of playing more of the pop-type music and more of the melodic stuff is that it helped me with my melody. I mean, I can still write heavy stuff but it will have melody now. One of the things that cut us off from a lot of our core audience is that the drumming changed; it got very simplistic. And I listen to Jimmy playing a natural beat when we start writing something. First we get the part right, then we get the beat right, then we get the sections right, then I'd say , 'Now you know where all the sections are—just play lead drums.' That's what Nick used to do, and that's when we were the most famous: when Nick was playing lead drums. And most of his drum parts, I wrote. And I'm not going to say I'm a drummer and I'm not as good at playing drums as Nick is, and I'm definitely not even close to Jimmy, because Jimmy is a master. He's a bona fide drum master."

"But what we're doing right now is we just promised we won't tell anybody what it sounds like. Because with **The World Needs A Hero**, we said, oh, it's going to be a return to **Countdown To Extinction** and **Rust In Peace**, a little bit of **Youthanasia**, and we got everybody's hopes up. And when it came out, everybody's expectations were so incredibly high that there was no way, even if it was **Rust In Peace** Part II, they wouldn't have accepted it as **Rust In Peace**, Part II. So we're just making songs right now, having fun doing it and David Ellefson told me two days ago, he said I feel closer to you right now in these last three months than I've felt in many years. Because we're just being together as a band again. And that's important. It's like being in a marriage. If you hate who you're with, it won't work."

As for production personnel or philosophy on the proposed next album, Dave figures, "One thing with us, we have our own sound, and it's something we need to stay true to. **Risk** and **Cryptic Writings**, that was not really our sound. I learned a lot from those two records how to make what our core bass, rhythm guitar and drums sound is, sound better, and where to put ear candy and stuff like that. Because any reviewer who is worth his salt is going to have to review ten to maybe 50 records a month and you don't have time to live with that record. And a Megadeth record, you cannot... I notice that you cannot hear a Megadeth record one time and grasp the entire record in one spin—you just can't. Because it's like trying to speed-read through Tolstoy. You know, you can't do it. Change the production sound? Do I want to have some nu-metal guy do it? No. Do I want to go to some slick producer that does stuff like Bob Rock or a Beau Hill? No."

"I like what I did on the last record. And the freedom and the liberation in telling the management not to come to the studio, telling the record company, don't come to the studio, and each of us doing what we did—it felt very much like when I was making the demos for **Rust In Peace**. Because I had just graduated from engineering school and I was working by myself, and I had an engineer in there assisting me, trying little tricks here and there. And when we did **World Needs A Hero** it was the same thing. I was in charge but I had a great engineer working with me, but I wasn't really using all the tricks that I had learned because I was just so excited to be free. It's kind of like, if you're a slave and you're set free and you start running, it takes you a couple minutes to realize, hey man, I'm naked (laughs). I'm just too busy running right now, I don't give a shit. And the freedom in trying to get away from trying to be reformulated was really good."

"Because I respect our previous record company a lot, and I respect our previous management a lot for what they tried to do with me," says Dave, the new management team being Larry Mazer and Steve Wood, Entertainment Services Unlimited. "They tried to make me be a better person, they tried to teach me how to work better within my industry. What happened to the music, I think... I stand by the records, I believe in them 100%. Could they be better? Sure. I can go back in there and mix what Dann and Jeff did for **Cryptic Writings** and **Risk** and could make them sound really great. I would love to go remix **So Far, So Good... So What!** because Michael Wagner mixed it and it's just like So Far... So Much Reverb (laughs). Do I plan on giving absolutely all I have for the next record? Yeah, everything I've got is what I plan on doing."

Simply put, Did Dave now want what Pantera and Slayer had?

"No, Slayer and Pantera are two totally different bands. They are nothing like Megadeth. Megadeth at one time was the state-of-the-art speed metal band and we were light years ahead of everybody and better than everybody. And I think because we were at the top of our field... I mean, at one point when **Countdown** and the **Black Album** was out, we were bigger than Metallica, which is really hard to imagine, but at one time we were more popular than they were. And I think if you try and compete with the likes of Slayer and Pantera, one, it's not worth it because they do what they do so much better than we do and two, we don't have any experience at it."

Asked if Mustaine felt the relationship those bands have with their fans is similar to what Megadeth had but then lost, he shrugs, "I don't know what their relationship is with their fans. I mean, I can tell you what I know about record sales and what I know about concert attendance and I can tell you what I know about what the promoters think of those bands, but that's a business point of view that should remain private out of respect for the bands. And for me, fans don't want to hear that shit anyways. They don't want to know about the behind the scenes stuff, they just want to hear great music. Both of them have been really great bands and I was hoping that there would come a time when Metallica, Megadeth, Slayer and Pantera could do like a coliseum tour. It would be enormous. I know there would be a lot of bloodshed out in the audience because there are a lot of loyal fans and there would be a lot of moshing going on and a lot of accidental and a lot of purposeful injury taking place, but I think it would be an amazing thing. And I've been talking a lot to Lars lately. And sadly, they've got some stuff they need to take care of before they can even perform to be part of a package like that. And I don't know if Pantera and Slayer are even interested in doing anything with the likes of two bands that everyone seems to think have sold out."

What about Anthrax? "I like Anthrax. I think Scott Ian is great. Charlie is a good drummer; the whole band is just really great. They're fun to be with, fun guys to be around and they've got good music. Should they be a part of that? Yeah, I think so. I think Anthrax should be part of it more than Pantera should because of the initial tenure there in the beginning. But Pantera is more popular than Anthrax right now so they deserve it based on their credibility right now. Is anybody in Anthrax as good at playing guitar as Darrell? Shit, Darrell's a genius. There are very few people in the music business as good as Darrell. And him and his brother together are a fantastic duo—they're just amazing."

The aforementioned DVD shoot and CD live album recording in Argentina was cancelled as part of the worldwide chill put on the entertainment industry after 9/11, with the band cobbling together a couple of Arizona dates in November instead, in order to build the live album and DVD, both called **Rude Awakening**.

"I think the **Rude Awakening** album is a pretty good legacy to leave behind, that encapsulates the best of what is Megadeth," said Ellefson, speaking with Sue Nolz in '02. "Making a live album really comes down to having a record company that's willing to back you doing it. Up until Sanctuary agreed to do it, we were at the mercy of our previous label and it was never in our contract with them. Sanctuary came to us and they saw the excitement, and that the fans had been requesting it. So they decided to do it, and we seized the opportunity."

Contrary to Mustaine's above stated plan for the album, *A Secret Place* and *I'll Be There* were not part of the track list, but Dave does dedicate the package to the band's Argentine fans. The 24 track CD version of the package was issued March 19, 2002, and the DVD (truncated to 20 tracks) on April 9th. In the interim, in February, the band issued a deluxe, remixed version of the debut **Killing Is My Business**, deftly brought up to date by engineer Bill Kennedy, who is co-producer with the band on it plus the live album as well.

Then Megadeth was no more.

"I didn't leave the band—the band broke up!" says Jimmy. "I don't even know if the band broke up. Dave quit the band. He called me one day. He was... you know, after the **World Needs A Hero** tour, when we did **Rude Awakening**, he called me, he was having some issues, whatever, and a couple months after we mixed the live record, he called me up one day and says, 'Hey, just want to let you know, I'm leaving the band.' And I'm like, OK. 'I want to do music with a more positive message.' I never understood that. And I said OK, and that was kind of the end of the conversation; haven't talked to him since."

"It worked out anyway, because you know, honestly at the time, I was burnt out from being on the road so much," continues DeGrasso. "And it was a thing where I just wanted to chill, because I remember, right after Megadeth, I think the next day, after Dave called, Ronnie Montrose called. And he was like, wanted to know if wanted to do anything. And normally I would jump at this, because I was a really big fan of Ronnie's. But I just didn't want to go back on the road. I just wanted to hang out for a while at home; I was starting a family and stuff like that. So I took a year off, and then the phone started to ring, and Ronnie called again, and I went and did that for a couple of years, and then David Lee Roth called, and I went to do that for a couple of years. So I'm lucky—the phone keeps ringing."

"Some of the Megadeth was really cool," reflects Jimmy, asked about highlights of his time with the band. "I remember playing Woodstock back in '99. That was really cool, as far as getting to see a lot of bands on the day. Things like that are fun, where you get out and watch a bunch of bands and get to play at the end of the day. It's a great experience. Something you'll always remember. Yeah, with Dave, we always had a good time..."

11
THE SYSTEM HAS FAILED
"Why don't you just leave me alone?"

Dave Mustaine, band-less, soon found himself relapsing, ostensibly due to pain medication administered to him in the process of getting a kidney stone removed. While in Texas undergoing rehab, Dave suffered a freak injury that, in wry demonstrating of Dave as an everyman, well, every man and woman can relate to. His damn arm fell asleep, or more accurately, Dave fell asleep in a chair, with his left arm at an odd angle, draped over the back of the chair, and he suffered severe nerve damage, specifically a crushing of the radial nerve. This is the type of thing that can be the kiss of death for a guitarist, and reminds one of the very sensible preference of Steve Howe from Yes not to shake hands with fans. It also brings to mind Neil Young cutting himself while putting together a sandwich and even pro football players who miss games due to motorcycle or jet ski accidents.

Apropos of little but I gotta say it, Dave's particular injury is the type of thing that has parallels as well with the whole idea of... you know how people say if you die in a nightmare, you die in real life? Namely, this fear that the commonplace really can be dangerous. Another example—this is my book and I figure here's the place to say this—I seem to think of Foghat guitarist Rod Price probably once every few days, namely at home when descending a skinny staircase in the dark or when carrying something, counting the steps. Why? Because the poor man died falling down his own stairs. Both of those examples, and Dave's unfortunate incident, are in this same realm of being bitten by the mundane, which was supposed to be mundane, but proved otherwise. With Dave's thing, the idea is, who hasn't woken up in the middle of the night with an arm completely dead to the world and shaken the hell out it while envisioning certain amputation? Exactly. End result: Dave goddamn Mustaine pops into my mind every time my arm or leg falls asleep.

So Dave now had a nasty case of Saturday Night Palsy or more formally, radial neuropathy, and his arm and hand was rendered useless, certainly, as far as being thrash's bitter shred eccentric was concerned. Come April 3rd of 2002, Dave gave his band (and brand, and alter ego) Megadeth its last rites and underwent four months of physical rehab, not particularly so he could be Mega-Dave again, but just so he could live a regular life. Amusingly, there was the subtle distinction that Dave was quitting Megadeth—the rest of the band, presumably, did not see fit to continue in his absence.

A slapdash contractual obligation album was put together erroneously called **Still Alive... And Well?**, a title that brought back Megadeth's love of punctuation, a title that was an answer Dave ventured when asked what he might want to have put on his tombstone (hence the tombstone art).

The album, issued on September 10th of 2002 when there was no band, featured six live tracks (mostly no-nonsense classics) from The Web Theatre in Phoenix Arizona, circa November 17, 2001, plus six selections from the last studio album, **The World Needs A Hero**. **Still Alive... And Well?** would mark the last appearance on a Megadeth record for Dave Ellefson before Mustaine and Dave Jr. would break but then patch up relations eight years hence. In the meantime, July of 2002, Dave very publically set about auctioning off the tools of his trade, while Al Pitrelli finds other employment, replacing Jack Frost in Savatage.

Chris Poland had told me, as this long period of downtime for Dave wore on, specifically July of 2003, that, "I've been hearing things about a reunion. He hasn't really spoken to me about it. It's just every once in a while we speak about what's going on just with his life. I haven't spoken music with him, no. But I know he can play again, so that's a good thing. It's possible, but it's still to be seen, though. I don't know, for some reason, everybody keeps—in like the grapevine—talking about my brother Mark being the drummer. But this is all just conjecture and rumour (laughs)."

As for Dave's growing religious convictions during this period, Chris says, "You know what? It's always... he was raised, I think they were Mormons? (actually Jehovah's Witness). So he had that kind of instilled in him. Anybody that's raised with religion for the first ten years of their lives, whether they want to be an atheist or not, I don't think it's possible. I think there's somewhere inside them that they have to look to that religion at some point in their lives. So I think Dave's always kind of had that, his belief in God. His wife and his family, I think is what drew him to that. That's just me just speculating."

Poland had also talked about an impending release of some **Rust In Peace**-era demos. "Yeah, that we did together, which will be with, I guess, Capitol Records' permission too. That should be interesting. Because I remember playing it, thinking how fun it was. This was after I got sober, and I was going to join the band again, and I went down there. I got an offer from Capitol/Enigma to do the **Metalopolis** record, though, and I thought, you know what? Do I really want to join Megadeth again and possibly not have time? I have all the songs written already, and they wanted to sign me, and this was something I really wanted to do. And my brother was really into it too; he helped me do all the pre-production on the songs, so we could get them all sussed out before we went in and did them. So this is '89, the fourth record. It was Nick Menza on drums; it wasn't Chuck Behler. So yeah, I'd come back and almost rejoined for the fourth record, and did demos for that. Those songs are great. That's like my favourite—not that I don't think the third record is good, even though everybody hated it."

"So yeah, he tells me we're going to release that. And I'm like, that's awesome. Because there is some stuff on there that was really, really good, that wasn't like **Rust In Peace**. The versions that were on the demos had more of a blues thing going on, personally, which is what I like, but fans may not like it. But at least they can see the progression of the songs. I didn't really do anything but solo. I'm not sure what Dave did. I think I only play on four songs."

But then, of course, Chris was out again, making way for the arrival of Marty Friedman...

"You know, what it comes down to, I played some solos on this stuff, because we were signing contracts too, as far as getting monies, where the money would just come to me directly from the label. You know, just for my performances. We were talking about me joining—I was talking about joining, and he was asking me to join. It was hard, because I didn't want him to think that I had went and just not really considered it. I did consider it. It took me weeks. Like, wow, should I do this? And the more I thought about... at the time, my manager was Janie Hoffman, and she was like, you know what? You're in a position where you can do what you want. If you want to do your own music, you can. And I thought, well why not? Isn't that what I want to do? So that's what I did. Because then he spoke about having Marty Friedman coming in if I didn't do it. And I thought well fuck, you can't lose there. And so it wasn't like I was leaving him in the lurch."

"As you can see, when I left Megadeth, I did **Return To Metalopolis**. That had the Megadeth imprint; that was the kind of stuff that I wanted to approach Megadeth with, but it wasn't until later, like years later, that Dave even let anybody approach with parts and stuff. So I had already written it, and it was like, it wasn't something I felt I wanted to do forever, but it was something that I'd written. I was out on tour with the Circle Jerks playing bass when I wrote a lot of that, and I just felt like, you know what? I'm going to do this instead."

In May of 2003, however, Dave reports that he and his fretting arm are back and that he will be working on a solo album. He didn't talk about a reunion situation, nor were there any promises to release any of the **Rust In Peace** demos. However, the ensuing record would have the long exiled Chris Poland playing a role.

As for Dave "Jr." Ellefson, he found himself flying below the radar but keeping his hand in the game. "I worked with Dave on **Prophecy**," notes Sepultura/Soulfly legend Max Cavalera, that record emerging March 30, 2004. "He played three songs on the record, and he did the video, *Prophecy*, with us. He almost became a Soulfly member. Yeah, it became this close. But he was working with Peavey at the time, and we didn't want to influence that, so we just had him jam on the record and do the video with us, and did a couple shows with us. Dave is a cool guy, a really nice guy. And every time I see him, it's nothing but good vibes with him."

"I didn't hang out too much with Mustaine," continues Max, asked about Mustaine. "In Australia, we did a tour and we went to dinner together, and that was pretty neat, with his wife and his daughter with him, at that time. He didn't have his son, but his daughter. That was pretty cool. He's a good guy. I think he gets a lot of shit from the Metallica stuff, but I think once you get to know him, he's a cool guy, actually. I think he gets a bad rap."

And as for an assessment of Megadeth's place in metal history, Max says, "I really like them. Myself, I think it's really cool and original, almost like jazz, in some of the early stuff. **Peace Sells** and **Killing Is My Business**, there are some kind of jazz fusion ideas, which is really cool and new in metal. It was different, and I think it was even different from Metallica. That was really cool that he came out and did something not exactly the same as Metallica. **So Far, So Good... So What!**, excellent record. I don't know too much of the newer stuff. Mark Rizzo, our guitarist, is a big fan. He likes the new stuff a lot. He always talks about, 'Yeah, you should check out the new Megadeth, man. Pretty cool!' But I'm so I'm glad they're still going, still doing their thing. Both Daves are cool guys."

As 2004 wore on, it would come to pass that the Dave Mustaine solo album would become a Megadeth album, predictably, in the grand tradition of this happening and making sense, as was the case with Tony Iommi and **Seventh Star**, Ritchie Blackmore and **Stranger In Us All**, and even, in a sense, with Alice Cooper and **Welcome To My Nightmare**.

"Yeah, it's been pretty painful," mused Dave talking to our mag Brave Words & Bloody Knuckles about the record that would emerge, namely **The System Has Failed**, issued on September 14th of 2004. Bossman Tim Henderson took this particular interview, eager to maintain relations with Mustaine despite fireworks that emerged after **The World Needs A Hero** received a 4/10 review with us two years back.

"I don't know, I think a lot of it was just that I had an opportunity to make things right," continued Dave, first wanting to talk about the catalogue reissue program that very smartly accompanied the release of the long-awaited new material. "You know, working with a co-producer, sometimes you have to cooperate and sometimes you compromise and when Capitol gave me the opportunity to go back in and make all of these reissues the way that I hear them in my heart and in my mind when I think of these songs versus, you know, what's on record, I jumped at it. The two records I wanted to fix the most were **So Far, So Good... So What!** and **Risk**. Probably the two that I didn't want to touch the most was **Countdown** and **Cryptic**. You know, it's kind of hard to go after two records that sonically are really well recorded and produced. So basically those two records were just kind of paring away some of the stuff that was over-produced."

On the rebirth of Megadeth as a viable recording and touring act, Dave says, "If you read the wording in the press release that we put out in 2002 I think it was, about the breakup and me going into retirement, it did word it in a way where it left the door open. The thing though, when I went to make this record, it wasn't to make a Megadeth record. I was in California last summer and I knew that... when I retired there was a fire inside of me that just loved to play and I thought that after a while of not playing that, that fire would just go out—it didn't. If anything it just got more and more painful for me to think, 'You know what? This is not the way that you want to be remembered.' I decided I was going to do a solo record and then management went to EMI publishing and they said, 'Dave's going to do a new record, we owe you a Megadeth record, will this solo record count?,' and they said 'No.' He said, 'Well, I guess then he's a free agent,' and they said, 'No, we own him until he gives us that Megadeth record.' So that's basically why it's a Megadeth record and not a Mustaine record. There's a lot of people that say that it's me by myself and not Megadeth and I don't fuckin' get it because I've listened to this record and it sounds like Megadeth."

"I've lived through things most other people would die just watching," adds Dave, on the new record's considerable fire. "I'm a fighter and a survivor. I've made some questionable records and I've rebounded. I've taken the criticism and it doesn't feel good but you know what, I know that the people that are saying this, some of them are fans and they just don't want to see the band that they grew up on turn into something that they don't recognize any more. Like I said, part of being a good leader is you have to compromise. Sometimes it's like being a parent; you tell the kid, 'Don't touch that fuckin' stove' and they keep doing it and you say 'OK, I warned you.'"

Megadeth to the core, says Dave, and that includes the **Rust In Peace**-vibed cover art, featuring our old friend Vic Rattlehead, "actually handing out what is the equivalent of 'get out of jail free' cards to all those people in line. You know, because the system has failed, these guys can buy their way out of jail time. Look at Martha Stewart today, perjuring herself and committing insider trading—she only gets five months? And then she's going to appeal it? Obviously the courts are for sale. We're gonna see... honestly right now it's so ironic; I'm talking about the court system and now I'm involved in it."

What Dave is wryly referring to there is the legal action that was taking place between himself and Dave Ellefson. Ellefson initiated, citing breach of contract and loss of publishing and merchandise revenues he claimed were owed. Ellefson, in a suit filed July 12th, 2004, had been seeking $18.5M in damages, to which Mustaine, on July 29th, counter-sued, stating that on May 14th, Ellefson had signed a settlement agreement giving up his 20% stake in the band. Ellefson countered, stating that he had signed under pressure and the agreement was later withdrawn.

Once inside **The System Has Failed**, things get off to a rousing start with *Blackmail The Universe*, a chunky thrasher containing all those things you know and love about Megadeth, obtuse, percussive riffing, novel vocal melodies, and Dave spitting nails over world politics. As well, there's a surprise switch from the opening thrash velocities to mid-paced crunch and then a further collapse into a half-speed break.

"*Blackmail The Universe* wasn't so much about Bush's plane going down," cautions Dave, referring to the shocking opening sequence. "It was just about the President's plane going down and that nobody wanted to go get him. Actually that song was based on a book by C.S. Lewis called **The Great Divorce**. It's kind of scary, the whole topic of that song—plane goes down, nobody wants to go get him so they fire up the old nukes. But it had nothing to do with the Bush administration because one thing that really cranked me up... I was over in Europe and all the Europeans were telling me all these bands that are American that are coming over saying they fuckin' hate Bush and stuff like this. Every president since I was born was criminal to some extent. Kennedy was a drug addict, Nixon was a liar, Carter and Ford were bumblers, Lyndon Johnson got us into a war that killed literally hundreds of thousands of people unnecessarily. Everybody thinks Clinton is such a rock star. Well yeah, he does have a certain schmaltziness about him but that's because he made us all rich; the economy was booming. If America had been in a recession they would have said, 'This guy's a horrible president and he gets blow jobs from fat chicks.' Certainly Bush isn't the best President America has ever had, but whoever replaces him isn't going to do any better. There's always going to be somebody disinterested or dissatisfied somewhere."

"You know, I'm an American," continues Mustaine. "I love America. I also know that when you travel, the reason most Americans get treated like shit when they travel internationally, it's not because they're Americans, it's because they behave like assholes. For me, going to different countries... for example, I lived in Spain for awhile and just the pace over there is totally different. You just don't go over there and beat the table and say, 'I want my order.' I think that probably has a lot to do with how America is all about self-advancement."

Die Dead Enough however—catchy chorus and all—tempers things, and sends the message that there's going to be evocations of the **Youthanasia** period on **The System Has Failed** as well. "There are some people that are panning on the record," notes Dave, "saying it ain't fuckin' **Rust In Peace** Part II. Well, it will never be Part II because I'm not a 28 year old swingin' dick anymore. I'm 42. Sure, I can still play like that but it would sound totally contrived."

The plan was for *Die Dead Enough*, the album's first of two singles, to be used in **Tomb Raider II** and then the **Saw** film; neither happened, but at least a production video got made for it, featuring Dave and none of the other guys, which makes sense because there really was no band at this point. Joining Dave on the record were Zappa great Vinnie Colaiuta, who clearly was not going to become Megadeth's drummer, Christian music and country session bassist Jimmie Lee Sloas (ditto), and, as lead guitarist on all tracks except *I Know Jack*... one Chris Poland.

"Well, Dave just called me," explains Chris, on the surprise merger, "and said hey, listen, I'm making a record, and I don't have a lot of options, and I just think it would be great if we get together again. And it was, actually. Anything you heard after that was basically attorney/management problems. But it was great working with Dave, and it was great working on that record. It was very challenging. They have a certain thing they want, and you know, I have a certain thing I want, and I had to kind of step back and just give them what they wanted, so."

And Poland's role? "I just soloed. On all of them. I was very curious, because the reason... you know, Dave called me up and said, 'Listen, Vinnie Colaiuta is playing drums on it.' And as soon as he said that, I was like yeah, I'm in (laughs). There's some really great songs on it. Like *My Kingdom* is... God, recently it's been my favourite Megadeth track. I know I played on that and I'm a little biased, but I love that song, man. And I love the first song on the record too. And there are a couple other tunes. There are some things on there I wouldn't consider Megadeth material, but it was cool. I kind of consider that his solo record, and I think it was great that he got that out of his system. You know, he's a really great writer, and I'm not going to sit here and dis him or anything. Because I learned a lot from that guy."

As for the chance that Poland would join Dave on the tour for the album, Chris says, "No, no, no. Dave knew... I know he kind of joked around about it, but this thing I do here, this is what I'm going to do until they put me in the ground."

But yes, that was Dave's band for the album, Mustaine co-producing with Jeff Balding, recording the album at Oceanway and Emerald Entertainment in Nashville (hence, Jimmie), with additional recording in Dave's backyard at Phase Four Studios, Tempe Arizona. A number of extras are dutifully listed in the credits, but Dave smartly kept it simple, the core band remaining consistent, even if in solo album fashion, this would not remotely be the band to promote the record live.

Third track in now, *Kick The Chair*, an attack on the justice system, is another selection that helped reviewers proclaim that Dave was thrashing hard again. This direction... well, I'm just being myself, Dave seemed to say.

"Yes, well, when I went out to New York with management to go talk to the record company... in America it's a little weird because when you make a new record you've got to put everybody on notice: you've got to notify your publishing company, you gotta notify your record company. We notified them and when I went out to talk to the record company the president said, 'Dave, you know what? At one point you held the flag for the thrash/speed metal, heavy metal generation in America and you just kind of walked away from it.' I knew what he was saying, but part of me didn't want to hear it. He just said, 'You know what? Get your flag back, man. Don't fuckin' make this record for anybody but yourself.' I thought that this was really cool; this is a record company that puts out a shit load of money for a band, band breaks up and they've done nothing but believe in this group and they've been nothing but fucked by everything that's taken place yet they still believe in me enough to say, 'Megadeth/Mustaine... we don't care, we just want your music and we just want you to make music for yourself.' I walked away from that meeting thinking this is such a beautiful way to feel about making music. It was freeing, very liberating."

Kick The Chair was issued May of 2004, four months before the issuance of the album, as an advance free download, Megadeth always game to work with the internet in forward-thinking ways, including at this time, regular blog postings.

"I think there's a good way that the internet can be used," mused Dave. "Anything can be used for good or for band and I've found a way that the internet can be used to promote and further my career, also to stay in close contact with fans. Although, too close is dead when you get to the point where you are answering every email and posting on every thread and stuff like that; it gets to be a little crazy. There was a point where I really was concerned about keeping in close contact with everybody. But right now, like I said, everything has kind of been suspended because I know that people are watching what I'm saying and can use it against me. I'm just sitting back right now, just seeing how things are going to pan out. I know the fans are waiting to see what's going to happen just as much as anybody else is. I like the fact that you can use the internet as a marketing tool, that you can put up medium, whatever, if it's music or video or anything like that, photos and stuff like that. And it can be used for purposes that are instant gratification for people. It's so hard to promote a group nowadays. Just the pure fact that the music business is suffering so bad, bands are dying, record companies are being acquired by other record companies to the point where there are no record companies anymore and the record companies that are out there, they are in trouble. It's good to be able to make use of something that if you don't have marketing money to do something, you can use things on your own."

Back to the record, *The Scorpion* is another **Youthanasia/Cryptic**

Writings-type rocker, with Dave crooning low over a percussive mid-pacer with pregnant pauses. Lyrically, Dave paints a psychological portrait of your basic despicable human being, equating his loathsome personality traits with those of a scorpion. He's been there before, Dave has, only the summary of the scumbag would include more allusions to drugs and what they do to one's moral compass. Indeed, as one might expect, Mustaine's admitted as much that it's a portrait of himself as a junkie, only it could easily be about Gar or the newly returned and long rehabilitated Chris Poland. Dave has also said the scorpion dimension to the song was inspired by Aesop's fable, where the moral of the story is that killing is simply part of the scorpion's nature.

Speaking in general about the material he'd used on **The System Has Failed**, Dave explains that, "Basically what happened was from about 1990 to about 2001, when I was doing soundchecks or when I'd be at rehearsal or anything like that, I would... one of the reasons I don't like to practice is that when I pick up my guitar I write and I'm not always taping so I don't want to write if I'm not recording because then that potential riff is gone forever. So it's really hard for me to want to do that unless I'm set up. So whenever I would rehearse or soundcheck or anything like that I would tape and I had 150 sound files. The press release says songs but it wasn't necessarily songs; it was just files. One of the files would have maybe one riff on it, one of the files would have an entire song, maybe enough for two songs in it; it just depended. And oddly enough, when I got all that stuff loaded into my machine and I started going through it, that's when it really started to become clear to me which direction the record needed to go in because I wanted to make a metal record, there was no doubt about that, but I just didn't know which songs I was gonna pick."

"There is one song that didn't get finished and actually I had 22 songs because I was going to go into the studio with Jeff (Balding, producer) and record all 22 songs at my leisure so then I could release these two Dave Mustaine solo records in a row, in my timing, whenever I wanted to. Sadly it ended up being a Megadeth record so I figured, 'Shit, I'll just do the Megadeth record;' that way there won't be any fudging of the books or anything like that because I've tried to be really conscientious of exorbitant expenses in the studio. I had my vision of what I wanted it to sound like and ultimately, in my head, there were certain parts that I knew were going to sound a certain way, but you never really know until you're done, what it's gonna look like. I'm going to try my best to not think about radio or MTV or selling records. I want to play the shit that I play and makes me feel good, the stuff that's complicated heavy Dave Mustaine metal Megadeth riffs."

Toxic love lament *Tears In A Vial* is the first of two tracks on the album in possession of a New Wave Of British Heavy Metal vibe, here, most notably in the galloping melodic riff. it's an interesting direction for Megadeth, quite melodic and mainstream but not in a manner that sounds second-guessed toward modern rock. This is very much down a pathway toward Deverill-era Tygers or early to mid-years Saxon, pure groove, conventional construct, memorable.

The next track with a NWOBHM vibe is actually a nostalgic look at metal's golden days. Although Dave mentions denim, leather, thunder, lightning and wildfire (!), his paean to heavy metal shock power is really about the birth of thrash. Apropos of nothing, it is prefaced by a 40 second intro called *I Know Jack*, which celebrates Lloyd Bentsen's classic debate cut-down of mental lightweight Dan Quayle back in October of 1988. Nonetheless, *Back In The Day* is yet another great Megadeth track that finds Dave riffing intelligently and with intense note density, while still managing to come out the other end wholly accessible.

Something I'm Not is another thumping mid-paced metal tune with percussive stops and starts. It's generally believed that the song is about Lars Ulrich, with Dave having been recently re-stung by his experience with the **Some Kind Of Monster** confessional documentary assembled by Metallica.

"You know me," Mustaine says, asked about it by Tim Henderson while it was still fresh, "the whole time since I've left Metallica those guys have just railed me, said I was unimportant, said I was a temporary guitar player, a shitty lead guitarist and now all of a sudden I'm so goddamn important I gotta be in their movie? America was attacked September 11th, 2001, and that was filmed September 13th, 2001, two days later. We played Vancouver on the 12th and I couldn't fly home for my 40th birthday. Now, that was a milestone in my life. The fact that when you hit those milestones, they're important and I couldn't go home. I drove all the way from Vancouver down to San Francisco and spent my 40th birthday with Lars, being videotaped. And when it was over I signed a piece of paper and said, 'I don't know about this man. I want to see it before you put it out; let me approve it.' And they said they would. They sent it to me and I didn't approve it and then Lars does this spin saying, 'Fuck man, I don't know what to tell you man. Fuck, we were trying to see why he would say no; we didn't know if it was him or his manager.' Well who cares if it was me or my manager, we said no. I know that I told that director and producer, 'I don't want you to use it.' If I'm so unimportant, and if I was such a non-important part of the band, if I was such a shitty guitar player, why do I have to be in your movie? Why don't you just leave me alone?"

"I've got a pretty quiet home that I live in," continues Dave, asked about how the rest of life was treating him as of 2004. "I bought a horse recently. I'm trying to get used to just being normal; it's really hard. I would rather be a normal person that works for a living now than be really self-important and be starving in secret. If I didn't work it would drive me crazy because the music is such a big part of what I do. And now that I've been able to get back to what I do and not what everybody wants me to do... yeah, it's really hard. When you're in a band it's like you've got three wives. Especially when you've got management that is trying to tell you what to do. Then all of sudden you've got five wives."

Up into the last third of **The System Has Failed** is thrash ballad *Truth Be Told*, which oscillates from mellow and sorrowful verse to **Rust**-crunchy thrash chorus. It's probably the album's proggiest track, given its switchbacks and various speeds, and at 5:40, it's the album's second longest. Lyrically it's a history-sweeping declaration of war on war, same mistakes being repeated since the days of Cain and Abel.

Of Mice And Men... well, John Steinbeck has a novel(la) called that, but then again Metallica have a song called *Of Wolf And Man*! As well, the song is clearly biographical, Mustaine expertly working his way through his years, pulling knives out of his back, likely on some level knowing that he is writing a huge Megadeth classic, one of the band's best of many solid songs in the 2000s, a deserved second single from this record.

Shadow Of Deth is an involved intro, a military march of pageantry that uses an English-accented recitation of *Psalm 23* as it thumps toward closing (but brief) epic *My Kingdom*, a crunching Megadeth saga and journey, **Rust In Peace**-like in temperament and high-minded musical goals, lyrically all swords and chalices and kings, although Dave gets in a curious line about possessing the right to bear arms, a clue as to future and fervent political, er, fevers to befall Dave as he "wakes up," according to the definition of that state offered by talk show inciter and exciter Alex Jones. The Latin at the beginning of *Shadow Of Deth* translates as "my help comes from the Lord," Dave willing to put his Christianity out there—God is thanked before family in his personal thanks list in the booklet—honestly although not proselytizing with it.

And that was it, fans and critic s alike accepting **The System Has Failed** as a Megadeth record, the album rising to No. 18 on Billboard, moving about 170,000 copies by December of 2005 (and 14 months earlier, 46,000 units in its first week of release). *Die Dead Enough* as a single hit No. 21 on the Mainstream Rock charts but has not persisted as a Megadeth staple.

As all eyes turned to the return of Dave Mustaine on stage, Dave figured, non-committally at the time, "Well, the 20 dates that I had mentioned was for North America, obviously including cities that matter. The rest of the world, obviously there's a lot of market places that Megadeth matters and it's just that right now everything is kind of in limbo, with the record coming out and this thing with Ellefson, we just don't really know what's happening. Would I like to play? Sure, I'd like to play. Am I gonna not play? No. Is it gonna be right away? Well I was hoping so, but I don't know now. I can't talk about the lawsuit or anything like that but I can tell you this much: it's going to take more than that to kill me."

Intriguing was the idea that Dave would finally close that circuit with Canadian metal legend Jeff Waters, the baby Dave Mustaine, the sustainable thrash icon on a lower level but known to the knowing just the same.

"I've been talking to one of your countrymen about playing with me and it looks pretty good," said Dave at the time, gearing up for touring **System**. "We've been talking quite a lot and my only fear is that he's so good and he's a leader of his own thing and this is an institution here. It's a worldwide thing. I've already had some struggles with bringing in a hired gun that was a leader of another situation with Alan (Pitrelli). Alan's a good guy, good player. I don't think that he really could take going from being a leader in Savatage and TSO (Trans-Siberian Orchestra) to being, you know, second, or actually fourth, in Megadeth. I don't think he could handle it. That's my only fear about working with Jeff is that he's a leader of his own thing. But, we're talkin' and we're talkin' and I'm passionate about what I want to do and it may very well happen. We've obviously started a friendship and I've known of him for years. It may just be that this is a combination that will put him on the map and give me some stability because I have a lot of friends that are Canadian and every one of them is just fucking righteous."

The association goes back to the late '80s. Or does it? Replacing Jeff Young back then... Waters was discussed in the press, as was Dimebag Darrell and eventual hire Marty Friedman.

"Honestly, that never was the case because I never spoke with the man," clarifies Mustaine. "I would like to have said that we talked. I may have made a phone call or someone may have made a phone call on my behalf, but I don't remember ever speaking to him. It's not like that period was a blur because I was very coherent at that time and if it would have come down to me listening... because I had the **Alice In Hell** record and I thought, 'This guy is great.' I know that if I would have sat down with him and just said, 'Here, this is my vision' and presented my case, if anybody was willing to be at the top I know they would have come along for the ride. I think right now that is one of the things that I'm most hesitant about because I don't know what I'm going to do. I don't know, with this whole thing with Ellefson right now, if it's going to be the end of Megadeth, if it's the end of me period, or what. I've pretty much put everything on the blocks for right now."

"Yes, we are talking a lot!" noted Waters this second time, back in 2004. As for 1989, Jeff's recollection is as follows: "Chuck (Billy, Testament singer) stormed into my hotel room and told me Dave was on the phone. We spoke. I was in shock. Tell me *you* wouldn't remember talking to a legend! He wanted Side B of **Peace Sells... But Who's Buying?** learnt and then mentioned that he might want to re-record my song *Crystal Ann* (from 1989's **Alice In Hell**) on his next CD."

Flash back seven years, and Jeff had told our mag, "It worked out perfectly for them 'cause I don't think I would've worked out. I would've been fired pretty quickly 'cause back then drugs and drunken binges were the norm. I was drunk back then all the time, so I think the combination of me going down into a big successful band would've killed me."

But in 2004, he was saying, "Look at it this way, Mustaine is a metal legend. I am a budding legend. He rules and I rock. If it is meant to be, then it will be. But know this, all ye metal fans, what an honour to even speak with a musician of his calibre! I hope things work out for him and Megadeth, regardless of my involvement. Still, how could I not ponder the magic that he and I would create if we were both to sit down someday and write together? As for myself and Annihilator, well I am here: ten studio CDs; the latest, **All For You**, is selling better than *all* Annihilator CDs since the mid-'90s. New video just coming out for title track. US deal done so there will be a US domestic release soon. Just returned from a triumphant tour with Judas Priest in Europe last month; asked to 'possibly' do their world tour next year. Planning fall/spring headline touring as we speak. Not too shabby for a kid from Ottawa, Canada eh?"

Never happened, but Megadeth persisted and resisted death. In fact, little did they know, but a wholesale face-wiping of personnel expectations was about to take place within the empire that was Megadeth. Dangerously close to collapsing into circus status, Dave rapidly unwound (quite publicly) and then found a tactical unit of unknowns and unexpecteds, folks who would string and thread together a sense of stability and continuation for years to come.

Who were these people? Well, after the disappointment of losing Nick Menza to a Bill Ward-styled collapse of suitability, Canadian Shawn Drover was to be added to the in-flux mix, a natural choice, as new Megadeth hire guitarist Glen Drover had brother Shawn in his back pocket as technician willing and able to take up the cause. Both Glen and Shawn were from quality, multi-album franchise Eidolon, with Glen additionally having served as King Diamond's guitarist. On bass was to be Iced Earth's James McDonough, a more than capable minted metalhead who would remind one of later hire Chris Broderick, in superman characteristics characteristic for the job. All three, along with dear leader Dave Mustaine, incredulously back in action, would be featured in the video for superlative Megadeth statement of class and intent *Of Mice And Men*.

The ensuing tour, coined as *Blackmail The Universe*, would commence in October of 2005, Exodus in tow, Megadeth later transitioning to Europe supported by Diamond Head and Dungeon. Fuelling interest for the dates, along with the recent studio album, was June 28th of 2005's **Greatest Hits: Back To The Start**. This was followed by more excellent documentation of Megadeth's career through physical product in the vast and detailed DVD video collection **Arsenal Of Megadeth**, issued March 21, 2006.

It is of note that **Arsenal Of Death**, along with **Rude Awakening** and **That One Night: Live in Buenos Aires** all achieved gold status in the US as videos, but disconcertingly, there have been no new album certifications to date since **So Far, So Good... So What!** reached platinum back in 1998. Of course, this goes for the band's new records in the 2000s but also the back catalogue, which can mean two things: a) the hit albums have sold really slowly through the '00s or b) we've got one of those labels on our hands, i.e. the exiled and bemoaned Capitol, that doesn't find themselves sufficiently motivated to investigate whether, say, **Rust In Peace** or **Countdown** deserves any sort of elevated awarding.

But back to the compilations, all of this impressive output was semi-vigorous enough business as usual compared to the brilliant business manoeuvre that was to represent Dave's prescient shift toward focus upon the live arena, a seemingly modest concept crudely monikered—and then deftly brand as—Gigantour.

12
United Abominations

"Maybe I'm from a bygone era"

As 2005 sweat bullets into 2006, Megadeth found themselves smartly transitioning to lording-over headline act through their Gigantour metal-reviving festival concept. Until this point, public perception had been that their band of Dave-and-whoever would forever remain strong "sandwich" act on exciting festival-type billings, legends that had lost their lustre but still gamely brought to bill that catalogue of rough and challenging thrash songs with just enough group and groove to warm the headbangers up for the *real* survivors of the metal wars.

The first incarnation of the fest saw the band working with Dream Theater, Nevermore and Overkill, Dave building a bill that was overtly and intently pure metal, the three bands mashed together essentially representing what Megadeth was: thinking man's thrash, thrash with lots of prog flourishes. Ergo one's a thrash band and the other two are two sides of the progressive metal coin, the metal in the alloy of both being two flavours of... thrash.

Other early accompaniers included Fear Factory, Anthrax, Dillinger Escape Plan, Life Of Agony, Symphony X, Dry Kill Logic and Bobaflex, again, a big pot o' progressive and thrash with a little alternative and industrial thrown in for variety's sake.

Late 2006, September and October, Megadeth started out in the states with Lamb Of God, Opeth and Arch Enemy sharing a main stage, Overkill, Into Eternity, Sanctity and The SmashUp rocking a second stage. Over to Australia in the latter part of October, and Megadeth were joined by Soulfly, Arch Enemy and Caliban.

Early 2007 was given over to the construction of a follow-up to the well-received **The System Has Failed** album, a solid and meticulous thrasher, but somewhat lessened in the eyes of fans due to Dave's complete lack of a real band of banging brothers on which to hang one's hat. On the one side, there was scepticism that Megadeth had in fact survived Dave's personal turmoil, and on the other, it was obvious that Dave was one of the great metal songwriters of the second generation borne of the post-NWOBHM '80s.

United Abominations, issued May 15, 2007 through a new deal with Roadrunner, would find Dave introducing on record his new band-fer-real (but not-fer-long), James LoMenzo on bass (replacing the short-lived James

MacDonough) and Canadian brothers Glen Drover and Shawn Drover on guitar and drums respectively.

"It was great because it was like joining a retrospective," says LoMenzo, already a veteran, having worked with White Lion, Pride & Glory, Ozzy, David Lee Roth and Black Label Society. "It was kind of being given a vocabulary of thrash metal music, which I was aware of, but never immersed in. I just had no reason to do it, when thrash metal was coming up. With White Lion, I guess I was kind of in the middle or on the tail of that. Probably behind it, actually, come to think of it, chronologically, with Metallica. But you know, for me, that was a lot of fun. At that point of my career, I had just finished with Black Label Society, which was kind of the big and plodding sound, which I enjoyed. To move from that to the precision and speed of a lot of the classic Megadeth stuff, it was a challenge for me. And I enjoyed that challenge—it was really something to think about and to do. And to say that I didn't go in with some trepidation... I told Dave Mustaine immediately, I said, 'I don't know if I'm your guy, because I'm kind of a blues basher. But I certainly want to give it a go.' And he was very gracious to that. He goes, 'Well, you know, Megadeth is kind of blues only really fast' (laughs). So I took his advice on that and I said okay, I suppose I can handle it."

"In regards to heavy metal, I think I've been nailed to the cross," continues James, wondering how he wound up here—actually the first contact came through a friend of his, Alan Steelgrave, who said that he had a shot at this big metal gig, but for now, he couldn't tell him who the band was. "Whoever calls he says, 'We're playing, you know, you're a heavy guy, come play.' The truth of the matter is, I love all kinds of music. I always have. I started out listening to pure pop music on the radio, which turned into rock music. And by pure pop I mean, you know, I'm not a young guy. I used to listen to Frank Sinatra, Ray Charles, people like that, along with the Beatles and the Rolling Stones, back in the '60s. Rock 'n' roll radio, AM radio, was vital to bringing you new music. Next to going out and buying the single, you didn't know what singles to buy unless you were listening to AM radio. So as a kid, I was immersed in all of that stuff, and the more trite the hit the more excited I got about it. I could listen to something like *Classical Gas*, which is a really weird song, Mason Williams playing the gut string guitar. I mean, to me that was very compelling, because that was something that was so different from just having a guy sing."

"On television when I was a kid, everybody got a TV show," continues James, on the journey that eventually deposited him in Megadeth. "Glen Campbell got a TV show. So what we know as country music now was actually just a pop form back then, but it was mapped as country music. I mean my eyes, my ears, all that stuff, as a little six or seven-year-old, I was just soaking all this stuff in. So, flash forward to the future, it wasn't until after the White Lion band... I guess White Lion was on tour with Ozzy

Osbourne and all these heavier bands, White Lion was a strange band. I always felt that we postured as a heavy metal band, but we weren't necessarily a metal band. We were really a pop music band. But we made it sound a little heavy because of the guitar, because of the three-piece forum, and because it was so much like Van Halen. So it started sounding like more of a rock band than a pop band. So right after that, I hooked up with Zakk Wylde, simply because we were on tour. Directly from that we started our Pride & Glory band, which led eventually to Black Label Society. So all of a sudden I started getting all these calls for heavy metal bands. Frankly, you know, for the most part, I wasn't that interested. I liked playing some heavy metal music. I loved Judas Priest, Iron Maiden; bands like that used to really thrill me because their thing is to sing. But I think what heavy metal does best… it had a very fascist approach, kind of there's one way. A band had a tight variance, which is kind of cool, because it was easy to latch onto—it gives you something to get behind and it becomes a way of life. And that's where I appreciated that whole thing, kind of the following and the lifestyle, the way that people devote themselves to heavy metal. But as far as playing the music as a bass player, I found it kind of boring—until Megadeth, many years later."

But don't kid yourself, Dave Mustaine grew up pretty much the same way, taking comfort in pop as well as the heavy stuff. "You know what, it's very interesting you should say that," reflects James. "Because we used to listen to an awful lot of classic rock, Zep and Bad Company, and stuff you wouldn't expect, Al Green. We'd use the sound system backstage when we would travel, and you know, backstage before the shows went on, him and I, we used to love listening to that stuff. And we would grab instruments and jam to it, just something to divert. So at least at that time anyway, and I don't know if it was my influence, I doubt it, but Dave was open-minded and listening to a lot of stuff. So, no, I don't think I drew him one way or another. But he certainly drew me in a direction that I didn't expect, which, I appreciate to this day. He brought out a part of me that I normally wouldn't bother with."

"I've never been in the Roadrunner offices," noted Mustaine at the time, talking with Tim Henderson about career, a topic he has always found ripe for reflection. "The last time I even talked to Roadrunner was before I signed to Combat. It's been good so far. It's nice to be one of the big dogs at that label. Obviously there are other bands that are our calibre and then some. There are some other people there that have set an example for us with respect to what the label can do. My goal is to be one of the top successes of the label. It seems like a no-brainer. There were other labels that offered us more money, that didn't have as much credibility and other labels that had seemingly more in the credibility department as far as being a major label, but the money really wasn't there. It's not really about the money, but it's about being able to finance business. When you go into the studio and a guy gives you a million bucks to do the record but he doesn't know how to do anything with it... 'Well, sorry, when this money runs out, the record dies.' I'd rather deal with a label that believes in the band and knows how to get it to the masses and has a relationship with people who are in our market/genre."

"It's really hard to trust people in the world," continued Dave, always easy and honest when it came to our mag, BW&BK. "So I try do the best I can and you just get people who you like to deal with and that way, when they let you down, 'cos they all do, it's not quite as difficult when there is somebody you don't like who lets you down because you are ready to pounce on them."

"Basically we have all new people, everything is all different. Shawn and Glenn are playing. We rented John Bonham's drum kit for Shawn and he was beside himself. He went to England as a young man and came back a seasoned veteran because the way he is playing, I didn't know he had that talent. I knew he had a gift. He even surpassed my wildest dreams for what drums should sound like on a Megadeth record. It's really rewarding to go through all the extent that we did and the difficulty to make everything happen because I believe sonically what we've got down right now is probably some of the heaviest bass and drum sounding tracks that we've had in a really long time. As far as the speed and the tempo or anything like that, that's up to other people to listen to and see if they like it or not. Tone-wise what we have right now is really cool."

"Glen has four songs done," explained Dave in this pre-release chat. "I just started my overdubs on Monday and I'm doubling my tracks so I'm about four songs into it. The record consists of 12 songs, 11 for an American release and 12 for Japan. Unless Roadrunner adds an additional track from something previously and puts out all 12 tracks around the world, which I think would be cool. I'd like to see all 12 tracks go around the world and give Japan a live track or something. As for song titles, these song titles change everyday! And I won't know the record title until I committed to the damn artwork, which is kind of going along the lines of the **Star Wars** trilogy. You know how it went back in time? Basically the direction for the artwork is going back in time."

Musically, Dave framed the upcoming slab as, "the music that I want to write and play, because there is no longer any outside pressure from people to write music that will provide income for them, whether it's management or other band members and stuff. I'm feeling good; I'm in a zone. I don't want to say I'm playing really well; I'm getting my work done and it's effortless, so... It hasn't been quite as hard as the last couple of records have been because even though the songs were returning to form, there are some things that I picked up along the way. I'm proud of how I learned to do vocal melodies with this music genre because there is not a lot of people who play music like this who have vocal melodies while taking the time to think about guitar solos. That matters to me. Maybe I'm from a bygone era. I really think the heavy metal community needs bands like Megadeth."

"Well, as you know, the band was laid to rest in, I think, 2001," begins new guitarist Glen Drover, asked about his hiring into the ranks of Megadeth. "So it was after they did **World Needs A Hero** and all that... Of course I wasn't there, but David had injured his arm, didn't play for a while, and the band was laid down. And then in 2004 he did—let's see if I've got this right—but I believe what happened was, he recorded **The System Has Failed** and he wanted to call it a day. But I think he was under contract; he owed Sanctuary another album under the name Megadeth. I'm not 100% on this one, but I'm pretty sure on that. And the responses were good, if I can remember at the time. So I think at that point he said yeah, he wants the band back together, and maybe do a farewell tour. And that's what it was originally. Putting the band together was supposed to be for a farewell tour. But I think because of how well it worked, how much fun we were having, we were kicking ass. We really were kicking ass. We were fuckin'... We were really, really working hard, and just toured everywhere, and everything else, and he just decided to continue."

As for Glen's and Dave's paths crossing... "The way he found me, oddly enough, we were doing this thing for the Wacken Festival, as Eidolon. We played there a few years previous, and there was a fan from the UK that came, and we were walking around the field and watching the other bands and this guy comes up and says, 'Hey, I'm a big Eidolon fan and I'm looking forward to your set.' Him and Shawn were blabbing and they exchanged contact info, kept in contact, email. And he was also talking to Dave McRobb, the website guy for Megadeth, the main guy. So basically what happened was, this guy Sam, the fan guy, was talking to McRobb, and McRobb put the word out about possibly Dave looking for people, and then he said, you know, there's this guy Glen, he played with King Diamond, played with Eidolon, check this out, might be a good match. And it basically went from there. I got an email from Sam one morning, and he said, 'I recommended you for the gig.' And I said oh, okay, Saturday morning, okay, little too early in the morning for this. And within a couple days, I was actually on the phone with Dave Mustaine. So it happened very, very quickly. Then we went and supported the **System Has Failed** album, toured that first. We did a lot of touring, toured for a year or two, and then we went in to do the **United Abominations** album."

Stepping back however, there was definitely some enticing intrigue as to who would comprise the new post-break-up Megadeth. "Yes, well, when we went in to rehearsals, and what happened, it was me and Nick Menza, because he'd been recruited before I was there, right before me. Then after me it was James MacDonough from Iced Earth. So that was the initial band rehearsals. But after about a week in rehearsals in Arizona, it wasn't working out with Nick, and in the end, Nick... There was something between him and Dave. Maybe past stuff, who knows? It just wasn't happening. You could tell. There was a lot of tension there, and there was personal issues. Anyway, Dave goes, 'Well I know your brother plays, I like the Eidolon stuff, what about him?' So Nick was let go, and Shawn came in the next morning. It was that crazy. This was like six days before the first show. We were doing 20 songs, and Shawn had to learn these songs, and how are you going to do that, right? He did it. He learned them all in six days, he went out and played all the songs. Dave was like, 'Oh, we can cancel the first two.' And Shawn's like, 'Fuck that.' And this is before iPods. So he's got the Discman, just listening over and over and over. Like a sponge. When he learns it, he's got it. Just repeated listens. Practicing. And he got the gig, and that was it."

"Actually, one thing, before James McDonough was actually hired, Dave had asked me if Adrian Robichaud from Eidolon would be interested. So initially it was going to be Adrian Robichaud, Dave, me and Nick—that's who was supposed to do the gig. Because Dave said, 'Well what about your bass player?' And that didn't work out, because Adrian is a finger player, and Dave wanted a pick player, like Ellefson. He just wanted that particular sound. It's just the way he wanted it. That's the style he wanted. He wanted to continue that whole thing. It makes it tighter. You have to follow Dave all the time; he does that stuff, intros and so forth."

"The first tour was Exodus; shit, there were so many," continues Glen, whose first actual show with the band was a headlining slot at the third annual Dubai Desert Rock Fest, March 16, 2006. "And we would work on writing stuff at soundchecks. Dave is always doing that. He is always messing around with stuff. And he'd just come up with a riff and we would just start off playing it. And it was, 'Hey, that sounds pretty cool.' But Dubai, I had a different idea what it was going to be like, like a tourist spot, but it wasn't like that. We were in the desert; it was fucking the middle of nowhere. Everybody was cool, but it was different. We are not at home here."

And who attended this thing, mostly locals?

"Yeah, pretty much. Sure looked like it anyway. It was fucking jammed. It was an outdoor, open-air festival, probably 20 or 30,000. It was an open air festival, with a lot of bands. Testament were there, plus the band with hit song *Kryptonite*—3 Doors Down (ed. also Reel Big fish and local band Mannikind). That was weird. It was that kind of festival. There was a heavy band, and then there was a band like that. Everybody's on stage at the end of their set, 'You guys looking forward to Megadeth?' 'Yeah, me too.' That was funny."

"Dubai was perfect," adds LoMenzo." That was the first gig I did with Megadeth—touché, by the way (laughs). And the trick to that one was really remembering all the songs. Because it was an awful lot thrown at me in a month's worth of time (laughs). It was a 20+ song set. Trying to remember all the songs, that was in my head a lot. But going out to the desert to play, what a trip. Dubai back then, they had a lot of money pouring into it, a massive amount of construction everywhere. It kind of reminded me of the summer camp I went to when I was 13. It was the first year the place opened up and it was a co-ed camp and they really hadn't figured it all out (laughs), the people putting the camp together. So it was ultimately chaotic fun, and that's what Dubai reminded me of. I met people who were young people like in their twenties and stuff from the states. One found a job as a photographer and another one was just vagabonding around. So you have that faction of people that were there which was interesting, because they just figured, it's cheap living, there's no rules here, we're going to have fun. And then there was this, you know, workers on the highway, just wearing turbans walking down the highway. And you look at a stretch of 20 miles forward and 20 miles back with nothing there, and I was wondering where they were walking to. So it was very strange. I mean, we rode camels, we went on the dunes, which is a trip everybody should do, a little dune ride with some cars when you can. Because it feels like you're in the middle of absolutely no place in the world. So we really explored and had a great time. And the band was really well received—nothing like playing *Holy Wars* in the middle east, you know?"

As for his other fondest moments playing live with Megadeth, James says, "You know what? Heaven & Hell. Iron Maiden was great, although I'd been out with them with Black Label Society (for the record, James was with that band circa 2004's **Hangover Music Vol. VI** and the following year's **Mafia**). Judas Priest was terrific, because they were all very giving. Ian Hill, of course, just being a bass player, but he's a gregarious fellow so he was fun. Glenn was surprisingly nice. Everybody in the band was pretty cool. And again, I'd met them when I was on Ozzfest with Black Label. A lot of people that we went out with were people I would run into on tour over the years and years and years. There's a really good feeling about seeing everybody still out there and standing. Especially some of our elders, because I don't have too many left (laughs). But no, that's a great feeling, because in a strange way, because of the recognition. I mean, Geezer Butler, on the Heaven & Hell tour, it's funny, because I had met him many times before, and having done stuff with Zakk and Ozzy Osbourne, all that stuff, he came up like first day, 'Hey, LoMenzo!' And it was kind of like Bugs Bunny: 'He knows my name!' I was excited. It's Geezer Butler, so of course. But it's kind of funny, because I find myself doing that with younger bands now as well."

With respect to the level of challenge playing live with Megadeth, James asserts that, "You know what? I didn't find any of them particularly hard to do initially. To me it was a memory game. My fingers turned out to be pretty good. They were moving pretty good. All kudos and hats off to Ellefson, because he wrote some great, great stuff, and I was really privileged to be able to pick up some of those songs and play them as best I could. And I tried to be as faithful to his style as possible, because I thought it would sound better that way. But I don't think there was ever anything that was a particular bear to me. If you broke them down into patterns and sections, none of it seemed that difficult. To me the real trick was performing it. Because what we had was a big stage, and we were all wireless, and it was a question of getting good enough to be able to find those little spots to take my hand off the neck for a minute and raise my hand up to the crowd, because they were so into it. Do that thing you do on stage, try to join with people. That, to me, was the most exciting part, like playing those really complicated parts and finding the spaces to perform them. So I think that was my biggest memory about all those years in Megadeth, was getting stagecraft together with the music."

New drummer Shawn Drover did in fact make attempts to channel the spirit of the great and passed and never surpassed Bonzo, during the making of **United Abominations**. Having sent our mag a photo of himself with the drums, he had indicated, "Bohnam's pieces are the black/white striped drums. The kit is a circa 1975 setup and the *only* Bohnam kit available to rent from a vintage gear rental place somewhere in England. It was a surprise from Dave. Needless to say, I was indeed both surprised and very happy. I used John's drums in several places throughout the recording of the new Megadeth record."

"So yeah, I did use Bonham's, but they were put in with the set I was using. In other words, I wasn't just using Bonham's four-piece drum set. They were combined with the huge drum set I was using in the studio. On certain songs, I would use more of Bonham's kit than on others, depending on what the song was. Certainly a song like *Sleepwalker*, with all it's double bass drums, I used the kit that was in the studio. Something like *United Abominations*, at the end of that song it's all Bonham. A lot of overdub stuff we would use on certain songs would be John's stuff, like the bass drum or the snare. He had a huge 20-inch floor tom which sounded like a cannon. So I used that as much as I could within the songs that I played. When we played (bonus track) *Out On The Tiles*, I tried to play that as close to the record as possible, but still adding my own thing. I didn't want to do a direct rip-off because nobody can directly rip-off John Bonham anyway. I tried to keep it close out of respect for the song and out of respect to him. But I added my little thing to it as well. Having the kit there in itself was pretty inspiring."

"He surprised me with it," said Shawn, on how the idea came about. "Dave said, 'I've got a surprise for you, but I'll let you know when you get there.' So we got into the studio and he says, 'By the way, I got you the only Bonham kit that is available for rental out of this place that has vintage rock star equipment in it.' I was floored, I couldn't believe it. That kit is so expensive to rent—I can't even tell you how much it was it was so ridiculous. But it was worth it."

"I can't wait for it to be released," continued Drover, "because we've been working on it for so long. It's cool for myself of course being that it's my first record with Megadeth. That just heightens the anxiety and excitement for me. I'm just really glad it's finally going to come out after us working on it on and off for over a year now. Being the drummer, all my stuff gets done first and everything else is finished later. Even with Glen and Dave going back to England to finish the record the last time, there were still a lot of things that were yet to be completed. Melody lines, solos, finishing touches. So when I finally did get the records, it was a surprise for me to see how Dave and Glen finished it all up."

Having been the main songwriter in his and his brother's well-regarded Eidolon project, Shawn said, "It was coming from a different view point—I welcomed the change. Being that I did most of the songwriting in Eidolon, it was a nice change, a different way of approaching a record. In terms of the drums, it was a completely collaborative effort. We would go in to do a song and I would do it with my vision and Dave would interject and say, 'Why don't you try this?' A lot of times it was something better than what I thought of. Balancing what I was doing off of the engineer and Dave turned out to be a really pleasant experience. In terms of songwriting, we went through the whole process of the songs and always made suggestions, but obviously the core of the material is Dave. But it didn't bother me at all. I had no problems with him steering the ship in that respect. We went through it all in demo form. Once we went into the studio, we had scratch guitars recorded and I'd play along with that. In some instances, Glen or Dave would play along with what I was doing. For the most part it was scratch guitars and not the final guitar takes that helped me get through the songs."

United Abominations opens with a spirited mid-paced thrasher called *Sleepwalker,* on which Dave gets to apply his wry sense of humour to all manner of violent death, committed, presumably while the perpetrator was sleepwalking. It is one of many example of Megadeth songs that are considerably heavy, thrash and even progressive, but somehow contain enough of the old school, the NWOBHM and the melodic to emerge from the sausage grinder as an accessible thrash uniquely attributable to Megadeth.

The same premise applies to the second track *Washington Is Next!,* although this one is even more melodic and four-on-the-floor. The added invitation to agitation however is that Dave assaults us with an intense blast of politics. Mustaine's new world order tale rolls and roils and Dave spits out a warning that all of this was prophesied from ancient times in the cradle of civilization. Apocalyptic imagery is legion, and to his immense credit, Dave makes it all work with a brisk yet mournful and Maiden-mad musical backing track that pays inspiring tribute to the NWOBHM.

"My political mindedness comes from the fact that I'm a patriot," said Dave, asked by Sam Dunn about the source of his interest in politics. "I love my country. I've been around the world and I know there are a lot of countries that... they want to be Americans for a reason, because where they live is like a step up from poverty. We've gone to places like in Brazil, in the favelas there, where people live inside of what we manufacture trash-cans out of, and that's their home. It costs six weeks' worth of a man's salary to buy a ticket to see Megadeth in Brazil, and that bothers me. I don't like knowing that a person has to work six weeks to come see me play music that comes effortlessly. I want to be able to give back to the fans. Especially when it comes to playing live. We did Rock In Rio in '92 and several people died at that concert. It was not a cool experience for us. They were sneaking people in and a police officer killed a fireman there; somebody fell off the balcony there. Death has its way of following us. We had a death in the very beginning with the drummer and a soundman that worked for me, and then we had two deaths at Castle Donington in '88. We had a death in Denver, somebody died sniffing hairspray for Halloween that was following us. Yeah, there's been a lot of things that have followed us. Those things all end up in a song somehow. It may not necessarily be the occurrence but the emotion will show up."

"Look, if you can't tell that I don't care what people think, then I'm not doing a very good job," continues Dave, on not following trend with his lyrics. "I have no tattoos. I am an anomaly. I don't follow trends. I don't spout clichés. How long have we been talking? How many one-liners have you heard me say? None. I don't need to. I speak the truth. Truth is way more cool for me than trying to be funny and use one-liners. I write what I feel. I write what I feel because I know you feel it, too. I know you know what it feels like when your car's just about to run out of gas, and you're thinking, 'God, if I get stuck at this light I'm going to be pushing this fucking car.' You've had that feeling. You had to have, at least once in your life. I have it every once in a while. Back when I was married I had it a lot because people would drive my car and I'd get in there, and I'd get going, usually get in a car pool lane where there's no escape, the light would come on and it's like, 'Oh my god, I'm not going to make it.'"

"I was very outspoken," says Dave, thinking back to the tone of his lyric canon. "Sometimes I said stuff about people and I meant it. Sometimes it was a joke. But just because you say it as a joke doesn't mean it doesn't hurt. And at the time we didn't care who we hurt. It was pretty much... we were one speed that was full stop. We're either asleep or we're going full-bore, and that's how we lived, and anybody who didn't get on the bus got under it. And I think that was prevalent with a lot of the metal bands in the latter part of the '90s. You started to see a lot of bands really get forced to reinvent themselves during the flannel years and the goatee years. I tried growing facial hair for a while and every time I just ended up looking like some mad Nazi, so I just figured I don't want to do that. So I've been sans beard almost my whole career. I've watched the music industry right now, and it's all made up of people who wear camouflage cut off shorts. And it's like when the hell did that ever get into fashion? I'm watching things, and I've been around long enough to see it went from leather pants to tight blue jeans to wearing stuff you could get off a dummy outside of Home Depot. I guess it's just that kind of anti-rock star thing."

"I'm always charmed by *Washington Is Next!*," offers James LoMenzo, back to the record, asked for his favourite tracks from his two-record run with the band, "just because it was a song that I had a creative bond with. I just remember it as being a big, really wide-open song. It had a lot of space for these big open heavy metal bass parts, like with Iron Maiden or even The Who. And Dave was very cool to let me have all that space to kind of slather on a melodic part on that, which wasn't, to me, typical of Megadeth at that point."

As for talking politics with Dave, James says, "Here's the thing, okay? I went to the band probably just to the right of liberalism (laughs). I mean, I still grumble every time I have to get on a plane to this day. With that face on. You know, we're trying to protect ourselves—I get that. But I see the value in both sides. So Dave's politics? I tried to stay the hell out of it. You know why? Because he's very, very mired in his beliefs, as he should be, and as you would guess, listening to the music over the years. So let him go. Whatever he's doing was fine. I neither backed it up or portrayed it one way or another. My job there was to play music. It would've been interesting to talk politics, but I think we both kind of sensed that we were standing on different sides of the platform. Honestly, swear to God. That's the reality. So it wouldn't be healthy (laughs). I mean, we're closer on religion than on politics, that's for sure. On my behalf, I was raised a Roman Catholic, so I sit on that traditionalist slant. That's where I come from.
But we didn't talk about religion very much either. We respected each other. So I think that's the way it should be, especially when you're locked in a band with people. Because it's a moving family that you have."

Next track on **United Abominations** is old school Megadeth album title in waiting *Never Walk Alone... A Call In Arms*, which is the only track not solely credited to Mustaine, given its Glen Drover co-write.

"I came up with a little bit," recalls Glen Drover. "And what made it to the album was a song called *Never Walk Alone*, part of that song. The rest of the album was all Dave. Basically, most of that song came about when we were doing the finishing touches on the album. We went to Andy Sneap's studio in England. It was just me and Dave, and we went to do finishing touches, which is solos, plus he did some vocals and some rhythm parts he needed to do to finish up the album. Because it was quite a long process. We went through two producers. Andy came in at the end, because the first producer didn't work out. That was Jeff Balding, who did **System Has Failed**. So we were finishing up that song and I came up with this middle section, which is a riff that was actually a spinoff of an old Eidolon thing. I was messing around with the riff of a song called *Priest* from **Seven Spirits**, the old independent album we did, and Dave went, 'What's that?' And I said, 'Oh, it's kind of similar to an old thing we did.' So we just used that, some of its guitar themes."

Indeed a chunk of the reason that the album missed its initial October 2006 release date by six months was the gut-check the band put itself through, namely this switch from producer Jeff Balding over to steely UK thrash knob-jobber (and before that, Sabbat guitarist) Andy Sneap.

"**United Abominations** was a fun time, especially at the end when Andy Sneap came in," says Glen. "He's such a great guy; we just hit it off like that. We just became brothers very quickly. We just see eye-to-eye. It was as if we'd been working together for a while, as odd as that sounds, comfortable and very productive. He took what we had done, which was about eight songs. Plus we recorded two or three with him at the end, to add the album. What happened was Jeff Balding had done the album, but the record company wasn't really happy with the end result, and we parted with him, and then Andy came onboard to basically bring the album, hopefully, where we needed it to go. He'd done all these great bands, like Arch Enemy, and he knows the shit; he knows his history. Listen to the last two fuckin' Accept albums—that speaks volumes right there. He definitely made his presence known, because compare the original version to the version that came out, it's quite different."

And what is that difference?

"The difference is the guitars are more metal. The original one had kind of a brown sound; it was a little too old school, too laid back. I remember hearing the album all the way through, and it didn't hit me. So Andy basically did his thing, engineering-wise. We might have re-recorded a few things along the way. But he definitely made it his own, even though he jumped in late in the game. He definitely brought the guitars where they should be, drums, everything. And Dave was singing more aggressively, I think at the end, more so than the beginning. Everything was just, 'Okay, let's just do this; fuck it, it's Megadeth.'"

"We worked at a few different studios in total," offers Glen on the geography of the record. "We started in a really interesting place, somewhere outside of London, this mansion that was owned by David Gilmour for many years. It's basically this mansion, and the studio was built in a barn, beautiful place, centuries old. Who owned it at that point was Trevor Horn, from Yes. That was great, because I'm a huge Yes fan. So I talked with him and his wife. Beautiful place, amazing trip to be having. He's up at the house. We were in one house, and he's got his... You'd have to see the layout, but it was very, very nice."

"But it didn't stop there. I think we got the drums and the bass done, and that's about it. We also worked at a place called The Steakhouse, which is a studio in Hollywood owned by Steve Lukather from Toto. We were there for a couple weeks or so. Did a lot of demo work, before we started the album. We did a lot of demo work, closer to where Dave lived at the time. Not Vic's Garage—that came into play after my time. That was only built a few years ago and didn't exist then; he just moved to San Diego toward the ends of my days. And aside from that, where else did we record? Well, Andy Sneap's place. Those were the final recordings, and that's where the mixing and mastering happened."

The idyllic locale of which Glen speaks was in fact SARM Hook End Studios, London. The Steakhouse was indeed in Studio City, California, with additional studio credits going to Big Fish Encinitas, Backstage Productions, S.I.R. in Hollywood and Mustaine Music, Fallbrook, California.

Adds James LoMenzo, remembering England, "**United Abominations** was interesting because it had come off **The System Has Failed**, which started giving Megadeth and Dave some notoriety again. So it was a bridge between that, because some of the songs could have easily been on **System Has Failed**. Some of the songs were moving in a classic Megadeth direction, but it didn't go all the way for me. Which was fine, because I don't think I was completely prepared to contribute to that anyway. But I enjoyed the process. We went to a studio in England that used to belong to the guitar player from Pink Floyd, and the guy that was in The Buggles, Trevor Horn. That was exciting, to sit in that environment, an 11 bedroom mansion that we stayed at, which was right off the studio. So I mean, the whole thing felt rather bigger than it should have. It was exciting to me, after all these years—it was like, here's another one."

"Dave was very charged about getting Megadeth... I wouldn't say back on track, but more back in the public consciousness a lot more. And so he was really into making a good record, and I sensed that immediately. I was thrilled and delighted to find out that he wasn't the tyrant that everybody was telling me he was. He's very giving, and he gave us a lot of space to create and be part of the music that he had written. I had just met the Drover boys early on. We did some shows and then we went into the studio, and they were a delight to work with, because they were really into it as well. It was a painless, kind of mellow working environment."

As for Trevor Horn, co-saviour of Yes back in the early '80s, "We met him once or twice, kind of roaming... (laughs), he would roam the grounds. I think we met his dog more than we met him. The place was essentially haunted, we were sure of that. Which lent a sense of occasion. But the best part of it was after it had come out. It garnered an awful lot of interest and it did very well, for its place and time. And I was excited to be part of that, and then Download Festival, Monsters Of Rock, all the big festivals. We were getting really good spots on that—did Gigantour—it was really good; it really felt like the band was moving in an upward direction."

"It was somebody's decision," reflects James, on the whole switch from Jeff Balding to Andy Sneap. "I wouldn't say it was Dave. I thought it was just a decision that other people make. I was as surprised to find out what had been going on as everybody else (laughs). And I don't think a lot of it was wasted. I think it was all kind of used one way or another. But both guys—and this may sound diplomatic—I really enjoyed working with both of the fellows. Andy Sneap had a really good grip on it, because he came to Megadeth as more of a heavy metal fan. And like I said, this kind of corroborates that notion that it really was a bridge from **The System Has Failed** to **Endgame**."

"I've not heard anything that has really blown me away for a good couple years, really, to be honest," says Andy Sneap, proving his comfort inside of a situation like Megadeth. "I've been going back. I've been involved with an Accept album, Megadeth, Exodus... I've sort of gone back to the old guys again. Because for me, that's where my heart lies, really. I hear more in the players from 20, 25 years ago, that I'm interested in as a player and a producer, than anything that the newer kids are doing. And I'm kind of getting bored of the productions I'm hearing. It's all sounding very samey and safe. Some of the danger in the playing of the old school guys... they actually had to learn to play back then, and there wasn't the trickery in the studio that you could do, so you had to learn your craft, really."

"Now, you're almost looking at the music more than you're listening to it," continues Sneap, asked what kinds of tricks are infused into metal-making in the modern era. "You can tune anything to an inch of its life, you can snap all the drums to the grid, you can cut and paste the guitar parts so it's identical all the way through a song, and I'm hearing that all the time. And it's one thing I'm really trying to get away from. But with the older players you can do that, because they actually have the talent to do it. The amount of times I get kids into the studio now, they can't actually play a song all the way through. So to me, the quality of playing has really dropped over the last ten to 15 years. And I think it's because people have gotten lazy. And I also think—and actually KK Downing said this to me, because we were talking about this—but back in the day, bands actually had to rehearse a lot more because they didn't have any way of recording the songs. You would be lucky if you had a guy with a four-track in the band. So you actually had to go to rehearse it, to know how the song went. But I call it laptop metal now. People actually write the songs on computer even before the band gets together. So a lot of the times, kids would get into the studio, and they haven't actually played the song as a band."

As for his first interaction with this particular old school band, Andy says, that he "got involved in **United Abominations** quite late in the game. They had done the album with Jeff Balding, the engineer, Dan Huff's engineer from Nashville. And Dave was sort of in the driver's seat, and Jeff was sort of engineer/co-producer on that. And it was turning into more of a rock album than anything else. Dave was really trying to push towards these sort of radio-friendly ideas, that rock direction that Megadeth went to in the last few albums. So the label felt it needed a bit of metalling up, and I got the call to come in and push it that way a little bit. And as soon as we got working on it, me and Dave got on really well, and we realized how things need to start going on it, and it worked out so well from there. I did some live stuff with him the following year; we did that box set and DVD, one or two DVDs."

"So I riffed it up, really," continues Sneap, clarifying how the record was made heavier through his goodly guidance. "With any song, if it's a good song, you can kind of play it in any style, and we sort of took it from the rock side of things... we did some guitars again, and even re-did bits in the same key, but rewrote the odd riff, re-did some of the drums on it so it wasn't so simple. Just those sorts of things really; we re-did all the vocals again, actually got more aggressive on the vocals, because he was singing it quite a lot. So we took it from a metal point of view to more of a thrash point of view. I think if I had been involved from the beginning on that, we could have had it quite a lot heavier. But it was kind of late in the day when I got involved. There was really only so much that we could put into it. So that gave us a good starting point for the **Endgame** album. There were a few lyrics changed, but not a whole heck of a lot, but only because Dave had got the chance to go back and do it and he decided he wanted to change bits and pieces. It was more for the performance that we went back and did all the vocals again."

"I can't blame anybody but myself," said Mustaine, reflecting on England within a few months from the experience (and, I might add, completely contradicting Andy's take on things). "The decisions that were made to employ people who didn't finish the project... either they weren't qualified to do it in the first place or something happened with the dynamic between the two of us during the project. When I hired Jeff Balding, I said this has to be a metal record period. **The System Has Failed** was a return to form. **United Abominations** had to be a spot-on-form Megadeth record. It had to be. And as we started getting through the record, there was stuff that he didn't have to do. It was apparent to me... even though Jeff and I are the same calibre as far as success and producers and stuff like that, we're not from the same cloth. Andy is from the same cloth. When we come in from the same background it makes it a little bit easier. Now, I found out from Mike Gitter (A&R Roadrunner) that Andy started playing guitar because of me, and I thought that was really neat. For him to go full circle from picking up the guitar because of me to doing my record... I had no idea, but he's magic. We worked really well together and he's got a really funny sense of humour, English wit. We kind of exchanged barbs at times. I think that Andy could go to a whole other level. He just needs to get the right representation and somebody to protect the farm."

"Huge fan of his production," adds Shawn on the subject of Mr. Sneap. "I had Testament's **The Gathering** when it first came out. Like, 'Who is this guy?' To me that record is monstrous. All the subsequent records—Nevermore's **Dead Heart**—there are so many records that just blast out. I'm a fan of that in-your-face production. When his name was mentioned to work with us, to me it was a no-brainer. It was just a matter of everyone having to agree on that. Once he got in there... I loved it. He's a great guy and his direction was very focused on what he wanted us to do—it was a great match."

As for Mustaine, "He's a lot like Glen and myself in a lot of respects," says Shawn. "He's very driven. So are we. He's a perfectionist in certain ways, as are Glen and I. In the live situation, if something goes wrong that night, we'll always be the first to say let's make that a little better next time. It's a pretty common goal. I think maybe some people can be scared or whatever. Dave has no problem telling you good or bad if something's up. He'd be the first to tell you, 'Dude, you really played great tonight.' And that's the way Glen and I are as well. That's kinda the way I'd want him to be anyway. If he was real lackadaisical, I wouldn't dig that a whole lot."

Back to the **United Abomination** track sequence, and third selection in we've got the title track, second longest on the record at 5:33 after opener *Sleepwalker*. This one's more of a **Youthanasia**-like groove rocker with a proggy, melodic chord sequence for a pre-chorus and chorus, but again with lyrics that pack a political punch, Dave compiling about as complete a diatribe against the United Nations as can be fit in a song not of hip-hop word count. It's a natural position for Dave, if only for his political activist bent, but there's extra vitriol given the new world order angle, the UN being about as literal and material an expression of one world order that there is, followed closely by Brussels.

"We both did a lot of guitar tracks," notes Glen. "I think I did pretty much all of the clean stuff on the album. Certain tracks I did distorted rhythm tracks like *Sleepwalker* and *Never Walk Alone*. *Sleepwalker* in particular, but the majority of the tracks I did. Dave of course is still on there—he's on all the tracks. For the most part you've got to have his rhythm tracks in there because that's the sound. But there's definitely a fair amount of me in there. It's not like it was with King Diamond where I went in with that one album and Andy LaRocque did the rhythm tracks and I did solos. I didn't do anything else except for my guitar solo spots and that was it. It was fine, but it was nice to do this album where there is so much more of me in there throughout all the songs."

"For me, it's kind of a mixture of older and newer Megadeth," continues Glen. "I think me and Shawn bring the heavier element in. Dave did write the majority of the album of course—I have a credit on one song. But I think our influence is there because we grew up with the older albums. So we bring that element in and try to bring back some of the past. 'Cause a lot of the Megadeth fans want to hear the older-styled stuff with the heavier, aggressive sound. We worked on the album for ages—from the time we started working on demos to the time we finished it was about a year-and-a-half. The songs really started to take shape as we went along. There was a period where the album was pretty much done and then we decided to make some changes. It really started to get stronger as we went along. It's definitely been a long stretch. I learned a lot of different things. Not just little tricks with the mechanics of recording, which always interests me, but I had a better understanding of what Megadeth is all about. How Dave shapes his songs and his approach and how he comes up with these riffs. He's got so many unique ideas and it's all signature stuff. A lot of these songs, when you listen to them, you know they are a Megadeth song. Dave has a really cool and unique way of writing. I learned a lot about how he phrases things and plays rhythm patterns and so forth."

Gears Of War swings a similarly weighty sledgehammer at the machines of war, with the same sort of thrash band take on AC/DC's particular charms as the track before it. Lyrically this one's quite brief and its message more oblique, Dave outlining the impersonal (dehumanizing?) nature of advanced weaponry. The song is used within the soundtrack to the video game of the same name, interestingly, in its original instrumental format.

Blessed Be The Dead, a frightening and apocalyptic celebration of the four horsemen, is so much tied to an AC/DC tradition, its opening—although not central—riff evokes the Aussies' *What's Next To The Moon*. Nonetheless, it's still a plodder with a big one-note bass line, interesting in its laid-back, almost meandering turns.

Play For Blood is distinguished by a rhythmic, descending riff that reminds one of *Killing Is My Business... And Business Is Good!*, with the other parts being equally memorable, some licks proggy, its central premise as straight forward as *Symphony Of Destruction*. Dave and Glen trade solos extensively on this tale of violence on the streets.

Glen estimate that the soloing on the album is "about half-and-half, maybe a little bit more me," between himself and Dave. Asked about Mustaine's particular strengths as a mad axeman, he figures, "It's hard to describe, man. His lead playing is a combination of a lot of different things, but there's a lot of rock 'n' roll, I find, in his playing. I hear some Motörhead, more of the classic stuff, in his playing. I would say he's more loose, although his rhythm is very tight. He's not laid-back. I find it more about rock and classic metal; New Wave Of British Heavy Metal for sure; there's probably some that in there too."

One gets a sense that Dave himself understands what Glen is getting at, this idea that Mustaine could be tight but loose, that he's somehow dragging these sounds out of his guitar. "When I pick up the guitar," says Mustaine, "I still feel like it's an inanimate object and I'm wrestling with a wooden anaconda, you know what I mean? Other guys can get the guitar and play it and massage it and play all these great sounds and stuff. I gotta punch my guitar in the stomach to get it to work. But I like it like that because I use it as a weapon instead of coming up with some feather. I like to have the guitar that's going to be responsive and is going to be a tool for me to be able to do what I need. I've had guitars that have faltered on me and sadly they're out of existence. They're in pieces. That's a bad habit I have. If I have a guitar and it doesn't work I tend to smash it up a little bit. But that's to make sure no one else has to go through that problem with that damn guitar."

As for his own style as applied to Megadeth, Glen says he's a "mixed bag of different things that have influenced me throughout the years. But there's no question, we both have different styles. And hopefully that came across in the albums. I was really a fan of the earlier King Diamond albums, where you had Andy and then you had Mike Denner, where you had a complete contrast between guitar players, so you knew who was doing the solo. Rather than having two guys that sound the same where you don't know who's who. Some people might say that might not be a big deal, but for me as a guitar player, I thought it was cool to have that contrast, that dynamic, the different styles. Mike Denner is a very melodic player, so maybe it's better he plays more melodic sessions and Andy is more the aggressive heavier stuff. So that was my goal anyways, to try to make sure that you could tell who's who, type of thing. Whether we achieved that I don't know, but that was the goal."

"When we did *A Tout Le Monde*, that was supposed to be a b-side for a Japanese album, Martin," Dave cautioned when we had been talking about the album a few years hence, concerning incongruent track No. 8 on the album. "It wasn't supposed to be a single on that record. I don't know if you've heard that story or not, but we sped it up a little bit, we had Christina (Scabbia, Lacuna Coil) sing on it, and we had a bit of an extra section in there so Glen could make that solo his own. I said, you know, we'll do one more pass, because the solo was two phrases long. We'll make it three phrases long, and you can have the beginning phrase where you kind of *Freebird* it a little bit, and then you drop back into the original solo and you finish out on the melody that everybody knows. So we really tried to keep things fresh and stuff like that. But that song was not meant to be on the domestic release."

Indeed it had been the label that had insisted it was on there, and from a business aspect, it did help the record, as well as tying in with the original version. The song remains a live favourite, one on which Dave sings quite conventionally—oh, there are snickers, but even the hardcore thrashers can be seen digging the connection this song brings, in the live setting, between fan and band.

"It depends on the song," muses Glen, on how much Dave would croon on the record and how much he would thrash attack from the throat. "It's what is calls for. If it's a more aggressive song, he'd do that. If it's a mellower song, you do that. He doesn't want to do the same thing all the time. He wants to do different things, some melodic stuff, some heavy stuff. He doesn't want to be doing just one fucking thing all the time. He just doesn't want to write *Peace Sells* over and over and over. He said that before—I'm quoting him."

A few different guest vocalists were considered for the remake of this contentious song, but Christina got the nod, given Dave's favourable impression of all she had accomplished with her band of gothic Italian metallers, Lacuna Coil. For her part, she had said she was honoured to take on the role, having always admired the song.

Amerikhastan perpetuates the mid-paced vibe of the album, as well as its heavy politics, Dave attacking US involvement in the middle east and the breeding of more hate that it does. The song brings back the celebrated Megadeth trope of Dave preaching from the pulpit in spoken word. Both Glen's and Dave's guitar solos are some of the tastiest on the album, and even their placements underscore the track's novel construct.

You're Dead finds Dave back in thrash vocal mode, over a proggy, pounding musical backtrack of slow-burn thrash, which nonetheless picks up for a classic Mega-shred late in the revenge story sequence. Then it's onto crushing closer *Burnt Ice*, a warning about the evils of crystal meth, set to yet another twisted progressive thrash soundtrack that is tempered and made accessible by sticking to sensible speeds.

"It was fun for a while and then after a while it was in such excess that you tend to kind of appreciate it," says Dave of his drug days. "I think we all need to have a bit of that recklessness once in a while to know what it's like. But living in **Caligula**... the '80s were fun, and for people who remember it, they probably weren't really in the middle of it that much. There was a lot of people who died in the '80s. I remember our bassist was at the hotel when Nikki Sixx overdosed. And there's so many people that we know that died during the '80s. The glamorization of cocaine and metal... of course we didn't think coke was cool; we thought it was kind of juvenile. Heroin was the drug of choice for the real metal people. But then again, that was our own telescopic view, and we were really the only ones that were really doing it. It wasn't a drug that was really popular with metal. I think the thing you'll find most popular with metal is adrenaline. Booze. And that, for me, is fair game. I think it's fun to go out there and have fun with your friends and have a couple of drinks or something like that. But the whole drug blizzard that went into the '80s and even carried over to the '90s left a lot of people in road kill form. Look at the guys in Aerosmith right now. After all of that fucking 'holy roller' finger-pointing bullshit…"

United Abominations sold 60,000 copies instantly upon release, opening at No. 8 on Billboard. Japan got a pretty cool bonus track in the aforementioned bulky version of obscure Led Zeppelin classic *Out On The Tiles*. Musically, the band jam it hard (throwing in a couple extra riff "quotes" toward the close), but Dave doesn't take risks with his range, turning in one of his punky, snarling, almost spoken vocals.

Both Guitar World and Brave Words & Bloody Knuckles would go on to herald **United Abominations** as the top record of all of 2007. Touring for the album found the band putting Gigantour aside for a support slot with the revered and reconstituted Black Sabbath vehicle known as Heaven & Hell, otherwise known as Ronnie James Dio-era Black Sabbath.

"Heaven & Hell, that was a great tour," remembers Glen. "To be honest with you, if I had to pick one tour that was the highlight of me being in the band, of those four years, it was that band. Being friends with Ronnie, who was such a genuine person. I'm sure you met him and I'm sure you know. I don't have to tell you too much. All the guys were like that; Tony was very cool with me. Here's the guy that fucking started me off playing guitar, and I remember one time we were playing in, I think it was Connecticut or something, and I used to always… when they were doing soundchecks, Tony would actually go out a lot of times by himself during their soundcheck, and he'd just go play riffs and walk around and check out the place. And I'd be around just watching him, just hanging out and talking to his guitar tech and stuff like that. And one time, it seemed like they were pretty busy, so I didn't want to interfere, so I just hung back. He says, 'No, Glen, come over.' And I'm thinking this is not happening. This is Tony Iommi. It was just very surreal. Just one example of, wow, wait a minute, this is the band, this is fuckin' Black Sabbath here. So it was very thrilling; they're all great guys. Vinnie Appice too, he's great. Became really good friends."

"The second concert I ever saw when I was 11 or 12 was the **Mob Rules** tour in Montreal," adds Glen. "And my favourite albums are **Mob Rules** and **Heaven And Hell**. And if I had to pick one Sabbath album, it's probably **Mob Rules**. That's my favourite era of the band. But like I say, everybody was very nice to us, very kind. There were no egos anywhere, from the crew to the band. I talked to Tony a few times. I spoke to Vinnie when we would be at catering. We had some great chats with Ronnie—he'd tell us some old Rainbow stories. I think the Heaven & Hell idea was great, just to play songs from that era and lineup. There's definitely enough material, plus the three new songs. There's not a bad note on any of these records."

Dave at this point in time, post-**United Abominations** and well into the swing of giving Megadeth a second or even third life, seemed to be finally moving toward contentment.

"I've got a pretty square life," Dave told our mag. "I've been able to separate who I am on stage with who I am on the street now. As the two grew apart, there was a dynamic I was able to see that made it easier to get into character and to get out of character. I think a lot of these other people are so stuck in character non-stop, day in, day out, get off stage and drink and pound and party, 'cos I'm on stage, I'm always on stage. For example, there's a lot of people in the music business that I hung around with in the beginning, people who think they are born with a JD bottle in their hand. A guy that comes to mind is Slash. Another one is David Lee Roth. All the props, you know. I don't know if Dave ever drank a bottle of JD on stage. To me, showbiz says you put iced tea in there. That could've been what it was. I know that Chris (Holmes) from W.A.S.P. was in a raft in a pool in **The Decline Of Western Civilization** guzzling clear liquid out of a vodka bottle. I know what vodka tastes like and drinking it that fast, your gag reflex... I dunno, maybe he doesn't have a gag reflex; maybe after all those years in W.A.S.P. he doesn't have it. I was able to separate those two. By living my life normally, I could experience being fully charged on a record again."

"Things have totally changed," continues Dave. "I had to have my life pulled out from underneath me. I have everything, but I was so driven that it wasn't enough. All of a sudden you have to hit that end of the track and then just say, things aren't that bad, you need to really appreciate where you are at right now. When you are so disillusioned because you are surrounded with people who are preying off your insecurities, who keep propping you up on stage and keep giving you false accolades, false sense of security and false hope... and everything is just a lie and then at the end of the day you are sitting there all alone and these guys are laughing all the way to the bank. There's been some painful periods. I just got an email from somebody asking me about ex-band members. It's sad."

"Justice just turned 15," says Dave, turning to family. "Kids are a really big catalyst for life change, especially when they have to suffer from the bad decisions you make. One time Justice came home and some piece of shit on the school bus had said something to him because the **Behind The Music** thing had just come out. And the kid said something to Justice like, 'Your dad's a crack-head.' I was never a crack-head. The guys that can afford drugs don't have a drug problem. When you run out and start sucking dick and selling your stuff and other people's stuff, that becomes a problem. I was just a heavy drug user, but that lifestyle has changed for me. But when I saw it affect Justice I called up the other dad and said, 'You know, I think you need to talk to your kid.' Sadly, the kid that had done that, the parents had just divorced. Same thing—he's crying out for attention. He's fighting with another kid, trying to put another kid down so he would feel good. Unfortunately Justice was the kid he was trying to put down because he had his own pain. I'm a product of a divorced family. It's so amazing how all this stuff ties back to lack of love and that's what made this record so fresh with me. I just felt that when Glen, Shawn and James came in, it's the last component for this new incarnation of Megadeth. We just had this 'symbiotica' between all of us."

"The Drovers have their own brotherly thing—brothers get along the way that they do," says Dave, at the time showing himself to be amused that he had brothers in the band and also that his half his band was Canadian. "You sometimes see two brothers get along and you want to act like you're a brother too and you just can't. It's apples and oranges. Plus, with three brothers, there'd be two in the end after one of them got killed. There's also a really neat balance in the band; you've got the two veterans and you've got the two rookies. And we all are excited. So it's just this ebbing and flowing of energy of good and bad and different, bringing each other up, correcting each other."

Is Dave capable of taking advice? Does he listen?

"Of course I do. That's part of the folklore." To which he offers a revealing anecdote... "I put on a pair of pants the other day—sometimes before we get ready to go onstage we make sure we don't look like a fuckin' idiot. Enough guys have gone out there with Reeboks on, you know what I mean? So I put some pants on. I've been trying to put some weight back on after my pending divorce with my wife—I lost a lot of weight because I was stressing a lot. So the clothes I was wearing wasn't fitting. And James goes, 'That doesn't look so good, boss.'"

"I really look at the way the project kind of laid itself out," muses Dave, on the house-cleaning taking place so that Megadeth could live. "Some of the people were removed by divine intervention, others were just asshole-isms. We had to make numerous changes with management, with the agency, with personnel that were in the recording process. The A&R work on the record, we went round and round about stuff that ultimately ended up being 90% of the way it was in the beginning anyway. Had difficultly with the art department trying to tell me to censor my artwork. To keep things from getting ugly legally, we took some precautions on a particular piece of image and to find out it doesn't even matter. I had to make a clean album cover and we were told by the label we needed to do this and I said, 'Are you sure?' So after struggling for weeks with this clean image, we find out that we don't need it. That pushed things back. The formatting, Gigantour... we didn't want to blow Gigantour out. I knew the record was coming."

Back into the mechanics of **United Abominations**, Dave figures, "It was really important for me to have some perspective in between the songs. I would go and listen and think, you know what, this could be just a little bit more articulate with the pedaling on the guitar part, or maybe a little run in there or maybe put a solo in there where there are just some chords. Or maybe take a solo out. There was a lot of stuff in there too like ad-lib vocal stuff that was taken out, and some was put in. I really pushed myself on this record to go back on the stuff that made me happy and I didn't care what anybody else was saying. But I'm also stuck in a place where I have to be a leader and there's domestic harmony that I have to keep with all these band guys 'cos unfortunately they are playing on my insecurities that we all have and then they hold you hostage by saying if you don't give them what they want they leave. And then what happens? I go back to the same place I was as a four-year-old with my family breaking as a divorced child. And I'm like, fuck, here I am again. Band members leaving. Crew guys saying, 'My ex-band that I was out with offered me more money to come back. I'm thinking about going back.' They're trying to play that game. Dude, I've seen it all. At this point right now I'm no longer desperate. When you are finally honest with yourself, no matter what happens, you are OK with things. If it all ends today, I'm finally OK with it. If it would've ended before, I would have felt like I was unfulfilled."

Coming back 'round to his **United Abominations** bandmates, specifically his Canuck wing, Dave comes off as genuinely interested in what makes them tick. "Glen is a very unique individual because all that matters to him is the guitar. He's a huge music fan. Of course his wife and son are very important to him. This is a guy that when I think of a guitar player I think of him. In most in our genre, there's usually only one musician in the band and the rest are players. Because Glen is at the level that he is, the musicianship has gone up in the band. Now Shawn is a guitar player too. When I think of somebody who plays drums and is a drummer, I picture him. Everywhere you go it's like 'I play guitar'—like shit you do. I used to goof around in concert and I would say, 'Anybody that plays guitar stick your hand up. OK, how many of you play like me?' 'You lie! I was just playing around.'"

"I found that in most bands that are successful," continues Dave, "there's usually one person, maybe two, like in the Beatles, that always start to pull the fabric apart because of money and insecurity. And then somebody comes in and says, 'Get rid of these guys; take the front guy and make him a star.' Well he's already a star; he just has a small supporting cast. And that's some of the stuff that happened in the beginning that's not here right now. The four of us all love what we do so much that we really challenge each other in there. Like I was doing a solo and Glen said, 'I wouldn't change a note of that.' Pardon me? I completely respected what he said. And I went, 'OK, I won't.' Now another part was like, 'Uh, you know what, I always second-guess myself. I'm not sure because somebody is gonna say it's a sloppy solo.' That part was overruled by Glen's passion for the band, his love for me as his band leader and brother. It's not like he stood up to me. He's proud of me and wants me to know when enough is enough. Because I'll keep going until my fingers get hurt if I know I'm not doing it right. And I've done that before and I really hurt myself."

"Making this record with his ability to play, I just wrote whatever I felt I could possibly push myself to the limit of knowing that I could teach it to him and he'd be able to get. Now, some of it happened by way of listening to the garbage that he listens to. He'll put stuff in his iPod that is so awful and I'll say, 'What is that?!' And he'll say it's Regurgitated Baby Anuses or something like that. I remember one time we went into this crab shop in Boston and there was this band playing on the radio and I hear this guy in the background going, 'Ooh, yeah, yeah!' And I kept making fun of him every time he did that. Like, that's really kooky-sounding. And Glen says, 'Oh man, that's Celtic Frost—he does it every song, every record.' And every time I would hear this guy I would think, 'God, he does that every song?' The riffs are really heavy because they are so far ahead of its time. But it's not a riff, it's a chord thing. I don't think there are any movements of fingers; it's just bar chords shifting around. I thought it was really fun and it kind of lit a fire inside of me listening to that. I actually went back and listened to some Mercyful Fate, even though it's against my judgement to listen to stuff that's really hardcore Satanic shit anymore. But I love the music and I've got to the point where I can block the lyrics out. I just don't even hear it. I guess a lot of it is that I've conditioned myself to hear guitar in bands so much that the lyrics go by and I don't even know what they are and then days later I'll hear it and go, 'Whoa, where did that come from?'"

"This is what I've been trying to do for a long time," answers Dave, upon the supposition that with **United Abominations**, he's created a record with retro appeal, a record that people want to hear from Megadeth. "Some people want to see people fail. And for a long time it was fashionable to see me fail because I was the bad guy. People change, and even though there is a part of all of us that's capable of being angry and being the bad guy. Like when you're playing hockey, there's times when you knock the shit out of somebody and then you go have a beer with them after. That's a beautiful thing about a real warrior. You know when you are at battle and you know when you are at peace. I'm finally at peace with myself. All the times I think I've been mad at people, I wasn't really mad at them at all, I was mad at something that I saw in myself. It wasn't until I got to the point where I was a millionaire living on some dope-fiend's couch last year smoking cigarettes again, facing divorce because I'd left my family because I just couldn't deal with things anymore. There was just one day—oddly enough it was Yom Kippur—I just prayed and said, I'm so sick of all of this. What am I afraid of? Why won't I let anybody in? Why is there this 'You can come close but don't get too close or I will fuck you up' kind of shield that I have? Why do I have that? It goes back to somewhere in my childhood—something went wrong, or something didn't go right. I gotta let that go and move past that, because I've been given a gift to play music."

"I've got so many friends in my life that count on me," continues Dave. "I bring them hope and happiness and stuff. I look at my kids and think, is this anything like you thought it would be? I have fear, because I know when they go off on their own, chances are living like we live is going to be hard for them to do it on their own. My daughter's got the gift. She can sing and play the piano. My son, I think is going to be an actor. He's really handsome. His mom's Dutch, so that helps. And he's really a good actor. I've seen him act a lot. First role he ever got, he got the lead and I was like, holy shit! 'Cause I'm pretty critical about acting. Even though I want to be one, I'm not very good at it because I haven't had much schooling in it. I watched him and went up to him after the play was over and lifted him up and hugged him and I said, 'Son, we are forever—you and I—united on a totally different world right now. You and I both command the stage in our family.' It was a really cool moment."

"So the world being my oyster right now, I've got to remember where it comes from because it ain't by my doing. I tried so long and so hard to do it on my own and every time I messed up. I would just justify, 'You don't understand; this is what happened' and blame other people: 'Yeah it was Junior's fault, it was Friedman's fault, it was Menza's fault. He lied, he cheated.' I picked them. And I could've stopped it right in the beginning or the first time it happened. I wish them all well. I know that they are going to do well at whatever they are going to do. I guess this is a by-product of finally growing up."

At this point talk turned to Gigantour, an increasingly dependable touring brand that is flexible enough to lie in wait, break glass when needed.

"We're talking about bring a Gigantour up here just for Canadian bands. Well, not necessarily Canadian bands, but bringing Gigantour up here and having a lot of Canadian bands on it. There will be obvious ones, but it won't necessarily be in arenas either. If the bands that come along in the headlining position have enough weight or credibility, it may go from a theatre to a hall to a smaller arena. My whole thing is that I'm so grateful for what has taken place in my career, I want to be able to use what I have left in the touring capacity to be able to open doors for these other bands. Like Into Eternity; they aren't a national act. They certainly aren't an American act. They are relatively unknown in a lot of places. I took them out, took 'em under my wing and protected them. They were very respectful. I hope they had a good time."

"I know that that's the kind of stuff I needed when I first started. Alice Cooper tried to talk to me when I went out with him in the beginning—Alice is my godfather. He sat me down on his bus one night. He was sitting there with eyeliner on and I'm just out of my mind. And I'm going like, 'Cool, Alice

Cooper—we are going to get wasted.' I didn't know he had stopped drinking at the time. He goes, 'You know what? You really gotta cool it.' It really kind of put a damper on things. But you know what? There's a way that you can be out there and try to help people in a way that you don't discourage them, but you can also show them that there are some good things to do and there are some not so good things to do. The choice is yours. If you have any problems, call me. I will always be here for you. And that's the way I feel about all the band's I've had at my festival."

As we conclude this lengthy, introspective chapter, I had talked to Marty Friedman—bit of an aside, I know, although it's nice to keep track of what the family is up to—about his **Loudspeaker** solo album that seen release in the US two months before the issuance of **United Abominations** (and a year earlier in Japan).

"I think I wanted to do what was most natural," explained Friedman on his new, lively, entertaining record of smart shred. "Especially because over the last two years in Japan, I've been everything but natural in terms of what I've been doing. I've been doing a lot of music and TV stuff, but it's stuff that is completely out of the ordinary. When I came to Japan, I came to do Japanese pop music and Japanese rock music, which is really what I love to do. And I started doing that and it was all great, but all of a sudden I started a TV show, a brand new show I was asked to do, and I had no experience in TV whatsoever, other than just normal TV music, promotional stuff. But I did it and the show took off all of a sudden, and I started doing too much TV, and it started to whack me out musically, because it was so different and alien to what I was doing."

"And I was just enjoying it so much, it came time to think about doing a record, and I'm like, I'm getting my rocks off in so many different ways, it would be really, really easy to go and make a full-on aggressive record. Because I get to do all the ballad stuff and dance stuff, and the TV stuff sometimes doesn't have anything to do with music at all. It's really an exhilarating experience. It's a very fast-paced environment, a good overall experience. Kind of a life experience, and it's a good influence on music, I always think. If you're concentrating on music 24-7 all the time, it's really hard to have a life."

As for the lifestyle that has accompanied Marty's surprise relocation... "I live in downtown Tokyo, in a high-rise, and it's just insane, man. It's everything I wanted it to be and more, really. Just having all those kinds of outside life experiences really, first of all, confused me about what I wanted to do musically. Because everything was working out no matter what I did. Music-wise it goes all the way from full-on techno to ultra idol teen pop to full-on death metal stuff and everything in-between. And I was just loving all of it. And it's really, what do I do? What do I really want to do? So when I made a record, I didn't want to just put something out. So it took the 13 months to make the record, and I would basically go in for a day or two here and there, a week. Every month I would get in for a couple of days, between my other schedule, which was mostly TV stuff. So it was really fresh to come into the studio and bash out some full-on metal after reading cue cards all week."

"And that kind of freaked me out, because it was so natural to make this record the most aggressive record I've ever made," continues Marty. "And kind of, when I started, I thought this was really easy, this is what I want to do. I think the whole thing with me is like, what comes most easily is probably playing full-on aggressive rock, or metal. And the fans that have supported me over the years, what do they want to hear about from me? It's probably the same answer. And it was an easy solution. And the reason I'm still happy to do that is because I took my time doing it. When I was in the studio doing it, it was a change of pace and it was very fresh and fun to do. I think I needed that outside stimulation to make the record as good as it was. If I was doing this kind of stuff 24-7, 365 days a year, I would probably go out of my mind, because there's so much I wanted to do."

As for **Loudspeaker** specifically, (the middle record of a dozen at this point, depending on what you count)... "It's definitely loud like Megadeth, but I think it's about a thousand times more aggressive, and modern, and pretty deep. Without analysing it too deeply, I think the most interesting thing is the song structures. The framework of it is full-on aggressive—I guess you'd call it metal. It's pretty heavy stuff. But if you look deeply into it, a lot of the key changes and the way the songs are laid out are pretty much influenced by J-pop and visual K music and things that are not necessarily metal, but done in a completely aggressive way that it comes out as a really fresh kind of metal, to my ears."

"I don't really ride the subway so much anymore, because it's insane," offers Marty, feeding further my curiosity about this reportedly crazy-ass celebrity life he's been living in Tokyo. "When I first moved here, I was full-on into the subway and the trains and all that stuff, and occasionally I would run into fans and stuff. But ever since I started doing the TV stuff, it's really kind of impossible to really go anywhere. I don't mind being recognized, and I love chatting with fans, but I can't really do the public transportation things so much. So I either take taxis or my manager has a special car for me and he takes me to my events and stuff. Yeah, Tokyo is a great city. It's sort of like New York on speed, really (laughs)."

Family, wife, kids?

"Single guy, man. Still living it up."

13
ENDGAME

"I like that album more than the one I played on"

There was a cluster of bridge product that helped perpetuate the improbable rebirth of Megadeth that Dave Mustaine had been proposing. September 4th of 2007 marked the release of **That One Night: Live In Buenos Aires**, which harbours a point of significance in that it was at that Obras Sanitarias stadium show (Pepsi Music Rock Festival, October 9, 2005) that Dave announced that Megadeth would continue its run both as a touring band and on record. Also of note, the mammoth CD and DVD package is the only Megadeth album to feature the bass guitar services of James MacDonough.

Hot on the heels of this release was the **Warchest** box set, issued October 9, 2007, followed by **Anthology: Set The World Afire** on September 30, 2008. Keep cranking out retrospective celebrations like this, and the point starts to sink in that what we have here is a band making a shift from fair-sized metal-munchers from an era not too long ago, toward classic rock band that has earned its prominent place.

But **Warchest** was quite the piece of work, Once past the nifty moulded plastic bullet belt packaging, it contained four action-packed CDs plus a DVD. The fourth CD documented the band's last show on the historic Clash Of The Titans tour, October 14th, 1990 at Wembley Stadium, which they thrashed to pieces with the help of Anthrax, Slayer and Suicidal Tendencies. Amongst the first three CDs, album tracks were interspersed with demos, soundtrack selections, interview clips, live tracks, and even the band's cover of Kiss' *Strange Ways*, recorded for the high profile **Kiss My Ass** tribute album but not included on it. The DVD featured in the lush package was a live show documenting the band at their commercial peak in 1992, but playing the intimate and venerable Hammersmith Odeon. One other interesting CD track was the band's live performance of *A Secret Place* from Woodstock 1999, not so much for the quality of the rendition (or the mainstream song itself), but for the fact that Megadeth was even at the event, playing alongside Metallica but mainly a pile of trendy "hard music" acts of the day, at a commercialized debacle that turned into a riot, thanks to Limp Bizkit.

And whither Dave Ellefson at this point in time? What is it the fat-stringer was doing all day, now that he was not killing' it with Megadeth?

"The eight or nine hours of work a day for me is probably like most people," Ellefson told me back in October of 2009. "A ton of emails, phone calls. We just finished up a tour of Scandinavia with this group together with Andreas Kisser from Seputura—we've got a group called Hail!, which is basically classic metal hits and things like that. That group is a perfect example of whenever we work, the phone rings, and if you stop working too long, the phone doesn't ring. That's it in a nutshell of how our music career works. Probably any career, in that the more you're active, the more you're visible. The more you're visible, the more people want to be around you, as people gather and the phone rings and email happens. So that's just kind of music business 101, and it's been like that from when I was 12 years old and grew up in Minnesota and putting my first band together and trying to have our first gig, to now. Here I am all these years later, and it just seems to work like that. The good news is that information comes via email, MySpace, Facebook and Twitter. Whatever it is you do, that stuff comes directly to you or to your doorstep through you and your management and you can field these things and do some touring."

At this juncture however, Ellefson had only recently broke the ice and thawed relations with Mustaine. "A couple weeks ago, I guess, yeah. The truth of it is, he quit the group in 2002 because of some incidents that were happening in his personal life. He walked away from the group, and thus the band was over. And as much as, I think, he desired me to stay around and still work with him, it was... unless we're working as band, there's nothing to do. So I was looking at that and going, you know, this is probably the time where I should just keep moving forward. That was what, seven, eight years ago, still fairly young, and industrious, energetic, enthusiastic man that I am, I had other artistic things I wanted to do."

"I was happy being in one band for all those years," continues Ellefson. "I was never like, 'Dude, I can't wait to do my solo album.' I was never that guy. And that's probably why I was in the band for probably 20 years. Because I was happy there and happy being a formative part of those many years. But when he walked away from it, partly, I was happy for him, if it meant his own preservation, you know? But yet, time marches on, and so I moved on to new things, and when he called me a couple years later to come back, the arrangement for me to come back was much, much different than what it was when we ended. There was still a big record deal on the table, there was a lot of stuff there, so by nature, there was money involved, attorneys get involved, and unfortunately, because his side did not want to communicate directly with me... and there's reports that I regret this lawsuit, and the thing that I regret about it, is that I didn't maybe make a better effort to go to him personally and try to have some sort of communication directly with him. Instead, it went to his manager, and then it went to the attorneys, who, as you know, by that point, once an attorney sends you a letter, then guess what, now you're hiring an attorney to essentially defend yourself. So that's kind of in a nutshell how that relationship went, and then it just eroded from there."

"Now we've had communication, over the years, even this summer, to the point that I went and hung out with him in the summer for a short while, for an afternoon. And it was good, it was enjoyable, it kind of felt like, you know, old times. But I gotta tell you, I'm a little bit guarded on these things, because to some degree, a business arrangement is much like a divorce. You know, finance and romance, those are two things that are very hard to make work again. And I just went and saw the Creed reunion the other night. It's hard to capture lightning twice, as my friend Dale, singer in F5, so poignantly put it to me. And I think because there maybe might have been some hope that there would be us working together again and that did not happen, that there's now hard feelings again, which is always the danger."

"I mean, that's the thing, and I'm very guarded about that. Especially with someone I've spent so much time with. But yet, I also realize I'm not the only one who's been here. So to some degree, I don't take it personally. I try not to fuel that fire, I try not to engage. It's easy when somebody says something, especially in the press, where the whole world sees it, that you want to retaliate, get back at a person. And with all due respect to the media, there is, as an artist, as a musician... handling the media—and I'm not saying running away for the media—but handling the media is something that takes a very diligent step, especially when it's a hot spot, hot topic. So you know, I think everybody can find me on the web, they know what I'm doing, I'm active, I'm out doing things, I'm always ready to keep the door open, and still do, quite honestly, to reengage with someone at that point. But it's gotta be the right time. Because otherwise, again, those opportunities can be spoiled, and then the whole thing is lost, and I don't think any of us will want to see that happen."

Asked about how the money side of things works in bands, just from a general standpoint, Dave says, "It's funny, a lot of people get together in bands, and they're like, 'It's all about the music, bro; don't worry about the money.' Until one day a check shows up, and it's sitting on the table, and you're looking at your neighbour going, 'You know, that guy didn't write anything, and I do all the work, and I answer all the emails,' you know what I mean? So I think that's that something that, if you're serious about, or your group gets to that point, that's an inevitable conversation you're going to have. And it can quite honestly be a dividing conversation with your band mates. You know, you split everything equally, that's one less thing to argue about, is the money. That's when one guy goes, 'I wrote the tunes, so it's mine.' Then you get into that, 'Yeah, I wrote the chorus.' 'But how about my guitar solo?' I think you just open that can of worms. Or the merchandising dude, you know, 'Split it all.' Or, 'Hey man, I'm the one who created the logo, and I came up with the...' whatever. I think any time someone tries to divide it up, it immediately starts to... And it may not happen today, but in ten months, when you've been out on the road, in the van, and you're tired, we all hate each other, and your breath stinks, and I don't want your dirty socks in my head rest, you know what I mean? When you're at that point, you're gonna remember that son of a bitch who said he oughta have some of it. 'You took all the money from the merchandise,' is just one more argument to throw fuel on the fire. And then you're in Charlotte, North Carolina and the band breaks up, and everybody's going home and it's all over, because of those kind of issues. So my thought is, if there's an arrangement that works, be as equal with it as you can."

But it wasn't just money that Megadeth could fight about. "Early on, you know, there were drug issues in the band," says Dave, understatement of the year, given that it's a rare band where every last member winds up on heroin. "You know, we've been very public about that, like the VH1 **Behind The Music** special. Sometimes those things can only be handled by having to sever a lineup and reform the band. And those are difficult because none of us were exactly choirboys. So it's kind of like, you see the Axl Rose/Steven Adler situation, and why should I quit partying? They were all partying too. So it's the pot calling the kettle black syndrome. But at some degree it became about preserving the group and being able to move on. I personally have; I think I've mended fences with those people back in those days, which is good."

Explaining another subplot of Megadeth's dramatic behind the scenes tale, Dave says, "In other times, having to make management changes is very difficult, because good management... they become the fifth wheel, like this extra member of the band. Management can either advise you to bring people together, or do the divide and conquer routine, where they start singling members out, and it's like the **Rock Star** movie. For me, probably through the **Rust In Peace**, **Countdown**, **Youthanasia**, that era, we happened to have a manager who was just like us. He started out as a tour manager for Armored Saint, had long hair like Bruce Dickinson and was a metalhead. And he fundamentally got what we were about, and he got everything about the group, and that was a great time and one of the most profitable times and certainly just a period that I felt really strongly about. But importantly that relationship changed over the years, and then that change had to be made. And for me, I don't like changing people. Metallica, they had one manager with Q Prime; I admire that—it's cool when you keep the team together. Rod Smallwood with Iron Maiden. He's almost like the talking head, the figurehead, the sixth, seventh Beatle. How many guys do they have? Well anyway, I use those as great examples of management. If you can find a team like that... because being an artist is really about being a team."

Inevitably management issues get tangled up with the making of the music. "Yeah, well, the last album we did for Capitol Records, **Risk**... that was not a happy time. Quite honestly, most because of management at that time, that advised us. The **Cryptic Writings** record—which was actually very good and successful—was a point in time when everybody in the band wanted to listen to direction; we felt good about the direction. Right previous to that we actually made a decision whether we were going to work with another very well-established manager or go with the manager that we did go with, and I think it was good. Because it actually reinvented the band and it gave us another probably five or six years of a really good career, especially at American FM radio, and probably here in Canada as well."

"But then by the time the **Risk** album came along, unfortunately management, in my opinion, overstepped their line, and to some degree, internally in the band, pulled the divide and conquer routine, sort of singling certain members out, pushing others back, and I never liked that. Because at the end of the day, I remember many times being out, and you used to go to the label, you get your money, you record an album, you get on the road... all that money that you get from them is not yours to keep. You have to recoup that. In other words, you have to pay that back to them. So here you are, six months later, you're on the road, you are in your van, you're all beat-up and feeling burnt-out, and people are sick and just worn out from the work of that. And meanwhile, back at home, there is the manager, who has already collected their commission and made their money. And then to make it, they have to continue to keep the band out and working."

"You know, it's interesting, because if we open a McDonald's, and we hire a manager, he gets his money first. He would make his money and salary, and maybe make a bonus based on his ability to improve our business together, the owners of the McDonald's. But in the music business, the managers usually take their money first, and as a result, leave us, as the artist, holding the bag, having to pay that money back. And that is the model, but it's starting to change. To some degree, and to the manager's credit, they are often the ones that take the risk, do a lot of work for maybe years and months in hopes of there being a payback. Because at the end of the day, the manager is going to be the famous one. So for years later, we can write books and join other bands and do other things."

"Lots of time it comes down to just ethics," notes Dave. "And having to, again, be on the road, now you're in debt, you can't go home, because if you stop the gravy train you're dead. Basically you're done. So you have to stay out there, you have to keep taking advantage of opportunities. And I think the trick at that point is do the ones that make sense, and not to the ones that just try to grab a quick buck. I have a good friend who gave me some advice years ago, on a non-music business related matter. I said, should I do this or not? And he says, well, first of all, why don't you take the money out of it? So take the money out of it; now looking at it without any money, would you go do that? And that was probably one of the best pieces of advice

I ever got in my life. Because it's easy to get financially motivated, especially if you're in a band and you're broke. You have no money, and you have to work, and sometimes taking your money out of it keeps your eyes on the prize. Are you really doing this because this is what you're artistically called to do?"

Back in Dave Sr.'s world, the man's 12th album **Endgame**, would represent a venomous Mustaine maximus far from the recorded works of the careerist "joiner" who was trying to sound right at home with the hipsters breaking stuff at Woodstock 99.

"I think **Endgame** is probably the heaviest album they put out in years," says guitarist Glen Drover, shockingly out of the band for this next studio record, replaced by Jag Panzer's Chris Broderick. "And to be honest with you, I like that album more than the one I played on. Andy Sneap knew where the band needed to go, because he grew up with this stuff too—he had a clear vision. And I think **United Abominations** and **Endgame** show that. He had more to do with **Endgame** because he went in fresh, rather than jumping in after eight songs or ten songs were done, like he did with **United Abominations**."

Asked about Glen leaving the band, bassist LoMenzo figures, "You know what? Here's the thing. Megadeth was, at that point, because it was moving on, spending 289 days a year touring. It was never going home. And some people enjoy that and some people enjoy it less. And I think at that point, Glen was pretty much enjoying it less. I can't speak from his perspective, but from my angle, I think that's where it was going. As for getting Chris, Chris was actually referred by Glen, if memory serves. I think it actually was Glen who brought him up although it might have been Shawn. They both knew of him from Jag Panzer. So they got a video of him and brought it by and showed it to Dave. And that was it: 'Well, let's get this guy in; check him out.' Turned out to be the nicest guy. Friend of mine to this day. I mean, love him, love him to death. Really, I mean, a craftsman, he loves his instrument, he loves to work at it. And he's just a great guy."

Asked to critique Broderick as an axeman, James explains that, "He had a way of playing really dexterously and very cleanly, more so than anybody else. Mustaine, in my estimation, his style, as a fan kind of looking into it—and I don't know if many people would get this—but he's got a Jimmy Page swagger about his thrash metal (laughs). You know, he's very accurate, but at the same time there's a very humanistic feel to it. There is almost a tight rope kind of thing, where it's like he could possibly lose it, and yet he never does—that's very exciting about his style. And I think that's what gives Megadeth its sound. And Chris was—as Marty Friedman was—able to address that and do a counterpoint to it. I think that's his best facet to the band, to this day, too. I really think he's a wonderful counterpoint to Dave's rhythms. And Dave on lead... he's no slouch playing lead either."

Contrasting Chris with Glen, James says that Drover "was a great guitar player who just really loved the notion of playing guitar in Megadeth. So that lent itself to a lot of excitement. And Glen was rather meticulous in his own way—he took the music very seriously. Chris, on the other hand, he came in, and I mean, he was in many ways overqualified for the band. I don't mean that to sound like he's way too good for Megadeth. But in some ways, his musical reach went beyond what Megadeth should be. So it was fun watching him get on board, get directed and to figure out his place. Once he did, it was really scary, because Dave very wisely found a way to incorporate his vast talents, and kind of make more statements with Megadeth, and kind of make him, I would say, the new Marty Friedman, you know, the stand-up guitar player in the band. And I think that's what we immediately recognized about Chris."

"Shawn is your blue-collar metal drummer," adds LoMenzo, turning attention to what it was like being half of the Megadeth rhythm section with Shawn Drover. "He came in, you know, as tight as bones, and again, another big fan of the band coming in. He was there about a year before I was. He helped me get on board and caught me up with the history of the band in many ways. So I appreciated him as a person, and for his help. And as a drummer, he's sterling. I played with great drummers, and they all have something different to offer. I just did a show in Estonia with Vinnie Appice, and that's a whole other flavour, you know? But I find the better the drummer—you'd be surprised—the more humble they are behind the scenes, and the better people they are. Anybody who is into their craft generally has this level of thankfulness, and Shawn definitely fits that bill. He loves what he's doing, and he really works at it."

New hi-octane lineup in place and there it was: **Endgame**, a blisteringly heavy and aggressive new Megadeth record to add to the pile, the album arriving September 15th of 2009 into an environment with more metal bands than ever, but every album selling a tenth of what it might have just ten years earlier.

After a Maiden-like romp of an instrumental introduction called *Dialectic Chaos*, the album opens proper with *This Day We Fight!* and off to the races we go, the newly extra carnivorous Megadeth thrashing hard, Dave and his new six-string maestro Chris Broderick turning in a riff that is so note-dense it's hard to tell what's going on. The track was inspired by Aragorn's speech in **Lord Of The Rings**, but outside of that slightly embarrassing tidbit of background, the rest of it is all business.

"Everybody was saying it was **Rust In Peace** II, and where were we coming from on this?," chuckles producer Andy Sneap, asked to contrast **Endgame** with **United Abominations**. "I mean, we weren't really A/B-ing. A lot of the starting points of the songs, we went back and listened to... Dave has hundreds and hundreds of riff tapes he'd been compiling over the last few years and we put them all into a ProTools rig. So we went back and listened to all these ideas from when we were jamming, stuff from **Countdown**, stuff from **Rust In Peace**, stuff they were jamming on at soundcheck, and we'd pull little snippets out, 'Oh, that's a good idea; that's good,' just so we had little starting points to work from. And the way the studio was, we had everything set up in the back room, so we would get these ideas and go in and jam on them and sort of build from that. And although Dave had already written the stuff, it was really me and Shawn going, 'That's cool, that's cool, that's what we like, let's try this bit,' and then Dave would come in and listen to it and go, 'Okay, I like that, I see where you're coming from there.' So there's a lot of bouncing ideas off of each other, which is quite nice. So it wasn't just all Dave. He kind of trusted us, which is the way it had worked on the last album. We'd come together—it built trust between us. So it felt very cooperative on the whole thing, between the three of us, and then James and Chris would come in and put their side of things in."

Adds LoMenzo on the record's first track proper, "*This Day We Fight!* is an incredibly dexterous song for everybody (laughs). That was a crazy one to play. I was thrilled to find somebody had gotten a hold of a naked bass track of mine, and on first listening, it sounds like a racket. It sounds like just a bass going down the stairs. But on second listening, it's really pretty fast (laughs). And I imagine I played it pretty well. People who listen to those things rate it as very good, so I'll go with that."

"When we went in to start that record, the objective was to bring it back," continues LoMenzo, "you know, to try to get more of a classic heavy metal vibe on the whole thing, more so than on **United Abominations**. That's where we were going. So it was funny, because immediately I thought, you know, simplify. Don't make things more complicated than they have to be. After all, it's metal, if you think about it. And Dave seemed to be in agreement with that as well. It wasn't until the… Because even as we did it, there were a couple of ballad-type songs on there and stuff. So I didn't really get the picture. But then the critic started coming around, and this is when we already started touring the songs. They started just coming off the hook and saying exactly what you're saying. This is it. You guys have come back to being Megadeth and it's heavy as ever. That's when I started listening to it and going, oh yeah, okay, yeah, I guess it is (laughs). When you're in the middle of all this stuff, it's a microcosm from minute to minute and you don't really know."

"*This Day We Fight!* is a pretty brutal song of the modern era Megadeth," agrees drummer Drover. "It's arguably one of the heaviest songs we've written since Dave reformed the band, I would say. Because it's a pretty violent, speed metal song; we played that one for a while live, and that was fun to play."

Next up was *44 Minutes*, which opens with a mournful and melodic riff plus recorded emergency footage that kicks off the story of a violent bank heist, namely the North Hollywood shootout of 1997, one of the heaviest exchanges of gunfire caught on camera outside of war. Although this one's classic rhythmic Megadeth with a gnarly bass tone, it marks the first chunk of extremely hooky melody on the album, come chorus time.

"I think that's probably what sets Megadeth apart is more the melodic stuff," noted Dave, speaking with Sam Dunn. "I've learned how to play heavy stuff because I like the way it makes me feel, but deep down inside in my bone marrow there's a degree of musicianship. Even though I'm self-taught and don't really know what I'm doing, I still know what I like to hear. That's like saying just because you don't know how to cook you don't like to eat. Just because I don't know what I'm playing doesn't mean I don't like playing it. There's a lot of stuff I'd really like to learn. Our guitar player, Chris, this guy's crazy. He plays guitar 13 hours a day. I look at him and it's cool because you can set him in a corner, go about your day and he'll still be there playing guitar. I couldn't do that. I love playing guitar but not like that."

"I haven't really followed their arrangement ideas," counters Dave, asked if the songwriting of old classic pop enters into his thought process. "I think songs should climax no matter how they start. I also believe a song can be a two-part song. I've seen a lot of songs that have reprises where they'll come back to the song a little farther down the record, and I like having those twists and turns with music. For me, one of the worst things is having a record that you listen to once and you can digest everything in one sitting. There's a lot of bands that are like that. I was playing Krokus this morning for my son to show him what happens if you sound like somebody else. And I said, 'Tell me that doesn't sound like Bon, and tell me that doesn't sound like Angus.' I said, 'You're never going to get anywhere if you try to sound like somebody else.' I very easily could have tried—without James and Lars around I don't know how successful I would have been—but I could have tried to follow the Metallica formula but I didn't out of respect for them and out of self-respect. I wanted to do my own thing. I didn't want people going, 'Eh, he's just like'..."

But Megadeth's respect for melody has been key... "I think so. I think it's why the choruses every once in a while will have a bit of a hook in it that's a little bit outside the realm of what thrash metal does and makes it a little more appealing to some other people. Music in general for me is always something I've taken seriously. Whether I was listening to stuff as a kid, listening to the Beatles or Cat Stevens with my sister, or listening with my older brother-in-law who listened to bands like Paul Revere & The Raiders or Gary Puckett & The Union Gap, Righteous Brothers, and stuff like that back in the '60s. I was just a kid at the time but I'm listening to this stuff and I'm getting some musical nurturing. My three sisters are all older than me and they're listening to Motown so I'm getting some funk, so I'm growing up a bit with some rhythm, and I'm growing up with a lot of hooky songwriting stuff. And I discovered the Beatles and Led Zeppelin and it's all over. So that's where I actually started as a musician, was with the British invasion. Then as far as my guitar playing style, it was pretty much crafted around the New Wave Of British Heavy Metal. So thank god for England or I wouldn't be able to play a note."

Funny car-racing tale *1,320'* is one of these two-part songs of which Dave speaks, although the second part is not a full-on vocal-based composition but more of a flameout to support soloing. The it's onto *Bite The Hand*, a brisk mid-pacer with a hard end of NWOBHM vibe and a half-time breakdown. Lyrically, this one's about the type of capitalism that Tea Party types can all get behind as bad, a little something called crony capitalism, systemic high level corruption, an American aggravation that just might result in hard right wingers with a libertarian bent contemplating a tumultuous break with the Republican party.

Back, however, at the music end of this one, crazy guitar duels ensue, its buzzing hive of business serving as sonic metaphor for the lyrical anger enclosed.

"When Chris first got involved, I think he was a bit out of water, really," explains Sneap concerning the Jag Panzer wizard. "He didn't quite fit in, and he was sort of thrown in, 'Right, learn this, learn this,' 30 songs to learn in three weeks or whatever before a tour. And actually, when he stepped up to the mark on this album, he did well. Actually got a lot of ideas figured out. Dave would listen, 'Oh, I don't quite like that bit there, and tweak this bit here.' But they are very different. Chris is very, very thoughtful; the way he worked it out, it was like a mathematical equation for him, and then Dave would come in and dribble as he's playing his guitar solo (laughs). So it's sort of like a front row seat at a gig when Dave is doing his solo. He's almost bouncing off the walls and gritting his teeth, and I actually liked that. It's a very stark contrast to Chris' style of playing, where Dave's playing has really got some energy when he gets going, some real fire, and that's what I like. You can get all the sweeping arpeggios and everything worked out, but all that minute detail can get very sterile for me. I like the passion and passionate playing when I hear it. But solo-wise, I would say it's 60% Chris, 40% Dave."

"I was very much in the driver's seat when we did this album," continues Andy, on whether Dave tended to take the reins. "Dave had trusted me to track the other guys, so he would just sort of come in, because he's got a lot of other things going off in his life. He's trying to write his book at the same time, and run other parts of things. So he would leave me to it, come in, listen to it, add a few ideas, go off and come back in the evening. And we would go over things again. Make notes and get changed little things he wasn't happy with. So it was quite good, from the working side of things, bouncing things off of each other. All told, I tried to keep more of a live feel to it. I didn't want to get too sterilized about it."

Not sure Andy succeeded on that front, as really, the modern-day Megadeth albums sound fiercely professional, locked-down, and with **Endgame** in particular, blurry of note densities and progressive thrash flourishes. In other words, fans who on the surface really had nothing to complain about instead complained—and not many of them; most were digging the new material—about Megadeth giving the fans too much of what they wanted and, heaven forbid, expected. This new and efficient Megadeth, heavy as it was, seemed to try too hard, in the eyes of some, to compete with the young pups coming up.

Stay hungry, says Dave (and Dee Snider). "I listen to these guys that say, 'Man, there's no competition.' I just think, you moron, why do you think there's numbers on the charts? We're all competing for No. 1. And anybody that tells you they'd rather play a small place than a big place has never played a big place. When they say that stuff it's like, 'Are you kidding? Do the math! How much money are you going to make playing at the Whiskey versus playing at LA Stadium? Hello?' Some of these things people act so pious about. What they're willing to do for their fans... well if you really love your fans, you'd play really inexpensively like we do. When we do our tickets for the American Carnage, we've got tons of $10 seats. We do that because we know who we're playing to. We're playing to ourselves. Granted I got lucky and I made a lot of money, but you know what? I still love macaroni and cheese, man. I'm a normal guy."

And he knows his fans want Megadeth to bring the metal, which is what **Endgame** delivered, like the cover of **Fistful** and the cover of **Vulgar**.

"I think the musical climate is a little more accepting of bands that diversify themselves, and at the time I think a lot of people expected certain stuff out of me, and because I hadn't really made clear what I was going to do, I don't think a lot of people were really open-minded to me experimenting like that. Now if I had been doing that in my career earlier, I know people would have said hey, it's okay for you to do this. But I was pretty much sticking to my guns in the beginning of my career, with my music, with the songs, with the arrangements, with the style and stuff. And when **Youthanasia** came out, that was pretty much the beginning of the end with us. **Risk** was the nail in the coffin. I pretty much said, 'Guys, it's done, we're not doing this any more. I'm not listening to Capitol any more, and we're leaving the label.' And we left. There was a guy that worked there and he comes into the studio, and I'm in some Adidas trainers, I got a jump suit on, like sweat pants and a sweat jacket, and he comes in and he goes, 'Har har, you going to a soccer game?' And it's like, look, I didn't make fun of you coming in here with your guy from the record label, and the two of you are dressed like twins. Why are you making fun of me? I'm at work here."

"The spirit of heavy metal, I think, is loyalty," continues Dave. "To inebriating levels, when you think about it. We like the brand of liquor that we like, and there's not much that will move us from that posture. We also smoke certain cigarettes, and we'll smoke other cigarettes if we have to, but for the most part, we're so conservative when it comes down to tobacco. Same thing with the stations we listen to, television we watch, cars we drive, shoes we wear. The integrity of the heavy metal audience is so much more so than most of the other people that are fellow happy trudgers, out there walking the road of destiny. For me, I look at it like, sorry man, I won't drive a Lexus. It's a high-priced Toyota. If you can't afford a Beemer or a Mercedes, then don't drive one. Look at it like this, you've got Heineken, you've got Amstel Light, and then you've got Miller High Life. So the Mercedes is obviously the Heineken, the Beemer's the Amstel Light for the yuppies who can't afford the Mercedes, and then you've got the Lexus which is like... and that shit always gave me a headache, too. Miller High Life? I could drink one bottle and it would be like someone hit me in the back of the head. I would get a headache."

"And that's how people go through life," furthers Dave, on a roll. "They want to be the real deal, they want to get into thrash metal, they want to play like us and be like us, but man, you know what?—you can't fake a lifestyle. You can't. Sharon Osbourne was talking to me over in Spain recently and we were talking about one person in particular, and I won't name him out of respect for the guy, but she said something, 'Out of everybody in the entire music industry, he's the only one that's not like any of us.' And I went, wow, that's really peculiar because the person we were talking about, and what she was talking about, it was true. He was the only one in heavy metal that has this one particular facet, and none of us do."

"When you look at the things that drive us, I'm still hungry," reflects Dave, even if now he was fully four records into his post-**Risk** turn-around and... not really in a rut, but producing at an almost annoying level of efficiency. "Yeah I've got a nice car and I've got a nice place where I live and I've got money. But it's not mine. It was given to me by the fans. They believe in me. I believe I'm under worked and overpaid. I think that the beginning of my life was really hard. The ending is quite a lot better so far. I'm a better finisher than I was a beginner with things, and I look at a lot of things I've gone through and either I get upset about it or I look at it and say, 'This is going to make me a better person,' or I'm going to share what I did to get through this mess with somebody else. So many kids come up to me and they say, 'God, you have no idea what *Darkest Hour* means to me' or what *A Tout Le Monde* means to me and I go, 'Yeah I do. I wrote *Darkest Hour* the day that Cliff died.' My heart broke that day. I went straight downtown, bought some heroin, and I came back to my apartment, I got loaded and just wept. I played my guitar, just tears streaming down my face and was asking the same question we always ask when somebody we love dies: 'Why?'"

"Where does your fire come from? It comes from that little boy inside me that likes to do stuff that people can't do. I like to set the guitar down and say, 'Show me you can do that.' And there's so many people that are better than me and I know that, but I have fun at what I'm doing. Put somebody in my perspective, find somebody that's almost 50, that can play guitar and sing at the same time, like I do, as good as I do, and I'll be impressed."

More of that very impressive singing and strumming takes place on **Endgame**'s next track, *Bodies*, I'm sure at least elliptically named after a classic by the Pistols, a band we know Dave identifies with. In truth though, this is a choppy mid-pacer wedged in spirit between **Peace Sells**, **So Far** and... **Youthanasia**. Lyrically, it's not about abortion like the original, but instead mortality, Dave in self-deprecating mode about his own insignificance but also belligerent about idiots that have crossed his path and become dead to him along the tumultuous way.

In one sense, *Bodies* is a chugging intro salvo to the album's intensely metallic title track, *Endgame* which finds Dave tormented by the new world order like his friend and obsessive orator-of-another-sort Alex Jones. Musically, it's a serving of that slightly incongruous neo-thrash folks of a slightly younger generation like Shawn Drover might symbolize. I would say Chris Broderick, stoker of the engine room, but he is in fact of the self-same generation as Dave, so we can't blame him for cutting edge skilfulness beyond what Mustaine would ever want in—or from—himself.

"We put a lot of time into it," muses Andy, on the clearly well-crafted banquet of metal that **Endgame** is. "Six months of my life down there in San Diego doing that. I think we did a good album. I don't see any way we could have improved that album, at the time. I think there's room for improvement on the next album, as things are thought-out a little bit more, that if there will be actually songs written before we start, it will be better. Because it really was a case of starting from the ground up on it. Even in the studio, we did demos of everything, came back to it, started tracking it, and it would be nice if the band could actually rehearse the songs and demo songs before I actually get involved the second time."

Do you think it's the heaviest Megadeth album ever?

"Sonically I think it probably is, yeah," says Andy, typical of a producer, answering the question off-topic towards the near abstract concept of sound. "You know, people will always go... I love **Peace Sells**, and I love **Rust In Peace** as well, and I think those are actually classics. Would I say this is a classic? I would say it's very good, but I think you only know if it's a classic five or ten years down the line. I've heard the album more than anybody else on the face of the planet, so for me to judge it, it's hard to say, really. I need time away from it. Ask me that in a year's time."

The Hardest Part Of Letting Go... Sealed With A Kiss is a bitter love song (originating from darkness within Dave's marriage) possessed of an epic, balladic vibe, although it mostly rocks hard like memorable uptempo Dio or galloping Maiden. The melody is rich and easy on the memory circuits, and all told, the song is a smart foil to the mayhem that is the rest of the record, tracks like the shockingly fast and note-dense *Head Crusher* which comes next. No *Crush 'Em*, that's for sure, this one is a vigorous and enthusiastic celebration of the torture device of which the title bemoans in writhing pain. "I think we were after a really aggressive sound for that whole CD," notes Broderick, and *Head Crusher* is very, very in-your-face and that's what we were looking to do."

"There's lot heavy stuff on that record, but I'll always lean towards *Head Crusher*, which is a song I wrote," notes Shawn, who indeed garners his lone credit on **Endgame** with this master blaster. "I just think it has all the elements of a really good Megadeth tune. It's heavy, it's violent, it's got a lot of cool thrashy parts to it."

As for the writing of it... "It's a pretty similar situation to what happened with *Built For War* from **Super Collider**. It was just a matter of, hey, guys, got any ideas, yes, I got this idea, and it was a full idea I had recorded—I had a full song constructed. The first half of the song started off as more of a medium tempo song, almost like a sped-up *Symphony Of Destruction* kind of tempo, if you can visualize that. And then it kicks into the heavy fast part, which ended up being a big chunk of what ended up being *Head Crusher*. Dave was like, 'I don't dig the first half of the song; I like the second half of the song.' And that kinda threw me for a loop, and I tossed it aside for a while. But near the end of the record, he looked at the song again and he said, 'Man, I don't really dig the first half of the song, but I like the second half.' So he started writing, you know, filling in the blanks of that song, which ultimately became a collaborative effort between Dave and myself, and ended up as *Head Crusher*. So it ended up where the whole song is pretty much up-tempo and violent. He supplied the missing pieces, you know; all the verses and the stuff was mine. I can't remember all the parts that were mine. It wound up pretty much a 50-50 split during that song, musically speaking, but it all stems from a song idea I had. We ended up using half of my song and he supplied the missing pieces."

So Shawn can be counted on to bring the metal, and so, evidently, could Mustaine in this new mind frame. But all are in agreement that Andy Sneap was a big part of lighting a fire under Megadeth, as Drover explains.

"Well, yeah, Andy obviously was the guitar player for Sabbat, so he was full on into metal, and still is to this day. We had a really good relationship with Andy. He's a friend and all that; he's just a really good producer. And he really worked well with all of us. Still, we all kind of had... when we went in and did the **Endgame** record, we already heard, by the time we were going in, a lot of the musical ideas that Dave had submitted, and all of us submitted, and we really tried to focus on making good heavy songs. And I think Andy did a really good job with it. I really have a lot of good memories recording that record. That was the first time we recorded at Vic's Garage, which is our studio in San Marcos, and that was a really good time. Me and Andy stayed at... Dave had a beach house down in Southern California, where we stayed when we were down recording. We both stayed at Dave's beach house. I have a good memories of it and it's certainly one of my favourite Megadeth records the band's ever done."

Moving forward, *How The Story Ends* was inspired by Sun Tzu and **The Art Of War**, and musically, we're back to a high quality traditional mid-metal, Dave's riff being of a type that would support a central pillar of a great Dio, Priest or Maiden album (or more like Bruce solo circa **Chemical Wedding**).

Endgame grinds out a victory by submission with the circular doom-thrash of *The Right To Go Insane*, a song dedicated to those slipping through the cracks of the American dream. "*The Right To Go Insane* is extremely cool, that half-tempo, plodding thing," comments bassist James LoMenzo. "It's a favourite of mine, along with *This Day We Fight!*, because of the big open bass parts of the song, which is cool for a bass player."

It is of note that **Endgame**, as framed, a very heavy Megadeth album, emerged a year after Metallica's **Death Magnetic**, a much vaunted return to a somewhat purist thrash (and if unpure, it's because of proginess and sheer song length, more than anything). I asked Sneap if there was something in the acceptance or perceived coolness of thrash in the late 2000s that might have been causing bands like Metallica to return to the fold.

"I don't know, really. I mean, I'm actually one of those guys who really likes the Black Album, and I think the **Load** and **ReLoad** album is a good album—if you combined the best bits off of those two, you've got a good album as well. I don't know, with Metallica, it's hard to say, isn't it? These bands, they get such a bubble around them, and a close-knit community, and they're in with the management and there are so many yes-men and people telling them what to do, that they kind of lose... music is a very personal thing. Thrash, when it first started, it was very angst-driven, and it was a passionate form of music, and I think when people get into a comfortable life, you don't really feel the same anymore. It's difficult to start writing riffs when you're not feeling it. I think a lot of these bands, with the success they've had, it took them away from what thrash was all about. Gary from Exodus was saying, what we should do with the Metallica guys, is give them food for each good riff they write, get them writing hungry in a garage again. Pass them a burger under the door for each good riff (laughs). But the thing is, it's a good sort of analogy, really. Because I think that's what sparks thrash, is that anger of sort of late teens, early twenties, and there was that energy to it, wasn't there? I think, these bands, they get into midlife, and they've got the nice house, family, nice car, they're not quite as angry as they used to be. And if you go back to rediscover it again, it's quite difficult to do. With Megadeth, I mean, a lot of it was me and Shawn Drover, who sat down, sort of pushing Dave on this album, really trying to dig deep and prod him a bit, goad him a bit, and just get the riffs out. And I knew as a Megadeth fan what I wanted to hear out of it, so that's the sort of benchmark I gave it, when I was working on it. So hopefully, the thrash thing has never left me. I've always been 100% into it."

I talked to Matt Heaffy from Trivium—successful next gen thrashers compared to Megadeth and Metallica all the time—about Megadeth's accomplishments in the world of thrash, versus those of Dave's competitor class comprising Metallica.

"I think when it came down to Metallica, yeah, Metallica was technical; Metallica did create some of the absolute greatest songs in thrash metal, and still do. But Megadeth is a band that embraced a whole new set of technicality that was pretty mind-blowing. I mean, Slayer is technical, but Slayer is more so right hand technical—it's a matter of endurance. And it's a matter of stamina, to play this stuff. Where it came down for Megadeth— lead playing aside, because the lead playing was insane, especially when Marty Friedman was part of the picture—but with Mustaine, the rhythm guitar parts he would always write seemed to be like rhythm parts that a singer/guitar player shouldn't be able to play and sing. They are so paradoxical to what's going on from the guitar to the vocals. And I think that's a huge thing that Trivium have. There are a lot of things that we are creating that David was pushing for, that I was like hey, man, I cannot play and sing this, because the rhythm is so different. It's not easy to deal with. And so when I look at things like that, vocal parts that don't go with rhythm guitar parts that a singer/guitar player that has to play live, that's more so Megadeth than it is Metallica. Metallica has difficult stuff to play and sing, but there's always a way to put the vocal rhythm into the guitar rhythm. But I think with Megadeth, sometimes that's not even there—I don't know how Mustaine does it."

Commencing June 16, 2010 at Sonisphere in Poland and marauding around Europe over seven dates for a couple of weeks was the stupendous and historical Big Four tour, which found Megadeth sharing huge stages with Anthrax, Slayer and headliners Metallica. The event was captured in CD and DVD form with the arrival of **The Big Four: Live From Sofia, Bulgaria**, filmed and recorded on the fourth date, June 22, 2010. Another show would take place on April 23, 2011, in California, one at Yankee Stadium in New York, on September 14, 2011, with five European dates wedged in between during festival season, early July. Sub-plot of course included Dave's hard feelings with the Metalli-cats, but with Slayer as well, and then Slayer didn't have a lot of good things to say about Metallica either, during the whole **Load** and **ReLoad** era. The show used for the physical release was also broadcast live to more than 450 theatres across America and an additional 350 outlets across Canada, Europe and Latin America.

And yet, before the **Big Four** package dropped in October, a month earlier the band had sent to the stores **Rust In Peace Live**, featuring the band crashing through that classic live back on March 31, 2010, at the Hollywood Palladium. Issued in CD, Blu-ray and DVD formats, the set also included six non-**Rust** selections, Dave gamely including the likes of *Trust* and *She-Wolf*, always the honest supporter of the whole catalogue, in both interviews and on disc.

Keeping Dave's dance card full in 2010 was the large imprint publication of his memoir, an oral history of sorts that he co-write with Joe Layden.

Interviewing Dave about the project at a Toronto hotel, Mustaine told me that, "Joe was a person who was introduced to me, and they told me his resume, and they said that he was a sportswriter, essentially, and I thought, you know, this is going to be good, because he's not caught up in all the typical same ol' same ol' same ol' words that everybody uses in metal. It would be somebody who can write, and they use a bunch of different verbiage, as well as somebody who doesn't really know me, and who will be a very unbiased party. Because I don't want this to be presented like a Dave Mustaine sales pitch. I wanted it to be the truth, warts and all, and I think anybody who has read this will see that I'm not making it like some kind of way to vindicate myself. It's just telling the story before I get too old and forget it."

"I did have some very important criteria that I wanted to go over," says Dave, on the dangers—and temptations—inherent in taking what was likely to be his one shot at a tell-all. "And this being my first book, I didn't really know what I was doing. This was a whole new area for me, so I read a couple other people's bios—like I read Manson's bio, I read several political figures that I respected, I read Slash's book, AC/DC's book—and I just wanted to see... like other stuff that happened to me was better left out of the story. There was stuff that I did which was better left out, and there is stuff that needs to be told. But because of the way human nature and how litigious everybody is now, it could never be told. But having said that, I wanted it to be as much as I could about who I am, and not about, 'Buy Megadeth records' for Pete's sakes, because they already sell. So this is more about like, okay, so now that this whole Big Four thing has now proven to the world that there isn't any feuds anymore, what's next? And more Big Four concerts, hopefully, and a new record for us. But in the meantime it was me being able to say, OK, now, if you want to know who this guy is who has been the villain for so many years, well, here I am. This is who I am and this is what makes me how I am. and it's not so much as, like I said, selling Megadeth—it's about explaining Dave Mustaine."

I wondered if getting all this out on the table would help clear the air, so to speak, in terms of Dave's relationships with various people in his orbit, and indeed, the way in which they now would deal with him...

"I don't know how it's going to change people," posits Dave. "And I didn't really do this to have an effect on other people. It wasn't like some self-righteous bloodletting or something, for me to come into it as an enlightened soul. It was really just me just telling the story. And you know, like I said, I didn't want to hurt anybody in the process. But there was a lot of stuff that was really funny in the book, like the story about the scorpion and the girl we threw in the bushes—it's just funny stuff. I look at it, and I think, man, that's rock 'n' roll. But then I also think about, well, why did Ozzy get happy faces tattooed on his knees? You know, there are questions like that I had about other people, and I'm just wondering, did I answer some of those questions in my book? Yeah, I did—there are places where I say why I did the things I do, and why I am the way that I am."

"Like for example, on the way over to do the morning television show here, what's that called? **Breakfast TV**; it's huge, right? And on my way over there, our driver... we had this retard, and he takes us all around town to get there, and he takes me right past the Greyhound station. And I was like, 'Aaaarggh!' when I saw a Greyhound bus, because that's how I went home, right? So it's funny how it reminds me of this story about this guy who was a tour manager for ZZ Top who worked for us said that the dancers for ZZ Top, out on their tour, every night they would get a whole bunch of mud wrestlers to come out and dance for them, and they would stay on the tour for a little while, and then they would all get cocky and want to have more money or more this and that, and then whenever that happens, they would take everything out of their dressing room and leave a bowl of mud in there, for them to remember who they were. Now I don't know if this is true or not. The guy who told me the story doesn't work for us anymore, but I thought wow, what a great way to break it down for the lowest common denominator? A bowl of fucking mud, you know what I mean?"

But still, there's got to be some catharsis to doing this, a poignancy, perhaps, some sort of realization that this cast of characters have been, to various degrees, a part of the circus that is Megadeth and frankly, we're all just at a place where we as a metal community have no choice but to grow old together.

"Well it's really funny that you say 'we.' Because for the longest time I never felt like I was part of the we. And a lot of that was sadly the feud, and everybody trying to be hip and think that it was cool to be a Dave hater. And it's like, I said a lot of stuff, that I think anybody in their circumstances would say when they're backed into a corner or hurt or whatever. And you know, it's funny because I was talking with Kerry King the other day, and he flat out said, 'I don't even remember what I was mad about. It was so long ago.' And I was like yeah, I don't even know what you were mad about either. So we just laughed about it, because we were kids at the time."

"But you have a fan that takes this popular figure or a person they're pining for, it takes on a life of its own. So I feel like part of 'we' right now—that in itself is a rush. A lot of that started when I started to see my name showing up in articles about influencing other guitar players. Because I never saw it. And then you start seeing people say that no, they were influenced by Dave. And yes, you listen to them and you can hear it. But I wouldn't take credit for it. A lot of kids playing out there right now are also brilliant. And there are some people out there right now that I think are a little bit too brilliant, and they need to remember what this is all about. It's not about being out there and soloing, it's about expressing yourself. You know, I love to express myself to the music, and that's one of the things that I think caused one of the biggest problems, is expressing yourself. Some people don't want to hear it."

"I think just for continuity and not only the respect for friends, but self-respect for myself, I think it's important that I was trying to keep it as accurate as possible," answers Dave, asked about the need to which he had to connect with old acquaintances to make sure he had his facts straight. "So a lot of it was easy to just go back and look at like, there was a knife put into the ground at a particular time. We'd say, okay, this happened during the **Peace Sells** era. Well, **Peace Sells** was only between those two years, and then this happened in the summer, and through process of elimination you figure out what the facts are. It wasn't really hard to determine a lot of this stuff, and I still have pretty good use of my faculties, and there are so many fact-checkers out there. But over the years, you forget certain things. Sometimes I'll be talking about a story and I'll go off on a tangent and I'll go, 'Oh, what the fuck was I even talking about?' (laughs). But that's probably the worst thing that is going on with me right now as far as storytelling. I don't really have a hard time remembering when things went down, but sometimes you will go talk to some people who were there, and I don't necessarily put their face at that place at that time, so I sometimes I don't remember that they were there. But I remember the events, the key players."

"It's not really like there's bad and good," reflects Dave, asked if the writing and the personal reading of **Mustaine** reveals a happy story, a tale, on balance, filled with more good than bad. "There's life and then there's, for me, what's going to be the afterlife. And how I deal with things right now makes a difference in the world, because I missed out on a lot of stuff. When **Countdown** was No. 2, did I care? No, I was furious about fucking where Billy Ray Cyrus was. And I was upset because the Recording Industry Association of America would let a country artist in the pop charts. You know, put him in the country charts! Let me have my fucking No. 1! For once, OK? And you know, I didn't even realize, if I never make it to No. 1, then I'll be the No. 1 person at being No. 2. And it's just some perspective—an aperture kind of clicks into focus. You know, I've got a great life. I stopped wanting everything, and I started looking at what I've got, and I realize I have more than most."

"And that this is part of being a little kid. You know, you want to get everything you can. And you know, you go to the buffet and you pile up all the sprinkles and shit on your ice cream, and you know you're not going to eat it, but boy, you want to make sure! I look at my life right now, and like as I said before, not trying to be clever, I've been overpaid and under worked. I think about what George Harrison said about when you become popular, you exchange your nervous system for fame, and he's absolutely right. I have a hard time when we travel in certain areas. If I want to be left alone, or if I'm going through something and I'm having a bad day, you know, you're always going to run into somebody who is going to see you, and you've got to be able to (snaps fingers), snap out of it, because as a public figure, you're not really allowed to have bad days. And I think that's another thing, that in the beginning of my career, I was open about those bad days. Fortunately for me, in the long run, it's come around full circle, and you know, I was a pioneer at being honest. I think a lot of musicians nowadays, they're saying that being honest to your fan base is the key to success. It's the key to longevity. You know, you can hide stuff, but it will come out. And you can bullshit your fans, but they will abandon you."

Talking to Dave just two days after the massive Big Four celebration of thrash, it seemed appropriate to ask if some wry combination of what's said in the book at length about Metallica and what had just happened live... was there some satisfaction in quietly demonstrating to Metallica, through deed, that yes, Megadeth had been a successful life lived?

"I don't know if I wanted them to know that I was successful," ponders Dave. "I think that if there was anything that I wanted, it probably boils down to just wanting to be treated with respect, you know, just like any other man would. And even though our partnership ended, I think probably what I wanted was the friendship to continue. You know, just because you don't work together with somebody doesn't mean you have to be at odds with them. I think that probably was the motivator for me, over those years, is that I never lost a job before, and had never lost a friendship like that. And it was hard for me to deal with, because I didn't have a dad to turn to, and say, 'Dad, what the fuck?!' You know? (laughs)."

"And looking back at it now, we've always been friends; it's just that the press made money selling magazines that had shit in it. When we met the other day at the restaurant, Lars and I sat down and talked for a while, and it was just like old times. And when we did this roundtable thing for Metal

Hammer, Lars had said something about, you know, we have our relationship, and then there's the relationship that the press thinks we have. And we've been friends for years; this whole thing has been over for years and we've always talked. But it's just like every once in a while something would come up and depending on where any of our headspace was, was whether we got baited into it. Now I know no matter what, that if anything is said, I just don't care about it anymore. You know, I've made amends with James and with Lars and with Kirk, and never had a problem with Robert. So if there is anything that is said by anybody, I know it's just bullshit. You know, even if it's not bullshit, we made peace. Everything is... it's all good. There's no problems anymore. So for me wanting them to know that I'm successful, I don't know if I ever wanted that. I just wanted to keep the friendship."

Even outside of the massive Big Four stand, Megadeth appeared, perceptively to have turned a corner, quietly, like the bigger Rush and the smaller Clutch, becoming a band viewed as elder statesman, characters that belong to the world, crafters of some of their best music now but also a fun past to mine and celebrate communally.

"Record labels saying that we need to change our music, cut our hair and stuff like this," sneered Mustaine, "It's funny, right now, it's so ironic that we would be our most successful now when the record company is the worst, and we would be playing to sold-out arenas and amphitheatres like tonight, and we would just be basically doing no wrong. You get to look back, and it's like... because I have one more record for the label we're on right now, we're going to be moving on. I've looked at the way things have happened, and I'm a pretty fair dude. If things were going good, I would say that we would be more than happy to stay where we're act, but it's just the music industry is so upside down right now. Like I said, there are no good A&R guys around anymore, so who knows what's going to happen?"

"I do know I'm going to keep recording, because before Junior came back, it was looking like it was a just a tour whenever it came time to play and stuff like that. But things just transpired over the last six or seven months, Martin, and made it so fun to play again. I mean, you've seen me and known me for a long time, and we've had our ups and downs with the magazine and everything like that, but I really care about that and I know that you guys have a right to think like that and say what you want and I support you in that, so I think that's one of things that's kept our relationship really clean, was that there was always mutual respect. And I like the fact that right now, with my career, where I'm at, it's the purest it's ever been, because I'm not caught up in the whole Hollywood machine anymore. I mean, I live in San Diego. My band, one guy lives in Atlanta, another guy lives up in Thousand Oaks and another that lives in Arizona. We don't all have Hollywood addresses—we're just normal guys now."

14
THIRTEEN
"I'm going to do a little Budgie part"

On November 1, 2011, Megadeth unleashed upon a complacent, smug and spoilt metal world the best record of their long and twisted road thus far.

Thirteen (or, aggravatingly, **Th1rt3en**) was a blast of crafted mass hysteria that offered everything we'd want from a Megadeth album, in judicious doses, all thumb-pressed into the right places. If **Endgame** could be argued to be the heaviest Megadeth album ripped from Dave's spleen, **Thirteen** might just be the record that built most on a fine predecessor, the band taking all the best philosophies and tempering them just enough so that a Mega-masterpiece emerged as cogent and deftly balanced as was **Rust In Peace**.

Of course I'm well aware that I'm being provocative here and half of youse are saying yer out of your mind. But a part of me believes this, just like a part of me knows that for any heritage act, there's a bevy of abstract magicks swirled around the legendary old records that can never be reconjured. It's a long discussion and it can never be won on either side—this is art we're talking about here. But suffice to say, **Thirteen** is a helluva metal album if the composite of the Megadeth metal experience (foot on the brake, foot on the gas) is something you are inclined to appreciate.

Thirteen marked the return of Dave "Jr." Ellefson to the Megadeth fold, and all of a sudden, half the band was originating principals, with the other half having been part of the fold since the last record. Megadeth was starting to feel like a gang again, and inside of it, you now had your street metal version of Page/Plant, Richards/Jagger and Perry/Tyler.

"They're both great," says drummer Shawn Drover, asked what it's like to be part of a rhythm section with LoMenzo versus Ellefson. "I mean, add James MacDonough to that too. I played with three bass players in Megadeth, and of course I didn't really get into recording with James MacDonough, but he was a fantastic bass player as well. Having David, it's funny, because when David came back in the band, it was right before we were going on tour for the 20th anniversary of **Rust In Peace**. Again, I love James, he's a fantastic bass player, but it's cool to have somebody who helped write all the songs with Dave, who was the guy who played on the record, did all those world tours back in the day. To have him come back into the band, and me looking out there going wow, there's Dave and David, the nucleus of Megadeth for all those years, definitely brought a smile to my face. I gotta tell you, at those initial rehearsals, it was like putting on an old pair of shoes that you found in the closet; they still fit really well, you know what I mean? It was just cool to have that. Again, nothing against anybody else, because I love playing with all three guys. I thought they were all great, and extremely talented musicians. It's fun to play with different people. Everybody brings a little different element to the table. But ultimately when you're playing in Megadeth, or playing with a band that has a catalogue of music, you gotta keep it pretty close to what has already been recorded. You really can't deviate a whole lot from that. Because that's ultimately what the fans want to hear."

Remarked Mustaine, in conversation with Music Radar's Joe Bosso, "It was obviously more fun, and that's not to take away from any of the guys who played with us while Dave was on his... his 'time out,' so to speak. When he came back, we were writing the song *Sudden Death*. I was just getting ready to play bass on the track–that's right where things had ended with James Lomenzo–but Dave was there and I said, 'Hey, do you feel like recording something?' We were discussing doing the **Rust In Peace** tour, but it was only going to be a month's worth of dates to see how it went. We just wanted to see what it would be like. After the month, we were able to say that it had gone great. Dave had revived his career, and our friendship was very hearty. You know, when things went down with us, I didn't want that. I didn't want those problems. I love the guy. But that's what a relationship does–it's a living, breathing organism. But it was very painful when all that stuff happened with us. I was secretly hoping that we would be friends again, but I didn't know if we'd ever play together."

"Even during the time we were estranged from one another," Dave told Jeb Wright, "I still cared for him; he was like a little brother to me. You don't get into fistfights with other people to protect a friend that you don't care about. Dave got some funky direction from somebody who told him that I was doing something wrong, and I wasn't. The lawsuit was dismissed. One time, I was going through Phoenix and I asked if he wanted to have dinner together. I still loved him even though he sued me for 18-and-a-half million dollars—that is a lot of money. I still loved him and I wasn't going to let money, or material stuff, get between our friendship. We went out to the California Pizza Kitchen and he said, 'You know, that was the dumbest thing that I've ever done. I apologize.' I said, 'Dude, I love you and I forgive you.' A couple of years later, we are playing together again."

"I think that is the cool thing about heavy metal that people don't see," continued Mustaine. "There are friendships and bonds and loyalty and forgiveness and reconciliation. What a great example of how to break down those boundaries that we put up for ourselves. A lot of our fans have problems with how they are brought up; their parents aren't doing very good jobs. The parents know it, but forgiveness is such a massive thing. When we get pissed-off and hold grudges against some of our very best friends, then we cheat ourselves of really great friendships. A lot of people wrote us and told us they were having a grudge, or a fight, and that they were not friends anymore and, then when they saw that Dave and I got back together, they ended their grudge. I've got my old best friend back and I've got my band back too. It is just kind of a cool, feel good, warm and fuzzy thing all around."

Thirteen opened with a jazz chord over a tribal rumble and then a shred as *Sudden Death* got going. Dave's lyric is classic apocalyptic, poetic, and laced with his still somewhat quixotic but now long-time embrace of Christianity. *Sudden Death* might even be called "white metal," in the manner that, that epithet had been applied to the violent, fire and brimstone admonishments from Trouble on that Chicago doom band's first three records. Improbably the track was nominated for a Best Metal Performance award at the 53rd showing of the Grammys, although it lost out to Iron Maiden's *El Dorado*.

Says Dave of David, "When he sat down to do the bass line to *Sudden Death*, he sat in the control room with the door open. He said, 'I'm going to do a Diamond Head part right here'—and Diamond Head is one of my favourite bands. That aroused me a little bit. Then he goes, 'This next part, I'm going to do a little Budgie part'—and Budgie is another one of my favourites. I was like, 'Oh my God, this guy's messin' with my head, bringing up all these bands that I love. If he's playing me right now, he's doing it pretty good!' (laughs)."

"He had everything to do with it. I sucked without him," joked Dave, speaking with Pat Prince on the topic of burying the hatchet with Ellefson. "I'm just playing with you. Yeah, Dave added an element of excitement and fun to the band. Every player who plays an instrument is gonna have their own way that they handle the neck and the strings and stuff like that. We could have had the last guy who was playing before Dave do this record and play exactly what Dave played but it still wouldn't have sounded the same. We just knew it was gonna work out. So, yeah, I think he added a really great element but I think there are a couple other guys in the band that aren't so bad either."

Remarks Chris Broderick on *Sudden Death*, "That was written for **Guitar Hero** and we knew that they wanted a lot of guitar soloing on it. It was one of those things where we went and wrote the song around the solos and then expanded the song from there. Dave and I went back and forth taking solos and we really wrote the solos first and then the song was arranged around that. It was a backwards way of doing it but it really worked. We all present ideas. If you're a musician then you're always writing music, but at the end of the day, we have to look at what fits Megadeth."

As for whether Chris likes to craft his solos or just let 'er rip... "I really do both, but at the end of the day, I prefer to compose the solos. When you have time to think about what is going into a part of the song, then you can think more complexly than if you just solo over the top of something. When you just solo over the top of something then you're at the whim of your technique and you're at the whim of what you're thinking about at the moment."

The album's second track and lead single, *Public Enemy No. 1* got the attention of the Grammys as well, given a nomination at the 54th (losing to *White Limo* by Foo Fighters), while third song on the album *Whose Life (Is It Anyways?)* garnered the same accolade at the 55th (you can see why we scoff at this institution).

Public Enemy No. 1, inspired by the life of Al Capone, was one of those hooky, memorable tracks from the mind of Dave, like souped-up NWOBHM, packed with one-liners, blessed with a chorus that can't be erased from the memory circuits, and a verse vocal melody that is as chorus-like as the chorus.

"A song is only as good as its parts," Dave told Bosso, asked about this infectious track. "And the main riff in that one shows up at least three different ways, just alternating the picking pattern in one place, and going from a riff to half of a riff with some chords. Then we play the riff but double up in intensity and speed. I think the song is very simple, and that's what made so much of the New Wave Of British Heavy Metal so cool. During the '90s, when **Countdown** came out and on **Youthanasia**, we experimented a bit with chords, but a lot of that was because we were forced to. The music industry was turning on itself, and Nirvana were huge at the time. There was no place for metal; it was being forced underground. We were used to surviving at a pretty high level, so that was hard on us."

"I like melody, actually, most of all," says Broderick, asked about favourite ingredients in his metal. "I like the fact that you can incorporate a number of different styles of music within metal, which suits me very well. A lot of my background is classical guitar. It enables me to be able to put that in there, flamenco guitar, and also classical music, and composing classical music pieces in the form of metal, so it's pretty accommodating as far as a style of music goes. The thing I've seen recently that has really blown my mind... I used to give guitar instruction, and a lot of my younger students were showing up with Iron Maiden and Megadeth, Blind Guardian, bands of that sort, so that's always encouraging. Metal is a great place for guitar players. I think it stems from the roots of virtuosic guitar playing, because back in the '80s, every guitarist was trying to be the best. It was all about how well you can play."

Although he doesn't play seven-string with Megadeth, Chris says his use of the instrument outside of the parameters of the band has affected his writing. "I would say that within the confines of metal, the fact that I play a seven-string definitely changes it. The rhythms I try to come up with are definitely a little more syncopated than what you would normally consider metal to be. And probably a little bit more on the progressive side of things, than just straight metal."

Speaking with Jeb Wright from Classic Rock Revisited, Chris said that compared to **Endgame**, **Thirteen** "has a lot more melody. I'm a guitar player, so I guess I like to play songs like the ones on **Endgame** better, but if you really look at some of the melodies and the guitar playing that was put down for **Thirteen**, then you see how it is so much more appropriate for the music. Personally, I think most people are going to gravitate towards **Thirteen** than your average guitar player would."

"I don't feel like I have been a game-changer," continues Chris, modestly, on his role in the band. "But I do bring my knowledge of harmonization and functional tonality to the band. I also bring my influences, as well. I would think that anyone in my position would bring something to the band. There should be some inflection of personality to the band and I think that's what I bring. When I first joined, I didn't even have time to think about the people who I was trying to replace. I just knew I had a lot of work to do, in terms of getting the music down, and trying to learn it accurately. It wasn't until maybe a year ago that I could even think about where I was positioned as a guitarist. It is to the point that you don't even recount half of it anymore because there is so much going on, constantly. It has just been awesome."

As for key influences, Chris says, "Jason Becker, Paco de Lucia and players like that, in general, inspired me. I was definitely always into harder rock but I was also into the whole classical thing. Early on, I was into jazz but I can appreciate any genre as long as it is played and executed well. I just consider myself lucky to even have got into the position that I'm in. I am glad people really like what I do and how I play but I realize that there are a lot of other great players out there."

On the subject of having Jr. back, Chris told Jeb, "I would say I noticed the element of friendship that they have between each other right away. They have a great camaraderie. Dave and Dave have such a history that they can really read each other's mind, which is awesome. Ellefson is a great bass player, who is very professional. I can't say enough about getting to jam with him. This album was one of the smoothest albums I've ever been involved in. From start to finish, we were able to start the songs and finish them and move onto the next. It really was an easy album to make."

Oddly, Chris Broderick receives zero writing credits on the **Thirteen** album. Perhaps even more curiously, it's producer Johnny K who is in like a dirty shirt, his name showing up on fully six of the album's 13 tracks.

"Yeah, he was certainly part of the lyrics," says Shawn. "He kind of went over with Dave... you know, to be honest, once I do my drum tracks, I'm done.

I'm the first guy in line, and so if a song is changed, or the musical ideas are exchanged, or somebody submits something, they're going to get credit for it. So thinking back, honestly, I can't say how much or how little Johnny was a contributor to **Thirteen**, although obviously he was, because he was credited as such. It's probably that some lyrical ideas were exchanged between Johnny and Dave during that time."

To elaborate, Johnny "K" Karkazis is a Chicago-based producer, engineer, player and writer who has worked with the likes of Nonpoint, Stained, Sevendust, Disturbed, Machine Head, Enuff Znuff, Drowning Pool, Mushroomhead, Finger Eleven and Soil. Prior to Megadeth, his credits had been pretty much alternative rock or alternative metal, but here he was in the thick of **Thirteen**, appreciated enough to return for the next Megadeth record as well.

When asked, during the making of **Thirteen** in June of 2011, about the switch from Andy Sneap to Johnny K, Mustaine told Pure Grain Audio's Aaron Willschick that, "one thing with Megadeth is we've always tried to keep it current with our production team, you know, not getting too attached to any one person although a lot of the guys we've worked with have been great and there was no clear reason for having broken up the team other than keeping it fresh."

"With not working with Andy Sneap, he just wasn't available," continued Dave. "Andy had some stuff that came up right in the middle of the time that we were available to do our work. Usually when a band is ready to go in the studio they go in and they stay in; they don't go in and come out and go back in again. And I've found that to be really difficult for me because I lose stride and it just wasn't going to happen for us. We weren't going to get the record done in time because we had this Monsters Of Rock Energy Drink Mayhem Tour, whatever it is; it's the Mayhem Festival this summer and we had to get this done before we leave. You know, we have more Big Four dates coming up."

"When Johnny's name came up, I didn't even know who he was and I said something to a couple of the other guys, and they were like, 'Oh Johnny K! Oh really! Wow!' And I was like, 'Hmm, OK,' kind of like you know when someone says, 'Try this; it tastes like chicken.' So he came out here and we talked a little bit. We went an entire month, the entire first month, not one disagreement. There were some moments where we were trying to align our thinking and you know I think because we're two different guys from two different sides of the country and different histories I think there was a necessity for us to get our lingo in order. But as far as us having a desire to make this project a success, I think that we all have that first and foremost in our heads and that's what we want to do. So right now Shawn finished all of his tracks, he's gone; we left the drum kit up there in case we decide that something needs to be fixed or changed or whatever. And I'm doing guitar today and Dave Ellefson and Chris Broderick are coming in Monday to finish up bass and the other guitar and then it's singing, solos, ear candy and then we're done."

Back to the finished product, *Whose Life (Is It Anyways?)* wraps in a big ball, a one-and-four punk verse, a NWOBHM-like pre-chorus and a jagged **Peace Sells**-era chorus, with chords that are a little hardcore, a little stupid, a little Anthrax, quite loveable. The lyrics are brief, with Dave getting nagged... but by who, a significant other or by demanding fans? The track was strong enough to be considered as the record's first single, but became essentially the second featured track after *Public Enemy No. 1*, which was sent up nicely in a Western-themed production video.

We The People is pure Second Amendment, new world order, Alex Jones world conspiracy theory stuff, a never-ending rabbit hole Dave found himself boring into more and more as America split left and right harder... through need of a hobby as much as anything, through need for a diversion, an escape from boredom while Rome burned. This one's got all of it to the point of manifesto... one religion, the Illuminati, the founding fathers, liberty, constitution, secret brotherhoods, and in a final utterance, one world everything.

Next up is *Guns, Drugs & Money*, a groovy rocker far away from thrash, a mid-speed riffster one could see coming out of Marty Friedman as he drifted towards the end. It's a Mexican drug deal gone wrong, and it's followed by *Never Dead*, which is blessed by some of the greatest riffing ever on a Megadeth album, a hidden gem on this record that floats all boats around it. *Never Dead* finds Shawn laying down a relaxed groove, but the riffing out of Dave and Chris is all furtive thrash, until chorus time, where they establish an almost Lizzy-esque melodic pattern. Again, judicious balance, airtight songwriting, headbanging heaven. *Never Dead* was to be used in the promotional trailer for Komoni video game **NeverDead**, with *Sudden Death* also being used for a video game, **Guitar Hero: Warriors Of Rock**.

Moving on, *New World Order* grooves like *Guns, Drugs & Money* but with a degree of intellectual riffing and equally brainy counter-rhythm.

"*New World Order* was really, really old," Dave told Pat Prince. "We had never really officially recorded that and some people had said stuff about Nick Menza, and, you know, yeah, he wasn't a really busy writer but he did write a couple good things and *New World Order*, he had a hand in writing some of it, so it's kind of cool. I don't know what he's doing right now but I do know that when he wrote that, it was very modern-sounding. So when I came to do that song on this record, because we hadn't done it officially, it was a no-brainer."

"I've become more active in politics and more concerned in my fellow man," continues Dave, "because of my own discoveries and decision-making. I know if someone would have told me, 'You couldn't do that,' I would have said, 'Watch me.' Because it's just part of my nature. Not that I'm defiant just for the sake of being defiant because that would become kind of predictable, and there's nothing cool about being predictable. It all just kind of goes back to what you want to do with your life."

Dave tells Pat that he does indeed believe the world is sliding toward one world government: "Yeah, I do. You hear China say that they are preparing to go to war with the U.S.—they said that on Fox yesterday—that's not small potatoes, bro. But it is the elite that are doing this. But I gotta tell you, the elite have been running the government and all this stuff for a long time. People with the IMF and with the Fed and it's all the Rockefellers and the Rothschilds, they're the ones that call the shots. I just think right now that the American people are getting screwed so bad and they just don't know it. They cannot see the forest for the trees. Actually I think there's lot of stuff that's going on right now—I read a lot, I study a lot, I watch the news a lot because I'm a political writer. Not by choice. I started off writing about cars, *Mechanix*, and jumping into the fire. That had nothing to do with peace selling. This whole nonsense... if you watch what's going down with the super committee (on deficit reduction), I called that before it even started—that it's a joke and it's not gonna work. And it didn't work."

Fast Lane is pure **Youthanasia** chug with thrash overtones and thrash intensity. In essence, as metaphor for what makes **Thirteen** so inspired, it's the kind of song that could be performed, arranged and recorded to be placed on **Cryptic Writings**, or treated the way it is here, intensely metalized, drenched in electricity, and thrashed within an inch of its life regularly just so it remembers where it came from. Lyrically, it's Dave and his addiction to speed... through his love of cars. He's written about it before, and he'll likely do it again.

Black Swan is even more melodic and reclined, one of the most commercial tracks on the album, but again, supported by melody that is dark and richly metallic in the spirit of English metal from the low '80s.

Explained Dave to Ultimate Guitar's Steven Rosen, "*Black Swan* was a song written and it was released to all of our fans through our fan club as a bonus track for people who ordered the record ahead of time so it was never released. But I wanted that song to get released and so we re-recorded it and finished that and it's a totally different song now. I think it's one of the best songs on the record personally. *New World Order*, that song was around and it was never released officially because we never recorded it officially. There was a demo tape floating around. Same thing with *Millennium Of The Blind*; there was a demo tape that was floating around and so we re-arranged *Millennium Of The Blind* but we just left *New World Order* like it was and rerecorded it.

Millennium Of The Blind and *New World Order* both feature Marty Friedman in the music writing credits, with Ellefson receiving his only

Thirteen credit on the latter, which also, as Dave has explained, includes Nick Menza on lyrics. To clarify, *Black Swan* was a bonus given to members of the fan club who had pre-ordered 2007's **United Abominations**. Updating it for **Thirteen** was at Johnny K's suggestion. *Millennium Of The Blind*, inspired by the movie **Highlander**, had been recorded in demo form back in 1991, and had been included as a bonus track on the 2004 reissue of **Youthanasia**. Mustaine has said that they never went any further with the track at the time because it was too similar to a song he was writing called *Absolution*, which would morph into *Trust* on the **Cryptic Writings** album. *New World Order* also goes back to 1991, having been penned during the Clash Of The Titans tour. It also can be found on that same **Youthanasia** remix/remaster/reissue. Ellefson says reviving it was Shawn's idea; Shawn says it was Mustaine's.

Asked by Rosen whether these songs were revived because they still resonated with Mustaine, Dave figures, "To a degree but probably not. I think the reason I wanted them on there was I didn't know if I was gonna be able to play anymore and I had the songs that I had left. It required me writing new material and I didn't know if physically I was gonna be able to do that. I don't want to be a bleeding heart or anybody feel sorry for me. I see people like Kerry from Slayer who has been playing as long and hard as I have and he doesn't have the problems I have because he was smart enough to stretch out and exercise before he went onstage. I wish I would have thought about that but that's what sets people apart is their difference and uniqueness. I didn't think I was gonna be playing too much longer and I used the songs I knew I had. And the rest of the stuff, when we say we wrote it on the spot, yeah, we did because we didn't have any songs left."

So does that mean **Thirteen** could have marked the end for Megadeth?

"Absolutely. I just had my neck fused together. Did you know that? I went to the Watkins Spine Institute in Marina Del Rey on my wife's birthday of all days and I had to undergo spinal surgery. So that's the beauty of this thing even happening. When I went in to go do the procedure, they found a bone fragment that was in a vertebrae that was in there pushing against stuff it wasn't supposed to push against and it was causing me all that excruciating pain. At the end of the last festival we did, the Mayhem festival, we had to play like half sets for all those shows because it was just unbearable for me to endure the pain and play, but I wasn't gonna cancel. Thank God for John Reese, the guy that ran the thing. He was cool enough to let us continue and finish out with whatever else I could play instead of saying, 'Man, you can't play long enough. Get out of here.'"

Asked by Steven if having Dave Ellefson back has given the album an old school Megadeth vibe, Mustaine says, "To a degree, yeah. When it's the same talent, it's gonna be there to a degree but I think there's a freshness to it. With David Ellefson coming back, to a degree the bass is the same but it's not. Dave has been woodshedding the eight years we've been apart because I know how good a guy he is. I can listen to somebody and in just a couple minutes determine if they're a hack or not. I know where Dave was at with his playing when he and I parted ways. He was really good and he was in that pretty untouchable league. And then he came back and he played again and I heard what he was doing and it was like, wow, man, he's gotten so much better in so many areas. He's just playing much more mature, aggressive bass playing and I was excited. The songs sounded fresh and new again. When you play 'em in the studio, they're awesome and then when you get out on the road you kind of get away from it. You kind of push and pull and you speed up here and you kinda slow down there and you forget a part here and you overplay there. When he came back, we were playing the songs and I was like, damn, these things sound just like the studio. It was amazing."

Nearing the end of this easy-drinking feast is comedic "girl gone bad" anthem *Wrecker* and the liquor continues to flow, Dave and Co. drenching a near AC/DC riff in thrash ethics, again, striking the balance found within **Countdown**, slightly less so in **Youthanasia**, and then less again for **Cryptic**.

Millennium Of The Blind finds Dave excoriating the sheep of the world Alex Jones-style, essentially calling for an awakening as to their unseen enslavement. Musically, this one's darkly balladic and epic, a pause that refreshes against the solid yet rock 'n' rollsy rest of this less heavy record than **Endgame**.

Deadly Nightshade is yet another one of these tracks where the band pulls back on the throttle and wallows in doom, with Dave Jr. allowed to rumble alone here and there, reminding us that he's back providing foundation—this one's central riff goes back to the mid-'90s.

"The song *13* is much more melancholy in mood," said Dave to Music Radar, of the album's title track closer. "And it's basically about the same thing as the memoir. You get to feel it a bit more. It's not like Spinal Tap in D minor, though (laughs)."

"If it's done right it's really cool," figured Dave, concerning the use of true acoustic guitar, something Megadeth usually avoids, as evidenced by the mellow parts of *Millennium Of The Blind* being picked on electric. "If it's done wrong and it's jangly, it won't work in Megadeth. It's gotta be in the right surroundings and it needs to work. Megadeth has done stuff with acoustic guitar for years and years and years but it has to be done right."

On the whole idea of "13," Dave opined that, "The number 13 was bad for the Templar Knights, the knights who helped Solomon's temple. Those dudes were all rounded up on Friday the 13th and burned at the stake or something like that. I think people don't know about that and they kind of just connotate the number 13 with marijuana and that it's bad, you know. I was born on the 13th, I started playing guitar when I was 13 and this record's my 13th record."

And then it was time to tour this well-received 13th record, although well-received is a relative term in these tough times for CD sales. Selling 42,000 copies in its first week, **Thirteen** had peaked at about 120,000 copies a year later, having gotten to No. 11 in the Billboard charts, a slight drop from **Endgame**'s No. 9 placement.

Was it all too much too soon? Indeed, there was a palpable sense that it was good to have dependable ol' Megadeth around making albums, playing the hits, touring regularly, even emboldening their lineup with the reinstatement of Dave Ellefson. But in another sense, with all these substantive records coming regularly, like clockwork, it's as if we were getting too much of a good thing, too many songs to digest, too many riffs to swallow. Stupid complaint, really, but Dave, through gritted teeth, had to keep hearing and enduring them. It was of no mind, the band would continue to deal with the mixed feelings of the faithful, while quietly gathering up younger fans with their leaner, meaner metal sound represented by the histrionics of Chris Broderick all over these last two... place-holders.

"I'm glad I picked Motörhead and Volbeat," said Mustaine, agreeing with journalist Pat Prince's assessment of Megadeth's tour mates for the **Thirteen** campaign. "I think that all the bands that are on Gigantour this year are gonna be great. They all have a certain type of cool factor. Motörhead has that straight-forward 'I'm gonna kill you' kind of music, and Volbeat is that kind of dangerous kind of music—kind of like Elvis metal. And listening to Lacuna Coil with the two singers, it's very dynamic and they've got good guitar players in there. It's also cool that at one point we had Christina Scabbia sing a song with us. We haven't discussed having her come up and sing *A Tout Le Monde* with us each night. We probably should but we haven't talked about that yet."

Also along the tour talk tack, I asked Shawn Drover how Dave had been holding up in his advanced years, voice-wise, each night. Surely there must be a vocal coach of some sort that is helping him bark his highly pressurized spiels city after city...

"Not really, not that I've ever known. Certainly not someone who's come out on the road with us, you know, a vocal coach for eight weeks in a row. Never anything like that. I mean, he does vocal warm-ups backstage. That practicing a little bit before you go on stage, it loosens you up and gets you in the mode to get out there and perform. It's funny, because obviously, as you get older, your voice changes. You can't have the same voice when you were 22 as when you're 50, 51 years old. So things change over the course of time. You can listen to **Killing Is My Business** and listen to the new record, and obviously his voice isn't quite as shrill as it was back then. But that's just how he sang at the time. It was such a violent time for music, and I really think, as being a young man at that time, he probably sang as violent as he could, because those songs were such violent songs."

A fortunate situation to be in, to be sure, Dave carrying and coddling an increasing arsenal of songs where there's more crooning than shouting, very much like James and his evolving job fronting Metallica.

"And that's good way to put it," agrees Shawn. "It's not as violent as it was back in the day, although I don't know why. Again, it's what the songs call for, but that goes for singing, guitar solos, drums or whatever. If we wrote a record of the most extreme music that we've ever written, I'm sure he would sing a little more violent to accommodate that. But at this point in the game, you really have to be careful with your voice, as you get older. You tour a lot; you don't want to do anything that's going to damage your voice. When you're 22, you don't even care. You probably don't even think you're going to be a band two years later."

Any magic elixirs involved?

"Well, he always has green tea; he has it on the side of the stage and drinks a little bit. I don't know how much green tea he drinks or doesn't drink during the show, because he's in a different section than I am on stage. But he always has it up there. And he always has Lays potato chips, regular Lays potato chips. There's just something that makes your throat... like it greases your throat up or something like that. It's kind of weird, but he heard that somewhere like in Nashville years ago, and so that's something he's been doing ever since I joined the band. 'Why are you eating Lays potato chips?' (laughs)."

As for Shawn and his own job up there, he makes sure, like a vocalist, that he doesn't paint himself into a corner with crazy performances on record he can't reproduce live...

"No, nothing too tough. I mean, I'll never do anything that I can't reproduce live. I don't see the point in it. Because then you're a fake. Whether other bands do that or not, I can only speak for myself. If I was asked to do something that I just couldn't physically do, or some kind of weird drumming, I would say look, I don't want to do this, because I won't be able to reproduce it live. But really, there hasn't been anything that is too hard. I have to be comfortable with doing it. When you record, you have to be comfortable doing it. You don't want to do something so excruciatingly impossible to do that there's no way you're going to play it live. I don't want to ever be in that situation."

15
SUPER COLLIDER

"You know I'm a very polarizing figure"

Perpetuating the band's robust run of record-making—and record-making with provocative attitude—Megadeth returned June 4, 2013 with their 14th album of easy-drinking thrash at the premium quality price point. **Super Collider**, no surprise, was to garner the band mixed reviews but more than anything, that's just because poking Dave Mustaine in the riff cage has become a cyclical sporting event long democratized by the Internet, and celebrated every couple of years like the toggled Euro and World Cups.

Not that Dave didn't fuel the fire, given his choice of pre-release taster single for the album, using the record's group hug title track of insanely hooky arena rock proportions, notwithstanding a vocal melody that marries Zeppelin's *In The Light* to the **Sesame Street** theme.

"Well, it was a real simple song," Dave told me, doing press duties for the record as well as the upcoming Gigantour dates. "I think that a lot of people... and you know, Martin, you know I'm a very polarizing figure. People will find fault in anything I do, no matter what it is. It's the nature of the business and who I am. Was I apprehensive about that song? Sure I was. Was I apprehensive to put out *Built For War* too, and that's one of the most aggressive songs on the record? But I think that's probably just that little tiny seed of self-doubt that we all have. I mean, the whole reason I got into playing guitar was because I wanted to fit in. I was picked on in school, and I was a skinny little kid, and as soon as I started playing guitar, I mattered. And deep down inside, I still want to do songs that matter. I don't get the same kind of... It doesn't reward me in the same way, because that hole's been filled a long time ago, but you still want it to matter, and you still want people to like them. And there's a lot of guys that make records to get out of record deals that are just rubbish. I can never do that. As much as we were unhappy with our last couple of labels, all those records, they were legitimate, serious attempts at making records that fit the music industry at that time. People don't look back and say, well, shit, when **The World Needs A Hero** came out, there was something called nu-metal and nobody was playing solos, and the climate of music back then was so both bizarre, or when **Endgame** came out or **United Abominations** came out, it was a whole true metal thing; if you didn't have six billion mile-an-hour solos, then you weren't true metal. Excuse me, I'm one of the four horsemen."

"I gotta tell ya, I've lived a lot longer than I thought I was going to," reflected one of the four horsemen, talking with Tim Henderson about getting to this stage in his career. "It's not like I'm fantasizing dying or anything like that, but when you are young and you are homeless, you kinda wonder if you are going to make it through the night. You know enough about the past and the way me and Dave Ellefson lived. When I turned 50, I thought, God, I'm old. And I look in the mirror and I don't look 50 and I get up on stage and I don't feel 50. Is 50 like the new 30? And I'm watching TV and I'm seeing all these people I watched growing up dying, and it's like, shit, death is inevitable, make the best that you can, while you can, and that's why I've tried to appreciate things more."

"It didn't start off that way honestly," Mustaine continues, asked if **Super Collider** represents a Megadeth once again pulling back on the thrash throttle. "It started off with *Kingmaker* and Shawn and Chris had *Built For War* and *Beginning Of Sorrows* up their sleeves, so we knew it was going to have a lot of heaviness to it. But there are also songs like *Don't Turn Your Back*, *House Divided*, *All I Want* and stuff like that, that didn't make the record which were heavy too. When you have 14 songs and you give it to the record label and you trust 'em, you just kind of go with it. And with our jump from Capitol into the independent market (band imprint at Universal, Tradecraft), it was like jumping into a pot of boiling water and it was a reality check. We never had to work so hard to try and get our ideas out and really feeling like you are alone. It wasn't really that the labels were doing it, it's that they were incapable of doing what we needed at a major label level. So we went back to Universal and they gave us control to do whatever we wanted. We turned the record in, they liked it and it's been a great experience."

"The label thing was a gift, a complete surprise," continues Dave, painting the strange Tradecraft/Universal arrangement in its best light. "When we signed there I thought we are signing direct to Universal and then they said, 'Hey, you want your own label?' and I was like, are you kidding? It was like going up to young bachelor and saying, 'Hey do you want this bus full of Hawaiian Tropic bikini models?' And put it in perspective, I was like a kid in a candy store, although I'm not able to sign anybody right now because we're still working on this campaign and developing the label. At some point we will, and I think it's really cool because I know how to treat a band because I'm in one."

"Being a label head now, is a little different," says Dave, who none of us can picture actually running a label, not from inability, more so from it being a low priority. "You tend to know what it takes and what you need to do. Sometimes you give advice to bands, they'll listen and once you walk out the door they'll say, 'What an asshole—he thinks he knows everything.' I made a lot of mistakes in my career, but I've always gotten through it and been victorious and I've never given up and never let adversity hold me down.

Who would you rather have telling you how to get up off the floor, somebody who's never been knocked out or somebody that's being knocked down and has to find that intestinal fortitude to stand back up? I remember when I got my blue belt, I had to fight two guys for two hours, and after I passed that test, all the black belts lined up and either punched me or kicked me in the stomach. And this one guy kicked me so hard he put me on the ground and I could not get up. But I kept saying, 'Get up Dave, you got to get up,' and I stood up and I was ready to puke and my Sensei said that he was gonna take that instructor's black belt and bring it back down to a brown belt again because it was unnecessary. I was standing there, I wasn't going to block it, I was just taking it. And that was part of the initiation. Some were trying to fake me out trying to see if I would flinch and I didn't. Some of them would just tap me and some of them would give me a bruise. I was pretty beat-up after the two hours, because getting assaulted for two hours by two guys is a long, long time. An old Dave went down and a new Dave stood up, and I think that is the secret to life. You fall down seven times, you get up eight."

Just as Dave was taking a beating, Megadeth would attract a few sneers for the softer contours of **Super Collider**, which in fact, did come as a bit of a surprise after the hard and heavy ramping up over the course of the 2000s.

"Yeah, but that's a handful of trolls, you know that. Our real fan base respects what we do. They know that Megadeth isn't limited to just thrash nomenclature. We've never fit within those parameters, and anybody that has ever asked us what our music is like I've always said we're just Megadeth. Like a jazz, classical, punk-influenced band that plays all different kinds of songs. We're the guys that wrote *Black Friday*, but we're different. We're not like AC/DC, we're not like Motörhead, our songs aren't really similar, straight-forward rock songs. It's straight-forward metal. Some people like 'em, some people don't, but I think with the internet, you can have a guy with a hundred email accounts talking smack on these bottom-feeder websites. People read that and think 'this guy is real' and he's not real. There's two or three people that their whole campaign is to talk shit about everybody. Not just Dave Mustaine, not just Megadeth, they hate everything. Half these little farts wouldn't say this to my face 'cos they'd piss their pants if they stood in front of me."

"If I kept doing the same record over and over, I would never feel fulfilled. You got to think about it. Like a dog eats the same thing every day, unless he gets a hold of the trash. You know why they get excited about that?—no more Kibble! It's just like me, I would feel very unfulfilled if I didn't try to do something, and merging metal with melody has been really hard. Because again, you have the metal purists, and all they want to hear is real whiny screaming vocals, growling shit and no singing anymore. Some of the people that we most respect in our genre are the people that sing. Like Bruce sings, James sings, I sing. And Rob sings. And we kind of lost that side of it. I really admire Phil Anselmo; I know he's really had his struggles, but I've always been a fan of him, even when we had our disagreements, but I respected what they did. I always told him that one of my favourite songs was *Cemetery Gates*, and he hates that song, because he sings in it. I said, 'Phil, you've got a great voice' and I remember one time as a gift at the end of a tour they played it for me and I was so thrilled. I'm still a big Pantera fan. I think we're in a phase with metal music right where it's coming back to singing. A lot of the new bands... I can't name a bunch of them, but my son is always playing new bands for me. And one time he came up to me and said, 'You got to check this new band called Havok; they are like a young Megadeth.' I said, 'Really, you think so?' When you hear somebody else say that something sounds like you, it's kind of like when someone says this guy looks like you and you look at the photo, and you say 'You must be blind'!"

Drummer Shawn gets it all too well what the band is up against. "You know what, I know," he laughs, somewhat unbelieving when I tell him *Super Collider* is darn well my favourite track on the album. "You're a hardcore metal fan just like I am. Some people aren't going to get it, and they're not going to like it. I knew it as soon as we wrote the song. This is one of those songs that Dave had written already. He had constructed it towards the end of the **Thirteen** tour. He had some ideas, let's go over some ideas, and it was one of those songs that was a 90% written thing. And it's obviously a simple song, somewhat like *Symphony Of Destruction*, very to the point, verse/chorus, bridge, solo and what have you. So it's a simple song, and it's not as heavy as *The Conjuring*. I mean, that's a fact. And that's going to piss some people off. And to me, I don't care, that doesn't bug me, you know what I mean? I grew up listening to Van Halen, Supertramp, Fleetwood Mac, Black Sabbath, Deep Purple. To me, good music is good music. If it's good, I like it."

Expanding on the temporal germination of the thing, Drover says, "During the end of the **Thirteen** world tour, we were on tour, Dave was assembling some musical ideas, and he had that song, that riff. So I heard that song before we even went into the studio to record this record. That was one of the four songs that was pretty much constructed, musically speaking. I like it too, man. I gotta tell you, I think it's a really good hard rock tune, end of story."

"It's heavier than *A Tout Le Monde*, and that's a live staple," continues Shawn, offering perspective. "That was a hit for the band back in, when they wrote that song. But I'm sure back then, some hardcore fans probably bitched about that song too. But it's one of the songs that goes best over in our set, you know what I mean? I get it. I get when certain... probably some younger fans and stuff, they want everything to sound as heavy as **Killing Is My Business**. It's just never been like that. No record has been as heavy as **Killing Is My Business**. That's the most violent record we have. And I get it, I'm an advocate for the heavy stuff—I'm that guy. The heavier the better as far as I'm concerned. But Dave likes to stretch out sometimes and do different things. And he's got the balls to do it. I'm not saying that it's right or wrong, but I think it's really cool that he isn't scared to try something a little bit different sometimes."

"A lot of people did not like the title track," Dave told Jeb Wright, "because they thought it was too poppy. But here's the thing: it is the first track for our new record label, which is a major label. They love the band and we showed them that not only can we write commercial metal pop songs that people can't do anymore, because they're either afraid, or they sound like they are hacking up a chicken bone; they just don't know how to do it."

"We also have the super heavy stuff on there and I think that is good because it really shows them everything we are capable of. I think it also opens up a door to a lot of people who just don't like metal. They are going to listen to that and think, 'I like that one song' and they are going to get the record and listen to the rest of the album and go, 'Man, I love this style of music. I've been missing out for a long time.' Then Dave has introduced another person to the metal community and it becomes like that shampoo commercial where they tell two friends and so on and so on."

"I think I am one of the few thrash metal guys who is brave enough to delve into melody," continued Dave. "There is a certain push-back from the heavy metal and thrash community when you start getting too melodic. Sometimes songs just tell you what they want. There are songs that you do that just have an awesome hook in them and that hook opens doors to other things."

Fan chatter aside—and there was lots of it—*Super Collider* turned out to be a canny choice for advance single, as it brought a lot of intrigue concerning what the rest of the record was going to sound like. Turns out Dave wasn't finished engaging and then challenging the Megadeth (variously) faithful, but more on that later. The man with a plan was sensible enough to open the new record with a digestible enough upper-mid-speed thrash galloper, *Kingmaker* setting a crunchy tone, Dave matching the old school power metal grimness of the thing with a curmudgeonly mutter of a vocal.

"The song *Kingmaker* was a lot about my struggles when I was having all my neck surgery done," explains Dave, "and it's no secret, when your neck is being cut open and put back together again, you're going to need pain medicine. Being an ex-junkie, having that stuff reintroduced into my life caused a lot of havoc again, but fortunately for me, I'm off the stuff. And it really made me aware of, you know, these pill mills, and these doctors, and the epidemic of narcotic addiction. A lot of people take it and they don't really need it. The bummer is, what if you get hurt and you need to take it? It's not going to work (laughs)."

Talking about the record with Classic Rock Revisited, Dave said, "People ask me what the first track I started writing on the record was, and the chorus riff to *Kingmaker* was one of the first riffs I wrote on the whole record. That song had so many different lyrics to it. I would sing something and go, 'Eh,' as it just didn't fit the intention to the song. I would do another lyric and it would be too extreme for the song because it would take the beauty of the heaviness and kind of cheapen it."

Adds Drover, "*Kingmaker* I like a lot. It's a good leadoff track, good heavy tune. We've been playing that live from the get-go on this tour now, and it's definitely a fun song to play live, because it's heavy, and I like the heavy stuff, of course. Again, it's a diverse record; it's got some heavy songs and a couple of curveball songs, and it's got some songs that are a little more accessible."

Kingmaker followed *Super Collider* as the second single from the album, also arriving (in Inboxes?) before the launch of the full record, a couple weeks early on May 18th—not that the word "single" means the same thing any more, especially for a metal band. Still, *Super Collider* was an actual track one could buy on iTunes, plus it was the subject of a proper produced video. *Kingmaker* was more so loosely labelled a single and authorized for streaming on youtube.

Next in the sequence, we're into the previously discussed-in-detail title track, with its languid expanse built upon a catchy bass line from Junior, and Dave's strong vocal melody, one that, come chorus time, adds to the band's repertoire a sort of southern rock swagger.

The super collider of which Dave speaks (and one supposes, tacitly uses as metaphor for Megadeth) is in fact the Large Hadron Collider, buried under the middle of Europe, the biggest science experiment ever, as depicted on the album cover.

"We're on tour for **Thirteen**," says Shawn, "and Dave saw a picture of the super collider. 'Wow, look at this picture,' and I'd never seen it before; didn't know it was. You know, look how cool this looks and the colours, and we're like wow, that's really an interesting thing. It looked cool visually, and over the course of time, Dave just started thinking about it, and you know, maybe we should do something like this for the artwork for the record? Okay, cool, and then it was, why don't we just call the record **Super Collider**? Pretty much how it went down. There wasn't a whole bunch of thought into it. We all agreed the visualization of the artwork would be a cool idea, and we just went with it."

Specifically, the stock shot used was of the Compact Muon Solenoid's Silicon Tracker's inner barrel, and at the centre of the dark area, there's a faint image of Vic Rattlehead. Quickly the original photograph was being circulated, with fan's griping that the cover seemed a lazy way out in an era that was calling for a return to old school illustration, an ouvre Megadeth (and Ed Repka) was instrumental in pioneering.

"That is over in Switzerland," says Dave. "The cool thing is that we were given permission by the official place to use the artwork. There was a time where people didn't think that thing existed and then only top secret people were allowed to go in and see it. Now, little old Meger-Deth had the official pictures of it. There are really vibrant colours in it. It really shows how the world has advanced. We don't even know about what they are doing in the world right now. I like the whole conspiracy theory stuff. But I was not the guy who wrote songs about aliens—that was Nick. I believe in spiritual forces and stuff like that, but as far as life forms on other planets... they've searched for how many centuries and not one of these planets has any ability to sustain life? There are not any other inhabited planets out there."

Burn! is a track that bummed out a few Mega-watchers, due to the somewhat awkward chorus and a "burn, baby, burn" refrain that doesn't quite work. The rest of the track rides a sort of mid-**Youthanasia** vibe, and again, Dave found himself thinking about where a track like this might sit with the band's demanding fans.

"Well, I guess, probably, when you look at the records as they progress over time, you can either copy and do the same record over and over again, and then your fans, some of them get what they want, but after a while they'll grow tired of it, because they're listening to the same record. Or you can make some experimentation and try some different stuff like we did with **Risk**, which went a little bit too far, or, you can stay kind within the goalposts of being melodic and being really heavy. The thing is, we've got, basically two kinds of groups of people that—and it's not that these groups are polarized—but there are people that want *Black Friday*, and there are people that want *Symphony Of Destruction*. And with us going back to Universal right now, it's been really a breath of fresh air, Martin, because, as you know I wasn't happy when we left Capitol, and I wasn't happy at Sanctuary and I wasn't happy at Roadrunner, and over here it's been just like, like I said, a second childhood; it's just amazing."

Burn! clearly is for those who want *Symphony Of Destruction*, but *Built For War*... that's closer to the *Black Friday* crowd, even if Megadeth at this advanced point, when they grind out a thrash, it's gonna feel shiny and impossibly light years from the rock-scrabble band of the desperation years.

Explains Shawn, who gets co-writing credit on *Built For War*, along with Dave and Chris Broderick, "That's just a matter of Dave saying, 'Hey, you got any ideas?' 'Yeah, I got some ideas.' 'Well let's hear 'em; what have you got?' So I'd record my ideas and stuff, and he liked a couple of things that I submitted. And he said, let's focus on this one riff, and it just so happened that Chris... one of the riffs that Chris had was the opening part of *Built For War*, before it jumps into the verse. And it fit really well with what I was doing, and then Dave—this is pretty much close to the end of the day—he said, 'Look, if you have any more ideas, I wanna do this kind of breakdown in the middle of the song. See if you can come up with something.' And I had an acoustic guitar, and I came up with this thing that night, and that was submitted into the song next day. And Dave actually contributed one little musical part to the song; I'm trying to think now. He had a small part that was kind of missing from the song, which he wrote. So that was a three-way collaboration, and that was the first time that happened in the band. So that was exciting. And it came together, literally within 24 hours of Dave hearing the idea, to constructing the song, to me going in to record the drums—that was a process of about 24 hours."

"Obviously there's a huge difference between them," continues Shawn, asked to contrast Chris and Dave as guitarists. "And they really complement each other. Chris can pretty much do anything you ask him to. He's a great player; that's obvious, he could do all the crazy wacky Marty stuff and the Chris Poland stuff, and he can emulate pretty much anybody you ask him to. Dave is obviously a complete originator; he completely has own guitar sound. Soon as you hear it, you know it's Dave. You can tell it's a Megadeth song just from Dave's guitar playing and that's a cool thing in itself. So I really think that those two styles really complement each other. Because now we've got everything we need. If you want a wacky blistering solo with all these weird exotic scales, there you go, Chris, you can have at it. If you want something more erratic and something completely in-your-face, wacky playing, Dave's your guy. They both provide a lot of cool and interesting different elements to the overall sound of Megadeth. I think it's great."

As for who's doing the solos on the record, "Pretty much, I would say close to half each," says Shawn. "Sometimes Chris or guys in the past, Marty, would have maybe a little more solos—just depends on the songs. But obviously like the song *Tornado Of Souls*, Marty does that, and there's no solo for Dave in that song. And he's cool with that. If something lends a solo section to the other guitar player, he has no problem letting them have at it."

Would there ever be a situation where Dave does the solo on the album but then due to him singing and otherwise having his hands full, he hands it off during a live situation?

"Nah, I've never seen that happen. If he does it in the studio, he's going to do it live, no matter how difficult—he'll find a way to do it. Sometimes (laughs), he'll go dammit, why did I play such a difficult solo, because when he's singing... sometimes he's singing and doing a solo at the same time, which... you can do anything in the studio, but then live you have to do it at the same time. But I've never seen a situation where he couldn't reproduce something live that he did in the studio."

"Every band member change brings a little bit different element to the table," continues Shawn. "Ultimately, most of the music is written by Dave. That's pretty much how it's been throughout the course of Megadeth's history. So honestly, it's not going to change a whole lot. The stylistic ability of the solos are going to be different from every player. Chris Poland is different from Al Pitrelli, and Glen is different from Chris. They all bring their own little flair to the table; no two guys sound alike. So nobody's going in the studio trying to emulate something that somebody's done in the past. They try to bring their own flavour to the table—for the new songs—not copy Chris or copy Jeff Young or what have you. They just kind of bring their own musical flair, in terms of solos, their flavour. But in terms of song structure and recording songs, Dave pretty much writes a big portion of every record. So it's not going to really change the band, bringing in other guitar players."

"There is something enamouring about Canadian people," says Mustaine, flipping the tables and commenting on the band and hand he's been dealt here after 30 years of building the Megadeth brand. "I have always felt that. I recently found out that my family actually lived in Canada for a while before they migrated down into Ohio. And Shawn had to be a smart-mouth and say that he knew that I was cool for a reason! I punched him. Truth be told, Shawn is one of the reasons why I keep it going out here. David Ellefson is like an ambassador and he's really great and stuff, but I am not as close with him as I am with Shawn. And Dave and I were best friends and such."

"But when Shawn and I met there was something that just clicked and there's been a lot of times he has taken me aside and said 'Check this out' or 'We should do this,' 'The fans kind of want this,' 'What do you think of playing this song?' And I will tell him, 'It's not going to be good. We will do it live, but I promise you, when we start the song, by the time we finish the song, the beginning of the song is hitting the back of the building it's so fast.' When you play those really fast songs in a big venue, it eventually starts to sound like mud. If we play *Devils Island* or something like that, and then he'll say, 'You're right; it sounded like shit. We should stick to songs that sound good live.' When you're in a smaller venue, you can play some of those other songs if you want, because in a bigger venue it loses all of the dynamics. And that is my main job. Our real fans are going to know the song and sing along to the song, but there's a lot of new people out there and we want to bring them along on this journey with us and get them interested in the music and what Megadeth is about. A lot of times, you lean on the songs like *Sweating Bullets* or *Symphony* or *Trust*, songs that are real hooky and catchy. And then you hit them in the face with a *Peace Sells*, *Tornado* or a *Holy Wars* and people go wow, these guys can really get it on. The hardest part of my difficult job is trying to pick out of our 200 songs we have. It's like if you have a whole bunch of kids and you can only put two of them in a life-raft, who do you choose?"

Back to our record survey, *Off The Edge* is another grim old school thrasher rendered at groovy speeds. Lyrically, Dave keeps it general and vague, but there's an autobiographical element within which finds Dave near the edge with anger and panic. Another reading might be distress at the state of the world. The interjection of politics—but only obliquely—is by plan.

"I kind of backed off that a little, because when we were recording the records, I would just leave the news on in the background," explains Dave, on cutting back the politics, even as his interest has taken him to the point where he's talked world affairs as a guest on the Alex Jones show. "And world events, Martin, you know, you live in a very peaceful country, and my relationship with Shawn is the best I've had with any drummer I've ever played with—he's a wonderful human being. And on my dad's side, they lived up in Canada for a while, so you know a lot about being able to coexist peacefully. Like I was saying to the last guy I was talking to, imagine if our Canadian neighbours were actually Pakistan, it would be a lot different now (laughs)."

"But what I found happening, watching the news all the time, it just really started to sour me, and I would say stuff about what I just watched on the news. Because you know I'm a pretty straightforward guy. You don't have to ask me about what I mean—I'll pretty much tell you. Some of the stuff I say, you know, being a long-standing journalist, that you can do an interview with me, and it's not going hit the wires for any amount of time. It could be days, weeks, months. But back in the day, when you started, when I started, we just had the biweekly the trades. Kerrang! would come out every two weeks. And we had the 'zines on like paper you have in a printer at home, remember that?"

"And stuff that I've said, I said so long ago, and you know, you learn, and you realize that there are ways that are more respectful and more responsible ways to bring about solutions, and part of that is being introspective and changing yourself. And so I think that, you know, there's been a lot of records that have been about politics. **Peace Sells** was, and that stuff is still relevant today. The thing is that if you're writing stuff that is timely and timeless, it's going to stand the test of time no matter what. If you're writing stuff that is about topics that are relevant today and they're gone later today, then people aren't going to get it. Like, as great as that song, *Hook In Mouth* was, you know, it's about the PMRC, right? And it was based off of 1984. Well, if it would have been based off of the PMRC solely, that song wouldn't be relevant at all. Because with the stuff that is going on in the states right now, that album has started selling again, and people were asking about that song again. So it's really cool. And that's a song that's from back in the '80s."

Taking with journalist of bud of mine Jeb around these topics of intelligence, Dave warned that, "Heavy metal fans look rough and tough on the outside, and a lot of times we play like we're dumb for a reason, but when you get to know some of these heavy metal guys, then you find out they are loyal and they are really intelligent, but a lot of people won't give us the time of day. There is such a dichotomy there. People look at us and they don't think we care and they think we're lone wolves and social misfits. I'm not; I got very high grades in college. I love that I got the opportunity to cover the National Democratic Convention for MTV and getting into the whole political process. But I had to pull things back lately because the news is so disturbing; I had to stop watching it. Every day the news showcases bad stuff for people. There's so much politicizing of things behind the news. When I was a kid, we had this guy named Walter Cronkite who delivered the news. He's got to be turning over in his grave about these guys reporting the news these days because it isn't about the facts anymore, it's like showbiz."

"Well, I'm Canadian," laughs Drover, proceeding to stay well away from the question of Dave and his politics. "I really don't get involved in that, to be honest with you. Being Canadian, obviously we have a different political system up there, and I really don't pay a lot of attention to that either, since I live down here (note: originally from Mississauga, west of Toronto, Shawn now lives in Atlanta). I've never really taken a lot of interest in all that stuff. Elections down here are so much different than Canada, as you know. If you have an election in Canada it's a month or two months, to elect a prime minister—it happens very quickly. Down here, you've got an entire year. There's all kinds of debates, and we spend millions of dollars. Dave... he watches CNN and all that stuff. He's involved in world events. He knows what's going on, and he has opinions about it. But it's not something where we sit down at dinner and talk politics. It doesn't have any more importance than anything else in our daily routine. If something comes up in the news that's interesting, we might talk about it. But it can be about a hockey game or the Masters, anything like that."

Moving forward through **Super Collider**, *Dance In The Rain* is one of those doomy mid-paced, near prog-level numbers Megadeth do so well. Dave begins with an introspective spoken vocal, then transitions to a croon and then a heavier vocal as the band work their way seamlessly through parts that build in intensity. David Draiman from Disturbed provides a guest vocal and the fans didn't like that either, the metal community still associating Draiman with nu metal despite his transition to card-carrying metalhead over the years. But again we have a song that helps build the record as a whole as multi-dimensional. Draiman was basically an extra doo-dad stuck onto the project and indeed, he's a speed bump here on a road that for Megadeth has been lacking in too many twists and turns over the course of the last few records.

"Not all of the songs are slow, performance-wise," noted Mustaine. "The beat-per-minute might be a little lower, but in the song *Dance In The Rain*, I challenge any guitar player/singer to play that part at the end and sing it. It is a pretty challenging song. The great thing about that song is having David Draiman on tour with us, so he gets to come out and perform that track with us. It is so powerful with him doing it. David Ellefson pointed out on a social site how blown away he was with David and I just smirked because I knew how good he was."

"None of our albums sound the same—you know that," adds Shawn, underscoring the record's sense of variety and surprises. "You can go to any one of the records in our catalogue. **Killing Is My Business** doesn't sound like **Rust In Peace** or **Youthanasia**. I don't think we've ever had, certainly since I've been in the band, any preconceived notions of what we're going to do musically speaking, or let's make a record like this, or let's make this song sound like that. We just kind of go in there with a bunch of ideas. With this record, we had about four songs pretty much ready to go, 90%. There's always tweaks and stuff, but we had about four songs ready to go, and the rest of it, there was a lot of ideas that Dave had. Some of it was stuff that I submitted and Chris submitted and David submitted as well. That's pretty much how it's gone since I've been in the band. And honestly for myself, we just go in there and write the best music we can. Whether it ends up being a complete thrash record or something that's not quite as brutal as some songs before, to the average metal listener or whatever, it's never preconceived. How it turns out is kind of how it turns out."

Pressed for where **Super Collider** fits among the four he's been part of, Shawn figures, "If you want to go by heavy, I would think **Endgame** is the heaviest of the four. **United Abominations** has some heavy stuff too, but it has the more sensible stuff as well. To me, if you're going to have a heavy contest, I would say **Endgame** would be the heaviest of the four. It doesn't mean I like it more than the other ones; that's just to answer that question. **Thirteen** has elements of both of those records. It has some heavy stuff and it has some stuff that's not quite so heavy. So that's more of a balanced record, whereas this one kind of veers off into... there are a couple songs that definitely go into a different directions."

Beginning Of Sorrow opens with Dave Jr. hammering away on bass before the band crash in with a melodic, textured run at the chorus. Once into the verse, it's gritty again, but still mid-paced, as the album begins to take on a deliberate, even-keeled personality. Indeed most reviewers of the record as a whole definitely picked up on the album's general commercial vibe, particularly against the last couple of corkers, so Shawn's assessment of the album is accurate. Add in the fans, and pretty much everybody noticed that **Super Collider** was a case of Dave doing what Dave has to do, with the title-tracked single serving as both calling card and lightning rod.

Ex-Jag Panzer master Broderick gets a co-credit on *Beginning Of Sorrow*, along with Ellefson and Mustaine. "Chris is, to me, a very gifted guitar player," says Mustaine with respect to Broderick, the first repeat second guitarist on a Megadeth record stretching back to Marty. "Best one I've played with. And that's not taking anything away from the other guys, because they were all really talented. But he's just like the complete package. Because, you know, with Poland, he was a great jazz player, but we had our problems. With Jeff Young, he was a great player, but we had our problems. With Marty, you know, Marty melted down. I don't know what happened, he just melted down. And after that, it was really just being lost in the wilderness for a while. And with Pitrelli coming in, nice guy, but he wasn't right—he know it; we knew it. And Glen, he fit a place for a while, and really helped us, and it was Glen who recommended Chris. But Chris was the only one who, believe it or not, of all that talent—and I've got to say, probably the second in line would be Drover—Chris was the only one who really studied the previous guitar players' solos and did them right. I remember, after Randy Rhoads died, Brad Gillis had gone out and played and Brad is such a great player, but he didn't do the solos the way the we know them. And it's kind of like, where's the solo? And I remember how that affected me, and I swore after that point, if there was ever a song played by a guitar player in Megadeth, that if it wasn't their solo, then it would be as close to the original solo as possible."

"Chris is such a cool dude," adds Mustaine. "Very interesting guy. I was telling someone about the way he practices 13 hours a day, and we were driving through Europe and he's in the back of the bus standing up playing guitar while we're driving. And I'm thinking, man, if this bus driver hits something or somebody, you're going to die with a guitar going right through your chest, man—that's probably the way he wants to go."

The banjo massaged into *The Blackest Crow* was a further lightning rod or red flag for those who grumbled that the album was in composite a little mainstream. It was the easiest culprit, next to the Draiman guest spot, for those who wanted their thrash and wanted it now. In fact, not only is it banjo, but there's fiddle as well, not to mention... brushes!

"*The Blackest Crow* is certainly one of those curveball songs," laughs Shawn. "That was a new thing for me. I've never done something where you're using brushes on the snare; I've never done that. It's really a departure for me, stylistically. So yeah, that's the most diverse record of the four that I've done. I don't think you can disagree with that."

Still, despite the hillbilly appointments, it's squarely a mainstream heavy metal song, and again, sophisticated and yet dark of melody. Apparently Dave's initial plan was to have Willie Nelson and Miranda Lambert sing on the song which would have sent the fans into fits. In any event, *The Blackest Crow*'s depressing lyric is inextricably tied with the album's next track, says Dave.

"There is no lyric that I'm more proud of than another one, but one of the ones that I've been getting a lot of attention for is *Forget To Remember*, which is about my mother-in-law's Alzheimers's that she has, which is really a bitch. And the song *The Blackest Crow*, is actually the first lyric I wrote about Alzheimer's, when I found out she had it. When the song was finished it was really, really dark, and I thought, you know, I just can't be singing this about my mother-in-law, because people die from Alzheimer's, and it was too heavy. And so I kind of shelved it and then put it back. So we were trying to write another track, and that's when *Forget To Remember* happened. And when we were doing the music for *The Blackest Crow*, it didn't, it didn't have a title yet, I thought, wow, I wonder if that lyric would fit? And it fit."

It's most definitely a production showpiece, with, incidentally, the production credit on the album going to Dave and Johnny K, who, underscoring the connection to Draiman, had produced the first three smash albums from Disturbed.

"Johnny had done **Thirteen** with us, and we had some success with that, and so we tried him again with this record," says Mustaine. "He's got a certain modern sensibility and some approaches to production that are pretty cool, with tonality and stuff. If you keep using the same producer over and over again, you tend to get yourself into a rut. There are so many great producers out there that we've had the chance to mix it up over the years, which is really cool. I mean, I don't know where we're going next, or what we're doing next, but I do know that it's been really, really cool to be able to work with so many talented producers. Not all of them have been amazing experiences; some of them have been just kind of so-so. Some of them, you know, they were really difficult—doing **The World Needs A Hero**, that was really hard. But there's been a lot of really cool stuff that I've learned from all of them."

"Actually Johnny, for most of my drum tracks, he wasn't there," adds Shawn. "I recorded most of my stuff in January of 2013, and Johnny had a commitment at that time. We had a engineer, who started the record, who was Cameron Webb, produced several Motörhead records and things of that nature. Great producer, good engineer. So he was there and we had a discussion. We all kind of agreed, look, let's just keep the ball rolling here, and let's get drum tracks going and get 'em done. And during that time it's pretty much what we did. Cameron and I, and Dave of course, we were in the studio, and so it's hard for me to say much about Johnny K, because he really wasn't there during my part of the record. Of course, he listened to everything back home in a studio in Chicago and had some opinions, but by and large, Cameron was the one who was there with me during the recording process of the record, him, myself and Dave. It was quite a lot of fun working with Cameron, so I've nothing but good memories."

Well, you essentially get a full-blown producer with Cameron... "Absolutely. That's why there was no panic. We weren't going to stop the production of the record, because Cameron was there from the start anyway. And the beginning, when we were assembling songs, Johnny was there with David and Cameron as well, and he stepped right in, and I got along with Cameron right off the bat. We were definitely on the same page—he's a real metal guy, he gets it, and he was a pleasure to work with."

"But Johnny was there for the entire process of **Thirteen**," clarifies Shawn. "That was a good experience as well. I have a lot of good memories, doing those drum tracks and stuff. But yeah, once the drums were set up for the beginning process of **Super Collider**, it's pretty much mic'ed the same way it was for **Thirteen**. Recorded in our studio, Vic's Garage, down in Southern California, so nothing changed at all. The kit was already set up, so we just kind of went with similar mic positions and all that. Right away got a great drum sound, within a day, as we did with **Thirteen**, and went with it."

Forget To Remember is most definitely yet another pure heavy metal track well away from thrash, a standard meat and potatoes chugger with a catchy, melodic chorus, something it has in common with the next track, *Don't Turn Your Back...* although this one is squarely a gleaming thrasher through and through. Killer chorus however, almost NWOBHM-magical, possibly the high point of the album and certainly in total, one of the grander and heavier tracks.

"You're probably going to laugh at this, Martin," begins Mustaine, asked about the lyric. "But when I used to live in Arizona, me and David Ellefson knew this guy who was an old guy that was in a 12 step program, a really a crusty old bastard. And he told my wife a bunch of times I wasn't going to live past Christmas. In California they had this thing that they'd show the kids in school to make them be afraid of the law, which is called **Scared Straight**. And they would go in these prisons. Have you seen this? Where the guy pops his eye out and says, 'I'm watching you.' Why have I been saying this? (laughs). Oh yeah, I know. I'm just laughing that I'm talking about this."

"So the guy, you know, he would say stuff to us to try to scare us, and one of the things that he had said—another random thing—he was talking about certain friends that you have. Because like, I had talked to him about *Sweating Bullets*, when it says 'True enemy or false friend,' and he had tried to one-up me and said, 'That's kind of like the friend you have that will steal your dope and help you look for it.' And I went, oh my God, I knew a few of those guys (laughs). But then I said, I don't want to put that in the song, because I don't live that lifestyle anymore. Granted, I had to go through it to know that I didn't want to live like that every day. I certainly didn't want to condone it by talking about it, but I said, 'Steal my things and help me look for it.' It could be anything. It could be your property, your old lady, it could be whatever."

Adds Shawn, "*Don't Turn Your Back...* I think I did that the last day, the day that I was leaving; I was leaving that night. I believe we got down *Cold Sweat* that day, and Dave said, 'I've got one more idea.' Because we had enough songs for the record at that point; we had 14 recorded or something. He says, 'Dude, I've got this idea for a song, that I have a riff for.' And OK, we listened to it, and it sounded really cool. Again, it was something I pretty much learned right off the bat, right there, listening to the riff. We constructed the song, went down there and cut the drum track, and it was done probably in about an hour or 90 minutes. It's just a cool up-tempo track, with the whole double bass drum onslaught in it, which obviously, I like. What's cool about *Don't Turn Your Back* as well, there's a really cool bluesy thing that begins the song, which that first sparked my interest when Dave played it for me. Because he played me that little part—OK, that's kind of different—and then he says, 'Listen to the riff going on to it.'"

Probably the heaviest song on the album, really... "Yeah, those are definitely my favourites. The heavier songs are the ones I gravitate to. I'm just that guy."

Big contrast to the one before it, *Forget To Remember*. "Yeah, that's a different kind of tune as well. It's not a complete metal onslaught and that's fine. But I think it's a good concise tune. Still, for me, the heavier stuff is usually what I gravitate to, so definitely, *Built For War*, the song that I wrote, and *Kingmaker*."

Super Collider tears out of the place with a cover of Thin Lizzy's *Cold Sweat*, an uncharacteristically pure metal track from **Thunder And Lightning**, Lizzy's out-of-step incarnation featuring John Sykes on guitar.

"I had about two days left to cut drums," recalls Shawn, "and this conversation came up, you know, what do you think about doing a cover tune? And that to me is a fun thing. And we started talking about bands. And I think Dave and I both mentioned, hey, what about Thin Lizzy? We all respect them greatly, and they're a fantastic band. And for me, I love all the guitar players in Thin Lizzy—I'm a huge Gary Moore fan and Scott Gorham fan—but doing something that Sykes was on to me was a real thrill—and *Cold Sweat* was a song he actually wrote."

Was there any other Lizzy track that was on the table?

"That was pretty much the song that was mentioned, and we said okay, let's do it. So I went in there, and I think I did three swipes at the drum track and it was done; probably in about 20 minutes, 25 minutes, I'd nailed down the drum track. I knew that song backward anyway. That was a lot of fun. There was no thought involved. When you're creating music, obviously you have to be really focused to try to nail each thing, remember each part that's going on. But doing that, I've known that song since 1983, so it was just a matter of going in there and trying to nail it and make it as good a track as possible, but keeping true, very close to the original, not deviating too much from the original track. And if you listen to *Cold Sweat*, Chris pretty much nails the John Sykes solo, the half that he did, note for note. Which I really appreciate him doing that, because Sykes is one of my all-time favourite guitar players."

Talking to Jeb about the inclusion of *Cold Sweat*, Dave remarked that, "There have been some smart-alecks out there that say that we did it because we wanted to do a Thin Lizzy tune better than Metallica, but we're not playing that game anymore. I did the song because we had wanted to do that song for a long time. It had been rambling around since **Countdown To Extinction** and **Youthanasia**. There are a lot of great Thin Lizzy songs but *Cold Sweat* just called my name because I'm a street kid just like Phil Lynott was. We have a lot in common and, of course, we have several things that are different, but when I listen to those lyrics, I really identify with them. In my estimation, some of the best Thin Lizzy music ever written was the title track to **Thunder And Lightning** and *Cold Sweat*."

"When you do a cover song there are three things you can do," continues Dave. "You can suck, you can do it as good as the original, or you can do it better. Our goal was to do it as good as the original, as we don't think we could have made it better. We challenged ourselves as we sped the song up just a little bit, which made it a little more exciting and gave it a different production tone. We made it a little more modern and relevant. I also added a little part at the end of the song. After we decided to do the song, I had the inclination to see if anyone else had covered it and, of course, 50 bands or so had covered it since we first talked about doing it back in the '90s. One thing that was in common with all of them was a high note that was sung in the third interval of the chorus that everyone was skipping. I didn't hear it; Johnny K heard it. He said, 'It's right there' and I said, 'Oh my God, it is there.' I think our version is the closest to the original that has been done, though there are some other good versions."

And with that said and done, and with the album ending on yet another traditional heavy metal track (even if Megadeth didn't write it), it became summer, and time for Megadeth to mount another Gigantour. Once more, the messaging falling out of the experience was that Megadeth had transitioning into rich instructors of metal, a band that had seen the wars and survived them, had tales to tell and venerable metal anthems to perform. In essence, Dave Mustaine and his one-in-same brand belonged to the world and they were now to be treated as beloved possessions.

Asked about set list this time out, Dave again helpfully (although vaguely) tries to relate to the fact he's speaking with a Canadian. "We have such a different relationship up in Canada than we have in a lot of other countries, so we've always played rare stuff every once in while. We've done things we've only played in one particular area. So there's no real telling what we're going to do. We did a lot of the **Countdown** record, so we pulled a lot of that out. We've got our program that we have; there's a lot of songs, but there are so many other songs from the past we'd like to bring up, because this year's Gigantour is very aggressive (laughs). I don't know if you've seen all the different bands that are playing and I don't know if you've heard the opening band yet, but just about everybody I've talked to is really, really impressed with this lineup. And then there are a couple people that are not fans of one or another band, but that's cool—that's why you have more than one band (laughs)."

"We talked, but not quite as extensively as I would've liked to," says Dave concerning Jason Newsted, who was pulling away from the paints and proposing for us his new pure metal outfit called Newsted. "But we have talked, and you know, the cool thing about Newsted is that we were friends long before he was in Metallica, from back in the Flotsam & Jetsam days. I've known him longer than those guys have. And he's a guy I've gotten close with. I knew him when he was really, really young; we've got a really unique relationship and I look forward to seeing him and playing. He had said something about us jamming a Metallica song or something, and of course, it's up to David Ellefson. He's the bassist in Megadeth, if he wants somebody else to come out there and playing on stage with him. But I know Dave, and I think you know Dave pretty well, and he's always been the nice guy in Megadeth (laughs)."

"I didn't when LoMenzo was in the band," continues Mustaine, asked if he knew Zakk Wylde as more than a passing acquaintance, Black Label Society being second on the bill for Gigantour '13. "But I do now. But when we had seen each other in passing back when James was in the band, I think there was some tension between the two of them, and I never really got a chance to get to hang with Zakk. I've always loved his guitar playing. Remember when he first came on the scene, chicks loved him, guys feared him, but I thought he was just totally bad-ass. And it's kind of a bummer that it's taken this long for us to do something together. But don't forget, there's always been those Ozzfests that we played. But this has been the first proper tour where we're going to get to roll and hang out. Crazy guy, man, energy for days. I talked to him on the way back from the last show in Paris. I was riding in a car for about three hours, and the next thing you know, I'm doing an interview with him for his sports show. I don't know if you've talked to him a lot, but I was talking with him, and it was like, 'What did he say?' 'Dave, comin' in from the Vatican' or something like that."

As for other features to pull Gigantour above the ordinary... "This year, we're having an MC. Jim Florentine, the guy from **That Metal Show**, is going to be out with us, and he's going to be hosting and interviewing fans and interviewing bands, and we're going to have a lot of activity at our site. In Oklahoma City we're doing a charity baseball game for the tornado victims there. We're going to be having a lot of opportunities for the fans to come meet the different bands, with VIP packages and stuff like that. And opportunities for people to hang with bands after the show. A lot of our venues that we're playing are going to be outdoors, so it's going to be good summertime music stuff, and you're not trapped inside of a building. You can actually get some sun while you're at it. To me, those are the fun kinds of shows, when you can get outside. I like playing indoors too, especially when it's raining or snowing (laughs)."

One interesting turn of events that took place as Megadeth was mounting its tour in support of **Super Collider** was the arrival of the long-awaited Dave Ellefson memoire, **My Life With Deth**, penned with esteemed British rock writing legend Joel McIver.

Somewhat surprisingly, the book was issued through a Christian publisher and its contents lean heavily upon Ellefson's faith, which is a dimension to his personality he can share with the boss, of course, making their renewed relationship that much deeper.

"When I was asked to write the book," Dave told Jeb Wright, "I had to be honest about what my life really is like and get behind the walls of what it is perceived to be like. Otherwise, someone else could have just written a biography of my life. When the story comes by your own hand, a certain type of journey lays itself out on the pages before you. So, that is what my book really is, the real story of my life, rather than just another tale of my life. Of course, the truth is I've been raised in a Christian household from the beginning. I was baptized at one month old and I've been in the fold since then, even though I don't exactly remember the ceremony. I was apprehensive about putting a lot of stuff in it because I have teenage kids, as well as many friends and family not in the music business, those who would not appreciate the tales of decadence and debauchery. So, once I told my story to Joel and looked at it on paper, there were certain things that became clearer as to what should be told, and what should be left out. I was not going to write this gruesome 'tell all' just to make a buck."

"The most important thing was that it is a story of a kid who was 'called' into rock 'n' roll. Not because I needed the approval, the girls or the drugs, but because the genuine desire was put upon me, for some strange reason. I was just a kid growing up in a cornfield in Minnesota and one day this music thing just came upon me. I didn't ask for it, I didn't seek it out—it just came to me. Rather than fight it, I went with it and it became my entire mission of my life, the reason to get out of bed in the morning. To this day, it is the thing that inspires me to create, take chances, meet new people, try new things and even gets me around the world to speak of my life to people who have suffered some of the same obstacles I have. To me, it is the real joy of living."

"There is nothing wrong with speaking of a changed life," continues Ellefson, "or of lessons learned during your path. But, to bring other organizations, or people, into those conversations you should have their consent first. That is why I tried to tell my story, and not everyone else's. Everyone has their breaking point and mine came before I was 25 years of age. I had, had enough and saw that if I kept going on the path I was going that my life wasn't going to get better; it was going to get worse. For me, it was obvious that the party was over, even in rock 'n' roll. If I was going to pursue the things important to me, I was going to have to step up and change how I was living my life."

"I don't just walk up to people and tell them to read the Bible, but, to anyone who suggests these questions, I do suggest they read the Bible and find the answers for themselves, because that is what I had to do to find the truth on these matters. The answers are all in there, and there are no shortcuts to finding truth. Just my experience. I was once told by a dear friend that I have three powers available to me at all times: the power of prayer, the power of example, or the power to jump in and make a mess of things with my own will power. Based on my own experience, clearly, he was right!

To me, faith isn't about church; it's about finding a strength that lies beyond our own finite abilities. Church is just a fellowship of like-minded believers, much like a rock concert is a fellowship of like-minded believers; plus, we all want to know where we came from. Scientists confirm we are all made up of atoms but who made the atom? I guess that is the answer we all seek at some point in our lives."

As for Megadeth's notorious demons of old... "Well, addiction is an equal opportunity destroyer and there are people in all walks of life who suffer its wrath. To understand it as an illness puts it in a much different light and takes the judgment off the people who suffer from it, much the same way you wouldn't judge, or behold, someone with cancer, heart disease, or other life threatening illnesses. With that said, rock 'n' roll certainly has applauded its decadence only to find it killing its own talent. I lived through some of that myself, so I saw it first hand. More than anything, I'm here to help if anyone reaches out. That alone is a good enough reason to stay in it, to actually be useful and contribute something good back to it. I've had quite a few people open up to me about their own struggles with addictions and faith, which has been very therapeutic for them. If the book can help people feel comfortable about opening up those dark corners of their life to embrace change for the better, then the book was certainly worth writing. I've found that faith, hope and heavy metal can all coexist, *but* they have to be in that order. Sometimes, I myself, tended to look at things as an 'either/or' scenario—either you're in or your out. But, my own experience says that if God brought you to it, he'll get you through it."

Back to the world of Megadeth and their newly invigorated mission to take the metal to the people, likely many memories that last a lifetime were to be forged on the Gigantour tour that was upcoming as we went to press.

But for Shawn Drover, none were likely to beat what represents a coming to full circle as it were, that gig from June 16th of 2010 featuring Megadeth alongside Anthrax, Slayer and Metallica.

"I would have to say obviously the Big Four shows were certainly a real high point in my career, doing this for nine years with the band," relates Drover. "For me, playing the first show that finally... the combination of 26, 27 years of wanting these four bands to play together, and we finally pull it all together and do it. The first show we did was in Warsaw, Poland, and depending on who you ask, there was between 100,000 and 125,000 people. I just remember, Anthrax is on, and I just looked out and it was a sea of humanity that was out there. And I though, oh my God, this going to be all right. Everybody was in such great spirits and so happy that we could finally do this. All of us were just really happy to do it."

"We played, probably whatever it was, 15, 16 shows over as the Big Four, but that one for me was the highlight, playing Warsaw, Poland to that many people. Playing Yankee Stadium was also a thrill. We were the first heavy metal bands to inhabit that venue—name one other heavy metal band that's played Yankee Stadium. That in itself is amazing."

"But Warsaw, there was no nervousness. I think we all had a feeling of just a lot of excitement. We're going to go out there and we're going to give these kids a great show. And we did. Everybody played great, it was a great day... yeah, a lot of good memories of all those shows. But Warsaw, being the first one, it was just electric. The feeling in the air was special."

Again, as we close, indeed, this gives a sense of events coming full circle for Mustaine and Megadeth. There's the obvious linking of arms with Metallica, but there's also a sense that thrash just might have topped, through this grand stand and plan, the genre's previous pinnacle. Arguably, that pinnacle might have been the Clash Of The Titans statement from 1990, 1991, in which this hard—and for most music buyers, hard to love—music plunked itself into arenas and stadiums for one triumphant middle finger in the air before Nirvana arrived and shoved metal back into a subservience never to fully strut its stuff the way it did during its golden run in the '80s.

"No, because we did that again," explains Shawn, not quite getting my view of it, but getting across the point that the band had already somewhat relived Clash Of The Titans in echo form already. "We went out on tour two or three years ago, with Slayer and Anthrax. So we really did that again, and that was cool in itself. But the only thing that they really talked about was having the Big Four, never knowing that it would really ever happen in our careers, and I'm really glad that it all finally came together."

But notwithstanding the levity of the Big Four bash, the significance of the original Clash Of The Titans was not lost on Drover either, even if he could only dream of drumming for Megadeth back in the early '90s.

"If you remember the time, when they did the Clash Of The Titans thing, what was that, '90 and '91, do you remember who the opening band was? It was Alice in Chains. Tides were about to turn in a dramatic way. If you remember, MTV was playing all the metal stuff, and then all of a sudden the light switched off, and they weren't playing rock anymore. It's Pearl Jam and Soundgarden, and obviously Nirvana was the catalyst for that, which is fine. But you're right, thrash got to that point, and it never recovered from there, in terms of popularity, because the tide basically turned a 180. A lot of bands didn't make it—they collapsed. I guess what I'm getting at, the fact that we're still here in 2013, and all four of us are still here and thriving, that's, I think, a testament to our fan base, and a testament to good music. At the end of the day, good music is going to stand the test of time, and these four bands are living proof of that. And you can add Exodus and Testament into that mix as well. We're always referring to the big four, but all those bands are still here, and we're all still creating good music, 30 years into the game. That speaks volumes, if you ask me."

Discography

I'm keeping this tight and disciplined for ya folks, this discography being designed to be a handy, dandy guide you might flip back to and reference as you read along and ponder the albums, a quick checklist for you to see which songs hail from where. Nice 'n' tidy. As with all my books, vinyl-era albums get a Side 1/Side 2 designation, and there's a notes section to point out anything else I figured was important enough to make known, such as changes in band personnel. I've not bothered to get into reissue details—this is about the record as God intended it. A videography is also included, deliberately with a lesser level of detail.

A. Studio Albums

Killing Is My Business... And Business Is Good
(Combat, June 12, 1985)
Side 1: 1. *Last Rites/Loved To Death* 2. *Killing Is My Business... And Business Is Good!* 3. *The Skull Beneath The Skin* 4. *These Boots*
Side 2: 1. *Rattlehead* 2. *Chosen Ones* 3. *Looking Down The Cross* 4. *Mechanix*
Notes: Production: Dave Mustaine, Karat Faye. Band personnel is Dave Mustaine: guitar and vocals; Chris Poland: guitar; Dave Ellefson: bass; Gar Samuelson: drums. RIAA designation: none.

Peace Sells... But Who's Buying?
(Capitol, October 1986)
Side 1: 1. *Wake Up Dead* 2. *The Conjuring* 3. *Peace Sells* 4. *Devils Island*
Side 2: 1. *Good Mourning/Black Friday* 2. *Bad Omen* 3. *I Ain't Superstitious* 4. *My Last Words*
Notes: Production: Dave Mustaine, Randy Burns. RIAA designation: platinum.

So Far, So Good... So What!
(Capitol, January 1988)
Side 1: 1. *Into The Lungs Of Hell* 2. *Set The World Afire* 3. *Anarchy In The U.K.* 4. *Mary Jane*
Side 2: 1. *502* 2. *In My Darkest Hour* 3. *Liar* 4. *Hook In Mouth*
Notes: Production: Dave Mustaine, Paul Lani. Guitarist Chris Poland is replaced by Jeff Young; drummer Gar Samuelson is replaced by Chuck Behler. RIAA designation: platinum.

Rust In Peace
(Capitol, September 24, 1990)
Side 1: 1. *Holy Wars... The Punishment Due* 2. *Hangar 18* 3. *Take No Prisoners* 4. *Five Magics*
Side 2. 1: *Poison Was The Cure* 2. *Lucretia* 3. *Tornado Of Souls* 4. *Dawn Patrol* 5. *Rust In Peace... Polaris*
Notes: Production: Dave Mustaine, Mike Clink. Guitarist Jeff Young is replaced by Marty Friedman; drummer Chuck Behler is replaced by Nick Menza. RIAA designation: platinum.

Countdown To Extinction
(Capitol, July 6, 1992)
1. *Skin O' My Teeth* 2. *Symphony Of Destruction* 3. *Architecture Of Aggression* 4. *Foreclosure Of A Dream* 5. *Sweating Bullets* 6. *This Was My Life* 7. *Countdown To Extinction* 8. *High Speed Dirt* 9. *Psychotron* 10. *Captive Honour* 11. *Ashes In Your Mouth*
Notes: Production: Max Norman, Dave Mustaine. Japanese bonus tracks are *Breakpoint* and *Go To Hell*. RIAA designation: 2x platinum.

Youthanasia

(Capitol, November 1, 1994)

1. *Reckoning Day* 2. *Train Of Consequences* 3. *Addicted To Chaos* 4. *A Tout Le Monde* 5. *Elysian Fields* 6. *The Killing Road* 7. *Blood Of Heroes* 8. *Family Tree* 9. *Youthanasia* 10. *I Thought I Knew It All* 11. *Black Curtains* 12. *Victory*

Notes: Production: Max Norman, Dave Mustaine. Japanese bonus tracks are *Crown Of Worms* , *Holy Wars... The Punishment Due* (live) , *Symphony Of Destruction* (live) and *Sweating Bullets* (live) . RIAA designation: platinum.

Cryptic Writings

(Capitol, June 17, 1997)

1. *Trust* 2. *Almost Honest* 3. *Use The Man* 4. *Mastermind* 5. *The Disintegrators* 6. *I'll Get Even* 7. *Sin* 8. *A Secret Place* 9. *Have Cool, Will Travel* 10. *She-Wolf* 11. *Vortex* 12. *FFF*

Notes: Production: Dann Huff, Dave Mustaine. Japanese bonus track is *One Thing* (4:38). RIAA designation: platinum.

Risk

(Capitol, August 31, 1999)

1. *Insomnia* 2. *Prince Of Darkness* 3. *Enter The Arena* 4. *Crush 'Em* 5. *Breadline* 6. *The Doctor Is Calling* 7. *I'll Be There* 8. *Wanderlust* 9. *Ecstasy* 10. *Seven* 11. *Time: The Beginning* 12. *Time: The End*

Notes: Production: Dann Huff, Dave Mustaine. Drummer Nick Menza is replaced by Jimmy DeGrasso. Japanese bonus track is *Duke Nukem* . RIAA designation: gold.

The World Needs A Hero

(Sanctuary, May 15, 2001)

1. *Disconnect* 2. *The World Needs A Hero* 3. *Moto Psycho* 4. *1000 Times Goodbye* 5. *Burning Bridges* 6. *Promises* 7. *Recipe For Hate... Warhorse* 8. *Losing My Senses* 9. *Dread And The Fugitive Mind* 10. *Silent Scorn* 11. *Return To Hangar* 12. *When*

Notes: Production: Bill Kennedy, Dave Mustaine. Band personnel is Dave Mustaine: guitar and vocals; Al Pitrelli: guitar, backing vocals; Dave Ellefson: bass; Jimmy DeGrasso: drums. Japanese bonus track is *Coming Home* (2:35). RIAA designation: none.

The System Has Failed

(Sanctuary, September 14, 2004)

1. *Blackmail The Universe* 2. *Die Dead Enough* 3. *Kick The Chair* 4. *The Scorpion* 5. *Tears In A Vial* 6. *I Know Jack* 7. *Back In The Day* 8. *Something That I'm Not* 9. *Truth Be Told* 10. *Of Mice And Men* 11. *Shadow Of Deth* 12. *My Kingdom*

Notes: Production: Dave Mustaine, Jeff Balding. Guitarist Al Pitrelli is replaced by Chris Poland; bassist Dave Ellefson is replaced by Jimmie Lee Sloas; drummer Jimmy DeGrasso is replaced by Vinnie Colaiuta. RIAA designation: none.

United Abominations

(Roadrunner, May 15, 2007)

1. *Sleepwalker* 2. *Washington Is Next!* 3. *Never Walk Alone... A Call To Arms* 4. *United Abominations* 5. *Gears Of War* 6. *Blessed Are The Dead* 7. *Play For Blood* 8. *A Tout Le Monde (Set Me Free)* 9. *Amerikhastan* 10. *You're Dead* 11. *Burnt Ice*

Notes: Production: Dave Mustaine, Jeff Balding, Andy Sneap. Guitarist Chris Poland is replaced by Glen Drover; bassist Jimmie Lee Sloas is replaced by James LoMenzo; drummer Vinnie Colaiuta is replaced by Shawn Drover. Japanese bonus track is *Out On The Tiles* . Pre-order bonus track is *Black Swan* . RIAA designation: none.

Endgame

(Roadrunner, September 9, 2009)

1. *Dialectic Chaos* 2. *This Day We Fight!* 3. *44 Minutes* 4. *1,320'* 5. *Bite The Hand* 6. *Bodies* 7. *Endgame* 8. *The Hardest Part Of Letting Go... Sealed With A Kiss* 9. *Head Crusher* 10. *How The Story Ends* 11. *The Right To Go Insane*

Notes: Production: Dave Mustaine, Andy Sneap. Guitarist Glen Drover is replaced by Chris Broderick. RIAA designation: none.

Thirteen

(Roadrunner, November 1, 2011)

1. *Sudden Death* 2. *Public Enemy No. 1* 3. *Whose Life (Is It Anyways?)* 4. *We The People* 5. *Guns, Drugs & Money* 6. *Never Dead* 7. *New World Order* 8. *Fast Lane* 9. *Black Swan* 10. *Wrecker* 11. *Millennium Of The Blind* 12. *Deadly Nightshade* 13. *13*

Notes: Production: Johnny K, Dave Mustaine. Bassist James LoMenzo is replaced by Dave Ellefson. RIAA designation: none.

Super Collider

(Tradecraft/Universal, June 4, 2013)

1. *Kingmaker* 2. *Super Collider* 3. *Burn!* 4. *Built For War* 5. *Off The Edge* 6. *Dance In The Rain* 7. *Beginning Of Sorrow* 8. *The Blackest Crow* 9. *Forget To Remember* 10. *Don't Turn Your Back...* 11. *Cold Sweat*

Notes: Production: Johnny K, Dave Mustaine. Various bonus tracks: *All I Want*, A House Divided, *Countdown To Extinction* (live). RIAA designation: none.

B. Live Albums

Rude Awakening

(Sanctuary, March 19, 2002)

CD1: 1. *Dread And The Fugitive Mind* 2. *Kill The King* 3. *Wake Up Dead* 4. *In My Darkest Hour* 5. *Angry Again* 6. *She-Wolf* 7. *Reckoning Day* 8. *Devils Island* 9. *Train Of Consequences* 10. *A Tout Le Monde* 11. *Burning Bridges* 12. *Hangar 18* 13. *Return To Hangar* 14. *Hook In Mouth*

CD2: 1. *Almost Honest* 2. *1000 Times Goodbye* 3. *Mechanix* 4. *Tornado Of Souls* 5. *Ashes In Your Mouth* 6. *Sweating Bullets* 7. *Trust* 8. *Symphony Of Destruction* 9. *Peace Sells* 10. *Holy Wars*

Notes: Production: Bill Kennedy, Dave Mustaine, Arthur Gorson. Band personnel is Dave Mustaine: guitar and vocals; Al Pitrelli: guitar, backing vocals; Dave Ellefson: bass; Jimmy DeGrasso: drums. DVD version features slightly reduced track list (20 tracks instead of 24), plus interview footage and bonus live footage, consisting of *Kill The King*, *Angry Again*, *Almost Honest*, *Train Of Consequences* and *A Tout Le Monde*.

That One Night: Live In Buenos Aires

(Image Entertainment, September 4, 2007)

CD1: 1. *Jet Intro* 2. *Blackmail The Universe* 3. *Set The World Afire* 4. *Skin 'O My Teeth* 5. *Wake Up Dead* 6. *In My Darkest Hour* 7. *Die Dead Enough* 8. *She-Wolf* 9. *Reckoning Day* 10. *A Tout Le Monde* 11. *Angry Again*
CD2: 1. *Hangar 18* 2. *Return To Hangar* 3. *I'll Be There* 4. *Tornado Of Souls* 5. *Trust* 6. *Something That I'm Not* 7. *Kick The Chair* 8. *Coming Home To Argentina* 9. *Symphony Of Destruction* 10. *Peace Sells* 11. *Holy Wars*

Notes: Production: Bill Kennedy, Dave Mustaine, Arthur Gorson. Band personnel is Dave Mustaine: guitar and vocals; Glen Drover: guitar, backing vocals; James MacDonough: bass; Shawn Drover: drums. DVD version features slightly reduced track list (17 tracks instead of 21), plus bonus feature *Symphony Of Destruction* (alternate track).

Rust In Peace: Live

(Shout! Factory, September 7, 2010)

1. *Holy Wars... The Punishment Due* 2. *Hangar 18* 3. *Take No Prisoners* 4. *Five Magics* 5. *Poison Was The Cure* 6. *Lucretia* 7. *Tornado Of Souls* 8. *Dawn Patrol* 9. *Rust In Peace... Polaris* 10. *Holy Wars (Reprise)* 11.

Skin O' My Teeth 12. *In My Darkest Hour* 13. *She-Wolf* 14. *Trust* 15. *Symphony Of Destruction* 16. *Peace Sells*
Notes: Production: Mark Adelman. Band personnel is Dave Mustaine: guitar and vocals; Chris Broderick: guitar, backing vocals; Dave Ellefson: bass, backing vocals; Shawn Drover: drums. Issued as CD, DVD and Blu-ray.

The Big 4: Live From Sofia, Bulgaria
(Warner Bros., October 15, 2010)
CD1: Anthrax (ten tracks)
CD2: 1. *Holy Wars... The Punishment Due* 2. *Hangar 18* 3. *Wake Up Dead* 4. *Head Crusher* 5. *In My Darkest Hour* 6. *Skin O' My Teeth* 7. *A Tout Le Monde* 8. *Hook In Mouth* 9. *Trust* 10. *Sweating Bullets* 11. *Symphony Of Destruction* 12. *Peace Sells/Holy Wars Reprise*
CD3: Slayer (12 tracks)
CD4, 5: Metallica (18 tracks)Notes: Production: Jim Parsons; executive producer: David May. Megadeth band personnel is Dave Mustaine: guitar and vocals; Chris Broderick: guitar, backing vocals; Dave Ellefson: bass, backing vocals; Shawn Drover: drums. Issued as DVD with CDs and Blu-ray.

Countdown To Extinction: Live
(Tradecraft/Universal, September 24, 2013)
1. *Trust* 2. *Hangar 18* 3. *Public Enemy No. 1* 4. *Skin O' My Teeth* 5. *Symphony Of Destruction* 6. *Architecture Of Aggression* 7. *Foreclosure Of A Dream* 8. *Sweating Bullets* 9. *This Was My Life* 10. *Countdown To Extinction* 11. *High Speed Dirt* 12. *Psychotron* 13. *Captive Honour* 14. *Ashes In Your Mouth* 15. *She-Wolf* 16. *Peace Sells* 17. *Holy Wars... The Punishment Due*
Notes: Band personnel is Dave Mustaine: guitar and vocals; Chris Broderick: guitar, backing vocals; Dave Ellefson: bass, backing vocals; Shawn Drover: drums. Issued as CD, DVD and Blu-ray.

C. Compilations

Hidden Treasures
(Capitol, July 18, 1995)
1. *No More Mr. Nice Guy* (3:02) 2. *Breakpoint* (3:29) 3. *Go To Hell* (4:36) 4. *Angry Again* (3:47) 5. *99 Ways To Die* (3:58) 6. *Paranoid* (2:32) 7. *Diadems* (3:55) 8. *Problems* (3:57)
Notes: Production: Max Norman, Dave Mustaine. Short LP/long EP compilation consisting of one on non-album tracks, one non-Megadeth compilation album track and six film soundtrack-related tracks.

Capitol Punishment: The Megadeth Years
(Capitol, October 24, 2000)
1. *Kill The King* 2. *Dread And The Fugitive Mind* 3. *Crush 'Em* 4. *Use The Man* 5. *Almost Honest* 6. *Trust* 7. *A Tout Le Monde* 8. *Train Of Consequences* 9. *Sweating Bullets* 10. *Symphony Of Destruction* 11. *Hangar 18* 12. *Holy Wars... The Punishment Due* 13. *In My Darkest Hour* 14. *Peace Sells*
Notes: Hits package save for two new tracks, *Kill The King* and *Dread And The Fugitive Mind*.

Still Alive... And Well?
(Sanctuary, September 10, 2002)
1. *Time: The Beginning/Use The Man* (live) 2. *The Conjuring* (live) 3. *In My Darkest Hour* (live) 4. *Sweating Bullets* (live) 5. *Symphony Of Destruction* (live) 6. *Holy Wars... The Punishment Due* 7. *Moto Psycho* 8. *Dread And The Fugitive Mind* 9. *Promises* 10. *The World Needs A Hero* 11. *Burning Bridges* 12. *Return To Hangar*
Notes: compilation of live tracks and selections from **The World Needs A Hero**.

Greatest Hits: Back To The Start

(Capitol, June 28, 2005)

1. *Holy Wars... The Punishment Due* 2. *In My Darkest Hour* 3. *Peace Sells* 4. *Sweating Bullets* 5. *Angry Again* 6. *A Tout Le Monde* 7. *Trust* 8. *Kill The King* 9. *Symphony Of Destruction* 10. *Mechanix* (2002 remix) 11. *Train Of Consequences* 12. *Wake Up Dead* 13. *Hangar 18* 14. *Dread And The Fugitive Mind* 15. *Skin O' My Teeth* 16. *She-Wolf* 17. *Prince Of Darkness*

Notes: limited edition DVD consisted of *Kill The King* (mega-mix video), Megadeth Live At The Fillmore intro screen, preview of upcoming **Arsenal Of Death** DVD, and live versions of *Prince Of Darkness*, *Holy Wars... The Punishment Due*, *In My Darkest Hour*, *Hangar 18*, *Sweating Bullets*, *Symphony Of Destruction* and *Peace Sells*.

Warchest

(Capitol, October 9, 2007)

CD1: 1. *Killing Is My Business... And Business Is Good!* 2. *The Skull Beneath The Skin* 3. *Peace Sells* 4. *Wake Up Dead* 5. *Devils Island* 6. *Set The World Afire* 7. *Into The Lungs Of Hell* 8. *Anarchy/Problems* (session take) 9. *Hook In Mouth* 10. *Liar* 11. *In My Darkest Hour* 12. *No More Mr. Nice Guy* 13. *Dark Themes...* (interview) 14. *Holy Wars... The Punishment Due* (demo) 15. *Tornado Of Souls* (demo) 16. *Five Magics* (demo) 17. *Hangar 18*

CD2: 1. *Keeping Score...* 2. *Symphony Of Destruction* 3. *Go To Hell* 4. *Foreclosure Of A Dream* 5. *Architecture Of Aggression* (demo) 6. *Skin O' My Teeth* (live) 7. *High Speed Dirt* (live) 8. *Ashes In Your Mouth* (live) 9. *Sweating Bullets* (live) 10. *Breakpoint* (session take) 11. *Angry Again* 12. *Train Of Consequences* 13. *Reckoning Day* 14. *New World Order* 15. *The Killing Road* 16. *Strange Ways* 17. *Paranoid* 18. *Diadems* 19. *A Tout Le Monde*

CD3: 1. *Trust* 2. *Almost Honest* 3. *Use The Man* 4. *She-Wolf* 5. *A Secret Place* (live) 6. *One Thing* 7. *Duke Nukem Theme* 8. *Insomnia* 9. *Crush 'Em* 10. *Kill The King* 11. *Dread And The Fugitive Mind* 12. *Never Say Die* (live) 13. *Moto Psycho* 14. *1000 Times Goodbye* 15. *Coming Home* 16. *Kick The Chair* 17. *Of Mice And Men*

CD4: (all live) 1. *Intro/Rattlehead* 2. *Wake Up Dead* 3. *Hangar 18* 4. *Hook In Mouth* 5. *The Skull Beneath The Skin* 6. *The Conjuring* 7. *In My Darkest Hour* 8. *Lucretia* 9. *Devils Island* 10. *Take No Prisoners* 11. *Peace Sells* 12. *Black Friday* 13. *It's Electric* 14. *Anarchy In The U.K.* 15. *Holy Wars... The Punishment Due*

DVD1 (disc 5; all live): 1. *Intro/Holy Wars... The Punishment Due* 2. *Wake Up Dead* 3. *Hangar 18* 4. *Lucretia* 5. *Sweating Bullets* 6. *In My Darkest Hour* 7. *Tornado Of Souls* 8. *Ashes In Your Mouth* 9. *Peace Sells* 10. *Anarchy In The U.K.*

Notes: Disc 4 is a live CD recorded at Wembley Arena, October 16, 1990. Disc 5 is a live DVD recorded at the Hammersmith Odeon, September 30, 1992.

Anthology: Set The World Afire

(Capitol, September 30, 2008)

CD1: 1. *Mechanix* 2. *Rattlehead* 3. *Peace Sells* 4. *Wake Up Dead* 5. *Devils Island* 6. *Anarchy In The U.K.* 7. *Set The World Afire* 8. *Into The Lungs Of Hell* 9. *In My Darkest Hour* 10. *Holy Wars... The Punishment Due* 11. *Tornado Of Souls* 12. *Hangar 18* 13. *Take No Prisoners* 14. *Go To Hell* 15. *Sweating Bullets* 16. *Crown Of Worms* 17. *High Speed Dirt* (demo)

CD2: 1. *Skin O' My Teeth* 2. *Ashes In Your Mouth* 3. *Breakpoint* 4. *Angry Again* 5. *Train Of Consequences* 6. *Reckoning Day* (live) 7. *A Tout Le Monde* 8. *The Killing Road* 9. *New World Order* 10. *Trust* 11. *She-Wolf* 12. *Insomnia* 13. *Prince Of Darkness* 14. *Kill The King* 15. *Dread And The Fugitive Mind* 16. *Foreclosure Of A Dream* 17. *Symphony Of Destruction* (live) 18. *Peace Sells* (live)

D. Videography

Rusted Pieces
(Picture Music International, April 1991)
1. *Peace Sells* 2. *Wake Up Dead* 3. *In My Darkest Hour* 4. *Anarchy In The U.K.* 5. *Holy Wars... The Punishment Due* 6. *Hangar 18*
Notes: collection of production video clips.

Exposure Of A Dream
(Capitol, November 3, 1992)
1. *Symphony Of Destruction* 2. *Foreclosure Of A Dream* 3. *Skin O' My Teeth* 4. *High Speed Dirt* 5. *Go To Hell* 6. *Symphony Of Destruction* (Edited Gristle Mix)

Evolver: The Making Of Youthanasia
(Picture Music International, May 2, 1995)
1. *The Making Of Youthanasia* 2. *Train Of Consequences*

Behind The Music
(Sanctuary, October 16, 2001)
1. *Behind The Music* 2. *Moto Psycho* 3. *Photo Gallery* 4. *Vital Statistics* 5. *Out-takes/Bonus Footage*
Notes: Megadeth episode from the music documentary/biography series.

Rude Awakening
(Sanctuary, April 9, 2002)
1. *Dread & The Fugitive Mind* 2. *Wake Up Dead* 3. *In My Darkest Hour* 4. *She-Wolf* 5. *Reckoning Day* 6. *Devils Island* 7. *Burning Bridges* 8. *Hangar 18* 9. *Return To Hangar* 10. *Hook In Mouth* 11. *1000 Times Goodbye* 12. *Mechanix* 13. *Tornado Of Souls* 14. *Ashes In Your Mouth* 15. *Sweating Bullets* 16. *Trust* 17. *Symphony Of Destruction* 18. *Peace Sells* 19. *Holy Wars* 20. *Silent Scorn*
Notes: Tracks 1 to 20 from live concert, Web Theater, Phoenix, AZ, November 17, 2001; tracks 3 to 7 in bonus material from live concert Rialto Theater, Tucson, AZ, November 16, 2001. Bonus material: 1. *Megadeth On Megadeth* 2. *Paul Gargano on Megadeth* (text) 3. *Kill The King* 4. *Angry Again* 5. *Almost Honest* 6. *Train Of Consequences* 7. *A Tout Le Monde*

Video Hits
(Capitol, January 11, 2005)
1. *Peace Sells* 2. *Anarchy In The U.K.* 3. *Hangar 18* (short MTV edit) 4. *Symphony Of Destruction* 5. *Train Of Consequences* 6. *Trust*

Arsenal Of Megadeth
(Capitol, March 21, 2006)
DVD1: 1. *Excerpt From Talk Radio* (1986) 2. *Peace Sells* 3. 1986 *Interview* 4. *Wake Up Dead* (1988) 5. *Penelope Spheeris Cutting Edge Happy Hour Interview* 6. *In My Darkest Hour* 7. *So Far, So Good... So What! Interview* 8. *Anarchy In The U.K.* 9. *No More Mr. Nice Guy* (1990) 10. *Marty Friedman Audition* 11. *Rust In Peace TV Spot* 12. *Clash Of The Titans Tour, 1990* 13. *Holy Wars... The Punishment Due* 14. *Excerpt From Headbangers Ball 1991* 15. *Hangar 18* 16. *Go To Hell* 17. *Rock The Vote* (3 promo clips) 18. *Countdown To Extinction TV spot* 19. *Symphony Of Destruction* 20. *Symphony Of Destruction* (edited) 21. *Skin O' My Teeth* 22. *High Speed Dirt* 23. *Foreclosure Of A Dream* 24. *Excerpt From A Day In The Life Of Hollywood* 25. *Sweating Bullets*
DVD2: (1994) 1. *Excerpt From Evolver* 2. *Train Of Consequences* 3. *Making Of The Train Of Consequences* 4. *Youthanasia TV Spot* 5. *1994 Interview* 6. *Excerpt From Night Of The Living Megadeth* 7. *Excerpt From MTV Most Wanted 1995* 8. *1994 Interview* 9. *A Tout Le Monde* 10. *1994 Interview* 11. *Reckoning Day* (1997) 12. *Cryptic Writings TV Spot* 13. *Trust* 14. *Making Of The Trust Music Video* 15. *Cryptic TV* 16. *Almost Honest* 17. *A Secret Place* 18. *1998 Interview* 19. *Excerpt From The Drew Carey Show* (1999) 20. *Risk Promo* 21. *Insomnia* (2005) 22. *Sweating Bullets* (live) 23. *Peace Sells* (live)
Notes: Above selections are music videos unless otherwise indicated or described.

That One Night: Live In Buenos Aires

(Image Entertainment, September 4, 2007)

1. *Blackmail The Universe* 2. *Set The World Afire* 3. *Wake Up Dead* 4. *In My Darkest Hour* 5. *She-Wolf* 6. *Reckoning Day* 7. *A Tout Le Monde* 8. *Hangar 18/Return To Hangar* 9. *I'll Be There* 10. *Tornado Of Souls* 11. *Trust* 12. *Something That I'm Not* 13. *Kick The Chair* 14. *Coming Home* 15. *Symphony Of Destruction* 16. *Peace Sells* 17. *Holy Wars/Silent Scorn* 18. *Bonus Feature: Symphony Of Destruction* (alternate track)

Rust In Peace Live

(Shout! Factory, September 7, 2010)

1. *Holy Wars... The Punishment Due* 2. *Hangar 18* 3. *Take No Prisoners* 4. *Five Magics* 5. *Poison Was The Cure* 6. *Lucretia* 7. *Tornado Of Souls* 8. *Dawn Patrol* 9. *Rust In Peace... Polaris* 10. *Holy War (Reprise)* (Bonus Material) 11. *Skin O' My Teeth* 12. *In My Darkest Hour* 13. *She-Wolf* 14. *Trust* 15. *Symphony Of Destruction* 16. *Peace Sells*

The Big 4: Live From Sofia, Bulgaria

(Warner Bros., October 15, 2010)

Notes: DVD track list same as CD version above. DVD exclusive footage consists of behind the scenes at Sonisphere, interviews and Am I Evil? rehearsal material.

Countdown To Extinction: Live

(Tradecraft/Universal, September 24, 1013)

Notes: DVD track list same as CD version above.

So Far, So Good... So Megadeth!

CREDITS

Interviews With The Author:
Michael Alago, 30th October 2009; Mike Albert, 6th February 2013; Chris Broderick, 2nd July 2004; Jimmy, DeGrasso, 31st January 2013; Shawn Drover, 13th June 2013; Glen Drover, 22nd June 2013; Dave Ellefson, 13th January 1998, 10th May 2001, 3rd October 2009 & 4th November 2009; Marty, Friedman, 27th May 2001 & 12th March 2007; Jeff Gilbert 2009; Scott Greer, November 2009; Scott Ian, 15th March 2010; James LoMenzo, 25th June 2013; Nick Menza, 30th January 2002; Dave, Mustaine, 1996, 13th January 1998, 10th August 1999, 15th August 2000, 9th October 2001, 29th July 2010 & 26th June 2013; Chris, Poland, 8th July 2003 & 4th February 2013; Andy Sneap, 10th February 2010; Brian Tatler, 11th April 2013; Neil Turbin, 13th November 2009; Michael Wagener, 6th May 2008; DJ Will, January 2010; Jeff Young, 20th May 2006 & 4th February 2013.

Additional Citations
Note: Some of these citations are incomplete as to date etc. If informed or corrected, I would be pleased to expand or amend any and all credits in future editions.

Aardschok America. Megadeth/Overkill concert review by Gene Khoury. Spring 1986.
Brave Words & Bloody Knuckles. Megadeth by Tim Henderson. Vol. 1, No. 4. August / September 1994.
Brave Words & Bloody Knuckles. Plunging To Megadeth... by Tim Henderson. Vol. 1, No. 6. January/February 1995.
Brave Words & Bloody Knuckles. Interview with Glen and Shawn Drover by Tim Henderson. 2007.
Bravewords.com. Megadeth's Dave Mustaine: "Half These Little Farts Wouldn't Say This To My Face Cuz They'd Piss Their Pants If They Stood In Front Of Me" by Tim Henderson. November 25, 2013.
Classic Rock Revisited. Interview with Chris Broderick by Jeb Wright.
Classic Rock Revisited. Interview with Dave Mustaine by Jeb Wright.
Classic Rock Revisited. Interview with Dave Ellefson by Jeb Wright.
Dunn, Sam. Interview with Dave Mustaine. February 8, 2009.
Dunn, Sam. Interview with Sean Kinney. 2009.
Entertainment Weekly. Rust In Peace record review by Jim Farber. Issue No. 37. October 26, 1990.
Grinder. 1984 Demo review by Jim Powell. 1984.
Hit Parader. Megadeth by Jodi Beth Summers. 1986.
Hit Parader. Megadeth: Days Of Destiny by Ernie "Spuds" McKenzie. 1988.
Hit Parader. The Story Behind The Song: Megadeth's Foreclosure Of A Dream. 1993.
Kerrang! Youthanasia record review by Jason Arnopp. No. 517. October 22, 1994.
Kerrang! I Could Murder Aerosmith! by Paul Rees. 1994.
M.E.A.T. Megadeth by Drew Masters. Issue No. 52. October 1994.
Metal Forces. Death Dealers by Bernard Doe. 1986.
Metal Forces. No Holds Barred by Bernard Doe. 1986
Metal Forces. Megadeth new album + new lineup by Bernard Doe. No. 26. 1987.
Metal Forces. Burning Ambition by Garry Sharpe. No. 29. July 1988.
Metal Hammer. Megadeth: So Far, So Good... So Mega! by Dave Dickson. Vol. 3, No. 3. February 29, 1988.
Metal Hammer. Simply Symphonic. 1992.
Metal Hammer. Youthanasia record review by Jerry Ewing. 1994.
Metal Maniacs. Megadeth: Rest In Peace by Sue Nolz. Vol. 19, No. 8. October 2002.
Music Radar. Interview: Megadeth's Dave Mustaine talks TH1RT3EN, Metallica and riffs by Joe Bosso. December 14, 2011.
Powerline. Thirteen appears to be a lucky number for Dave Mustaine by Patrick Prince. Dec 14, 2011.
Pure Grain Audio. Interview with Dave Mustaine by Aaron Willschick. June 7, 2011.
Raw. The Final Countdown! by Dave Ling. No. 99. June 10 – 23, 1992.
Rip. Megadeth: Trial By Fire by Steffan Chirazi. Vol. 7, No. 12. November 1993.
Rolling Stone. So Far, So Good... So What! record review by Jim Farber. Issue No. 522. March 24, 1988.
Rolling Stone. Rust In Peace record review by Robert Palmer. Issue No. 591. November 15, 1990.
Rolling Stone. Countdown To Extinction record review by Karen Csengeri. Issue No. 640. 1992.
Ultimate Guitar. Megadeth: 'People Have Usually Said We're A Thinking Man's Band' by Steven Rosen. October 12, 2011.

About The Author

At approximately 7900 (with over 7000 appearing in his books), Martin has unofficially written more record reviews than anybody in the history of music writing across all genres. Additionally, Martin has penned over 60 books on hard rock, heavy metal, classic rock and record collecting. He was Editor In Chief of the now retired *Brave Words & Bloody Knuckles*, Canada's foremost metal publication for 14 years, and has also contributed to *Revolver*, *Guitar World*, *Goldmine*, *Record Collector*, *bravewords.com*, *lollipop.com* and *hardradio.com*, with many record label band biographies and liner notes to his credit as well. Additionally, Martin worked for two years as researcher on the award-wining documentary *Rush: Beyond The Lighted Stage* and on *Metal Evolution*, an 11 episode documentary series for VH1 Classic, and is the writer of the original metal genre chart used in *Metal: A Headbanger's Journey* and throughout the *Metal Evolution* episodes. Martin currently resides in Toronto and can be reached through martinp@inforamp.net or www.martinpopoff.com.

Martin Popoff
A Comprehensive Bibliography

Motor City Madhouse: Going Gonzo With Ted Nugent (2017)
Rush: Album by Album (2017)
Beer Drinkers and Hell Raisers: The Rise of Motörhead (2017)
Hit the Lights: The Birth of Thrash (2017)
From Dublin to Jailbreak: Thin Lizzy 1969-76 (2016)
Wind of Change: The Scorpions Story (2016)
Agents of Fortune: The Blue Öyster Cult Story (2016)
Metal Heart: Aiming High with Accept (2016)
Ramones at 40 (2016)
Time and a Word: The Yes Story (2016)
This Means War: The Sunset Years of the NWOBHM (2015)
Wheels of Steel: The Explosive Early Years of the NWOBHM (2015)
Swords And Tequila: Riot's Classic First Decade (2015)
Who Invented Heavy Metal? (2015)
Sail Away: Whitesnake's Fantastic Voyage (2015)
Live Magnetic Air: The Unlikely Saga Of The Superlative Max Webster (2014)
Steal Away The Night: An Ozzy Osbourne Day-By-Day (2014)
The Big Book Of Hair Metal (2014)
Sweating Bullets: The Deth And Rebirth Of Megadeth (2014)
Smokin' Valves: A Headbanger's Guiide to 900 NWOBHM Records (2014)
The Art Of Metal (co-edit with Malcolm Dome; 2013)
2 Minutes To Midnight: An Iron Maiden Day-By-Day (2013)
Metallica: The Complete Illustrated History (2013)
Rush: The Illustrated History (2013)
Ye Olde Metal: 1979 (2013)
Scorpions: Top Of The Bill (2013)
Epic Ted Nugent (2012)
Fade To Black: Hard Rock Cover Art Of The Vinyl Age (2012)
It's Getting Dangerous: Thin Lizzy 81-12 (2012)
We Will Be Strong: Thin Lizzy 76-81 (2012)
Fighting My Way Back: Thin Lizzy 69-76 (2011)
The Deep Purple Royal Family: Chain Of Events '80 – '11 (2011)
The Deep Purple Royal Family: Chain Of Events Through '79 (2011)
Black Sabbath FAQ (2011)
The Collector's Guide To Heavy Metal: Volume 4: The '00s
(2011; co-authored with David Perri)
Goldmine Standard Catalog Of American Records 1948 – 1991, 7th Edition (2010)
Goldmine Record Album Price Guide, 6th Edition (2009)
Goldmine 45 RPM Price Guide, 7th Edition (2009)
A Castle Full Of Rascals: Deep Purple '83 – '09 (2009)
Worlds Away: Voivod And The Art Of Michel Langevin (2009)
Ye Olde Metal: 1978 (2009)
Gettin' Tighter: Deep Purple '68 – '76 (2008)
All Access: The Art Of The Backstage Pass (2008)
Ye Olde Metal: 1977 (2008)
Ye Olde Metal: 1976 (2008)

Judas Priest: Heavy Metal Painkillers (2007)
Ye Olde Metal: 1973 To 1975 (2007)
The Collector's Guide To Heavy Metal: Volume 3: The Nineties (2007)
Ye Olde Metal: 1968 To 1972 (2007)
Run For Cover: The Art Of Derek Riggs (2006)
Black Sabbath: Doom Let Loose (2006)
Dio: Light Beyond The Black (2006)
The Collector's Guide To Heavy Metal: Volume 2: The Eighties (2005)
Rainbow: English Castle Magic (2005)
UFO: Shoot Out The Lights (2005)
The New Wave Of British Heavy Metal Singles (2005)
Blue Oyster Cult: Secrets Revealed! (2004)
Contents Under Pressure: 30 Years Of Rush At Home & Away (2004)
The Top 500 Heavy Metal Albums Of All Time (2004)
The Collector's Guide To Heavy Metal: Volume 1: The Seventies (2003)
The Top 500 Heavy Metal Songs Of All Time (2003)
Southern Rock Review (2001)
Heavy Metal: 20th Century Rock And Roll (2000)
The Goldmine Price Guide To Heavy Metal Records (2000)
The Collector's Guide To Heavy Metal (1997)
Riff Kills Man! 25 Years Of Recorded Hard Rock & Heavy Metal (1993)

See martinpopoff.com for complete details and ordering information.